Waging War
ON TRIAL

Other books in ABC-CLIO's On Trial Series
Charles L. Zelden, Series Editor

*Look for more books in this series in paperback from Hackett Publishing Company.

Waging War
ON TRIAL

*A Sourcebook with
Cases, Laws, and Documents*

Brian R. Dirck

Updates to this book may be posted online at
www.hackettpublishing.com *as events require*

Hackett Publishing Company, Inc.
Indianapolis/Cambridge

For further information, please address:

    Hackett Publishing Company, Inc.
    P.O. Box 44937
    Indianapolis, IN 46244-0937

    www.hackettpublishing.com

Printed at Edwards Brothers, Inc.

Library of Congress Cataloging-in-Publication Data

Dirck, Brian R., 1965–
  Waging war on trial : a sourcebook with cases, laws, and documents / Brian
R. Dirck.— 1st ed.
    p. cm.
  Includes bibliographical references and index.
  ISBN 0-87220-739-0 (pbk.)
  1. War and emergency powers—United States—History. 2. War, Declaration of—United States—History. 3. United States. Congress—Powers and duties—History. I. Title.

  KF5060.Z9D57 2004
  342.73'0412—dc22

                                             2004012026

Contents

Series Foreword

The volumes in the On Trial series explore the many ways in which the U.S. legal and political system has approached a wide range of complex and divisive legal issues over time and, in the process, defined the current state of the law and politics on these issues. The intent is to give students and other general readers a framework for understanding how the law in all its various forms—constitutional, statutory, judicial, political, and customary—has shaped and reshaped the world we live in today.

At the core of each volume in the series is a common proposition: that in certain key areas of American public life, we as a people and a nation are "on trial" as we struggle to cope with the contradictions, conflicts, and disparities within our society, politics, and culture. Who should decide if and when a woman can have an abortion? What rights, if any, should those with a different sexual orientation be able to claim under the Constitution? Is voting a basic right of citizenship, and if so, under what rules should we organize this right—especially when the application of any organizing rules inevitably results in excluding some citizens from the polls? What about the many inconsistencies and conflicts associated with racial tensions in the country? These are just some of the complex and controversial issues that we as a people and a nation are struggling to answer—and must answer if we are to achieve an orderly and stable society. The answers we find to these disputes shape the essence of who we are—as a people, a community, and a political system.

The concept of being on trial also has a second meaning fundamental to this series: the process of litigating important issues in a court of law. Litigation is an essential part of how we settle our differences and make choices as we struggle with the problems that confront us as a people and a nation. In 1835, Alexis de Tocqueville noted in *Democracy in America* that "there is hardly a political question in the United States which does not sooner or later turn into a judicial one" (de Tocqueville 1835, 270). This insight is as true today as it was in the 1830s. In *The Litigious Society,* Jethro K. Lieberman notes that "to express amazement at American litigiousness is akin to professing astonishment at learning that the roots of most Americans lie in other lands. We have been a litigious nation as we have been an immigrant one. Indeed, the two are related." Arriving in the United States with different backgrounds, customs, and lifestyle preferences, we inevitably clashed as our contrasting visions of life in the United States—its culture, society, and politics—collided. It was to the courts and the law that we turned as a neutral forum for peaceably working out these differences (Lieberman 1983, 13). In the United States, it is the courthouse that provides the anvil on which our personal, societal, and political problems are hammered out.

The volumes in this series therefore take as their central purpose the important task of exploring the various ways—good and bad, effective and ineffective, complex and simple—in which litigation in the courts has shaped the evolution of particular legal controversies for which we as a people are "On Trial." And, more important, the volumes do all this in a manner accessible to the general reader seeking to comprehend the topic as a whole.

These twin goals—analytical and educational—shape the structure and layout of the volumes in the series. Each book consists of two parts. The first provides an explanatory essay in four chapters. Chapter 1 introduces the issues, controversies, events, and participants associated with the legal controversy at hand. Chapter 2 explores the social, economic, political, and historical background to this topic. Chapter 3 describes in detail the various court decisions and actions that have shaped the current status of the legal controversy under examination. In some cases, that will be done through a close examination of a few representative cases, in others by a broader but less detailed narrative of the course of judicial action. Chapter 4 discusses the impact of these cases on U.S. law—their doctrinal legacy—as well as on U.S. society—their historical, sociological, and political legacy.

Part 2, in turn, provides selective supplementary materials designed to help readers more fully comprehend the topics covered in the chapters of Part 1. First included are documents aimed at helping the reader better appreciate both the issues and the process by which adjudication shaped these matters. Selected documents might include court opinions (excerpted or whole), interviews, newspaper accounts, and selected secondary essays. Next comes an alphabetically formatted glossary providing entries on the important people, laws, events, terms, and concepts important to an understanding of the topic. A chronology provides the reader an easily referenced listing of the major developments covered in the book. Last, an annotated bibliography describes the key works in the field, directing a reader seeking a more detailed examination on the topic to the appropriate sources.

In closing, as you read the books in this series, keep in mind the purposefully controversial nature of the topics covered within. The authors in the series have not chosen easy or agreeable topics to explore. Much of what you read may trouble you, and it should. Yet it is precisely these sorts of contentious topics that need the most historical analysis and scrutiny. For it is here that we are still "On Trial"—and all too often, as regards these matters, the jury is still out.

Charles L. Zelden
Ft. Lauderdale, Florida

Preface and Acknowledgments

This book was written in the shadow of war. The editors at ABC-CLIO began discussing a volume on the legal issues of American warfare in the summer of 2001. Although at that time all agreed that such a volume would be useful, the subject's urgency and timeliness was not evident until after September 11. The legal and constitutional ramifications of warfare became even more relevant in the wake of President George W. Bush's internal security measures, the U.S. military assault on Afghanistan, and the war with Iraq. The second assault on Saddam Hussein's regime began just as this book was in the final stages of publication. Although it proved impossible to keep up with thealmost-by-minute changes on the Iraqi front, *Waging War on Trial* will nonetheless offer valuable historical context to these current events.

Part of the target readership of this book is undergraduates who have little background in legal or military history. Although the number of "nontraditional" students has been steadily rising in the last few years, it can be safely assumed that the majority of these undergraduate readers are young men and women in their teens and early twenties: the top end of "Generation X," or the bottom end of whatever is going to come next. These young people are of prime military age, and if the "war on terrorism" eventually becomes a large-scale "big war," they will feel the effect most profoundly. The events of September 11 have brought home the possibility of war to a degree that few would have imagined just a few years ago. Military service may once have seemed a remote possibility for college students and other young people, but no longer.

The precise nature of their response to this new state of affairs is not yet clear. Some have taken to the streets, protesting the administration's policies and plans for future military action. Others support the president and the war on terrorism and express a willingness to serve and perhaps be placed in harm's way. Many others go on with life as usual, hoping the storm will pass them by. My own impression is that most students fall into this third category. "Apathy" is an overused and much-abused term associated with modern youth, but sadly, in many cases it is appropriate. Student interest burned white-hot during the days immediately following the September 11 attacks, but when the events faded from the media's focus, so too did it fade in many students'—indeed, many people's—minds.

This is not to say that students do not care for war as a subject of study; on the contrary. I have noted both an interest in and shallow knowledge about war-related matters among my students. Enrollments for my course on the Civil War and a general U.S. military history course I teach called War and American Society are routinely high and generate a good deal of excitement. Students tend to have a good base of war-related trivia (thanks to The History Channel's various military obsessions and the recent Hollywood popularity of war movies in the *Saving Private Ryan* genre) and hold opinions on battles and military leaders with greater verve and tenacity than they do on most other subjects.

The shallowness comes through their lack of a profound understanding of the far-reaching social, cultural, legal, and political ramifications that radiate from the combat zone like ripples on a pond. Students know a lot about guns and bombs, but far less about how guns and bombs affect the home front, and vice versa. In making this observation, I am not engaging in the condescending finger-pointing, often noticeable among those who came of age during the Vietnam War era, at a younger generation that has not known war (or defeat) in any immediate fashion. Indeed, ignorance of war and military history is often most profound among those from the baby-boomer era who profess most loudly to have absorbed "the lessons of Vietnam." Nevertheless, there is among undergraduates generally a palpable lack of what might be called a thick understanding of war that goes beyond the battlefield and the weapons and into the culture, politics, and psychology of war.

There is certainly a deficiency of interest or knowledge in the legal and constitutional aspects of warfare. This is partly a by-product of students' overall indifference to—indeed, often serious dislike of— legal and constitutional history, which they associate with lawyers rather than soldiers. It is also indicative of a general lack of good, accessible books on law and war. The many available books on military history rarely address legal topics, and legal works on war are often too dense and technical for undergraduates.

An introduction to war's legal and constitutional ramifications seems urgently necessary for today's generation of college students, and that has been the driving impulse for this book. I have tried to make legal doctrines and concepts as accessible as possible and as free of technicality and jargon as circumstances allow. In editing the court cases that make up a substantial portion of the book's second half, I have whittled away information that would seem superfluous to the nonlawyer while trying to preserve the essence of each decision. My guiding question has been: Is this understandable and interesting to the average undergraduate student?

The tight focus on college students, along with the usual constraints of space and time that accompany any book project, required making hard choices. Law and war intersect at numerous points. Indeed, during a large-scale conflict such as the Civil War and World War II, nearly every legal question can assume a military dimension, and many purely military decisions have legal ramifications. In the interests of imposing manageable boundaries on these issues, I chose to define the book according to three broad areas of law and war: the war powers debates, civil liberties during war, and the operations of the military justice system (particularly the impact of military justice on civilians). More categories would certainly have been possible, but I believe these three have produced the most serious public debate and stand the best chance of acquiring front-page-news relevance for the post–September 11 world.

Even harder choices were necessary in deciding which court cases merited close attention. Legal history can be likened to multiple chains, whereby each court case is linked simultaneously to several others that in turn are linked to others, stretching back, via the doctrine of *stare decisis* and the importance of precedent, nearly *ad infinitum.* Each historian must decide how far to travel down this series of chains for each case. I have decided to keep these journeys to a minimum, for the sake of clarity and out of a desire not to overburden the text and documents with arcane explorations of case law. For the same reason, I have decided to keep the book's focus almost exclusively on Supreme Court cases. No doubt legal professionals would find gaps and omissions in the text, and military historians might regret the lack of attention paid to one or another important aspect of the nation's military history. My response to them would be that, for this book to function according to its stated purpose, a vigorous editorial hand was necessary.

Throughout, I have tried to maintain a balanced perspective on the often emotionally charged and partisan political issues that inevitably accompany America's history of war making. Neutrality is of course impossible—and really not very interesting—but I have tried to be fair to all sides, particularly on controversial, tendentious matters such as the intent of the framers of the Constitution in drafting that document's war-making provisions, the proper role of the presidency in determining when and how the nation should go to war, and the legacy of controversial events such as the Vietnam conflict. In doing the research for this project, I have learned a great deal, and I have come to think that we need a new national conversation on law and war, particularly the war powers debates and issues involving civil liberties. For better or worse, such a conversation must take place in the shadow of the new war on terrorism, and I hope that in the process we can be civil and evenhanded in our treatment of those who oppose this new war, those who support it, and the presidents, members of Congress, and judges who have the unenviable task of making difficult decisions in these extraordinarily difficult times.

Numerous individuals were instrumental in bringing this project to completion. Charles L. Zelden, the editor of this series and professor of history at Nova Southeastern University (and my long-standing and highly valued friend), first broached the idea for a volume on law and war, and during the ensuing months guided the project with skill and valuable insight. His expertise, advice, and friendship have been indispensable. Alicia Merritt and Gina Zondorak, editors at ABC-CLIO, have likewise been most patient and cooperative. The staff of Nicholson Library at Anderson University helped me acquire numerous useful sources; Jill Branscum of the Interlibrary Loan Department was (as usual) efficient and very supportive. I am also grateful to my colleagues in the Anderson University department of history and political science—Jaye Caldwell, Michael Frank, David Murphy, and Douglas

Nelson—for their willingness to read and critique portions of the manuscript. My students were also willing to entertain my ramblings about law and war with patience and, quite often, with useful insights and comments. Most of all, I would like to thank my parents and my wife and our children for their love and support.

Brian Dirck
Anderson, Indiana

Part One

Part One

1

Introduction

"My son kept saying, 'Mama, what's all the fog? Is it a fire?'" said Lea Perrera, a thirty-one-year-old Brazilian immigrant. She walked with her child along Roosevelt Avenue in New York City, just a few blocks from "Ground Zero," the smoking, dust-filled inferno where once had stood the twin towers of the World Trade Center. "There's panic in the air," observed another New Yorker. "People don't know where they're going or how they're getting there." The date was September 11, 2001, forever etched in the world's memory as "9-1-1," when thousands of Americans died at the hands of terrorists who attacked the World Trade Center and the Pentagon in Washington, D.C. (*New York Newsday,* September 11, 2001, E14).

A wave of anger swept the nation in the days following the attack. "This is the worst thing since Pearl Harbor," said one Houston man, "I think it's even worse. It makes me want to join the army and serve my country and protect it." An editorial in the *Toronto Sun* proclaimed, "It was a declaration of war on our American neighbours, and indirectly upon us, their allies. . . . Someone planned this for years. Someone funded it. Someone knows what happened. Find them." Others were less restrained. In a gathering of three World War II veterans at a Georgia diner, one man wondered how the United States could ever really stop terrorists from committing such heinous acts. "You can't stop them," declared a second man, "you have to eliminate them." The third veteran agreed. "Like vermin, like mosquitos, you have to kill them," he said (*Houston Chronicle,*

September 11, 2001, 6; *Toronto Sun,* September 11, 2001, 14; *Atlanta Journal and Constitution,* September 11, 2001, 10A).

Suspicion centered almost immediately on Osama bin Laden, a wealthy Islamic fundamentalist with a passionate hatred of the United States and a history of supporting terrorist assaults on American military and civilian targets. His network—known as al Qaeda, or "the base"—had agents in countries around the world. But its center, and bin Laden's home, was in Afghanistan, a war-scarred patch of earth run by Islamic fundamentalist extremists who called themselves the Taliban. Overwhelming evidence pointed to bin Laden and his allies as the sources of the September 11 assaults.

U.S. president George W. Bush wasted little time in publicly identifying bin Laden and the Taliban as legitimate first targets of America's new "war on terrorism." In an address to the nation from the floor of Congress on October 7, Bush promised immediate action. Listing them off one by one, he made a series of demands on the Taliban, including the extradition of Osama bin Laden and immediate cessation of all terrorist activities in Afghanistan. If they failed to meet even one of these demands, he made it clear, the result would be a military response. "Our enemy is a radical network of terrorists and every government that supports them," Bush said (George W. Bush, address before Congress, October 7, 2001; transcript available at http://www.whitehouse.gov). He offered the American people, and the world at large, a clear moral boundary between the friends and the enemies of the United States. Rarely has a president—for better or worse—drawn such a stark contrast between good and evil as a driving force in American foreign policy.

No one really expected the Taliban to comply with Bush's demands, and they did not. To pursue the military response he promised, Bush sought congressional support. Three weeks before his speech, Congress had debated a resolution backing the president's plan to launch military strikes in Afghanistan if necessary. The mood was defiant, even bellicose. "We're not interested in reading them their Miranda rights," declared Senator Bob Barr of Georgia. "We want to take them out, lock, stock, barrel, root and limb." The resolution authorized Bush to use "all necessary force" to defeat al Qaeda and the Taliban. Support for the Bush administration seemed universal; everyone wanted to vote for the resolution (*Baltimore Sun,* September 14, 2001, 16A).

One notable exception was Barbara Lee, House representative from California. Her constituency included the Berkeley and Oakland areas, with their strong antiwar pedigrees that dated back to the Vietnam era. Lee herself was a consistent critic of the use of military force, having voted against the U.S. prosecution of the Persian Gulf War and the Clinton administration's bombing campaign in Kosovo. "A rush to launch precipitous military counterattacks runs too great a risk that more innocent men, women, [and] children will be killed," she argued. Several other members of Congress had expressed uneasiness about giving the president carte blanche in prosecuting a war against terrorism. But when the moment of truth came, only Lee actually voted against the resolution. "I felt let's not do anything that could escalate this madness out of control," she said. "I felt that [someone] in this environment of grief needed to say let's show some restraint in our response" (*San Francisco Chronicle,* September 26, 2001, A1; *Baltimore Sun,* October 7, 2001, 5M; *Los Angeles Times,* September 23, 2001, M4).

The fallout from Lee's decision was significant and as prolonged as the wisps of smoke that were still rising from the debris at Ground Zero. Months after the World Trade Center attack, Lee's critics were still seething, and political opponents were lining up to take advantage of her plight. "For me it's so clear-cut," declared Audie Bock, a fellow Democrat and peace activist who nevertheless opposed Lee's vote. "The major, major issue is: The U.S. was attacked." Lee had her supporters; one journalist wrote that she "should be congratulated, not vilified, for daring to demur, ever so slightly, from government propaganda." Other Americans were considerably more harsh, accusing Lee of being a "peacenik," "a doctrinaire, radical Leftist," and clearly guilty of "breath-taking idiocy." She was bombarded by thousands of hate letters and e-mails, and at one point she was assigned extra security as a precaution against the death threats she received (*Los Angeles Times,* December 2, 2001, part 2, 1; *Denver Post,* October 28, 2001, F5; *San Francisco Chronicle,* October 28, 2001, C6; *Rocky Mountain News,* September 28, 2001, 44A; *San Francisco Chronicle,* October 22, 2001, A9).

Right or wrong, Representative Lee learned how difficult it is to oppose a popular military action, even in a free and democratic society, when there are American bodies to be buried and American fears to be soothed. Robert Prager had learned that lesson as well.

Robert Paul Prager was twenty-nine years old in 1917, when the United States declared war against his native Germany. Despite his heritage, Prager was not a German sympathizer; in fact, he tried to enlist in the U.S. Navy but was turned away because of his physical condition (he had one glass eye). A year later, while the American Expedition Force was preparing to meet a massive spring offensive by the German army, Prager labored as a baker's assistant and as a coal miner in Collinsville, Illinois. It was here that his troubles began.

Deeply concerned about the inequities that ran rampant throughout American society, Prager acquired a reputation as a radical among his fellow miners, who objected to his giving fiery speeches with socialist overtones. In America's superheated patriotic environment of 1918, distinctions between radical socialism and pro-German sympathies were hazy. When Prager applied for membership in the local coal miner's union, the union's president rejected his application, angrily denouncing him as a German spy. Prager just as angrily denied that he was anything of the sort, but rumors continued to swirl among the miners that the German émigré was part of a spy ring and that he was secretly stockpiling dynamite in his home with plans to blow up the mine.

On the evening of April 4, 1918, a mob of around 300 miners and others descended on Prager's home. They dragged the protesting German from his house and searched for a good spot to execute him. Fortunately, Prager was rescued by four policemen, who took him to the Collinsville jail for safekeeping. Unfortunately, the mob then stormed the jail. In desperation, the policemen shoved Prager under a pile of garbage in the basement, but he was discovered and forced to march barefoot out of the jail and down a city street, to the sound of cheers and the waving of American flags. Prager himself was wrapped in an American flag that he had been forced to kiss many times. He was then hung from a tree, with nearly 100 eager hands pulling the rope that killed him. "Dear parents—I must this day, the 5th of April, 1918, die," he wrote in a farewell letter minutes before he was hung. "Pray for me, my dear parents. This is my last letter."

Eleven men were indicted and placed on trial for leading the Prager lynch mob. At the trial, the defendants sported red, white, and blue ribbons and argued that theirs was a deed of "patriotic murder." It took the jury less than thirty minutes to acquit them. Although the deed was denounced in many quarters—one senator declared that the attack had been perpetrated by "a drunken mob masquerading in the garb of patriots"—others believed that Prager got what he deserved. "German Enemy of the U.S. Hanged by Mob," read the headline of the *Saint Louis Globe-Democrat* (April 5, 1918, 1). The *Washington Post* suggested that the incident "is a healthful and wholesome awakening in the interior of the country" (Kennedy 1980, 68; Ellis 1973, 433).

Robert Prager discovered in the streets of Collinsville that the mere appearance of opposition to a popular war can have a heavy price and that sometimes America's courts of law offer no remedy. Fifty years before Prager was murdered, John M. Chivington likewise negotiated the sometimes treacherous territory between law and the waging of war. Unlike Prager, Chivington was a soldier, and, also unlike Prager, Chivington would not pay for the experience with his life; instead, the lives of the 133 Cheyenne men, women, and children slain by Chivington and his men would go unavenged.

Chivington was a burly forty-three-year-old colonel in the Colorado militia during the fall of 1864, living in Denver, on the edge of the western frontier, as the Civil War raged in the East. Trained for the ministry in the Methodist faith, Chivington was anything but a mild-mannered parson. Outspoken and belligerent, with a penchant for violence, before the war he found himself in the dangerous position of espousing abolitionism in the slave state of Missouri. Undeterred by threats against his life, he arrived at the pulpit one Sunday sporting a brace of pistols and bellowing, "By the grace of God and these two revolvers, I am going to preach here today."

Such bravado was admirable, and Chivington had won praise and national fame in 1862 for his decisive defeat of Confederate troops at the Battle of Glorietta Pass (the "Gettysburg of the West") in New Mexico. Unfortunately, Chivington combined his fiery temper and aggressiveness with overweening political ambition and a passionate hatred of Native Americans. In Colorado this was a potentially lethal combination, where whites and Native Americans had been waging a low-grade guerrilla war of raids, counterraids, and reprisals. By 1864, Chivington was a candidate for Congress, and he knew that white voters would be attracted to a tough-minded Indian fighter. "My rule of fighting white men or Indians is, to fight them until they lay down their arms and submit to military authority," he said at a peace conference in September 1864. To his men, he was more blunt, telling them to "kill Cheyennes whenever and wherever found" (West 1998, 231; Brown 1970, 295).

At dawn on November 29, 1864, Chivington led 700 like-minded (and mostly inebriated) members of the Colorado militia on a surprise attack against approximately 600 Cheyenne Indians—many of them women and children—who were camped along Sand Creek in eastern Colorado. Their leader, Black Kettle, was a peaceful man who had been given permission by the U.S. Army to move his family and followers to the supposedly safe haven of Sand Creek. He had explicit assurances from army authorities that no harm would come to his people, and, as a symbol of his peaceful intentions, the Cheyenne chief flew an American flag over the entrance to his lodge.

Black Kettle's people were stunned to see the arrival of Chivington and his men, armed to the teeth and spoiling for a fight. What followed was a shocking paroxysm of brutality and atrocity, directed against the Cheyenne by white militiamen who were just barely organized enough to call themselves soldiers and who were too blinded by whiskey and racism to much care what sort of Indians they murdered. "All was confusion and noise," remembered one witness, with "men, women, and children rushing out of the lodges partly dressed; women and children screaming at the sight of the troops." Black Kettle's own wife was killed not long after he had told his people to calm themselves and "not to be afraid; that the soldiers would not hurt them." Chivington's men raked the camp with pistols, rifles, and grapeshot from the cannon they had brought with them. "I saw five squaws under a bank for shelter," an eyewitness later testified. "When the troops came up to them they ran out and showed their persons to let the soldiers know they were squaws and begged for mercy, but the soldiers shot them all ... there seemed to be indiscriminate slaughter of men, women, and children." When the soldiers finally left the Sand Creek camp later that afternoon, they carried with them grisly trophies of war, including many Indian scalps, and, according to one observer, "the private parts of females," which the soldiers stretched "over the saddle-bows and wore ... over their hats while riding in the ranks (Brown 1994, 89–90).

Many Americans reacted to the Sand Creek massacre with revulsion. "No one but a coward or a dog would have had a part in it," according to a disgusted Kit Carson (Brown 1994, 100). But others defended Chivington and his men, arguing that the raid was not a "massacre" but a battle, a bona fide military operation against a legitimate military target. "Among the brilliant feats of arms in Indian warfare, the recent campaign of our Colorado volunteers will stand in history with few rivals," argued an editorial in the *Rocky Mountain News,* which described the Cheyenne camp as a fortress, complete with rifle pits (*Rocky Mountain News,* December 20, 1864). Chivington himself vigorously denied that any atrocities had taken place under his command. He claimed to have killed 500 "warriors" while losing nine of his own men in "combat." In fact, many of these casualties occurred when his drunken soldiers fired upon one another (West 1998, 307–308).

John Chivington, Barbara Lee, and Robert Prager, each in their own way, illustrate the complexities involved when law and war have intersected in American history. The rule of law and society often clash, in greater or lesser degrees, depending upon the circumstances. But law and war clash in peculiarly contentious ways, throwing off brighter sparks than is usual. Why? The answer lies in the nature of war itself and in its innate incompatibility with the rule of law.

Chaotic Nature of War

War, at its core, is chaos. Abraham Lincoln called it a "mighty scourge," a "great difficulty," and "our national troubles" (Basler 1953, 8: 333; Dirck 2001, 210). His favorite author, William Shakespeare, referred in *King Henry V* to "the blast of war" and has Marc Anthony in *Julius Caesar* exclaiming in his famous line, "Cry 'Havoc!' and let slip the dogs of war!" Neither Lincoln nor Shakespeare was a professional soldier, yet both instinctively grasped that war is indeed a peculiarly intense and violent form of havoc, what novelist Stephen Crane famously called the "blood-swollen god" of combat that sends young men (and women) off to die like "methodical idiots."

Crane here let his moral outrage against war cloud his judgment, for the vast majority of soldiers are not "idiots." Yet combat does require a certain stoicism, a hard shell of psychological indifference that enables its participants to withstand the shock of witnessing— and the constant risk of—violent death. "We were inured to privations and hardships," wrote Sam Watkins, a veteran of the Confederate army during the Civil War. "[We] had seen our comrades slain upon our right and our left hand; had heard guns that carried death in their missiles . . . had heard the shrieks and groans of the wounded and dying. . . . We had followed the successes and reverses of the flag of the [Confederacy] through all these years of blood and strife"

(Watkins 1999, 197). Combat veterans such as Watkins, who have seen the battlefield, come face-to-face with war's brutal fury, and none walk away unscathed.

Anyone who has witnessed a war zone, even from the periphery, understands that the devastating effects of warfare are not limited to the battlefield. War has a centrifugal quality; it explodes outward from the battlefield point of contact between enemy soldiers, affecting people and institutions that are often only indirectly involved in the act of combat. "The whole outdoors alive with voices of soldiers. [I] hear wagons and cannon moving, rumbling, the country is now all excitement. I feel so nervous. Oh! so anxious," wrote Katherine Crouse, as the Civil War bloodbath known as the Wilderness Campaign engulfed her rural neighborhood in northern Virginia during the spring of 1864. "The crash of musketry is terrific[,] pop pop pop. The cannon shake the very foundations of the house . . . now we hear the shells whistling at a terrific rate. Oh, it makes me so weak[,] so generally wretched," she scribbled, "Yankees on one side[,] southern soldiers on the other . . . the Court House road is alive with yelling soldiers [and we] hear skirmishing at intervals all day up there. . . . Oh! God[,] human beings killing each other" (Cushman 1999, 2–4).

No soldier or civilian can help being affected by war's essentially destructive nature. "The soldier's concern is with death, not life, with destruction, not construction," military historian Stephen Ambrose points out. Ambrose described American GIs during World War II celebrating with glee the death of a German sniper during heavy fighting along the Western Front in the winter of 1944–1945. "Pvt. Roy Cobb . . . hit [the German] with his first shot. Pvt. Clarence Lyall, looking through his binoculars, said the hurt, perplexed expression on the German's face was something to see. As the soldier tried to crawl back to the cottage, Cobb hit him twice more. There were whoops and shouts each time he got hit." Ambrose's point here is not that American soldiers like Cobb and his comrades were bad men. Rather, the very bad circumstances of war produced an environment in which ordinary men come to revel in acts of destruction and death (Ambrose 1992, 234).

Americans have a peculiarly intense take on this process. The United States was a nation born in musket fire in 1776 and sustained four score and seven years later by the Civil War that cost at least 600,000 lives. In the twentieth century we participated in two bloody world wars and became the first (and so far only) nation to use nuclear weapons. At the dawn of the twenty-first century the United States is leading the way in a new war on the scourge of international terrorism, and is unhesitant in the use of martial metaphors to describe the hunt for Osama bin Laden and his followers. Military books routinely occupy the top of the nation's best-seller lists, and war movies are a time-honored genre in the nation's cinema. "Americans traditionally love to fight," says George C. Scott as General George S. Patton during his famous opening speech in the 1970 film *Patton.* "All real Americans love the sting of battle." War is endemic to American culture, and the United States' most respected military heroes—Patton, "Stonewall" Jackson, William Tecumseh Sherman, "Stormin' Norman" Schwartzkopf—have been men who waged war with pugnacious intensity. "War is all hell, and you can make nothing better of it," Sherman once said. On some deep cultural and psychological level, Americans prefer it that way (Weigly 1978).

The Laws of War, the War of Laws

Law and war might seem at first glance to have a natural affinity, for some people believe that the heart of the law is coercion, the credible threat of state retaliation—at its crudest form, the state-sponsored violence of the policeman's baton, the jailer's key, or the executioner's switch—against those who have in some way violated community standards of right and wrong. Legal scholar H. L. A. Hart identifies (and is critical of) the simple definition of law as an instance in which "conduct is no longer optional . . . one man is forced to do what another tells him, not because he is physically compelled in the sense that his body is pushed or pulled about, but because the other threatens him with unpleasant consequences if he refuses" (Hart 1961, 6). From this perspective, law is the habit of obedience to higher authority, instilled in a populace that understands that disobedience will bring unpleasant consequences (Austin 1954; Raz 1994, chap. 9).

In fact, the law is not merely a well-organized series of veiled threats, at least not on anything more than the most simplistic level. Certainly, to be effective, the law requires fear of punishment. But the law is even more a system designed to preclude the direct threat of coercion by establishing the legitimacy of legal authority. Citizens ideally obey laws not from fear of the policeman's baton but primarily out of respect for the judge's gavel. Such respect can be established in a number of ways: the belief that the judge represents the embodiment of a democratic process (and hence represents the judgment of one's neighbors); the belief that the judge speaks for a reasonable, orderly body of rules necessary for society to function efficiently; and the moral authority that resides in the judge's decisions, who in rendering a decision does what is "right," or what is "just," according to society's understanding of those concepts. "A state is legitimate if the constitutional structure and practices are such that its citizens have a general obligation to obey political decisions that purport to impose duties on them," observed legal philosopher Ronald Dworkin (Dworkin 1988, 190–191).

Whatever its source, the law's legitimacy is ultimately rooted in predictability. A citizen must be able to calculate ahead of time what sort of behavior will bring the unpleasant consequence of legal punishment. A regime in which the gavel can be banged merely at the whim of the judge sacrifices moral authority (who is to say whether a judge's whim is right or fair?), is likely removed from the democratic process, and is probably not very far removed from anarchy. "The only good government is a Republican government, a nation of laws, not men," John Adams declared, and his words have been echoed by Americans down through the decades to suggest that a basic governing principle of the nation is the idea that the clear, understandable words of written laws must govern the murky, often selfish and capricious motives of political leaders (Dworkin 1988, 146–150, 367–368).

Different legal regimes create the predictability necessary for legitimacy in different ways. Americans do so by elevating the written word of the law above the machinery of political power. Once a rule is properly recorded in the stark black letters and precise terminology of legalese—in court rulings, statutes, constitutions—it becomes accessible to the ordinary citizen, who is able to read the rule in the present and then predict whether or not a future action will bring unwanted legal consequences. There is likewise a long American tradition that written laws, particularly constitutions, possess a quality of authority and moral power that supersedes and controls the behavior of the men and women who wield power. "In all free states the constitution is fixed," according to a revolutionary-era edict, "and the supreme legislative power of the nation, from thence derives its authority." Put in more modern terms, written laws, arrived at by democratic means, should control the exercise of power, and not the other way around (Kelly, Harbison, and Belz 1991, 62–63).

Some jurists and legal philosophers read the connections between the legal written word, legitimacy, and predictability very literally, searching for pristine legal rules with universally recognized and agreed-upon meanings. They believe in the possibility of and the need for an objective reading of the law, independent of the personal biases of judges and lawyers. The most prominent spokesman for this point of view in recent years has been Robert H. Bork, a Yale Law School professor, a U.S. Circuit Court judge, and an unsuccessful nominee for the Supreme Court during the Reagan administration. Bork argues that judges, in order to maintain their legitimacy, must render decisions based only on the objective meaning of legal language as understood by the men and women who drafted that language. "A Court that makes rather than implements value choices cannot be squared with the presuppositions of a democratic society," he argues. In this view, legal decision making lies in the act of ascertaining, via neutral, detached reason and unencumbered scholarly inquiry, the original intent of the framers of the Constitution or the drafters of a given rule or piece of legislation, and in the process taking into account as little as possible of one's personal value system (Bork 1971, 6; Bork 1990).

Many legal philosophers doubt whether the sort of completely detached legal regime envisioned by Bork is possible or desirable. There are those who go to the opposite extreme and suggest that the law is nothing more than a reflection of the various biases of judges, lawyers, and law professors, most of whom throughout American history have been white and upper-class. The Legal Realism school of thought, which reached the height of its popularity among law professors and other intellectuals during the early decades of the twentieth century, offered a telling critique of classical judicial reasoning and its search for neutral principles upon which to base legal decisions. The Legal Realists argued that neutrality is impossible and that legal language cannot be understood apart from the sociocultural context in which it was written. The sort of neutral reasoning sought by theorists like Bork means that judges and lawyers detach themselves from the social consequences of their actions. What's more, the Realists argued, it is dishonest; judges define the law according to their personal predilections, not some high and abstract constitutional philosophy (Horowitz 1992; Kelman 1987; Altman 1990; Dworkin 1988, 271–273).

Although there is some truth to the Realists' analysis of legal reasoning, most philosophers (and probably most lawyers, judges, and political leaders) refuse to completely abandon the search for at least a degree of rational objectivity within the law. Most seek an accommodation between the rigid objectivism propounded by Bork and the often disturbing relativism of the Legal Realists. University of Oxford law professor Ronald Dworkin is the leading theorist of this middle-of-the road approach to the law. He argues that law is more than mere rules, to be applied in an entirely objective fashion (as Bork would have it) or discarded as mere window dressing for judges' class-based prejudices (according to the Legal Realists). Rather, legal rules are applied by judges and other legal thinkers on the basis of broad principles—fairness, due process, and so on. "Propositions of law are true if they figure in or follow from the principles of justice, fairness, and procedural due process that provide the best constructive interpretation of the community's legal practice," Dworkin wrote. Although they allow judges and other legal officials room for flexibility and interpretation, Dworkin and like-minded legal theorists do not deny the need for reason, predictability, and order for a legal regime to function properly. They seek a place where reason and predictability can function within the ever-shifting social contexts of changing times and circumstances (Dworkin 1988, 225).

Probably most modern legal thinkers fall somewhere in the neighborhood of Dworkin's view, valuing the calm, dispassionate rulings of informed opinions of judges and lawyers while simultaneously recognizing that interpretations of legal rules are open to flexibility, and rightly so. But no matter which school of thought prevails in any given situation, legal philosophers and practitioners of nearly every stripe believe, at some level, in the need for reason and predictability as the founding principles of any viable legal system. This is where the law's relation to war hits a snag.

The very characteristics that define war—its chaos, unpredictability, even insanity—cut across the grain of the reason, logic, and predictability that law tries to embrace. Indeed, it is difficult to imagine two human phenomena more diametrically opposed, more philosophically antithetical, than law and war. War is the realm of blood, filth, and death; it is a barely controllable release of violent and destructive force that threatens to harm everything it touches. Law, on the other hand, lies within the purview of academic philosophers like the Legal Realists and Dworkin, and austere judges like Robert Bork. Whereas the battlefield is a house of horrors, the courthouse is (we all hope) a house of reason, justice, and equity. "That is one of the indictments of war; its first casualties are liberty and truth," political activist Norman Thomas famously observed. He might have added another potential casualty: the rule of law, which ideally safeguards liberty and truth (Linfield 1990, 1).

Law versus War

War and law both seem to be indispensable features of human civilization; yet whenever they come into contact, they clash. The tension between law and war is endemic; it has never been resolved, nor can it ever be. Although few regimes would willingly wage war without rules—for the violence and friction that are the soul of war can too easily spin out of control—no attempt to legislate away war, to use the rule of law to negate entirely the use of force, has ever come close to success. Law cannot rid us of war, and war is rarely, if ever, waged without at least an attempt to corral its excesses with the rule of law.

Still, Americans have always tried to shackle the dogs of war with laws. Despite a history of aggressive war making and endemic social violence (the American nation is, after all, the breeding ground for those famously violent cultural icons, the Old West gunfighter and the Rambo-style action hero), Americans are uncomfortable enough with war-making institutions that those institutions are controlled with legal rules and regulations. The principle of civilian rule is elevated over the military to a nearly universal maxim, and has been done so with a remarkable degree of success (Wormuth and Firmage 1989).

The United States has never in its 225-year history been subjected to a military coup or a serious attempt at supplanting civilian with military rule. Quite a few generals have occupied the White House, and a strong military record proved to be a valuable political asset for Theodore Roosevelt, William McKinley, Harry S. Truman, John F. Kennedy, and George H. W. Bush, among others. Yet no president with a military pedigree has ever really confused his military loyalties with his duty as the nation's chief executive, and all have jealously guarded the presidency's prerogative as the place where final war-making authority lies. Harry Truman, for example, wanted so badly to join the army in 1917 that he ignored his relatively advanced age (he was thirty-three) and lied about his poor eyesight in order to enlist. Many of his closest friends were army buddies, and those connections were instrumental in launching his political career. Yet in 1951, he fired popular military hero General Douglas MacArthur because in his conduct of the Korean War, MacArthur had, in the president's opinion, tried to meddle in civilian political matters in a manner that was dangerous and inappropriate for an American military leader. "Truman's decision to fire MacArthur hinged on the relationship of the president as the Commander in Chief to his general and on civilian control of the military," wrote Assistant Secretary of State Dean Rusk (McCullough 1992, 102–105, 836–857). Truman's successor, Dwight D. Eisenhower, was one of this nation's most revered military men—the architect of the D-Day campaign and a chief reason why the Allies prevailed in World War II. Yet as he left the White House in 1960, he bluntly warned the nation about the perils of mixing civilian industrial might with military power and priorities. "In the councils of government, we must guard against the acquisition of unwarranted influence, whether sought or unsought, by the military-industrial complex," Ike declared. "The potential for the disastrous rise of misplaced power exists and will persist" (Richardson 1979, 186).

Thus, Americans have long been on guard against an inappropriate or threatening intermixture of public policy making and military matters. Still, there is serious tension in American society between law and war. There are blind spots, controversies, and unresolved debates concerning the proper relationship between legal institutions and war making, many of which have plagued the republic since its inception. The experiences of Barbara Lee, Robert Prager, and John Chivington each offer apt illustrations of this tension.

Who Declares War, the President or Congress?

Representative Barbara Lee became the unpopular critic of a popular war, and she did so within the context of the ongoing and sometimes acrimonious constitutional debate over who decides when and how America goes to war. The debate arises over the Constitution's division of authority between Congress and the presidency on military issues. Article I, Section 8 of the Constitution places the power to declare war firmly within the purview of Congress, and authorizes that body to "grant Letters of Marque and Reprisal"—that is, to authorize privately owned raiders to prey on enemy shipping—"and make Rules concerning Captures on Land and Water, To Raise and support Armies," and to oversee the training and deployment of the various state militias. Article I also contains one of only a handful of provisions in the Constitution that place a direct ban on state action by declaring in Section 10 that "No State shall . . . keep Troops, or Ships of War in time of Peace." The founders clearly wanted Congress at the center of military decision making.

But the president possesses considerable war-making powers as well. In Article II, Section 2 the Constitution names the president the "Commander in Chief of the Army and Navy of the United States" as well as the state militias when they are called into service. The framers wanted the nation's chief executive calling the strategic shots when war broke out. They were looking—almost literally—at one of the nation's most revered military heroes, convention president George Washington, when they drafted the Constitution's provisions for the presidency. It seemed entirely natural to them that, in a time of war, a man like Washington needed to be in charge. "The propriety of this provision is so evident in itself . . . that little need be said to explain or enforce it," wrote Alexander Hamilton in Federalist No. 74, "of all the cares and concerns of government, the direction of war most peculiarly demands those qualities that distinguish the exercise of power by a single hand. The direction of war implies the direction of the common strength; and the power of directing and employing the common strength, forms a usual and essential part in the definition of the executive authority."

But where exactly is the boundary between Congress's power to declare war and raise armies and the president's power to deploy those armies? Conflicts between these powers arise at multiple points, chief among them the definition of war itself. Congress officially declares war, yes, but can the president as commander in chief place American soldiers in harm's way without actually designating a given conflict a "war"? Congress has often tried to say no, but over 100,000 Americans have died in military actions taken by eleven presidents since Congress last formally declared war, in December 1941. And once a war—declared or not—is undertaken, what is the scope of Congress's authority to expand, limit, or terminate that war, particularly in relation to the president? Can Congress, for example, simply withhold the funds necessary to raise and equip the armed forces, thus fulfilling its duties under Article I, Section 8, and in so doing hamstring the president in his ability to wage war? Does Congress have oversight duties requiring it to convene special committees to investigate the way a war is being prosecuted?

Congress and the courts have been reluctant to impose significant restrictions on the president's powers as commander in chief, realizing that in a time of war, national security may well require a president to exercise extraordinary authority. But they have also been reluctant to give the presidency a blank check in defining when the United States is actually in a state of war and how that war may be prosecuted. Congress tries to act as watchdog over military actions initiated by the president. For example, the War Powers Resolution of 1973 requires that a president who commits American troops to a military action must either explain his rationale for doing so within sixty days or shut down the operation. The Supreme Court has held that presidents cannot unilaterally define any given situation as a "war" and subsequently exercise what would otherwise be excessive authority.

As we will see, war powers questions in general have a long and controversial history. When Barbara Lee offered her lone dissenting vote, she stepped directly into a thicket of constitutional and legal controversy. She understood this quite well. "I'm opposed to granting that broad power to any president," she told a reporter. "I believe Congress has got to be part of the decision-making process when we're talking about going to war against sovereign nations." Lee believed that the resolution authorizing President Bush to use force against the terrorist network in Afghanistan was an abdication of Congress's responsibility to oversee the war-making process. "I am an American who has tried to protect our democracy, who has tried to protect our system of checks and balances," she insisted. "We've got to make sure that the Constitution prevails at the same time that we increase our public safety." Representative Lee's reading of the Constitution placed Congress at the center of the declaring and waging of war; others believe that responsibility lies elsewhere or that it should be shared between the executive and legislative branches.

Treatment of Dissenters, Enemy Aliens, and Draft Resisters

Subjected to withering criticism herself for her stance, Lee expressed concern about the treatment of other dissenting American citizens, particularly those of foreign birth, as the nation pursued its war on terrorism. "Congress must keep those checks and balances in place so that our civil liberties aren't eroded in this moment of extreme adversity," she said (*Los Angeles Times*, September 23, 2001, A2). Lee might have been thinking of past incidents like Robert Prager's "patriotic murder," when the sentiments of a community galvanized by war and the need to maintain some form of internal security against foreign threats led to mob violence. The Prager incident illustrates the thorny legal problems caused by the manner in which dissenting voices are treated once the decision has been made to wage war.

The Constitution contains several provisions that may be used in a time of war to justify restrictive measures against American citizens and foreign nationals residing on American soil. Probably the most familiar such provision is in the preamble, which states that "we the people" created the Constitution to "provide for the common defense," and later in Article I, Section 8, which replicates the preamble's language by authorizing Congress to "provide for the common defense." This is a very broad, open-ended mandate that could conceivably encompass anything from a military draft system to government censorship of the press. Indeed, "provide for the common defense" has sometimes been used by Congress as an excuse to support projects that have little direct bearing on the nation's military establishment. In 1817, for example, Congress justified the funding of a large road and canal construction project by claiming that it would "render more easy and less expensive the means and provisions for the common defense." President James Madison found this rationale so flimsy that he vetoed the bill, calling the connection between war making and road building "an inadmissible latitude of construction" of constitutional language. Such direct clashes concerning the phrase "for the common defense" are rare, however. It is more often a political metaphor than a legal mandate (Hurst 1908, 8: 386–388).

Within the vague mantra of "providing for the common defense," what specifically does the Constitution tell us about acceptable (or unacceptable) wartime internal security measures? Not much. Article I, Section 8 authorizes Congress to "suppress Insurrections," and it would be possible to interpret as an "insurrection" behavior that impeded a war effort, such as resisting the draft or publishing military secrets. Section 9 allows Congress to suspend the "Privilege of the Writ of Habeas Corpus" during "Cases of Rebellion or Invasion." The writ of habeas corpus (Latin for "you have the body") is an ancient bulwark of individual rights, dating back to English common law provisions in the eighteenth century, in which the government is compelled by a person imprisoned for a crime to produce a legal justification for such imprisonment. If the government cannot do so, then the prisoner is set free. Suspension of the writ of habeas corpus allows officials to imprison people for indeterminate lengths of time without revealing the cause (Rehnquist 2000, 36–37; Levy 1999, chap. 2).

Aside from the habeas corpus and insurrection provisions, the Constitution has little to say concerning how far the government can go during a war to protect American citizens at home from real and perceived enemies, to what extent it can define criticism of its policies as disloyalty, and what measures it may take to protect military secrets and guard against breaches of national security. These matters have been left to the discretion of presidents, members of Congress, judges, lawyers, and other government officials, acting out of prudence, panic, or malice at various times in American history. Securing victory in war is a powerful, maybe even seductive goal, and it has led Americans to take extraordinary and at times repressive internal security measures designed to silence critics, punish draft resisters, prevent public dissemination of information, and so forth. "The war power of the national government is the power to wage war successfully," the Supreme Court declared in 1943. "It extends to every matter and activity so related to war as substantially to affect its conduct and progress . . . including the protection of war material and members of the armed forces from injury and from the dangers of sabotage and espionage." With this pronouncement, the Court unanimously upheld a curfew aimed only at Americans of Japanese ancestry living on the West Coast. "It is not to be doubted that the action taken by the military commander [imposing the curfew] was taken in complete good faith and in the firm conviction that it was required by considerations of public safety and military security," declared Justice Frank Murphy. "The Congress and the Executive working together may generally employ such measures as are necessary and appropriate to provide for the common defense" (*Hirabayashi v. United States*, 1943; Irons 1983, 234–250).

Robert Prager was not directly a victim of the government's internal security measures during World War I. But he was arguably a victim of the repressive atmosphere, encouraged by some agents of the federal government and theoretically sanctioned by the Constitution's war-making provisions, that directed a great deal of hostility at German-Americans, who, along with other ethnic minorities, were targeted by the government's Center for Public Information (CPI) as potentially dangerous subversives. The CPI produced leaflets, flyers, pamphlets, posters, and propaganda films (with titles like *The Beast of Berlin*) that stirred the sort of explosive "patriotic" passion that fueled the Prager mob. Had Prager lived, he might have been directly punished by government and military authorities, for the Woodrow Wilson administration and Congress—backed by a large segment of the American public—took extraordinary internal security measures during World War I, many aimed at Americans just like him: labor radicals and leftists who were allegedly allied with a fabled German espionage machine. Wilson administration officials and several congressmen publicly denounced the Prager mob, but they were partly responsible for creating the atmosphere that led to the mob's unfortunate behavior (Linfield 1990, chap. 4).

Of course, not all internal security measures taken by the federal government in wartime have led to excessive patriotic zeal or a license for violence. In fact, Americans overall have a pretty good track record in balancing the need for wartime security with the cherished American values of liberty and the freedom to dissent. But there are enough exceptions like the Prager mob scattered through U.S. history to inject a cautionary note that Americans, often despite the best of intentions and a constitutional system designed to protect individual liberties, are fully capable of allowing war to overwhelm the better angels of nature. At the very least, it will be seen that when war and law collide in the area of internal security and civil liberties, there remain many unresolved tensions and unanswered questions.

Battlefield Behavior and Military Justice

John Chivington's Sand Creek massacre raises a third set of issues at the intersection of law and war in America: regulation of the manner in which American soldiers behave when they are involved in what are ostensibly combat situations. When a soldier raises his weapon in the line of duty, he is at the cutting edge of war's darkest truth: the taking of another human life. He is at the very point of warfare that is the most difficult to control by rules or laws, but also the one most in need of such control. What, then, are the legal guidelines for permissible behavior by soldiers on the battlefield or when acting as an occupation force in hostile territory? How do we know that soldiers have crossed a legal line of acceptable behavior? Do civilian or military authorities create these guidelines and guarantee their enforcement?

The Constitution is largely silent on this matter. It charges Congress with the power to "make Rules for the Government and Regulation of the land and naval Forces." These responsibilities seem to flow naturally from the broader power to declare war. As one of the Constitution's framers, James Wilson, put it, "We all know the instruments by which an attack is made by one nation upon another. We all, likewise, know the instruments necessary for defense when such an attack is made . . . to raise and support armies—to establish rules for their regulation . . . these are the powers naturally connected with the power of declaring war" (McCloskey 1967, 1: 433–434).

Although Congress possesses broad authority to make rules for the nation's armed forces, in reality it has often deferred to the military on the day-to-day regulations necessary for training soldiers and conducting military operations. When the rules of behavior for American military personnel, the Articles of War, were first drafted in 1775, they were lifted directly from the British version, and the Continental Congress was given broad oversight responsibilities that were later embedded in the general provisions for congressional war-making powers in Article I, Section 8. The Articles of War were rarely revised over the ensuing decades; they were changed only four times between the Revolution and World War I, and these were technical rather than substantive changes, made by military men with little real input from Congress (Bishop 1979, 26). This does not mean that they were necessarily unfair or arbitrary. It does mean that civilian control over this area of the military establishment was often negligible at best.

The court-martial system likewise operated largely according to its own logic, independent of civilian courts of law. Although the Supreme Court has been reluctant to allow military courts to try civilians (even the civilian dependents of soldiers and sailors), it has usually allowed the military a free hand in trying its own soldiers (*Ex parte McCardle*, 1869; *Reid v. Covert*, 1957; *Kinsella v. United States ex rel. Singleton*, 1960). Throughout most of the nation's history, there was no way to appeal court-martial verdicts; not until after

World War II did Congress establish a court of appeals for court-martial proceedings. In the 1970s, the Supreme Court ruled that American military personnel possessed the same basic rights in a court-martial that civilians possess in a courtroom. These are both recent developments; up until about fifty years ago, the military legal system generally operated on its own and created its own guidelines for what was and what was not acceptable behavior by American soldiers. Congress was involved in military appropriations, it supervised the establishment and maintenance of the military academy at West Point, and it decided (along with the president) when to go to war. The matter of how war was fought and the process of rule making for soldiers in the field was normally left up to the soldiers themselves (Bishop 1979, 56–57; Generous 1973; Nufer 1981, esp. 2–5; Lurie 1992; *Gilligan v. Morgan,* 1973).

Congress could always investigate military behavior more closely; the Constitution's war powers mandate gives it the legal authority to do so. But the Constitution offers no specific guidelines concerning when or how such investigations might take place. As we will see, Congress has occasionally exercised this discretion. In December 1861, for example, Republican leaders in Congress felt justified in the wake of a series of Union defeats to create the Joint Committee on the Conduct of the War. There was considerable trepidation on the part of many congressmen, who felt that military setbacks should be investigated by military men. Others disagreed, arguing that the war-making provisions of Article I, Section 8 gave Congress clear authority to act. There were strong political reasons for creating such a committee as well: the Northern people were demanding to know who was responsible for the army's battlefield reverses, and congressional elections weren't all that far off. "We must satisfy the people of this country that things go on well," declared one senator. From the beginning, many viewed the committee as a partisan political tool for the radical wing of the Republican Party. Without a clear constitutional mandate beyond Congress's power to declare war, it was perhaps inevitable that the committee's work would become heavily politicized, often dependent on individual congressmen's reaction to press headlines (Tap 1998, 24).

Such was the case in the wake of the Sand Creek affair. When rumors surfaced in late 1864 that Chivington's "battle" was actually an atrocity-laden massacre, the Committee on the Conduct of the War responded to the public outcry by launching an official investigation. This was a difficult legal area. The committee was supposed to focus on the Lincoln administration, the behavior of the Union army, and Confederate excesses rather than the activities of a quasi-military western militia unit. Still, throughout the first half of 1865, the congressmen did the best they could, gathering damning evidence on the massacre and generating embarrassing headlines throughout the nation that turned the tide of opinion against Chivington and his men. "The committee's subsequent investigation kept the massacre before the public, certainly damaging Chivington's political ambitions," observed historian Bruce Tap. This was true. Yet in the final analysis, the committee was unable to directly punish the "butcher of Sand Creek," because by this point Chivington had resigned from the army. No one knew exactly what his status was in a military court, so an army attempt to court-martial him likewise proved fruitless (Tap 1998, 232).

In the end, Chivington escaped retribution for the Sand Creek massacre. He was never charged with any crime, nor were any of the soldiers under his command. Some in the government had a guilty conscience, however. In the Treaty of Little Arkansas, which the federal government signed with the Cheyennes and other tribes in October 1865, the army apologized for the atrocities committed at Sand Creek and promised reparations to its victims. The reparations were never paid. Four years later, Black Kettle would be murdered and scalped in another surprise military raid, this time by men under the command of another Union army military hero, George Armstrong Custer. Like Chivington, Custer would never be punished (West 1998, 307–308; Brown 1994, 168–174).

Conclusion

War powers debates, the treatment of domestic dissent in wartime, and the determination of what is and what is not an acceptable and legally recognized target in wartime—these three broad questions have thrown off the brightest sparks when law and war have clashed in American history, and they form the core of this book. These are contentious and unsettled issues. They were posed in the infancy of a nation born in war, and they haunt us still, more than two centuries later, as we launch a war on terrorism.

References and Further Reading

Altman, Andrew. 1990. *Critical Legal Studies: A Liberal Critique.* Princeton: Princeton University Press.

Ambrose, Stephen E. 1992. *Band of Brothers: E Company, 506th Regiment, 101st Airborne, from Normandy to Hitler's Eagle Nest.* New York: Simon and Schuster.

Austin, John. [1832] 1954. *The Province of Jurisprudence Determined.* Reprint, London: Weidenfield and Nicolson.

Basler, Roy P., ed. 1953. *The Collected Works of Abraham Lincoln.* 8 vols. New Brunswick, NJ: Rutgers University Press.

Bishop, Joseph W., Jr. 1979. *Justice under Fire: A Study of Military Law.* New York: Charterhouse.

Bork, Robert H. 1971. "Neutral Principles and Some First Amendment Problems." *Indiana Law Journal* 47 (Fall): 1–35.

———. 1990. *The Tempting of America: The Political Seduction of the Law.* New York: Free Press.

Brown, Dee. 1970. *Bury My Heart at Wounded Knee: An Indian History of the American West.* New York: Henry Holt.

Cushman, Stephen. 1999. *Bloody Promenade: Reflections on a Civil War Battle.* Charlottesville: University of Virginia Press.

Dirck, Brian R. 2001. *Lincoln and Davis: Imagining America, 1809–1865.* Lawrence: University Press of Kansas.

Dworkin, Ronald. 1988. *Law's Empire.* Cambridge, MA: Harvard University Press.

Ellis, Edward R. 1973. *Echoes of Distant Thunder: Life in the United States, 1914–1918.* New York: Coward, McCann and Geoghegan.

Generous, William T., Jr. 1973. *Swords and Scales: The Development of the Uniform Code of Military Justice.* Port Washington, NY: Kennikat.

Hart, H. L. A. 1961. *The Concept of Law.* Oxford: Clarendon.

Horowitz, Morton J. 1992. *The Transformation of American Law, 1870–1960: The Crisis of Legal Orthodoxy.* New York: Oxford University Press.

Hurst, Gaillard, ed. 1908. *The Writings of James Madison.* New York: G. P. Putnam.

Irons, Peter. 1983. *Justice at War.* New York: Oxford University Press.

Kelly, Alfred H., Winfred A. Harbison, and Herman Belz. 1991. *The American Constitution: Its Origins and Development.* Vol. 1. New York: W. W. Norton.

Kelman, Mark. 1987. *A Guide to Critical Legal Studies.* Cambridge, MA: Harvard University Press.

Kennedy, David M. 1980. *Over Here: The First World War and American Society.* New York: Oxford University Press.

Levy, Leonard. 1999. *Origins of the Bill of Rights.* New Haven: Yale University Press.

Linfield, Michael. 1990. *Freedom under Fire: U.S. Civil Liberties in Times of War.* Boston: South End.

Lurie, Jonathan. 1992. *Arming Military Justice: The Origins of the United States Military Court of Appeals, 1775–1950.* Vol. 1. Princeton: Princeton University Press.

McCloskey, Robert G., ed. 1967. *The Works of James Wilson.* 2 vols. Cambridge, MA: Harvard University Press.

McCullough, David. 1992. *Truman.* New York: Simon and Schuster.

Nufer, Harold E. 1981. *American Servicemembers' Supreme Court.* Washington, DC: University Press of America.

Raz, Joseph. 1994. *Ethics in the Public Domain.* New York: Oxford University Press.

Rehnquist, William H. 2000. *All the Laws but One: Civil Liberties in War.* New York: Vintage.

Richardson, Elmo. 1979. *The Presidency of Dwight D. Eisenhower.* Lawrence: University Press of Kansas.

Tap, Bruce. 1998. *Over Lincoln's Shoulder: The Committee on the Conduct of the War.* Lawrence: University Press of Kansas.

Watkins, Sam. 1999. *Company Aytch: Or, a Sideshow of the Big Show.* New York: Plume Library.

Weigly, Russell F. 1978. *The American Way of War: A History of United States Military Strategy and Policy.* Bloomington: Indiana University Press.

West, Elliott. 1998. *The Contested Plains: Indians, Goldseekers, and the Rush to Colorado.* Lawrence: University Press of Kansas.

Wormuth, Francis D., and Edwin B. Firmage. 1989. *To Chain the Dog of War: The War Power of Congress in History and War.* Urbana: University of Illinois Press.

2

Historical Background

War and the Constitution

Philadelphia's Independence Hall was full of lawyers in the summer of 1787. Of the fifty-five men who gathered there for the Constitutional Convention, thirty-four had some form of legal training. The extent of that training varied widely. Massachusetts delegate Nathaniel Gorham, for example, was a judge on the Middlesex Court of Common Pleas, despite his lack of a formal education in the law. Several other delegates had served as judges and magistrates, with various levels of expertise. Most of the lawyer/delegates had acquired their membership at the bar through the normal route available in early America: they read the requisite books, studied under an older, established attorney, and then were licensed to practice law after a brief examination. Some, however, were renowned legal figures, such as South Carolina's Charles Cotesworth Pinckney, who had been trained in the law in London and had attended lectures by the famous English legal expert, Sir William Blackstone (McDonald 1986, 220; http://www.archives.gov/exhibit_hall/charters_of_freedom/constitution/founding_fathers.html).

A constitutional convention teeming with attorneys made sense. Less apparent, however, was the fact that thirty-four delegates also possessed military experience, though some just barely so. Jacob Broom, of Delaware, made maps for George Washington before the Battle of Brandywine, his only recorded contribution to the patriots' war effort. Some had served in the ranks of the Continental army, others in various state militias. Hugh Williamson, of North Carolina, was a surgeon who in the aftermath of the Battle of Camden treated wounded soldiers on both sides. Thomas Mifflin was a Pennsylvania Quaker who found himself expelled from the faith when he received a major's commission in the Continental army; he was later involved in the efforts of the famous "Conway cabal" that tried to engineer George Washington's ouster from command of the army in 1777. And then there was Washington himself, America's premier soldier, who still looked every inch the commanding general as he presided over the Constitutional Convention. People looked at him and instinctively thought of famous military leaders from ages past. "Like Peter the Great he appears as the politician and the Statesman," wrote one delegate, "and like Cincinnatus he returned to the farm perfectly contented with being only a plain Citizen, after enjoying the highest honor of the Confederacy—and now only seeks for the approbation of his Countrymen by being virtuous and useful" (Brookhiser 1997, 59–60).

It is difficult to imagine a more thorough mingling of legal and military expertise than occurred at the Constitutional Convention. The proceedings were dominated by men who had expertise in the practice of law or of war, and often both. Few of the delegates did not possess either a legal or a military pedigree, and some even of these had made their mark in wartime policy making. Elbridge Gerry, a merchant from Massachusetts, was a member of neither the bar nor the army, although he had been dubbed the "soldier's friend" during the Revolution for his efforts in procuring equipment and pay raises for American soldiers. Another merchant, Robert Morris, of Pennsylvania, enjoyed a similar reputation during the war as a master of raising military supplies (Charleton 1986, 1–3, 5, 34).

The framers of the Constitution brought with them diverse backgrounds in the waging of war, but they had certain common cultural assumptions about the manner in which war should be waged. Chief among these was a long-standing American discomfort with professional armies. Before the Revolution, American colonists feared the presence of professional British soldiers in their midst as a potent weapon for use by the Crown and Parliament in bending the colonies to their authority. But this aversion ran deeper than the politics of empire. Many people believed that professional soldiers were lazy, dissipated louts, unable or unwilling to make a "real" living in the private sector. One New York City newspaper recorded rumors of the redcoats' "licentious and outrageous behavior," including allegations of robbery, property destruction, and attempted rape, observing that "such violence [is] always to be apprehended from military troops, when quartered in the body of a populous city" (Fields and Hardy 1991, 403).

Coupled with this fear of professional armies was a deep-seated suspicion of what might happen if a strong executive could combine political ambition with unfettered control of a professional army. The fact that in England the army's officer corps was drawn largely from the same noble class that advised the Crown and populated the House of Lords—the men who, according to the patriots, were leading the way in trampling American liberties—led many Americans to believe it important to avoid a melding of civil and military authority, because professional soldiers had a natural predisposition to act as a tool of the ruling class. "When there is any difference between rulers and subjects, [professional soldiers] will generally be on the side of the former, and ready to assist them in oppressing and enslaving the latter," observed one patriot writer, "for though they are really servants of the people, and paid by them, yet this is not commonly done in their name. . . . 'The King's Bread,' and the 'King's Service' are familiar expressions among soldiers, and tend to make them consider him as their only master" (Hyneman and Lutz 1983, 1: 198–199).

The fear of standing armies and of executive power had sometimes hampered efforts to prosecute the Revolutionary War. Patriots refused to create a single chief executive for the wartime government, relying instead on the Continental Congress, which could raise an army but did not have the power to raise the revenues necessary to maintain that army. As a result, the Continental army was a ramshackle affair run on a shoestring budget and beholden to overly suspicious state authorities for supplies, reinforcements, and money. General Washington and his aide Alexander Hamilton were driven to distraction by this state of affairs. "Aught not each State then be called upon to draw such supplies from the Country Manufacturers as can be afforded?" he wrote in a typical plaintive letter to Congress. "The distress most of [the soldiers] are in, for want of Clothing, is painful to humanity" (Grizzard 2000, 10: 334). Hamilton was likewise angry at the army's impoverished condition, though he tended to blame Congress as much as the state legislatures. "I hate Congress—I hate the army—I hate the world—I hate myself," he stormed. "The whole is a mass of fools and knaves" (McDonald 1979, 22).

The Americans' antimilitary attitudes served to embarrass Washington and Continental army veterans in other ways. In May 1782, a group of Continental army officers formed their own officer's club, the Society of Cincinnati (after the famous Roman citizen-general Cincinnatus), with Washington as its first president. The society was innocent enough, rather like an early version of the modern-day Veterans of Foreign Wars. Even Thomas Jefferson, who harbored his own deep-seated suspicions of professional soldiers, pronounced the organization a harmless one that "had absolutely no other basis but of benevolence and friendship" (Peterson 1984, 583). Be that as it may, the society aroused indignation and paranoia among patriots who saw in it the first stirrings of a dangerous professional military class. The assemblies in Massachusetts, Rhode Island, and Pennsylvania officially censured it, as did the governor of South Carolina. Washington was shaken by the ferocity of the assaults. "When this society was first formed," he wrote James Madison, "I am persuaded not a member of it conceived that it would give birth to those Jealousies, or be chargeable with those dangers (real or imagined) with which the minds of many, and some of respectable characters, were filled" (Rhodehamel 1997, 624).

Revolutionary War veterans such as Washington and Hamilton would remember these incidents when it came time to draft a new American Constitution. They would also remember the manifest shortcomings of America's first constitution, the Articles of Confederation, which barely provided for an organized army and had no executive to act as commander in chief. The preamble of the latter referred to the states entering "into a firm league of friendship with each other, for their common defense . . . binding themselves to assist each other, against all force offered to, or attacks made upon them." But the Articles created such a weak military establishment that the government could not credibly use the threat of force to persuade British troops to evacuate forts along America's western marches. The government also proved supine in the face of an armed uprising staged by impoverished Massachusetts farmers during the fall and winter of 1786–1787, led by Bunker Hill veteran Daniel Shays. In a series of violent skirmishes, the state militia defeated Shays's followers, many of whom wore their old Continental army uniforms, with little assistance from the national government. Again, Washington and Hamilton were flabbergasted. "To be more exposed in the eyes of the world and more contemptible than we already are, is hardly possible," Washington sadly observed (Rhodehamel 1997, 609).

When they attended the Constitutional Convention six months later, Washington and Hamilton strongly supported the establishment of a professional army and of an executive branch with the power to use it. Indeed, the Philadelphia convention as a whole possessed a heavy leavening of men who thought that the ongoing American fear of professional armies and powerful executives had perhaps been carried too far. But there were also many men at the Philadelphia convention who still believed in the dangers of a professional army, who feared the creation of a national military establishment that might be insufficiently guarded by civilian laws, and who wondered whether the provisions for a powerful new national army might not bring down the entire enterprise of writing a new constitution. Elbridge Gerry thought so, telling the delegates during debates on August 18 that "the people were jealous on this head, and great opposition to the plan would spring from" the lack of insufficient civilian checks on the national military establishment. Gerry believed there were already some radical Americans who were stockpiling arms to be used against any standing army authorized by the new constitution. He "thought an army dangerous in time of peace and [he] could never consent to a power to keep up an indefinite number," proposing instead that the army be limited to only 1,000 troops (Madison 1987, 481–482).

Gerry's proposal was impractical, and the framers wisely chose not to put such a rigid limitation on the army. Still, he was right about one thing: the American people as a whole distrusted professional armies. The framers could ignore such fears only at their peril. When it came time to draft those provisions of the Constitution related to war making, they therefore (as in so many other respects) had to strike a careful balance between power and democracy, between the need for a robust military establishment and adequate checks on the employment of that establishment. America's soldiers had to be equipped to properly fight a war, yes, but they also had to be ultimately subordinated to the democratic process.

The framers' chief device in this regard would be the separation of government powers by splitting war-making duties and powers between Congress and the presidency. As we saw in chapter 1, although the president would be the commander in chief of the armed forces,

Congress was otherwise given control of the nation's war-making apparatus. It had the power to declare war and to determine where and when habeas corpus could be suspended, and it was given sole jurisdiction over "making needful rules" for the military. The framers lifted this language directly from the Articles of Confederation, but now that the new federal government would have the power to raise money, the words had meaning. Congress could now raise, arm, train, and regulate a national military establishment without depending on fickle state legislatures for funding, and it would work with a powerful new chief executive, a president who commanded whatever sort of army and navy Congress saw fit to create.

With the creation of the presidency, however, a new question arose: Was Congress the only branch of the government that could involve the nation in a war? In mid-August, the framers debated a draft of Article II that gave Congress the power "to make war." Some delegates worried that the phrase "make" would hamstring the government, leaving it unable to act quickly in an emergency, particularly when Congress was not in session, since "make" implied a totality of power that excluded presidential action. James Madison and Elbridge Gerry moved to insert the word "declare" in place of "make," which would, as they put it, leave "to the Executive the power to repel sudden attacks" (Madison 1987, 475).

The debate that followed illustrates the difficulties the framers faced in fashioning constitutional war-making language that would preserve the delicate balance between Congress and the president, keep the nation strong enough militarily, but not too strong, and take into account the public's sensitivity on these issues. Some delegates wanted the war power invested entirely within the chief executive, arguing that the president "will have all the requisite qualities, and will not make war but when the Nation will support it." Gerry was troubled by such a cavalier assumption of vast executive power, stating that he "never expected to hear in a republic a motion to empower the Executive alone to declare war." Several delegates pointed out that since Congress would have the final say on matters related to declaring peace because of the Senate's treaty approval powers, then surely it should also have similar powers where declaring war was concerned (Madison 1987, 476–477).

The framers did change "make" to "declare" in the end, thus initiating the question that would thereafter lie at the core of the war powers debate: Does Congress's power to declare war prevent the president from placing American soldiers in harm's way? The Constitution created dueling military authorities in the executive and legislative branches, and the framers were probably not sure themselves how the inevitable rivalries between the president and Congress over control of the military might play out. The Constitution's war-making structure created the potential for confusion. However, at least one delegate wanted it that way. George Mason, of Virginia, bluntly stated that "he was for clogging rather than facilitating war." Efficiency in the waging and declaring of war might prove dangerous, so maybe confusion was itself a safety measure (Madison 1987, 476).

The subdivision of war-making authority between the president and Congress was a useful political tool for the Constitution's supporters—dubbed the "federalists"—to use in reassuring Americans that the new federal government could not use a professional standing army as a weapon of tyranny. Alexander Hamilton pointed out in Federalist No. 24 that the "whole power of raising armies was lodged in the *legislature,* not the *executive;* [and] that this legislature was to be a popular body, consisting of representatives of the people, popularly elected" (Rossiter 1999, 158).

At the same time, Hamilton painted a scary picture of the dangers the United States faced from enemies foreign and domestic. "Though a wide ocean separates the United States from Europe, yet there are various considerations that warn us against an excess of confidence and security," he wrote. Britain and France were still marshaling forces along the nation's western boundaries, with designs on contesting America's future claims to the continent. Hamilton pointed out that the country's Native American foes required constant vigilance and could easily unite with Britain and France to create a formidable anti-American coalition. "The savage tribes on our Western frontier ought to be regarded as our natural enemies, [Britain and France's] natural allies, because they have most to fear from us, and most to hope from them," Hamilton declared. Militias were useful, but alone they could not hope to long withstand the combined hostilities of America's enemies. A professional army was the only answer. Moreover, "if we mean to be a commercial people, or even to be secure on our Atlantic side, we must endeavor, as soon as possible, to have a navy" (Rossiter 1999, 158–161).

It is possible to discern in Hamilton's arguments echoes of the frustrated young Continental army officer who, while serving as an aide to General Washington, continually knocked his head against the prejudices and parsimony of state legislators who refused to properly equip or pay the nation's soldiers, even during the Revolutionary War. Thus, he rather uncharitably railed against some Americans' concerns about having a powerful standing army as the "dishonest artifices of a sinister and unprincipled opposition to a plan which ought to at least receive a fair and candid examination from all sincere lovers of their country!" (Rossiter 1999, 160). Hamilton also scoffed at the idea that state militias could properly defend American interests. During the war, he had seen the inadequacy of American militia companies on the field of battle. "I expect we shall be told that the militia of the country is its natural bulwark," he wrote. "This doctrine, in substance, had like to have lost us our independence. . . . The steady operations of war against a regular and disciplined army can only be successfully conducted by a force of the same kind" (Rossiter 1999, 166).

The various critics of the Constitution—lumped under the name "antifederalists"—weren't buying Hamilton's line, however. Nor were their objections "sinister" or "unprincipled"; quite the opposite, in fact. They feared what was to them the inevitable sinister machinations of a professional military establishment, and their objections were grounded in time-honored patriotic principles of limited government. They were particularly worried about the amount of power that would be concentrated in the hands of a president who could command a national military establishment to do his bidding. The president was nothing more than a "military king," argued one antifederalist, "with a standing army devoted to his will." Another referred to the Constitution's "standing army in time of peace" as "that grand engine of oppression." A spokesman for Pennsylvania's antifederalists wrote that "a standing army in the hands of a government placed so independent of the people, may be made a fatal instrument to overturn the public liberties . . . an ambitious man who may have the army at his devotion, may step up into the throne, and seize upon absolute power" (Kenyon 1966, 9, 57, 70).

As we know, of course, the supporters of the Constitution prevailed. In truth it must be said that the Constitution's three great areas of law and war—the war powers, internal security, and military conduct provisions of the document—were a strong but at best a secondary theme in the fight over ratification. They were subordinate to—or rather, imbedded deeply within—what seemed more pressing debates about states' rights versus federal power, the proper relationships between the government's branches, the vexed matter of slavery, and the creation of virtuous leaders for the new nation. By 1787, the Revolutionary War was already beginning to fade from a national consciousness that would evince a notoriously short memory for the hardships and dangers of war. The nation also had the reassuring presence of George Washington, the victorious general who would not be king, to soothe lingering suspicions about the motives of soldiers in peacetime.

This relative neglect of military matters would be a long and consistent feature of American debates over the nature of law and war. In the wake of such neglect lay a Constitution with fundamental, unresolved tensions concerning the legal limitations of war-making authority. Despite Hamilton's rather bland assertions, the nature of war making under the Constitution was far from self-evident or clear. This could be good or bad, depending upon circumstances. The diffusion of war-making power between the branches made it nearly impossible for an aspiring tyrant to create a banana republic–style military junta and seize control of both the nation's political and military establishments at once. On the other hand, Americans sacrificed certainty and efficiency with the Constitution's arrangements for waging war. The framers left a host of blank spots in the Constitution's war-making structure. What are the precise distinctions between "making" and "declaring" war? How do we legally control war and all of its attendant dangers once hostilities have commenced?

There are no definitive answers in the Constitution to these questions, and at least some of the framers wanted it that way. "We are acting a very strange part," Gouverneur Morris declared at the Philadelphia convention. "We first form a strong man to protect us, and at the same wish to tie his hands behind him" (Madison 1987, 475). Morris put his finger precisely on the central conundrum of America's attitude toward war making and its constitutional mandate. We want the power to unleash the dogs of war, in some cases terrible and "total war," and yet we want the law to keep those dogs tightly chained and unable to pose a serious danger to ourselves.

War and the Constitution before the Civil War

During the nation's first eighty years, unresolved legal and constitutional questions about war-making authority were muted. Throughout American history, the friction between war and the rule of law has been most starkly evident during times of great national crisis—the Civil War, World War II, the Vietnam War—when Americans have been compelled to confront directly the tensions and contradictions that are built into the constitutional system. But between the Revolution and the Civil War there were no profound national military emergencies, except the War of 1812 and possibly the Mexican War. These two conflicts caused some rumblings of dissent on the relative war-making powers of Congress and the presidency, but they were not pressed to the forefront of the nation's collective consciousness.

Americans were still unsure of the precise nature of the federal government's role in war, or even what a "war" was, in the constitutional sense of that word. In 1800, a Supreme Court case, *Bas v. Tingy,* established that Congress could authorize hostile actions against a nation that it deemed an enemy without making a formal declaration of war. This suggested that it was possible to wage war without declaring war, at least where Congress was concerned.

But what about the president's war-making powers? For example, what did it mean to call the president "commander in chief"? Was he expected to literally take the field in a time of war and command troops in battle? The ongoing American desire to keep civilians firmly in charge of soldiers would seem to have prevented such an overt—and possibly dangerous—mixing of civil and military rule. Yet President George Washington seriously considered taking personal command of American troops who were engaged in suppressing the 1794 Whiskey Rebellion, a series of violent disturbances centered in western Pennsylvania over a tax on whiskey production. Denouncing the rebels as "incendiaries of the public peace and order," the president laid plans to take the field, though he rather sadly wrote Edmund Randolph, "I cannot, constitutionally, command the Army whilst Congress are in session." The prospect of a sitting president commanding troops alarmed some Americans, but the rebellion collapsed before Washington could test his countrymen's sensibilities in this regard. No American president would ever do so (Rhodehamel 1997, 886).

Sixteen years later, the United States found itself again at war with its old nemesis, Great Britain. The War of 1812 brought in its wake a variety of disturbing events: British redcoats burned Washington, D.C., and incited Native Americans to slash and burn American frontier settlements; an American attempt to conquer Canada was badly bungled; and the underfunded and outnumbered American navy proved inadequate against Britain's bigger and better fleet. There was plenty of conflict to go around, from dissenters who openly traded with the enemy to incessant bickering between rival American generals. But the war generated little in the way of constitutional controversy. President James Madison had been reluctant to go to war against Britain—he knew full well how poorly prepared the nation was to fight a war—and seemed only too happy to pass Congress the responsibility. In June 1812, he asked for and received a formal declaration of war from Congress before pursuing full-blown military operations against Great Britain. To many Americans, the prospect of Madison, the erstwhile "Father of the Constitution," seeking congressional permission to wage war seemed to have settled the war powers debate firmly in Congress's favor (Miller and Maslowski 1994, 111–119).

This is not to say that presidents lacked the constitutional authority to put Americans in harm's way or that they did not do so during the relatively quiet years between 1812 and the outbreak of the Civil War. Throughout the early decades of the nineteenth century, American presidents authorized military actions—mostly naval operations—against a variety of foes. In 1801, for example, President Thomas Jefferson undertook naval action against the Barbary States of northern Africa to protect American shipping from depredations by Barbary pirates. He did so without any formal authorization from Congress, which later ratified American military action after the fact. Congress could at times grow annoyed when presidents pursued these little wars without their approval. In 1832, several congressmen grumbled about Andrew Jackson's little naval assault and marine landing in Sumatra; again, the goal was to suppress piracy. But for the most part, presidents understood that they could risk small engagements in the name of protecting American commercial and shipping interests abroad so long as the numbers were small, the casualties light, and the rationale reasonable (Boot 2002, 11–13, 47–48).

Something resembling a clash over the relative war-making powers of Congress and the presidency occurred during the nation's war with Mexico in 1846. The two countries were locked in a dispute over the precise location of the southern boundary of Texas. Mexico, still smarting over its humiliating defeat by Texas's upstart revolutionaries ten years earlier, insisted that the boundary was the Nueces River. The United States drew Texas's southern border 130 miles farther to the south, along the Rio Grande. The new American president, James K. Polk, was an ardent expansionist who had made a campaign promise to settle the Texas border dispute in America's favor, but months of fruitless negotiations had brought little more than a diplomatic impasse. Meantime, Mexican and American soldiers took up stations on the Nueces and Rio Grande Rivers, glaring at each other across the strip of no-man's-land between the rivers (Potter 1976, 1–3).

At this tense point in the conflict, Polk resorted to subterfuge and half-truths. After a brief skirmish between the two armies in the disputed zone, Polk called for an immediate declaration of war, informing Congress that "Mexico . . . [has] invaded our territory and shed American blood upon American soil." This was at best disingenuous and at worst an outright lie (McPherson 2000, 56–57). Once the truth was known, Polk's critics grew loud and numerous, among them an obscure freshman representative from Illinois named Abraham Lincoln. Lincoln demanded to know "whether the particular spot of soil on which the blood of our *citizens* was so shed, was, or was not, *our own soil*, at that time." In what came to be known as the "spot resolutions," he called for Polk to give Congress a full accounting of how he had managed to pull the nation into a war with Mexico and whether he had deceived Congress (and the rest of the nation) in doing so (Basler 1953, 1: 421).

This was not, strictly speaking, a constitutional clash between the legislative and executive branches of government concerning who was legally allowed to start a war. Like Madison before him, Polk requested a declaration of war, and Congress gave it to him. The dispute also did little to further Lincoln's political career. His future was damaged among Illinois Whigs, some of whom were embarrassed that one of their own had opposed what became a celebrated war (Donald 1995, 123–127). Nor did Lincoln raise any specific constitutional objections to Polk's actions as commander in chief. In fact, he suggested that in time of war, "good citizens and patriots [should] remain silent on that point, at least till the war should be ended" (Basler 1953, 1: 432). But this skirmish between president and Congress—or one congressman, anyway—small and insignificant as it was, did suggest that even in the wake of a popular war, Congress would not abrogate its oversight responsibilities on military matters so easily. Presidents would be given broad discretion in war making, but at least some members of Congress would demand a fair and honest accounting of what sort of war was being waged, and why.

Thus, in the years between the ratification of the Constitution and the outbreak of the Civil War, there were occasions during which matters of war powers and the legal authority to wage war did arise. But these were decidedly secondary matters in times that were dominated by other events. In fact, it may be that Americans grew a bit complacent on the issue. The various military actions the nation undertook between the Revolution and the Civil War were not of a nature that threw matters of war powers, internal security, or battlefield conduct into the sharp relief necessary to spark a national debate, and it may well be that antebellum Americans had come to believe that such matters would never really be a cause for concern. During the first half of the nineteenth century, the nation neglected its armed forces, shrinking the army and navy to dangerously low levels and periodically debating the wisdom of abolishing the military academy at West Point as an unnecessary expense (Miller and Maslowski 1994, 123–161). "All the armies of Europe, Asia and Africa combined, with all the treasure of the earth (our own excepted) in their military chest, with a Buonaparte [sic] for a commander, could not, by force, take a drink from the Ohio, or make a track on the Blue Ridge, in a trial of a thousand years," Abraham Lincoln triumphantly asserted in 1838 (Basler 1953, 1: 109). No doubt most Americans agreed.

When the sectional issues between North and South over slavery finally boiled over into civil war, an older and wiser Lincoln would learn that not all military threats to the United States would come from abroad. More generally, the Americans of his generation would discover that the framers' concerns about the constitutional and legal implications of war making were not quaint anachronisms, like powdered wigs and silk breeches. On the contrary, issues of the law and war would move to the forefront of the nation's attention, competing with (and even at times supplanting) the master national issues of slavery and race relations. During the Civil War, for the first time since the nation's founding, the legal ramifications of war making became vitally important.

Civil War: The Law's First Real Test

Debate over the legal ramifications of the war began in the North just weeks after the first shots were fired at Fort Sumter. As newly elected President Lincoln settled into his new office in Washington, D.C., he found himself in the midst of a sea of rebellion. The nation's capital was, after all, a Southern city, founded on land annexed from slave-holding states, Maryland and Virginia, that were seething with secessionist anger. Confederate agents and sympathizers in Maryland cut telegraph lines, destroyed bridges, and mobbed Union soldiers as they passed through Baltimore. Faced with an armed uprising almost literally in his own backyard, Lincoln acted decisively. He suspended habeas corpus and declared martial law in Maryland, and he allowed federal authorities to arrest several pro-secessionist state legislators (Neely 1992, chap. 1).

Lincoln took these actions without the consent of Congress, as required by the Constitution. He could not have asked for their consent, however, because Congress was not in session during the critical early months of the secession crisis. The president was, almost literally, all alone in a Southern city surrounded by Confederate sympathizers. "While I write this I am, if not in *range,* at least in *hearing,* of cannon-shot, from an army of enemies more than a hundred thousand strong," he wrote in September 1861 (Basler 1953, 4: 54). In the face of such imminent danger, Lincoln felt he had to act, and quickly, before the nation's capital was made untenable by pro-Confederacy elements operating in the largely secessionist-friendly Maryland countryside.

Lincoln's policies came under fierce attack by political opponents of his administration, who denounced him as a despot. Some Democrats started a rumor that Lincoln's secretary of state, William Seward, could, with the ringing of a little bell on his desk, arbitrarily order the arrest of any individual in the country (Neely 1992, 19). More serious than these rather predictable assaults from the Democrats was the outraged response from the chief justice of the Supreme Court, Roger B. Taney, who argued in *ex parte Merryman* (1861) that Lincoln had usurped congressional authority and exceeded his constitutional mandate when he suspended habeas corpus.

Lincoln's response mirrored that of his army officers: he ignored *ex parte Merryman.* Several months later, he did address Taney's arguments, in generalities if not specifically, in a special message to Congress on July 4, 1861. Admitting that the "legality and propriety of what has been done [in Maryland] are questioned," Lincoln asked, "Are all the laws, but one, to go unexecuted, and the government itself go to pieces, lest that one be violated?" Besides, he argued, "the Constitution, itself, is silent as to which, or who, is to exercise the power [to suspend habeas corpus] and as the provision was plainly made for a dangerous emergency, it cannot be believed the framers of the instrument intended, that in every case, the danger should run its course until Congress could be called together" (Basler 1953, 4: 430–431). He had a point—sort of. Article I does not really indicate who should suspend the writ "in Cases of Rebellion or Invasion." On the other hand, the clause is located in the section of enumerated congressional powers, so it is reasonable to assume that Congress must authorize suspension of the writ.

Lincoln was backed in this constitutional position by several leading legal authorities of the day, including Harvard's Joel Parker and Columbia University's Francis Leiber (Paludan 1975, 129–134; Hyman 1975, 90–92). Congress itself supported Lincoln's internal security actions in Maryland and elsewhere, and passed a resolution to this effect in August 1861. Two years later, in a show of support for the president and an attempt to assert its own voice in matters related to wartime internal security, Congress passed the Habeas Corpus Act of 1863. The act struck a balance between internal security and personal liberty, authorizing the president to suspend the writ while also requiring him to furnish lists of political prisoners to the courts, which could in turn release prisoners against whom the government's evidence was found to be unsatisfactory. This in effect allowed the Lincoln administration to continue its pursuit of wartime security largely unhindered. Although the president certainly had his critics, then and now—one historian lamented well over a century later, Lincoln was "a tyrant who would preside over the destruction of the Constitution in order to gratify his own ambition"—the Northern public generally supported his internal security policies as necessary wartime measures (Kelly, Harbison, and Belz 1991, 305–307; Anderson 1982, 193).

Lincoln was actually pretty lax in his treatment of white Southerners and Northern dissenters. He could be firm when the situation warranted it, as in May 1863, when he ordered the North's most notorious Confederate sympathizer, Ohio Democrat Clement Vallandigham, banished to the Confederacy after his arrest for publicly expressing "sympathies for those in arms against the Government of the United States." Lincoln did not directly order Vallandigham's arrest, but once the deed was done he stood by it, asking a critic, "Must I shoot a simple-minded soldier boy who deserts, while I must not touch a hair of the wily agitator who induces him to desert? . . . I think that, in such a case, to silence the agitator, and save the boy, is not only constitutional, but withal, a great mercy" (Basler 1953, 6: 266–267).

But such instances were rare. Lincoln was far more likely to overlook his Democratic critics and go easy on suspected Confederate sympathizers. Almost on the heels of his harsh Maryland measures, Lincoln authorized the War Department to release all "political prisoners" who agreed to abstain from any future disloyal activities (Rehnquist 2000, 59). In fact, he was a softy all the way around, routinely commuting the death sentences of Union soldiers who had been convicted of desertion. He referred to the review of sentences that occurred every Friday as "butcher day" and told one friend that he "must go through these papers and see if I cannot find some excuse to let those poor fellows off" (Davis 2000, 178). Lincoln had no stomach for harsh retribution against his enemies, North or South, and he accordingly applied a light touch in matters of national security and military discipline. "He was only merciless in cases where meanness or cruelty were shown," wrote his private secretary, John Hay (Burlingame 1999, 64).

In matters related to the draft, the Lincoln administration was likewise restrained and pragmatic. Both sides resorted to the draft early in the war to fill out their respective armies' depleted ranks; the Union and the Confederacy created the first such systems in American history. The North's version was at first aimed at the state militias. A decree issued on August 4, 1862, by the War Department required the militias to furnish the national army with 300,000 men (in addition to another call for 300,000 volunteers to serve out three-year enlistments in the national armed forces). This was followed a year later by the more direct Enrollment Act, which compelled enlistment by able-bodied men between the ages of twenty and forty-five. The Enrollment Act sounded stringent, but it had numerous loopholes. A draftee could hire a substitute, which in effect meant that rich men could hire poor men to get shot at in their stead. The law also allowed draftees to elude service by paying the government a $300 "commutation fee." This was no small sum in 1863, and, like the substitution provision, it served to give rich Northerners a chance to evade military service that poorer Northerners did not possess (McPherson 2000, 251–252, 356).

A conscription system of this nature was bound to create friction. There was a lot of grumbling and resistance, including a riot in New York in July 1863 that left 120 people dead and parts of the city in ruins (McPherson 2000, 388–389). The president himself was anxious to make the system as equitable as possible. Lincoln "intends to enforce the draft with such arrangements as will take from the present enrollment its present look of unfairness," Hay wrote. "He says he is willing and anxious to have the matter before the Courts" (Burlingame 1999, 70). Still, he would not tolerate draft evasion, and in September 1862 he took steps to curb the activities of draft dodgers and their accomplices by authorizing suspension of habeas corpus and application of martial law procedures for "all persons discouraging volunteer enlistments, resisting militia drafts, or guilty of any disloyal practice, affording aid and comfort to the Rebels" (Gallman 2000, 238).

The war powers question that would roil American politics during the late twentieth century—whether Congress or the president has the right to initiate war—was never an issue during the Civil War. Congress did not formally declare war against the Confederacy. It could not do so and maintain the central legal and political position that animated the Union side from the outset, namely, that there was no such thing as the "Confederate States of America" and that the South was simply an insurrectionary province filled with rebellious American citizens. To declare war on the South, according to the North's reading of things, would be an absurdity—a nation cannot declare war on itself.

The issue was not war but treason. But here the North faced a whole new set of legal problems. Treason cases have been rare in American history, because the charge is so difficult to prove. Article III specifies that treason can only be defined as "levying War against [the United States], or in adhering to their Enemies, [and] giving them Aid and Comfort." It further states that "No Person shall be convicted of Treason unless on the Testimony of two Witnesses to the same overt Act, or on Confession in open Court (Constitution, Article III, Section 3). During the early 1800s, the Supreme Court limited the scope of legal treason provisions still further, ruling that an act of treason must involve an overt, direct attempt to use force in bringing down the government (Kelly, Harbison, and Belz 1991, 1: 176–177).

Wholesale treason prosecutions against Confederates under such restrictions were impractical; in the end, the North couldn't even bring itself to indict Jefferson Davis. But if not treason, then what? Either the Confederates were foreign nationals, or they were wayward Americans. Both perspectives were fraught with difficulties. If the Confederates were foreigners, then Lincoln's entire theory of the war—that it was a lawful attempt by the North to thwart an illegal rebellion by misguided Southern Americans—was problematic. To admit that the Confederates were foreigners was tantamount to conceding the legal existence of the Confederacy, something the Lincoln administration could not do.

On the other hand, if they were still Americans, then Confederates possessed the entire panoply of legal rights guaranteed them as American citizens. Conceivably they could, for example, have sued the federal government for freeing their slaves, or at least demanded money for the privilege, meaning a million or so court proceedings for each and every slaveholder; this was even less practical than treason trials. How could the North justify such wartime features as prisoner-of-war camps for American citizens wearing Confederate uniforms? Weren't they civilian prisoners who possessed all the criminal law rights afforded American citizens?

In the end, the Lincoln administration, and the Northern government as a whole, was pragmatic in negotiating this thorny legal thicket. When it suited the federal government's purpose, Confederates were treated as de facto foreign combatants. Southern ports were blockaded, Southern soldiers imprisoned, Southern slaves freed, and Southern property confiscated as if the Confederacy was a legitimate foreign government. But the Lincoln administration never formally conceded the existence of a "Confederate States of America" and maintained throughout the war that Southerners had never actually left the Union (Hyman 1975, 224–231). The Supreme Court gave this perspective its imprimatur in 1863, when it ruled in the *Prize Cases* that the Confederates possessed dual legal status as both rebel insurgents and belligerent foreign nationals. "Civil War is never publicly proclaimed [but] . . . its actual existence is a fact in our domestic history which the court is bound to notice and to know," declared the Court's majority opinion.

The Court's opinion in the *Prize Cases* meshed quite well with the Northern government's general approach to constitutional matters. There was a remarkable degree of harmony among the three branches of the federal government concerning the need to be flexible and pragmatic in securing victory against the rebels. The accord between president and Congress became rather more strained, however, in the area of legal oversight of how the war was to be fought. In December 1861, Congress created the Joint Committee on the

Conduct of the War, the first real attempt by Congress to oversee at length and in detail the operations of an American army. There had been previous congressional investigations of military matters. In 1818, for example, a special committee had investigated Andrew Jackson's conduct of military operations against the Indians in Florida. But that committee had been short-lived and had offered no specific recommendations either condemning or supporting Jackson's behavior (Tap 1998, 33–34).

The Joint Committee was a different sort of animal. Ostensibly it was created to investigate a series of military disasters that befell Union forces early in the war: the disaster at First Bull Run and an ugly rout at Ball's Bluff in Virginia that resulted in the deaths of forty-nine Union soldiers, including Colonel Edward D. Baker, a former Oregon senator and a close friend of President Lincoln. Baker's death brought the defeat uncomfortably close to home for many in Congress, and there was a more general feeling that something had gone wrong with the Northern war effort. Rumors abounded that the army was peppered with disloyal officers, that commanding general George McClellan was "timid and weak," and that President Lincoln was too vacillating and incompetent to direct the sprawling Union war effort alone. "The massacre at Ball's Bluff is the work of either treason, or of stupidity, or of cowardice, or most probably all three united," wrote a State Department employee. Many in Congress had come to believe that these traits were sabotaging the entire military enterprise, and they wanted a committee to investigate before it was too late (Tap 1998, 12–24).

The Joint Committee's mandate was open-ended, and during its tenure it would look into a wide variety of war-making subjects: the conduct of individual commanding officers, the reasons for Union defeat in various battles, the treatment of prisoners of war, the creation of military technology, the negotiation of military contracts, and accusations of Confederate atrocities. Mostly the committee was a watchdog, keeping a wary eye on generals, war department officials, and the president. "The Creation of the Joint Committee on the Conduct of the War provided the means for impatient and patriotic congressmen to keep tabs on the administration and to ensure that Congress was kept well informed on the implementation of military policy," observed historian Bruce Tap (Tap 1998, 36).

The Joint Committee was a political entity that inevitably tangled partisanship and party loyalties with its investigation of military conduct. It was dominated by Radical Republicans, the wing of the Republican Party dedicated to emancipation, the prosecution of a vigorous war effort against the Confederacy, and a fundamental remaking of postwar Southern society. Accordingly, it tended to ask harder questions of generals with Democratic Party connections, like George McClellan, than it did with equally flawed generals who sounded Republican in their politics, like General John Pope. Although McClellan and several other Union army officers performed poorly enough that reasonable people could be led to question their competence—and perhaps even their loyalty—many Northerners thought the Joint Committee was more interested in conducting a political witch hunt than a serious investigation of the war effort. Even those more kindly disposed to the committee often thought it was guided by well-meaning but goofy amateurs. "They are a set of schoolboys playing soldier," fumed one newspaper editor (Tap 1998, 165).

Lincoln also had mixed feelings about the Joint Committee. The committee was dominated by Benjamin Wade and Zachariah Chandler, two Radical Republicans who sometimes criticized the president for being too accommodating toward generals like McClellan and for moving too slowly on matters such as emancipation. No American president has ever relished the idea of Congress looking over his shoulder, particularly in wartime, and Lincoln guarded the prerogatives of his office as assiduously as any other chief executive. He was apt to define his war-making powers as commander in chief very broadly and with a fairly high degree of exclusivity, and the Radical Republicans could sometimes seem as much a hindrance as a help. "Lincoln viewed the creation of the [Joint] Committee on the Conduct of the War with some anxiety," observed historian David Donald, "fearing that it might turn into an engine of agitation against the administration" (Donald 1995, 327). Nevertheless, Lincoln did not interfere with Secretary of War Edwin M. Stanton's cooperative attitude toward the committee, and he did nothing to protect McClellan and his Democratic friends from the committee's inquiries (Paludan 1994, 104–105).

Where the intersections of law and war are concerned, then, the Civil War offered both clarity and confusion: clarity, in that during its first real test, the nation's constitutional structure was equal to the task of prosecuting a war—the legal structure could destroy an enemy without destroying itself in the process; confusion, in that many of the constitutional lines of authority between the president, Congress, the Supreme Court, and the army were still tangled and unclear.

Imperialism and a World War

The Civil War provided the nation with its first extended trial of the three primary areas of law and war: war powers, civil liberties, and regulation of soldiers' conduct. But by 1890, the American legal structure had not yet been adequately tested in a conflict with a foreign power. The few military actions that the United States undertook before 1890—the War of 1812, the campaign against the Barbary pirates, and the Mexican War—had not been of a sufficient scale or duration to provide a true test of how the nation's constitutional war-making apparatus would operate in a conflict with a foreign adversary.

This mattered because war with a foreign power carries with it a wide variety of potentially troubling issues. Enemy combatants in a foreign war are likely to have different languages, religious beliefs, ethical values, political ideologies, and often skin colors from the American soldiers facing them in combat. Even foreign civilians friendly to American interests will likely differ from Americans culturally, socially, and politically in significant ways. This in turn creates a whole host of troubling issues concerning the possibility—in some environments, the probability—of American and enemy soldiers giving vent to the worst angels of their natures: racism, xenophobia, and even violent atrocities (Grossman 1996, 160–164). Whatever hatreds the "brother's war" that was the American Civil War might have generated between Northern and Southern soldiers could be eclipsed by the act of assaulting foreign men and women whose cultures were often very different from those of America.

During the nineteenth century, the United States had fought a series of wars with Native Americans, who could perhaps be considered "foreign" adversaries. But the Indian wars offered little in the way of guidance on how the legal system would cope with such an enemy. In terms of the war powers issue, the dynamic was quite different. The Constitution gave Indians a quasi-sovereign status as wards of the state, so it was hard to describe the various conflicts with Indians as constitutionally declared wars. Nineteenth-century Americans normally did not do so. Nor did the Indian wars constitute much of a test of the internal security aspect of war making. Indians' legal rights were subsumed under their ward status, whereby the ordinary structures of internal dissent during war—martial law and suspension of habeas corpus—did not apply (White 1991, chap. 4).

In the third area of law and war—legal restraints on the conduct of the soldiers serving in the field—the Indian wars did provide some precedent for how the constitutional system might operate with respect to war waged against a "foreign" foe. Rumors of depredations committed by American troops—mostly frontier militias—drifted east from the frontier throughout the nineteenth century, and from time to time reform-minded congressmen called for investigations. But Congress normally did not act on such requests, largely because there was no permanent congressional institution designed to do so. As noted in chapter 1, the Joint Committee on the Conduct of the War did feel compelled to investigate the 1864 Sand Creek massacre perpetrated by Colonel John M. Chivington and his men on Black Kettle's Cheyenne followers (Tap 1998, 232). Two years earlier, President Lincoln had believed it necessary to review the death sentences handed down to 303 Santee Sioux by a military court-martial after a bloody uprising by Native Americans in Minnesota. Lincoln went over the death warrants with the meticulous care of a career trial lawyer, and despite the vehement protests of army authorities, he commuted 264 of the sentences (the remaining 39 were hanged in the largest mass execution in American history). These were laudable pursuits; the Joint Committee was able to keep public attention focused on Chivington's excesses, and Lincoln was able to curb the bloodlust of an army tribunal that had obviously gone too far in its zeal to punish what one soldier called "a savage enemy" (Tap 1998, 232). But the actions of Congress and Lincoln in these matters were anomalous. Far more often, civilian authorities chose to ignore reports of military atrocities, allowing the army to decide for itself how it would deal with Native American combatants.

As the nineteenth century drew to a close, most of the nation's war-making provisions in the law and the Constitution had never really been tested against a bona fide alien adversary. But this would change. Even as the federal government declared the frontier officially closed in 1890, an entirely new frontier was about to open: that of American imperialism.

In a sense, the United States had always been an imperial power, if "imperial" is taken to mean an aggressive expansion of the nation's borders. Since the colonial era Americans had relentlessly gobbled up territory claimed by others—not just by Native Americans, but also by Mexicans, Frenchmen, Englishmen, and Spaniards—as the nation pursued its "manifest destiny" of stretching from the Atlantic to the Pacific coast. But many serious American policy makers had concluded by the late 1800s that the United States should pursue its imperial ambitions even further and acquire overseas colonies and possessions. If not, it was said, America would fall behind in global development and power. "Some stronger, manlier power would have to step in and do the work" of imperial expansion, Teddy Roosevelt warned, "and we would have shown ourselves weaklings, unable to carry to successful completion the labors that great and high-spirited nations are eager to undertake" (Healy 1970, 122).

There wasn't much in the Constitution on how the nation might go about conquering an empire. The framers were, after all, rebels against an imperial power and were not willing to overtly create a constitutional structure by which they could be what their own Declaration of Independence professed to despise. Article IV, Section 3 gave Congress jurisdiction over the western territories, and the Northwest Ordinance of 1787 provided a template for how those territories could be organized and administered. But both assumed that the territories in question would be placed on the path to statehood. No such presumption applied to overseas colonies, and therefore they fell outside the pale of the nation's constitutional structure.

The first major attempt by the United States to form an overseas empire came in 1898 with the Spanish-American War. The conflict somewhat resembled the Mexican War fifty years earlier, in that both were motivated ostensibly by assaults on U.S. military personnel (in the case of the Spanish-American War, a mysterious explosion on the battleship USS *Maine* while it lay anchored in Havana harbor was blamed on Spanish agents) but were on a deeper level attempts by American expansionists to acquire new territory. Both wars were also successful from an expansionist point of view. When the war with Spain ended in December 1898, the United States found itself in possession of what was left of the tattered old Spanish empire in the Western Hemisphere: the islands of Wake, Guam, Puerto Rico, Cuba, and—the grand prize in the Pacific Rim—the Philippine Islands. "It has been a splendid little war," exulted the U.S. ambassador to Great Britain, "begun with the highest motives, carried on with magnificent intelligence and spirit, [and] favored by that fortune which loved the brave" (Smith 1994, 238).

The Spanish-American War itself created relatively few legal or constitutional controversies where the war powers debate between president and Congress was concerned. President William McKinley was the last Civil War veteran to serve in the White House. "I have been through one war," he declared. "I have seen the dead piled up, and I do not want to see another." A genial, rather placid man, McKinley vacillated so much about the decision to fight Spain that hawkish American crowds burned him in effigy. For perhaps the only time in American history, a Congress bent on war had to force a reluctant president to act, rather than the other way around. McKinley was quite willing to let someone else take the final step. On April 11, 1898, he sent a message to Capitol Hill that in effect dropped the whole matter in Congress's lap. "I never wanted to go to war with Spain," he later asserted. This was not a man to quarrel with Congress over who had the power to go get American soldiers killed in battle (Linderman 1974, 28–29, 35).

Internal security was likewise a muted issue. This was partly a by-product of the war's relatively short duration—it lasted only twelve months—and low casualties; fewer than 400 American soldiers died in combat, and about 5,500 died from disease. There was not enough time or bloodshed involved in the Spanish-American War for real disenchantment to set in. The war also did not snatch reluctant civilians directly from their living rooms and turn them into soldiers. McKinley responded to the war's manpower needs by mobilizing units of the National Guard; the guardsmen griped a good deal about serving under the more strict regimen of the regular army, but such grumbling did not fester into the kind of open mutiny that would trigger a crackdown. Indeed, the government was swamped with volunteers eager to enlist and prove their mettle in what one observer called "the most popular war in which the United States has ever been engaged" (Linderman 1974, 63–64).

The war did create new and troubling issues regarding the conduct of American soldiers in a combat zone, albeit indirectly. With victory over Spain, the United States inherited both the potential and the troubles of the Philippine Islands. Many Filipinos had for years fought the Spanish authorities in an effort to establish their country's independence, and when Spain left, they turned their attention to throwing the Americans out. Violent confrontations in the Filipino countryside increased throughout 1899 and 1900, with insurgents destroying military targets, harassing and killing American soldiers, and persuading (by force, if necessary) wavering Philippine civilians to join the independence movement. By the spring of 1900, the United States found itself in a full-blown guerrilla war (Boot 2002, chap. 5).

The War Department responded with both a carrot and a stick. Army authorities tried to win the hearts and minds of the Filipinos by building roads, hospitals, and schools and making other civic improvements in an attempt to prove to the civilian populace that America's presence was a good thing. But the stick was there, too, and it was big: more than 70,000 American troops were stationed in the Philippines by early 1901. They were there to combat the often brutal tactics of the Philippine resistance, and in some cases American troops traded an eye for an eye, escalating their own capacity for violence and atrocity. Rumors abounded that American troops tortured suspected guerrillas and their civilian sympathizers, often treating the Filipinos with a contempt that was exacerbated by their different skin color. The rumors became so widespread and disturbing that Congress charged the standing Committee on the Philippines, chaired by powerful Senate Republican Henry Cabot Lodge, to investigate American military abuses during the Filipino War. Throughout 1902 (a year after the Filipino guerrilla movement had finally been subdued), the committee heard testimony from a variety of witnesses concerning the army's behavior, much of which was a sobering reminder that American troops were quite capable of allowing the dangerous environment of guerrilla warfare to blunt their moral sensibilities. One soldier named Charles Riley described for the committee the "water cure," a particularly gruesome device used to extract information from a prisoner. As Riley described it, the prisoner was "taken and placed under the [water] tank, and the faucet was opened and a stream of water was forced down or allowed to run down his throat . . . when he was filled with water it was forced out of him by pressing a foot on his stomach" (Boot 2002, 115).

The Committee on the Philippines's investigation marked the first comprehensive congressional attempt to monitor American soldiers' battlefield conduct since the Joint Committee on the Conduct of the War forty years earlier. Still, it is difficult to say what this initial congressional foray into the combat zone really accomplished. Lodge was a supporter of American imperialism, and he did his best to portray American involvement in the Philippines in the best possible light. Embarrassing episodes like the "water cure" sometimes surfaced, but since the committee did not issue a final report, its findings remained buried from the view of all but the most diligent researchers. Although the committee laid a foundation for later congressional inquiries into soldiers' conduct, it did not establish any uniform rules for evaluating that conduct, relying instead on vaguely defined "rules of civilized warfare" as a yardstick to measure soldiers' behavior. As the Filipino insurrection faded from America's collective memory, so too did the findings of the Committee on the Philippines (Miller and Maslowski 1994, 312).

Fifteen years after the Filipino insurrection died down, the United States found itself involved in a much larger conflict: World War I. At the time the worst war in human history, World War I looked to many Americans like an unfathomable European bloodbath that the nation should avoid at all costs. President Woodrow Wilson wanted nothing to do with the war. Like McKinley, he was haunted by the Civil War's distant but bloody legacy; Wilson was eight years old when Robert E. Lee surrendered to Grant at Appomattox, and he had vivid flash memories of injured Confederate veterans returning to his hometown of Staunton, Virginia. In 1916, he was reelected to a second presidential term with the slogan "He Kept Us Out of the War." But in 1917, a desperate Germany initiated unrestricted submarine warfare against American shipping, and Wilson reluctantly decided that the United States had no choice but to involve itself in a war that had already laid waste to much of Europe.

When Wilson finally decided to lead America into the conflict, he followed the precedents set by James Madison, James K. Polk, and William McKinley and formally requested a declaration of war from Congress. In calling for war, Madison could point to the immediate threat posed by an old enemy (Great Britain); Polk tapped into the nation's greed for land, and McKinley fidgeted uncomfortably before passing the buck to Congress. Wilson appealed to the nation's higher moral sense. In an eloquent speech before the House and Senate on April 2, 1917, he asked Congress to join him in waging a war "to make the world safe for democracy. It is a fearful thing to lead this great peaceful people into war," he declared, "but the right is more precious than the peace." Congress obliged, though not without some grumbling and latent isolationist sentiments. One senator, George W. Norris, of Nebraska, charged that the war had been generated up to help the rich get richer; it would "benefit only the class of people ... who have already made millions of dollars, and who will make many hundreds of millions more if we get into the war" (Kennedy 1980, 21).

Norris's words were greeted with cries of treason from the Senate floor. Although some antiwar congressmen agreed with Norris, many more felt that Germany's submarine policies had forced American involvement in the war. Others found Wilson's crusading rationale appealing and genuinely believed that the kaiser's Germany represented a threat to freedom and democracy. In the end, only six senators and fifty representatives voted against the resolution for war (Kennedy 1980, 23).

But there were ongoing areas of conflict between president and Congress throughout World War I. Wilson's critics in the Republican Party were numerous and loud, and they spoke for a significant segment of the American populace that was uneasy about the U.S. entry into the war. Some of the disagreements were about genuine differences of opinion; others were about partisan politics. But the root of disagreement between the president and Congress lay in the historical tug-of-war between the executive and legislative branches for ultimate policy-making authority. As we have seen, during the Civil War Lincoln proved to be a strong chief executive, and in many ways he established the presidency as the nation's foremost war-making authority. But presidential authority in general steadily waned in the decades after the war. Congress assumed ascendancy in nearly all major areas of policy making while the presidency groaned under the burden of impeachment during Andrew Johnson's presidency, corruption during the Grant administration, and mediocrity under just about everyone else (McDonald 1994, 277–279).

Teddy Roosevelt reinvigorated the White House in 1901 with his talk of a presidential "bully pulpit" that could shape public opinion; fifteen years later Wilson followed Roosevelt's lead in trying to restore presidential power and dignity. But Congress was not supine, particularly during a time of war. In the summer of 1917, Senator John Weeks, harking back to the Civil War, tried to create a new version of the Joint Committee on the Conduct of the War. The idea horrified Wilson. Such a committee, he believed, would make his job as commander in chief "practically impossible" (Kennedy 1980, 123). Throughout the war there were sporadic attempts, led by various congressmen, to seize control of the war effort from Wilson, including a proposal to create a special "war cabinet" of three private citizens that would have, in the words of historian David M. Kennedy, "effectively reduced Wilson to a figurehead" (Kennedy 1980, 125). He managed to beat back this proposal, too.

But the Senate did create a Committee on Military Affairs, which heard testimony on a variety of war-related matters, and after the war a committee chaired by Republican representative William J. Graham, of Illinois, investigated the executive branch's wartime conduct in considerable detail. The Graham Committee had ten Republicans and five Democrats, and its investigation quickly developed a reputation as a political hatchet job, with Wilson's Republican critics peering into the darkest corners of the war effort seeking out material to be used against the president. Army general Peyton C. March recalled, "I was asked about everything, from why General [Hugh L.] Scott was given a Distinguished Service Medal to the movement of Czecho-Slovak troops in Siberia. . . . These questions, of course, were perfectly outrageous." The Graham Committee's majority report castigated the Wilson administration for various administrative oversights and shortcomings, while the minority report, written by the president's allies, ripped the majority report as "biased, erroneous, and totally misleading. It is entirely useless for historical purposes except as an example of ingratitude on the part of some to those who bravely did their duty in the Nation's great crisis" (March 1932, 352–354).

In response to Congress's war-making initiatives, Wilson and his allies pressed for and, after much hard political infighting, received a sweeping affirmation of presidential war-making authority in the Overman Act of 1918. The act (named after Senator Lee Overman, of North Carolina, a staunch Wilson supporter) allowed the president, during a time of war, nearly unlimited authority in choosing how to arrange the various departments of the executive branch. Congress would no longer have any input on how the War Department, the Treasury Department, or any other executive agency was organized or how they would interact with other government agencies. Wilson called for this measure as a way of increasing efficiency, and his allies pointed out that the Constitution probably gave him these powers anyway as commander in chief. The act was also temporary; it would expire one year after the war ended. The administration's critics seethed over what they saw as a ham-handed use of presidential power, but in the end Wilson got his wish, and the Overman Act became law in April 1918 (Kelly, Harbison, and Belz 1991, 439–440).

A potentially more significant presidential mandate lay in the passage of the Lever Act, which allowed Wilson to exercise sweeping control of the wartime national economy. Americans were discovering that modern warfare could wreak havoc on a sprawling, complex, modern economy, and Congress responded—again, with a lot of grumbling from Wilson's critics—by giving the president wide latitude in manipulating market prices, supplies, and demand, particularly in the areas of food and fuel production. Under the aegis of the war effort, Wilson could set price ceilings, control distribution procedures, and even take over the operation of vital wartime industries, and he could do these things with relatively little input from Congress or the states (Livermore 1966, 50–55).

Wilson's war-making powers were also strengthened in the area of internal security with passage of the Espionage Act of 1917. American anti-German sentiment often shaded off into hysteria (as witnessed by the Robert Prager incident discussed in chapter 1), and many people worried about the presence of a German spy network in the United States that could sabotage the war effort. Congress responded to these fears with the Espionage Act, which gave the president broad power to suppress activities he deemed security threats. This included not just outright spying for the enemy but also draft resistance, publishing sensitive military information, transporting goods that might be of use to the enemy, and counterfeiting documents such as passports. Wilson's administration could use the Espionage Act to do much more than curb overt acts of disloyalty; it could suppress dissenting political opinions. The act's preamble stated in ominously vague language that the government could prosecute anyone who "shall wilfully make or convey false reports or false statements with intent to interfere with the operation or success of the military or naval forces of the United States, or to promote the success of its enemies, or . . . shall wilfully utter, print, write, or publish any disloyal, profane, scurrilous, or abusive language about the form of government of the United States, or the Constitution of the United States, or the military or naval forces of the United States, or the flag." The government could fine offenders up to $10,000 and imprison them for up to twenty years (Chafee 1941, 38–40).

Wilson wanted all these new war-making powers, and he used them. He organized the various executive agencies in charge of the war effort with less and less input from Congress as the war ground on, and quite a few people were jailed under the Espionage Act for doing little more than espousing leftist politics or openly criticizing the president. But it is important to keep in mind that the president did not just peremptorily seize these powers, like a generalissimo in a banana republic; rather, Congress voluntarily gave them away, with acts of legislation and a very broad interpretation of the president's war-making authority under the Constitution. In fact, Congress went out of its way to see to it that Wilson possessed the statutory means of victory. In May 1918, for example, Congress amended the Espionage Act so that it directly applied to individual "disloyal" acts and words, not just conspiracies, and it did so with broad popular support. "Individual disloyal utterances ... naturally irritated the communities in which they occurred," declared Attorney General Thomas W. Gregory, which in turn created "dissatisfaction with the inadequacy of the Federal law to reach such cases. Consequently there was a popular demand for [an amendment to the Espionage Act that] would cover such cases" (Chafee 1941, 40). Congress and the people gave away a lot to the president in the name of winning World War I.

So did the Supreme Court. Although the war ended before the Court could review most of the war-making measures pursued by Congress and the president, the one issue that did come before it— the wartime draft in the *Selective Draft Law Cases* (1918)—received unanimous approval. After the war, the Supreme Court largely validated the sweeping wartime powers awarded the president and the federal government in general. The Court upheld the constitutionality of the Espionage Act in *Schenck v. United States* (1919), in which Justice Oliver Wendell Holmes Jr. enunciated the famous doctrine that the government could act against words that pose "a clear and present danger that they will bring about the substantive evils that Congress has a right to prevent." In the same case, the Court upheld the controversial imprisonment of several individuals for their alleged seditious speeches. The Court also allowed Congress to keep intact its wartime powers to regulate key areas of the national economy, and even when it struck down some aspects of this authority—as in *United States v. L. Cohen Grocery Co.* (1921), when it invalidated that section of the Lever Act that set price controls on food—it did so cautiously, making clear that it did not dispute "the complete and undivided character of the war power" but rather had some mild objections concerning how that power was applied.

Nevertheless, there were thoughtful Americans who in the decades between the world wars tried to draw back from some of the implications of 1917–1918. Justice Holmes, in particular, who had validated government suppression of wartime speech so forcefully with his "clear and present danger" doctrine, had second thoughts about how far government censorship should go in the name of military success. In *Abrams v. United States* (1919), a case involving publication of antiwar documents by a Russian-born anarchist named Jacob Abrams, Holmes wrote that "nobody can suppose that the surreptitious publishing of a silly leaflet by an unknown man, without more, would present any immediate danger that its opinions would hinder the success of government arms." Holmes was a minority voice on the Court, which upheld Abrams's conviction, but a number of Americans also felt that matters of government power had perhaps been carried too far during World War I. The short attention span that has allowed Americans to consistently underfund the nation's armed forces has had one advantage: it has also left many Americans uncomfortable with allowing wartime expansions of government authority to remain unchanged once peace is declared.

Still, a line had been crossed. Americans were only directly involved in World War I for nineteen months, resulting in approximately 126,000 American deaths—a lot of funerals, to be sure, but paling in comparison with past big wars like the Civil War and the American Revolution and with the devastation the war had on other participants (France, for example, lost 1.3 million soldiers; Germany counted 1.7 million dead). Perhaps in a earlier era the American legal system would have shrugged off the effects of a war of such short duration and relatively low cost. But, for better or worse, the groundwork had been laid for a future expansion of government authority during wartime.

Law, the Constitution, and the "Good War"

The day after the Japanese bombed Pearl Harbor, President Franklin D. Roosevelt became the last American president to request a formal declaration of war from Congress. In a dramatic personal appearance on Capitol Hill, he invoked the now famous imagery of a "day of infamy" to describe the Japanese assault, and called on Congress to ratify the hostilities that were already taking place in Hawaii, the Philippines, Wake Island, Guam, and other American possessions under attack by the Japanese. "I ask that the Congress declare that since the unprovoked and dastardly attack by Japan on Sunday, December 7, a state of war has existed between the United States and the Japanese Empire," he solemnly intoned.

The national mood was such that Roosevelt had little reason to fear rejection of his request. "The facts of yesterday speak for themselves," he declared. "The people of the United States have formed their opinions and well understand the implications to the very life and safety of our nation" (http://www.yale.edu/lawweb/avalon/ wwii/dec/dec03.htm). Haunted by the images of enemy bombs falling on unsuspecting servicemen and the blackened hulks of American warships as they lay half submerged in the muddy bottom of Pearl Harbor, Americans were united in their desire for revenge against the Japanese (and their German allies; Hitler inexplicably declared war on the United States four days after the attack on Pearl Harbor) as never before in U.S. history. Congress granted Roosevelt's request and voted for war.

That vote marked the beginning of a generally cooperative wartime relationship between Roosevelt and Congress. Certainly the two branches were more cordial than had been the case between Wilson and Congress thirty years earlier. This was partly because World War I had laid the groundwork for a significant wartime expansion of federal authority. The prospect of a sudden expansion of federal power during wartime was not nearly so novel as it had once been.

FDR's response to the Depression during the 1930s had also established a constitutional foundation for granting the government extraordinary powers. When Roosevelt created a federal safety net for the millions of Americans devastated by the Depression, he did so in part by invoking emergency powers under his prerogative as commander in chief. He repeatedly conjured the image of a "war" against the Depression, declaring, for example, in a 1932 speech that "the fruits of depression, like the fruits of war, are going to be gathered in future generations" (Roosevelt 1938, 1: 847). This was the rhetorical flourish of a master communicator, but it was also constitutional theory. The Depression was as serious as any attack by a foreign nation, he warned, and as president he needed to be able to marshal his forces—social welfare programs, economic regulations, price controls, and so on—the way a general like Sherman had aimed his cannon or told the infantry where to march. "If we are to go forward we must move as a trained and loyal army," FDR reasoned, and he used this point of view to justify an extraordinary expansion of executive authority at the expense of the states and Congress (McDonald 1994, 402–406). Quite a few people found this argument spurious—the justices of the Supreme Court, for example—but by the time the United States was in a real shooting war, the Court and most other Americans had largely acquiesced in Roosevelt's robust new vision of presidential power.

Roosevelt further pushed the envelope of presidential prerogative in the 1930s with aggressive foreign policy initiatives designed to help the British—lonely and embattled by a Nazi juggernaut that controlled nearly all of western Europe by 1940—without actually declaring war on Hitler. In September 1940, FDR used an executive order to sell the British fifty obsolete warships in exchange for extended leases on several British-owned overseas bases. Congress squirmed a great deal at what came to be known as the "destroyer-base deal"; the idea of the president going this far toward war without congressional approval was worrisome, even among those who sided with the British in their fight against Nazi aggression. "Congress is going to raise hell over this," Roosevelt ruefully predicted, and he was right. Numerous congressmen railed against what Wendell Wilkie called "the most dictatorial and arbitrary [act] of any President in the history of the U.S." (Goodwin 1994, 147–148). Nevertheless, Congress acquiesced in the president's actions; in fact, the legislators were worried enough about the situation themselves to reinstate the military draft system in 1940.

By the time of the Pearl Harbor attack, then, Roosevelt had already transformed the presidency into a much greater instrument of national authority than had ever been envisioned by the Constitution's framers. George Washington, John Adams, and their generation would have been horrified by FDR's use of the Constitution's war-making powers to enact domestic programs, but most twentieth-century Americans had gone along with this process. There was criticism, to be sure, but with the terrible hardships created by the Depression, and with the rise of fascism in Europe and Asia, the nation and the world seemed to be facing unprecedented upheaval and danger. Most Americans had come to believe by 1941 that the times required extraordinary government intervention. Roosevelt was reelected to an unheard-of third term (and later a fourth term) on the basis of that belief, and a majority of Americans trusted him even as he grasped more levers of power.

After December 7, not many people were inclined to deny Roosevelt the authority he needed as commander in chief to defeat the Japanese and the Germans, and congressmen were even less inclined to pick any fights with Roosevelt that might be construed as obstructionism. Thus, they worked closely with the president to mount the most comprehensive and far-reaching war effort in the nation's history. Congress created new initiatives to deal with a bewildering variety of wartime problems, from labor shortages to price controls to industry regulations. The War Powers Acts of 1941 and 1942 authorized the federal government to regulate interstate commerce, the national forestry, industrial contracts, river navigation, and even postage services for American servicemen. Other legislation addressed exportation and importation of goods, the use of public lands for war purposes, the regulation of the merchant marine, the photographing and mapping of vital defense industries, the acquisition of industrial and farm labor, the establishment of a women's auxiliary to the armed forces, and the rationing of nearly every item that might conceivably be of use for the war effort. All of this was designed to facilitate the creation of an armed forces establishment numbering over 15 million men and women. In 1939, the federal budget was $9 billion; by 1945, it had ballooned to $100 billion.

Congress worried more about the wartime economy than anything else; it only infrequently ventured into direct investigations of soldiers' battlefield conduct. One exception was the Congressional Pearl Harbor Joint Committee, formed to look into what went wrong during the Japanese surprise attack, which had cost the lives of thousands of American soldiers. After months of investigation and hearings, the committee released its findings in July 1946. Among other conclusions, it exonerated the two principal military commanders on the scene, Admiral Husband F. Kimmel and General Walter C. Short, of outright dereliction of duty, but it did find that the two men had been guilty of "errors in judgment" in their failure to heed available warnings about an imminent attack and to take appropriate action (Clausen and Lee 1992, 287–290).

As with all such direct congressional forays into war making, the committee was either praised or criticized, depending upon one's political point of view. Some felt that the Republicans on the committee focused too much on trying to embarrass the Democrats; others believed that the committee's harsher conclusions fed the conspiracy theory (still entertained in some circles to this day) that FDR had known of the coming attack but allowed it to happen for political gain; and still others believed that the Democrats on the committee wanted to whitewash the entire affair in order to deflect criticism from their party's greatest president. Nevertheless, the committee's twenty-five recommendations did contain worthwhile suggestions, such as the development of greater coordination between the army and navy command structures and the creation of joint intelligence operations between the two branches. On this last point, one military observer wrote that "if such an intelligence agency had been in existence in 1941 and staffed with qualified people, as recommended, we wouldn't have suffered Pearl Harbor" (Clausen and Lee 1992, 293).

The most controversial area of the law affected by World War II occurred in the realm of civil liberties. World War I had set a precedent for significant curtailment of expressions of dissent and had blurred the line between criticism of government policies and outright treason. This mattered because, despite all the talk about universal American support for prosecuting "the Good War," there were Americans who, for various reasons, dissented from the majority view. Quite a few African-Americans wondered whether the war was an exercise in American hypocrisy, fought as it was in the name of freedom while Jim Crow segregation remained intact at home. Hispanic youths in poverty-stricken areas of California found little to rally their support for what many saw as a white man's war. Their open scorn for conventional society and outlandish dress in baggy, colorful "zoot suits" led to the four-day "zoot-suit riots" in Los Angeles in June 1943.

Conscientious objectors of various backgrounds likewise dissented from the majority's support of the war. Many of these Americans objected to the war on religious grounds, particularly those from Quaker, Amish, and Mennonite backgrounds. The government's response was considerably more lenient than it had been during World War I, when pacifists who refused to enlist were jailed. During World War II, the government created a special conscientious objector status—widely known as CO status—for pacifists and gave those who registered for the draft under this category the choice of either serving in the medical corps or performing some other nonviolent task considered of value to the war effort, such as war industry or relief work. More than 70,000 Americans served their country in this manner (Miller and Maslowski 1994, 208).

The government was less enlightened in its treatment of Japanese-Americans. Of all the Axis powers, American public wrath settled most heavily on Japan, the nation that had perpetrated the Pearl Harbor sneak attack, the Bataan death march (in which thousands of American prisoners of war were abused and murdered by their Japanese captors), and other atrocities. Add to this an undercurrent of racism that tainted many Americans' ideas about peoples of color, and Americans of Japanese descent found themselves with a target painted on their collective back. "A viper is nonetheless a viper wherever the egg is hatched," intoned the *Los Angeles Times,* "so a Japanese-American, born of Japanese parents, grows up to be a Japanese, not an American" (Dower 1986, 80).

Even people who were relatively enlightened on racial matters cast a suspicious eye on Japanese-Americans. Wild rumors abounded, particularly on the West Coast, of sneaky Japanese spies infiltrating the Asian-American population and plotting sabotage and mayhem. On the afternoon of December 7, with American ships still burning in Pearl Harbor, government authorities declared martial law in Hawaii and began arresting people among the islands' substantial Japanese population. Roosevelt authorized the FBI to round up anyone it thought was "dangerous to public safety"; four days later, 2,000 Japanese on the West Coast found themselves in jail (Robinson 2001, 74–75).

Roosevelt was subjected to overwhelming pressure, by the military and by the public, to do even more about the "problem" of Japanese-Americans. He signed Executive Order 9066 on February 19, 1942, authorizing the military authorities to remove civilians from areas it deemed vulnerable to sabotage and transport them to internment camps. The order did not specifically mention Japanese-Americans, but everyone knew whom the order targeted.

As a legal matter, the order was unprecedented. It eradicated American civilians' habeas corpus rights and subjected them to what was in effect martial law with no authorization from Congress. Even Abraham Lincoln, in the dark, early days of the Civil War, when the threat posed by sabotage to the government was much greater, had sought congressional approval for such measures. But the Overman Act's wholesale grant of power to the executive branch in World War I had laid the foundation for unilateral presidential action in wartime, and the War Powers Acts during World War II picked up on the theme. Roosevelt subsequently did not seek or legally require congressional approval of Japanese-American internment, and in any case, the mood of the country was such that Congress would not likely have interfered (Robinson 2001, 92, 97, 109).

As a moral matter, Executive Order 9066 was unconscionable. Approximately 112,000 Americans of Japanese descent were forced to abandon their homes and businesses and report to embarkation points for relocation to ten internment camps scattered around the countryside (Robinson 2001, 108). Four-year-old George Takei (who later portrayed Lieutenant Sulu on the original *Star Trek* television series) recalled waiting for the bus that would take him and his family from their home in California to Camp Rohwer in Arkansas. "All of us wore numbered identification tags," he remembered. "I was No. 12832-C." When they arrived at the camp, the internees "passed tall guard towers with armed soldiers staring down at us. Beyond the fence, a distance away, we could see internees who had arrived earlier lined up and waving forlornly. Beyond them were rows upon rows of black tar-paper-covered army barracks." George and his family found themselves in "a bare sixteen-by-twenty-foot space with raw-wood plank walls, three windows, and a floor of wooden planks" (Takei 1994, 19–23).

The plight of Takei and other Japanese-Americans technically does not qualify as a wartime suppression of dissent, for there seems to have been remarkably little dissent among this wronged group. In fact, throughout the entire war there was not one recorded example of an act of sabotage or espionage perpetrated by an American of Japanese descent. Many Japanese-Americans enlisted in the army. Despite this, by acts of commission and omission, Congress and the president allowed the internment of Japanese-Americans to continue even after the most flimsy excuses for doing so had passed. By 1943, no sane American could conjure the image of a Japanese invasion of the American mainland, aided by phantom legions of Japanese-American spies, yet most of the internees remained imprisoned in their remote camps until the very end of the war. Congress and the president did nothing. Even the Supreme Court went along with the program in its rulings in a series of cases on the government's internment policies (Robinson 2001, 112–113; Rehnquist 2000, chap. 15).

In the context of those terrible times, when millions of people died violently around the world and atrocities were commonplace, the treatment afforded Japanese-Americans may seem rather mild. George Takei was not the victim of any outright abuse while living in an internment camp. His biggest enemy was boredom, and, he wrote, "The most terrifying camp memory I have is of an Arkansas spring thunderstorm" (Takei 1994, 39). Certainly there is no reasonable comparison between Camp Rohwer and the barbaric prisoner-of-war camps run by the Japanese for their American prisoners of war, let alone the horrors of a place like Auschwitz.

But the internment of the Japanese-Americans was a serious miscarriage of justice and a failure of the nation's legal and constitutional system for waging war. Americans have long cherished the individual rights enshrined in the Constitution and the Bill of Rights—the first ten amendments—but the plight of the internees proved that an aggressive interpretation of the war-making powers of the Constitution could trump all of these other matters. The Japanese-American internment policy showed just how easy it was to upset that delicate balancing act in the Constitution between prudent and abusive exercise of the government's war-making power. Sometimes the Bill of Rights was not enough to trump the Constitution's war-making powers.

By the time World War II ended in 1945, the United States had fought six major wars—with Britain, Mexico, Spain, Germany (twice), Japan, and itself. Approximately 1 million Americans had lost their lives in these conflicts. U.S. soldiers had also fought countless smaller wars, in Tripoli, Sumatra, Samoa, and the Philippines, to name a few. When the lawyers and soldiers who framed the Constitution in 1787 thought of war, they thought of horse cavalry, cannon smoke, and smoothbore muskets that couldn't be relied on to hit anything farther away than the length of a modern football field. When lawyers and soldiers sat down 160 years later to work out peace agreements with Germany and Japan, they did so in the shadow of an atomic bomb's mushroom cloud and the future possibility of the human species' nuclear self-annihilation.

By 1945, the nation's legal structure for making war had been battle-tested in a variety of settings, times, and circumstances. In the three primary areas where law and war are concerned—war powers debates between president and Congress, civil liberties in war, and regulation of soldiers' combat behavior—what had transpired? How had the nation's legal system acquitted itself?

By 1945, it was established that Congress must place its stamp of approval on any extensive military action. Presidents had by themselves involved American soldiers in scores of small firefights, but serious and prolonged combat was a different matter entirely. Presidents who were reluctant to go to war—McKinley and Wilson—were only too happy to allow Congress the final say, whereas presidents who really wanted war—Polk and Roosevelt—or found themselves in a situation where bloodshed could not be avoided—Lincoln—had taken limited military action, but then quickly sought congressional support. No president had seriously asserted the right to create, maintain, and widen a war without any congressional approval at all.

Where wartime civil liberties were concerned, the overall trend had been toward a gradual and somewhat troubling expansion of government authority at the expense of individual liberties. Facing the perils of civil war and imminent national destruction, Lincoln had taken steps to suppress dissent and the personal liberties of suspected Confederate sympathizers, but he had done so with a degree of restraint and with more than adequate justification. The Wilson administration's more sweeping curtailment of civil liberties was less justifiable, and the government's treatment of Japanese-Americans during World War II even less so. In the context of how other nations have behaved in similar circumstances, the record of the United States in this regard was actually pretty good. But civil libertarians had a right to be worried, for it seemed that in the heat of battle, Americans were prone to shoving the Bill of Rights into the background.

Congress's sporadic attempts to investigate soldiers' battlefield conduct had not, on the whole, produced very encouraging results. The Civil War–era Joint Committee on the Conduct of the War set a standard for such investigations: committees could do some good work, but their activities were always heavily politicized and were frequently buffeted by partisanship and an intense distrust on the part of military authorities. The Graham Committee and the Committee on Pearl Harbor acted well within Congress's constitutional mandate, but their beneficial effects were limited. Far more often, Congress left the battlefield to the soldiers, for better or worse.

On balance, Americans at the end of World War II could look back over the nation's 150-year history and take satisfaction in the fact that the legal and constitutional system for waging war had acquitted itself well. There were problems, to be sure, but the dire predictions of the Constitution's critics had not come to pass. The United States had not degenerated into a military-led tyranny, the nation's armed forces had not become a permanent threat to personal liberty, and there had been no dangerous confluence of civil and military authority. The Constitution gave the president enough flexibility to respond to serious crises while still keeping the potentially awesome powers he possessed as commander in chief under congressional control.

But there were clouds on the horizon. Modern Americans would discover that presidents could overstep their authority and involve the nation in protracted battlefield bloodshed without congressional approval. As the United States assumed the role of superpower, and as the world became an increasingly dangerous place, even well-meaning chief executives might find themselves in over their heads, conducting wars in faraway places with no clear congressional or popular mandate.

Korea, Vietnam, and War by Presidential Fiat

Harry S. Truman confronted this scenario in the summer of 1950, when communist North Korea invaded South Korea, a protectorate of the United States and the United Nations. American GIs and their allies confronted tens of thousands of North Koreans—backed by Chinese money and weapons—as they poured across the two nations' border. U.S. soldiers found themselves penned into a small perimeter at the southern end of the Korean peninsula, their backs to the ocean. Telling the nation that "if the Communists were permitted to force their way into the Republic of Korea without opposition from the free world, no small nation would have the courage to resist threats and aggression by stronger Communist neighbors," Truman quickly rushed reinforcements to the beleaguered soldiers (McCullough 1992, 776–777). Through a brilliant series of moves by U.S. military commander Douglas McArthur, the Americans managed to push the North Koreans back toward their own border. Thereafter the war settled down into a protracted and grisly stalemate that lasted three years and cost more than 40,000 American lives (Miller and Maslowski 1994, 508–519).

The United States thus found itself suddenly thrust into a bloody war on the other side of the world fought in the name of containing communism but lacking any formal declaration or congressional approval. Korea was no "small war," coming in under the radar screen of Congress's attention and the American public's consciousness;

over 5 million men and women eventually served in the conflict. Nor did Truman seek Congress's blessing after the fact, as Lincoln had done in 1861. On the contrary, the administration defended its actions in Korea by arguing that the United Nations Charter provided a blanket mandate for U.S. military assistance to South Korea. This was the first time an American president had suggested that he could start a war without Congress's consent (Wormuth and Firmage 1989, 149, 183). Truman also created tension with Congress—and a considerable segment of the American people—when he fired McArthur in April 1951 over what he considered the mercurial general's insubordination and attempts to usurp civilian authority over the military. History has generally been kind to Truman on this score, for McArthur did in fact tread dangerously close to a serious breach of civil-military relations in making strategic decisions that could have had far-reaching diplomatic effects and were well outside his purview. But in 1951, "the reaction was stupendous, the outcry from the American people shattering," according to historian David McCullough. Congress led the way, with various members calling for Truman's impeachment, or, at the very least, a massive investigation of the administration's military policies (McCullough 1992, 843–844).

The McArthur furor aside, however, Congress's response to Truman's management of U.S. participation in the Korean War was, all things considered, fairly tepid. There was criticism, to be sure, but on the whole Congress seemed much more incensed by the McArthur firing (which was well within the president's constitutional powers) than by the president's unilateral assertion of war-making authority (which arguably was not). The Supreme Court did not involve itself in these matters much at all. The Court's 1952 decision in *Youngstown Sheet and Tube Co. v. Sawyer* did limit Truman's power as commander in chief by refusing to allow him to federalize the nation's steel industry as an emergency war measure, but it did not speak to the question of who may constitutionally initiate a major war.

Ten years later, another American president would start down a similar road, with more tragic consequences. This time the setting was Vietnam, another nation divided into a northern communist section and a southern democratic section. When soldiers and guerrillas under the command of North Vietnamese nationalist Ho Chi Minh threatened to overrun South Vietnam and reunite the country under a communist regime, American strategists again saw the specter of global communist domination. Throughout the 1950s and into the Kennedy years, the United States provided a slowly growing trickle of military advisers, hardware, and money to the government of South Vietnam. By 1963, the nation's commitment to South Vietnamese independence was considerable, occupying a growing portion of the defense budget and involving increasing numbers of American military personnel, some of whom were witnessing or participating in combat.

Unlike the Korean War, which created dramatic confrontations during its first weeks and captured a great deal of public attention, the Vietnam War snuck up on the nation. "It was almost imperceptible, the way we got in," recalled one observer. "There was no one move that you could call decisive, or irreversible. . . . Yet when you put it all together, there we were in a war on the Asian mainland, with nobody really putting up much of a squawk while we were doing it" (Schandler 1977, 3). Successive presidents—Kennedy, before him Eisenhower, and at a very early stage even Truman—made the critical decisions, with Congress largely rubber-stamping what at first seemed like yet another "small war" (McCullough 1992, 452). Since the days when Jefferson committed the American navy to thrashing Barbary's pirates, presidents have periodically deployed small numbers of troops in faraway places, on a scale that fit in that curious little constitutional space between the executive branch's "making" and Congress's "declaring" of war. Nearly all of these small wars had been short, relatively painless, and successful, requiring little in the way of congressional action and generating almost no controversy.

Not this time. The critical turning point came in 1964, when president Lyndon Johnson, responding to his military commanders' requests, ordered a massive increase in the number of U.S. soldiers and in the amount of materiel in Vietnam. By 1965, over 200,000 troops were serving in the war-ravaged little country, Johnson had approved military plans to carpet bomb enemy strongholds, and military expenditures had topped $400 million. Body bags brought more and more American soldiers home every day, and increasing numbers of young men were being drafted, willingly or not, to serve one-year tours of duty in the Vietnamese jungles. None of this was bolstered by a formal declaration of war, and Johnson refused to declare a state of emergency that might have placed the country on a war footing, fearing the political costs such a move might entail. Nevertheless, LBJ signaled a grim resolve to tough it out. "We will not be defeated," he declared during a speech at Johns Hopkins University. "We will not grow tired. We will not withdraw, either openly or under the cloak of a meaningless agreement" (Dallek 1998, 261).

Congress's Pendulum: The Gulf of Tonkin Resolution and the War Powers Act of 1973

Congress took a far more active role in the Vietnam War than it had during the Korean War. The Vietnam morass created two contradictory, seminal moments in Congress's long history of dealing with war powers issues. One involved an almost wholesale abdication of war-making authority to the president; the other was a landmark reassertion of its own claim to that authority.

On the morning of August 4, 1964, the USS *Maddox*, an American destroyer operating in the Gulf of Tonkin near North Vietnam's coast, reported that it was under attack by North Vietnamese torpedo boats. The *Maddox* claimed that it returned fire, sinking one boat and seriously damaging another. When he was told about the incident, LBJ's initial response was surprise that the North Vietnamese would even attempt such a brazen and hopeless assault on America's obviously superior forces. "The sons of bitches, what do they think they're doing?" he asked his advisers the next day (Dallek 1998, 148).

Surprise was soon replaced by shrewd calculation. In a manner reminiscent of Polk's stratagems during the Mexican War, Johnson seized on the incident to demand from Congress a resolution supporting immediate and powerful retaliation against North Vietnam. "I'll tell you what I want," he told Secretary of Defense Robert McNamara (within convenient earshot of the House majority leader), "I want the whole works destroyed. I want to give them a real dose" (Dallek 1998, 150). After a televised speech to the nation in which he characterized the attack on the *Maddox* as "aggression—deliberate, willful, and systematic," LBJ asked Congress to approve a resolution stating "that Congress approves and supports the determination of the President, as Commander in Chief, to take all necessary measures to repel any armed attack against the forces of the United States and to prevent further aggression." The resolution would expire when the president decided "that the peace and security of the area was

reasonably assured" (http://www.yale.edu/lawweb/avalon/tonkin-g.
htm).

Support on Capitol Hill for the Tonkin Gulf Resolution was overwhelming. Emotions were running high, and the resolution passed
easily: no dissenting votes at all in the House, and only two in the
Senate. Johnson was ecstatic, claiming that the resolution was "like
grandma's nightshirt—it covered everything" (Dallek 1998, 154). Indeed it did. "All necessary measures" could mean almost any number
of bombs, planes, bullets, and men. Thus, in 1964, Congress gave
Johnson a blank check to wage undeclared, prolonged war against
North Vietnam (Wormuth and Firmage 1989, 42–44, 218).

Eight years later, much had changed. Thousands of Americans had
died in the Vietnamese jungle, with victory never realistically in sight.
Thousands more Americans protested the war, evaded the draft, and
signaled their profound disillusionment with the government's policies. The war had become a deadly, pointless monster that devoured
America: its best young men and women, its sense of purpose, its
self-confidence. It devoured a president as well. Devastated by the
war and its travails, Johnson did not seek reelection in 1968. His successor was Richard M. Nixon, a war hawk who ordered new bombing raids on North Vietnam's cities and searched frantically for some
way to get out of Vietnam without making the United States look
like a loser.

In 1973, a sober, chastened Congress tried to undo the damage
wrought by its earlier abdication of power. It had already repealed
the Gulf of Tonkin Resolution, and now Republican Senator Jacob
Javits, from New York, sponsored a bill that would reassert
Congress's voice in when and how the nation went to war. The War
Powers Act asserted as its purpose "to fulfill the intent of the
framers of the Constitution of the United States and insure that the
collective judgment of both Congress and the President will apply
to the introduction of United States Armed Forces into hostilities."
The act then specified that future presidents must explain to
Congress in writing the reasons for any troop deployment within
forty-eight hours, and must end that deployment after sixty days if
Congress withheld its approval. The idea was to allow presidents
room for military action—like the founders, Congress realized that
some emergencies might require an immediate military response—
but to require eventual accountability to the people's representatives. President Nixon predictably vetoed the War Powers Act, but

his veto was overridden (Wormuth and Firmage 1989, 190–195; Ely 1993, 32–35, 48–53).

Meanwhile, the war in Vietnam ground down to its final, grisly end. Nixon gradually reduced American troop levels in Vietnam, so that by 1973 only a few thousand remained. All the while, he tried to convince the nation and the world that the almost pathetically weak South Vietnamese government could stand alone. This was not the case, however, and in 1975 the North Vietnamese launched their final, overwhelming assault. By then there were few American soldiers left in Vietnam. Nixon was gone, too, having resigned after the Watergate scandal and threats of imminent impeachment. The new president, Gerald Ford, reiterated America's commitment to a democratic Vietnam, but the words were meaningless without soldiers and guns to back them. South Vietnam buckled and collapsed under the treads of North Vietnamese tanks. Shocked Americans were treated to the spectacle of American helicopters frantically vacating the American embassy's roof in South Vietnam's capital city of Saigon, with communist troops only blocks away and desperate South Vietnamese clinging to the runners. American war making has never been the same since (Miller and Maslowski 1994, 600–601).

After Vietnam: Exorcised Demons?

For fifteen years after the fall of Saigon, U.S. guns fell largely silent. There were still small wars, to be sure. In 1980, President Jimmy Carter tried to rescue Americans who were being held hostage by the Iranian government with a miserably botched helicopter assault that seemed to confirm America's post-Vietnam doubts about its ability to wage war. In 1983, President Ronald Reagan ordered an invasion of the tiny Caribbean island of Grenada to rescue American citizens from the perceived threat of a Marxist island regime. Reagan's successor, George H. W. Bush, sent American troops into Panama in 1989 to end the despotic rule of Manuel Noriega and guarantee the security of the Panama Canal. The assault on Panama—like the Grenada campaign—was an efficient, largely bloodless, and professional operation (Miller and Maslowski 1994, chap. 18).

Operations of this sort have been around for a long time, with small groups of professional soldiers carrying out limited military and diplomatic objectives that created a minimum amount of fuss and publicity. But this time things were different. All military operations, large and small, were conducted under the cloud of Vietnam. Presidents also felt constrained by the War Powers Act, which rankled in a variety of ways. Some thought the requirement to consult with Congress on troop deployment matters was cumbersome and impractical. Gerald Ford, for example, deployed troops in limited actions in Cambodia and Lebanon during his tenure and found it impossible to report his actions to Congress until after those operations had been concluded. Later presidents usually didn't even try to comply with the War Powers Act; they deployed troops as they saw fit, and then informed Congress after the fact. No president except Jimmy Carter acknowledged the War Powers Act's constitutional legitimacy. Others viewed it as an unwarranted intrusion on their prerogatives as commander in chief. Congress, for its part, usually acquiesced in these fight-now-report-later arrangements as a necessary evil in an era of split-second military technology (Hall 1992, 911–913; Ely 1993, 63–65).

In 1991, the nation embarked on its first large-scale military operation since Vietnam. The target was Iraq, a nation that had fallen under the brutal rule of dictator Saddam Hussein. Hussein coveted the rich oil fields of neighboring Kuwait, and in August 1990 he launched a military invasion of that small country. Within a day Hussein controlled Kuwait, and there was evidence that he might then cast his sights on the even larger prize of Saudi Arabia. Alarmed by this naked oil and land grab, President Bush launched Operation Desert Shield, a defensive maneuver that placed thousands of U.S. troops in Saudi Arabia. Backed by the United Nations, the Bush administration began an intensive bombing and missile campaign against Iraqi targets in Kuwait and in Iraq. Plans were laid for Operation Desert Storm, a ground assault designed to remove Hussein's forces from Kuwait (Hiro 1993, chaps. 7–8).

For the first time since 1975, large numbers of American troops were about to be placed in harm's way. Although the Bush administration did not instigate a comprehensive draft, it did call up thousands of reservists to assist the frontline professionals. The specter of Vietnam haunted the nation, as antiadministration spokesmen and antiwar protesters (many of whom were veterans of the Vietnam-era marches) conjured images of a Vietnam-like "quagmire" in the deserts of the Middle East. Hussein himself did what he could to fan the flames of American dissent, warning that he intended to shed

American blood for every inch of Kuwait and that "the mother of all battles" awaited American soldiers (Hiro 1993, 330–341).

Worried members of Congress invoked the War Powers Act and asked President Bush to provide a rationale for the impending campaign. Like his predecessors, Bush refused to acknowledge the constitutionality of the War Powers Act and its requirements. But he did understand political realities. Although polls showed strong public support for the war against Iraq, there were many doubters as well. Bush was keenly aware of the need for a coalition effort against Saddam Hussein, both at home and abroad. He therefore asked for a resolution of support from Congress. Again, Vietnam was never far from anyone's mind; Bush's opponents in Congress worried about giving him carte blanche to wage war, as Johnson had received in the Tonkin Gulf Resolution. Bush supporters pointed out that the situation in Iraq was very different from that in Vietnam, that the United States had a moral obligation to intervene, and that Iraq's seizure of oil fields in the Middle East could have a potentially devastating effect on the nation's energy market. After an emotional televised debate, Congress gave Operation Desert Storm its support, but not without a good deal of hand-wringing and glances backward to Vietnam (Hiro 1993, 191–192; Ely 1993, 50–51).

In the end, the worst fears of those who opposed U.S. involvement in Kuwait and Iraq failed to materialize. Operation Desert Storm brought enormous military resources to bear on an Iraqi army that was much weaker than Hussein's blustery rhetoric suggested. For several months American missiles and bombers relentlessly pounded targets in the Iraqi desert, and then on February 24 U.S. commander Norman Schwartzkopf unleashed a crushing ground assault that obliterated the enemy. In the space of a few days, it was all over. The United States liberated Kuwait at the cost of only 122 battlefield deaths, while inflicting thousands of casualties on the dispirited and shell-shocked Iraqis. Bush stopped short of a total occupation of Iraq, calculating that such a move would exceed his United Nations mandate and undermine his political base at home. Saddam Hussein remained in power, albeit subject to harsh UN economic sanctions and a "no-fly" zone over parts of Iraq that were enforced by U.S. warplanes (Miller and Maslowski 1994, 638–642; Freedman and Karsh 1993, 410–427).

The Gulf War was by any measure a tremendous success. Many people felt the ghosts of Vietnam had finally been exorcised. But had they? No one could question the battlefield prowess of the U.S. military; the United States could bring to bear on any enemy unmatched technology, deployed by troops whose training and esprit de corps were superb. But in a constitutional sense, war making was more murky and unpredictable than at any time in the nation's history. By the end of the twentieth century, presidents routinely asserted their right to wage war without congressional approval, and Congress in turn cited a War Powers Act, the effectiveness of which was questioned by many observers. Civil liberties and the legal monitoring of battlefield behavior were relatively dormant issues, but they also contained blind spots and uncertainties. Perhaps most fundamental of all, Americans at the dawn of a new millennium could reasonably wonder whether a constitution drafted in 1787 was still useful and relevant when war was waged in the era of the nuclear bomb and the cruise missile.

References and Further Reading

Anderson, Dwight G. 1982. *Abraham Lincoln: The Quest for Immortality.* New York: Knopf.

Basler, Roy P., ed. 1953. *The Collected Works of Abraham Lincoln.* 8 vols. New Brunswick, NJ: Rutgers University Press.

Boot, Max. 2002. *The Savage Wars of Peace: Small Wars and the Rise of American Power.* New York: Basic.

Brookhiser, Richard. 1997. *Founding Father: Rediscovering George Washington.* New York: Touchstone.

Burlingame, Michael, ed. 1999. *Inside Lincoln's White House: The Complete Civil War Diary of John Hay.* Carbondale: Southern Illinois University Press.

Chafee, Zachariah, Jr. 1941. *Free Speech in the United States.* Cambridge, MA: Harvard University Press.

Charleton, James H. 1986. *Framers of the Constitution.* Washington, DC: Smithsonian Institution Press.

Clausen, Henry C., and Bruce Lee. 1992. *Pearl Harbor: Final Judgement.* New York: Crown.

Dallek, Robert. 1998. *Flawed Giant: Lyndon Johnson and His Times, 1961–1973.* New York: Oxford University Press.

Davis, William C. 2000. *Lincoln's Men: How President Lincoln Became Father to an Army and a Nation.* New York: Free Press.

Donald, David. 1995. *Lincoln.* New York: Simon and Schuster.

Dower, John. 1986. *War without Mercy: Race and Power in the Pacific War.* New York: Pantheon.

Ely, John Hart. 1993. *War and Responsibility: Constitutional Lessons of Vietnam and Its Aftermath.* Princeton: Princeton University Press.

Fields, William S., and David T. Hardy. 1991. "The Third Amendment and the Issue of the Maintenance of Standing Armies: A Legal History." *American Journal of Legal History* 35: 396–451.

Freedman, Lawrence, and Efraim Karsh. 1993. *The Gulf Conflict, 1990–1991: Diplomacy and War in the New World Order.* Princeton: Princeton University Press.

Gallman, Matthew, ed. 2000. *The Civil War Chronicle.* New York: Crown.

Goodwin, Doris Kearns. 1994. *No Ordinary Time: Franklin and Eleanor Roosevelt: The Home Front during World War II.* New York: Simon and Schuster.

Grizzard, Frank E., ed. 2000. *The Papers of George Washington: Revolutionary War Series.* Charlottesville: University of Virginia Press.

Grossman, Dave. 1996. *On Killing: The Psychological Cost of Learning to Kill in War and Society.* Boston: Little, Brown, and Co.

Hall, Kermit. 1992. *The Oxford Companion to the Supreme Court.* New York: Oxford University Press.

Healy, David F. 1970. *U.S. Expansionism: The Imperialist Urge in the 1890s.* Madison: University of Wisconsin Press.

Hiro, Dilip. 1993. *From Desert Shield to Desert Storm: The Second Gulf War.* New York: Routledge.

Hyman, Harold M. 1975. *A More Perfect Union: The Impact of the Civil War and Reconstruction.* Boston: Houghton Mifflin.

Hyneman, Charles S., and Donald S. Lutz, eds. 1983. *American Political Writing during the Founding Era, 1760–1805.* 2 vols. Indianapolis: Liberty Press.

Kelly, Alfred H., Winfred A. Harbison, and Herman Belz. 1991. *The American Constitution: Its Origins and Development.* Vol. 1. New York: W. W. Norton.

Kennedy, David M. 1980. *Over Here: The First World War and American Society.* New York: Oxford University Press.

Kenyon, Cecelia, ed. 1966. *The Antifederalists.* Indianapolis: Bobbs-Merrill.

Linderman, Gerald F. 1974. *The Mirror of War: American Society and the Spanish-American War.* Ann Arbor: University of Michigan Press.

Livermore, Seward W. 1966. *Politics Is Adjourned: Woodrow Wilson and the War Congress, 1916–1918.* Middletown, CT: Wesleyan.

Madison, James. 1987. *Notes of Debates in the Federal Convention of 1787.* New York: W. W. Norton.

March, Peyton C. 1932. *The Nation at War.* Garden City, NJ: Doubleday, Doran, and Co.

McCullough, David. 1992. *Truman.* New York: Simon and Schuster.

McDonald, Forrest. 1979. *Alexander Hamilton: A Biography.* New York: W. W. Norton.

——— 1986. *Novus Ordo Seclorum: The Intellectual Origins of the Constitution.* Lawrence: University Press of Kansas.

———. 1994. *The American Presidency: An Intellectual History.* Lawrence: University Press of Kansas.

McPherson, James M. 2000. *Ordeal by Fire: The Civil War and Reconstruction.* New York: McGraw-Hill.

Miller, Allan R., and Peter Maslowski, eds. 1994. *For the Common Defense: A Military History of the United States.* New York: Free Press.

Neely, Mark E., Jr. 1992. *The Fate of Liberty: Abraham Lincoln and Civil Liberties.* New York: Oxford University Press.

Paludan, Philip S. 1975. *A Covenant with Death: The Constitution, Law, and Equality in the Civil War Era.* Urbana: University of Illinois Press.

———. 1994. *The Presidency of Abraham Lincoln.* Lawrence: University Press of Kansas.

Peterson, Merrill, ed. 1984. *Thomas Jefferson: Writings.* New York: Library of America.

Potter, David M. 1976. *The Impending Crisis, 1848–1861.* New York: Harper.

Rehnquist, William H. 2000. *All the Laws but One: Civil Liberties in War.* New York: Vintage.

Rhodehamel, John, ed. 1997. *George Washington: Writings.* New York: Library of America.

Robinson, Greg. 2001. *By Order of the President: FDR and the Internment of Japanese Americans.* Cambridge, MA: Harvard University Press.

Roosevelt, Franklin D. 1938. *The Public Papers and Addresses of Franklin Delano Roosevelt.* 13 vols. New York: Random House.

Rossiter, Clinton, ed. 1999. *The Federalist Papers.* New York: Mentor.

Schandler, Herbert Y. 1977. *The Unmaking of a President: Lyndon Johnson and Vietnam.* Princeton: Princeton University Press.

Smith, Joseph. 1994. *The Spanish-American War: Conflict in the Caribbean and the Pacific, 1895–1902.* New York: Addison-Wesley.

Takei, George. 1994. *To the Stars.* New York: Simon and Schuster.

Tap, Bruce. 1998. *Over Lincoln's Shoulder: The Committee on the Conduct of the War.* Lawrence: University Press of Kansas.

White, Richard. 1991. *"It's Your Misfortune and None of My Own": A New History of the American West.* Norman: University of Oklahoma Press.

Wormuth, Francis D., and Edwin B. Firmage. 1989. *To Chain the Dog of War: The War Power of Congress in History and War.* Urbana: University of Illinois Press.

3

Cases

The "Least Dangerous Branch": The Supreme Court and American War Making

In Federalist No. 78, Alexander Hamilton tried to allay American fears of the new Constitution's Supreme Court by arguing that the Court had neither the power of the purse nor (more importantly) access to an army. "The judiciary, from the nature of its functions, will always be the least dangerous to the political rights," he claimed, "because it will be least in a capacity to annoy or injure them. The Executive not only dispenses the honors, but holds the sword of the community." The Court was the "least dangerous branch" because it seemed so far removed from the most crass definition of law that was observed in chapter 1: the direct application of force. Justices could not give marching orders to soldiers with guns, and that, Hamilton pointed out, meant that it had "neither FORCE nor WILL, but merely judgement" (Rossiter 1999, 432–433).

Of all the major areas of American policy making, the Supreme Court has had—on the surface—the least to do with the making of war. Perhaps this is due to the fact that few ex-soldiers have sat on the Court. Many of the framers had legal and military experience, and throughout the nation's history military men have mixed in the political environments of Congress and the presidency. Congress has always been well stocked with ex-soldiers, and twenty-four of our forty-three presidents have seen military action; nine were generals.

The Supreme Court, by contrast, has had relatively few military men in its ranks. Of the sixteen chief justices in the Court's history, only four saw military service. Of the ninety-two men and women who have sat as associate justices on the Court, only twenty-five possessed military records. On the current Supreme Court, only one justice, Chief Justice William Rehnquist, served in the military.

Nor has the Supreme Court been given a military mandate. Congress oversees the funding and regulation of the armed forces, and the president is the commander in chief. The Constitution, however, specifies no such tasks for the Supreme Court. When Congress first organized the federal bench in the Judiciary Act of 1789, it made no mention at all of a military role for the federal courts. The act allowed the federal district courts to review military sentences involving "no other punishment than whipping, not exceeding thirty stripes, a fine not exceeding one hundred dollars, or a term of imprisonment not exceeding six months." In reality, though, the courts usually left military discipline to the soldiers operating under the Articles of War.

Thus, the Supreme Court has had less to say about the legal questions surrounding American war making than might be expected. There has not been, for example, a Court opinion that definitively tries to settle the war powers debate between the president and Congress, although, as will be seen, the justices have found themselves involved in a variety of secondary issues that are related to war powers. The Court has been more actively involved in the questions surrounding suppression of dissent during wartime, because those questions tread on the familiar Supreme Court grounds of trial rights and freedom of expression. Taken altogether, the Supreme Court's involvement in war making has been sporadic and uneven, ranging from relative neglect to deep involvement, depending on the questions and the circumstances. It has never developed a consistent institutional philosophy on war making. It was probably never meant to do so, if the framers' unwillingness to mention the Court and war in the same sentence is any indication.

Defining the New Roles: The Court and War Making in the Early National Era

War was a minor theme for the Supreme Court during its first seventy years. The Court focused on cases that seemed more pressing and more directly related to establishing its institutional mission and fulfilling its constitutional mandate, such as creating its judicial review role and the federal judiciary's supremacy over state courts in key areas of lawmaking, finding a correct balance between federal and state powers, and offering legal answers to the many questions posed by the nation's burgeoning market economy. War and its constitutional consequences were far down on the Court's priority list, particularly in an era—between the Revolution and the Civil War—when the nation's military actions were mostly small, isolated affairs.

Those little battles, however, waged by the president in lieu of a formal declaration by Congress against the likes of the Barbary pirates did raise the question of when a war is actually a war. As seen in chapter 2, the framers left open a space between the power to "make" and the power to "declare" war. Congress was given exclusive authority to do the latter, but the Constitution allowed the president, acting as commander in chief, to do the former. Presidents could make war by sending American soldiers into harm's way. The framers seem to have intended this to be a limited power, taken by presidents when the immediate safety of the nation was threatened, and to be ratified as soon as possible by formal congressional action (Wormuth and Firmage 1989, chap. 4). Did that mean that the president's military actions prior to such a formal declaration amounted to a war per se?

The question would become relevant early in the nation's history. During the 1790s, America risked involvement in a real, honest-to-goodness war: the conflict between France and England that eventually engulfed the entire European continent. Despite pressure from Francophiles like Thomas Jefferson, President John Adams wisely resisted being drawn to France's side and tried to maintain a precarious neutrality between the combatants. Unimpressed, France announced in 1797 that it would forcibly seize American ships carrying cargo bound for its adversaries and that it would treat the crews of these ships as pirates (McKitrick and Elkins 1994, 537–538).

At the time, the United States hardly had a navy at all; the money to create one had been appropriated by Congress only three years earlier, and most of its warships were either under construction or still on the drawing boards. Desperate to find some way of encouraging American merchant vessels to help one another, Congress passed two laws. The first, passed in the summer of 1798, gave any American ship that rescued another American ship from the clutches of the French navy one-eighth of the ship's cargo in compensation.

The second law, passed a year later, sweetened the pot by giving the rescuer one-half of the ship's cargo if the ship had been captive for more than four days (Miller and Maslowski 1994, 102–106).

The precise language of each law was crucial. The one-eighth law did not name who was doing the capturing. The one-half law, on the other hand, stated that compensation would be due if the American vessel was captured by "the enemy" (*Bas v. Tingy*, 1800, 37). Everyone knew that France was committing hostile acts against American shipping, so of course France was an "enemy" by any casual use of that word. The law requires precision, however, and that innocuous word "enemy" would provide the fulcrum for the first major courtroom test of America's war-making powers.

On March 31, 1799, a French privateer seized the American merchant vessel *Eliza*. Several days later, the *Eliza* was retaken by the American vessel *Ganges*, commanded by a Captain Tingy. Tingy demanded one-half of the *Eliza*'s cargo as compensation. The ship's owner, John Bas, replied that Tingy was due only one-eighth of his vessel's cargo, because France was not, legally speaking, an "enemy." The way Bas saw it, France could only be an enemy if Congress had formally declared war, which it had never done. "The designation of 'the enemy' in that act, applies only to future hostilities in the case of a declared war," Bas's lawyers argued.

The justices hearing the case could see that more was at stake than merely the disposition of one ship's cargo, or even Congress's policy toward France. Here for the first time was laid bare the space between "making" and "declaring" war that had been left in the Constitution by the framers. If the Court accepted Bas's legal position, it would imply that Americans could engage in military activities only if Congress sanctioned those activities with a formal declaration of war. This could be good or bad. Limiting military action to only that sanctioned by a declaration of war would keep Congress—the most democratic arm of the federal government—in charge of American war making and might prevent overeager presidents or military leaders from drawing the nation into combat without the approval of the American people. On the other hand, such a limitation could rob presidents and the military of flexibility in dealing with complex and fluid situations that might require immediate action. Congress's deliberations are by definition deliberate—maybe too much so in a dangerous world that sometimes requires immediate military action to defend U.S. interests.

In *Bas v. Tingy*, the Supreme Court came down on the side of flexibility, rejecting Bas's claim that an "enemy" could be established only by a declaration of war. France and the United States were obviously "enemies" by any reasonable definition of the word, according to the Court. "By what other word [could] the idea of the relative situation of America and France . . . be communicated, than by that of hostility, or war?" asked Justice Alfred Moore in one of the majority opinions. "And how can the characters of the parties engaged in hostility or war, be otherwise described than by the denomination of enemies?" The hard reality of what Moore called "the scene of bloodshed, depredation and confiscation, which has unhappily occurred" between the two nations had created a de facto state of war with or without congressional action.

That being the case, nations could become enemies before Congress issued a declaration of war. Here the Court offered a distinction between two different types of wars. One type, according to Justice Bushrod Washington in a second majority opinion, was formal, deliberate, and based on actions taken by hostile governments. Such a war "is called solemn, and is of the perfect kind; because one whole nation is at war with another whole nation; and all the members of the nation declaring war, are authorised to commit hostilities against all the members of the other, in every place, and under every circumstance. In such a war all the members act under a general authority, and all the rights and consequences of war attach to their condition."

Justice Washington argued, though, that there was a second sort of war, whereby "hostilities may subsist between two nations more confined in its nature and extent; being limited as to places, persons, and things." He called this an "imperfect war" that was "not solemn, and because those who are authorised to commit hostilities, act under special authority, and can go no farther than to the extent of their commission." This was still war—soldiers fired weapons, property was destroyed, people died—but the combatants "are not authorised to commit hostilities such as in a solemn war, where the government restrains the general power." The hostilities between France and America constituted such an "imperfect war," Washington argued, and, "imperfect" though it may have been, it was still a war, and it still made France an "enemy." Mr. Bas lost one-half of his cargo.

The Court found itself on unfamiliar ground here, groping for the right terminology to justify a state of hostilities between America and France that was warlike but not quite requiring Congress's formal declaration. Washington tried to do this with his "perfect" and "imperfect" distinction; Justice Samuel Chase, in yet another majority opinion, called the situation a "partial war." It was clear in this first courtroom test of war-making authority that the Court wanted to preserve both flexibility of action in combat situations and Congress's overall prerogative to declare (and therefore control) the waging of war. It was also clear, though, with the multiple majority opinions and disagreements over terminology, that the justices were not sure how to fashion the legal justification for doing so.

While trying to decide when a war is legally a war, the early Supreme Court also found itself addressing questions of federal-state relations during wartime, particularly the controversy concerning when and how the national government could control the various state militias. During the Revolution, this had been a sore point for Americans who distrusted professional armies and feared that a national military establishment, run by career soldiers, could be used to control and overwhelm the citizen-soldiers who made up the militias. The militiamen themselves were likewise reluctant to be placed under the command of hardened professionals, who might impose brutal discipline and require obedience to orders that could carry them far from their homes. On the other hand, Americans with military experience during the war—George Washington, for example—believed that war required a strong, centralized authority. If the United States were someday invaded by a foreign power, its citizens could ill afford quibbling from militiamen concerning which part of the nation they would be required to defend and whose orders they would obey (Shy 1990, chap. 6).

The issue surfaced in the nation's first large-scale war since the Revolution. During the War of 1812, President Madison issued orders to various state militia units, getting them ready to defend the nation from a British invasion. A private in New York's militia, Jacob Mott, refused to obey the president, questioning the president's authority to command state militia troops, even as commander in chief during a time of war, and pointing out that, at the time, the president did know for certain that the British planned to invade New York.

Mott's lawsuit wound its way up to the Supreme Court, and in 1827, in *Martin v. Mott,* the Court quashed Mott's objections. Citing a 1795 law that allowed the president to call out the militia to "suppress insurrections, and repel invasions," Justice Joseph Story, speaking for a unanimous Court, argued that "the authority to decide whether the exigency [to call out the militia] has arisen, belongs exclusively to the President, and is conclusive upon all other persons." The Court worried about the sort of obstructionism possible if "subordinate officers or soldiers are pausing to consider whether they ought to obey." In such an event, Story worried, "the hostile enterprise [of an enemy nation] may be accomplished without the means of resistance." The Court therefore gave the president wide discretionary power over the state militia organizations, which might otherwise have become sources of confusion (Wormuth and Firmage 1989, 240).

Martin v. Mott and *Bas v. Tingy*, each in its own way, established the general point that in a time of war, the federal government's prerogatives were strong, especially those of the president. The *Bas* case on the surface had little to do with the presidency, but by allowing a state of war to legally exist without congressional action, the justices in *Bas v. Tingy* opened the door for future presidents by themselves to commit troops to the battlefield. In *Martin v. Mott*, the Court refused to allow state militia–centered obstructionism to hamstring a national war effort, communicating their belief that during a time of war, the needs of the federal military establishment should take precedence over the desires of state authorities.

As the Court created a broad war-making mandate for the federal government in the first decades of the nineteenth century, it also allowed the embryonic national military establishment to write its own rules and regulations relatively free from civilian interference. The U.S. Army and Navy adopted the Articles of War, which had been in use during the Revolutionary War after having been adapted from the British Articles of War. The Articles provided for a disciplinary code and court-martial system that was administered by and for soldiers, with no civilian interference. Congress authorized this, acting under its Article II power to "make Rules for the Government and Regulation of the land and naval forces," but otherwise it stayed out of the soldiers' way. Military men disciplined their own, and the military justice system remained a largely self-run institution throughout the first half of the nineteenth century (Lurie 1992, chaps. 1–4).

The Supreme Court did not have the opportunity to examine this state of affairs until almost the eve of the Civil War, when the proceedings of a navy court-martial came before it for review. In September 1854, seaman Frank Dynes left his vessel, the USS *Independence*, while it was docked in New York City's harbor. When the navy arrested him and brought him before a court-martial on charges of desertion, Dynes pleaded not guilty. Just what sort of defense he mounted is unclear; the court-martial acquitted him on the desertion charge but found him guilty of "attempting to desert." Dynes thought he saw an opening in this odd distinction. He argued that the navy had no legal authority to charge him with attempted desertion, since such a crime did not technically exist under the Articles of War or under the law passed by Congress in 1800 that enabled military courts to function. The offense of desertion existed, but not "attempted" desertion. Military judges had no right to make up new crimes, Dynes argued, and even less right to try and convict him for an arbitrary offense.

Normally this sort of dispute would have remained in the navy, as there were few ways for a serviceman to get his case out of the military courts and into the civilian system. Dynes's lawyer found a way. The navy compelled Dynes to serve his prison sentence in the District of Columbia; he sued the District's marshal for "assault and battery and false imprisonment," thus making the dispute a civilian matter, to be heard in the federal circuit court for Washington, D.C., and, eventually, the U.S. Supreme Court.

This clever method of making military justice a civilian problem notwithstanding, the navy's lawyers told the Court in *Dynes v. Hoover* (1858) that it should not meddle in affairs of military discipline. The navy had every right to punish its members as it saw fit. When Dynes claimed that his punishment of six months' imprisonment at hard labor was an unusual sentence running contrary to the "customs of the sea," the navy's counsel replied that "such customs and laws are not written in books, but exist as matters of fact, resting in tradition and practice."

Speaking for a nearly unanimous Court (Justice John McClean dissented without giving his reasons), Justice James M. Wayne pointed out that the military's court system was an entirely separate entity from the civilian court system. The judiciary was given its mandate from Article III, but the military courts derived their authority from Congress's power to regulate the armed forces. Congress therefore had exclusive authority to determine what those rules might be, and it had seen fit to establish the Articles of War as the standard for administering justice to American soldiers.

Wayne agreed with the navy's lawyers; the Supreme Court was ill equipped to pick and choose among time-honored military practices and their violation. "What those crimes are, and how they are to be punished, is well known by practical men of the navy and army, and by those who have studied the law of courts martial," Wayne declared, and "with the sentences of courts martial which have been convened regularly, and have proceeded legally . . . civil courts have nothing to do." If a court-martial stepped outside its boundaries of authority and tried to decide nonmilitary matters, that would have been another matter entirely, and the civilian courts might offer a remedy. On such an obviously military subject like desertion, however, the Court was better off deferring to the "practical" military men. Seaman Dynes lost his case.

Dynes v. Hoover reflected the Supreme Court's general demeanor concerning war making in the first half of the nineteenth century. The justices involved themselves in war only to a limited extent, preferring to give the other branches of the federal government and the military establishment wide leeway in establishing the rules under which they would operate. It was easy for the Court to do this, because during the early nineteenth century the nation fought relatively limited wars with small numbers of combatants, and its larger wars—the conflict with Mexico, for example—were of short duration and raised no pressing legal questions. The Court was uncomfortable with war making and gladly turned its attention to the economy, federalism, and other problems that seemed to fall more within its purview. As the nation approached the Civil War, however, the Court would find that it no longer had this luxury.

The Civil War: Libertarian Idealism versus Wartime Pragmatism

As war broke out between North and South in 1861, the Supreme Court was suffering from a tarnished reputation for the first time in its seventy-five-year history. Before 1857, the Court enjoyed nationwide respect for its careful, balanced approach to the difficult legal problems posed by the nation's remarkable geographic, economic, and political growth. The "market revolution," state's rights, territorial growth, industrialization—the Jacksonian-era Court had to negotiate a very tangled legal and political thicket, and most Americans thought it had done a good job (Newmyer 1986, chaps. 3–6). But then in 1857, in *Dred Scott v. Sanford* the Court tried to use its prestige to solve the vexed problem of slavery's status in the western territories. The result was a disaster; the Court's manifestly pro-South bias (it ruled that Dred Scott must remain a slave, despite his having been transported to free territory) and blatant racism made *Dred Scott v. Sanford* the most infamously bad judicial decision in American history. People who had once praised the Court for its evenhandedness and reason now decried its political bias and proslavery taint. "Rarely has the Court undertaken so much—but settled so little," observed historian R. Kent Newmyer (Newmyer 1986, 137).

The author of the *Dred Scott* decision, Chief Justice Roger B. Taney, was particularly distressed by the sectional crisis. He was considered to be one of the finest jurists of the time, the man who had ably filled the mighty John Marshall's shoes as the Court's sixth chief justice (Newmyer 1986, 149–151). The quarrels, though, between North and South, slaveholder and abolitionist, ate at him. He hated the Republican Party, and he hated abolitionists even more. "The South is doomed to sink to a state of inferiority, and the power of the North will be exercised to gratify their cupidity and their evil passions, without the slightest regard to the principles of the Constitution," he bitterly lamented in 1856. "I grieve over this condition of things" (Fehrenbacher 2001, 557). His grief led him to author a series of blatantly proslavery opinions from the bench, culminating in *Dred Scott,* where he famously referred to African-Americans "as a subordinate and inferior class of beings, who had been subjugated by the dominant race, and, whether emancipated or not . . . had no rights or privileges but such as those who held the power and the Government might choose to grant them. When the Civil War broke out four years later, many laid the blame squarely on Taney's doorstep. By that point, he was a frightened, bitter eighty-four-year-old man.

Taney remained loyal to the Union and he looked with dismay on the South's secession, but he blamed Abraham Lincoln far more than he blamed the white South. He was also a Maryland slaveholder, and the sitting justice in that state's federal circuit court (in those days Supreme Court justices did double duty on the circuit court system). As the Union army filled Maryland's jails with suspected Confederate saboteurs, Taney rushed to his circuit court seat in Baltimore, looking for a test case to use as a weapon against the Lincoln administration (Hyman and Weicek 1982, 239).

He found one in the predicament faced by John Merryman, a Confederate sympathizer who was dragged from his bed at two o'clock in the morning by army authorities and arrested for drilling pro-secessionist troops that he planned to offer to the Confederate army. Taney himself issued a writ of habeas corpus to secure Merryman's release; the army ignored it. Taney then issued a blistering opinion in which he denounced Merryman's arrest, made on the basis of "vague and indefinite charges, without any proof," as inimical to basic American principles of liberty and justice. He devoted the bulk of his opinion to delineating a rigid division of authority between Congress and the president where the wartime suspension of habeas corpus was concerned. Congress was given exclusive power to do so by the framers, Taney believed, "and if the high power over the liberty of the citizen now claimed, was intended to be conferred upon the president, it would undoubtedly be found in plain words in [Article II]; but there is not a word in it that can furnish the slightest ground to justify the exercise of the power."

Taney dismissed the notion that the dangerous environment of war justified extraordinary actions. Citing the Tenth Amendment, he asserted that the U.S. government was "one of delegated and limited powers," a fact that should not change "in times of tumult and danger." Like the Democrats (with whom he identified politically), Taney saw in Lincoln's Maryland policies an embryonic tyranny, using the excuse of civil war to suppress opinions the president disliked and to punish political enemies. The matter went far beyond even the suspension of the writ. That was bad enough, Taney argued, but the Lincoln administration had "by force of arms, thrust aside the judicial authorities and officers to whom the constitution has confided the power and duty of interpreting and administering the laws, and substituted a military government in its place." This was, according to Taney, unconscionable and un-American. "I can only say that if the authority which the constitution has provided to the judiciary department and judicial officers, may thus, upon any pretext or under any circumstances, be usurped by the military power," Taney concluded, then "the people of the United States are no longer living under a government of laws, but every citizen holds life, liberty and property at the will and pleasure of the army officer in whose military district he happened to be found" (*ex parte Merryman*, 1861).

In response to *ex parte Merryman*, Lincoln's attorney general, Edward Bates, issued an opinion arguing that Lincoln had acted as an agent of Congress during that body's absence. Moreover, Bates believed, the suspensions of the writ and declaration of martial law fell within the purview of Lincoln's discretionary powers as commander in chief. "It is the President's bounden duty to put down the insurrection," Bates argued, and "the manner in which he shall perform that duty is not prescribed by any law. . . . The end, the suppression of the insurrection, is required of him; the means and instruments to suppress it are lawfully in his hands; but the manner in which he shall use them is not prescribed and could not be prescribed without a foreknowledge of all the future changes and contingencies of the insurrection . . . if [the rebels] employ spies and emissaries to gather information, to forward secret supplies and to excite new insurrections in aid of the original rebellion he may find it both prudent and humane to arrest and imprison them" (U.S. Government 1880–1901, series 2, 2: 24–25).

In the final analysis, *ex parte Merryman* was one of the least effectual opinions ever issued by the Supreme Court. Lincoln ignored Taney, and while the *Merryman* opinion served as one of the rallying points for Southern sympathizers and Democrats, many of whom believed that the Lincoln administration was guilty of tyranny, it had little direct effect on the status of wartime detainees themselves. Lincoln continued to arrest suspected Confederate agents and suspend habeas corpus when he thought it necessary, and he enjoyed the support of most members of Congress in doing so. Taney himself would live only two more years, and when he died in October 1864 at the age of eighty-seven, public feeling ran so high against him—because of *Dred Scott* mostly, but also because of what many saw as the pro-South obstructionism embodied in *Merryman*—that Congress refused to appropriate the funds necessary to create a courtroom statue of the deceased chief justice, as had been the tradition (Fehrenbacher 2001, 578–579).

The Court recovered rather quickly from the opprobrium Taney had visited upon it, largely by acquiescing in the Lincoln administration's wartime policies and causing no further ripples regarding wartime civil liberties. This process began even before Taney's death. In December 1863, Clement Vallandigham, the notorious Ohio copperhead, appealed to the Supreme Court his arrest and conviction by a military tribunal on the charge of "having expressed sympathies for those in arms against the Government of the United States, and for having uttered, in a speech at a public meeting, disloyal sentiments and opinions, with the object and purpose of weakening the power of the Government in its efforts for the suppression of an unlawful rebellion." Vallandigham's lawyers argued that a military tribunal could not try citizens in a place like Ohio, where civilian courts were in operation, and that his rights as an American citizen had been violated by a harsh military justice system that did not give him a jury trial, the opportunity to confront his accusers, and various other due process rights.

The Court was unimpressed. Citing *Dynes v. Hoover,* the justices reiterated their desire to stay out of the military justice system by declaring that they had no jurisdiction over Vallandigham's trial. The military courts had been created by one set of congressional powers (the power to make rules for military), and the Supreme Court's appellate jurisdiction had been created by another set entirely (Article III's designation that Congress would supervise the scope of the federal government's judicial authority), and, as far the Court was concerned, ne'er the twain shall meet. "The appellate powers of the Supreme Court, as granted by the Constitution, are limited and regulated by the acts of Congress, and must be exercised subject to the exceptions and regulations made by Congress," argued Justice James Wayne. "In other words, the petition before us we think not to be within the letter or spirit of the grants of appellate jurisdiction to the Supreme Court." Vallandigham's military conviction stood.

Ex parte Vallandigham was consistent with the Court's hands-off approach to military justice, but perhaps it was also a manifestation of the Court's desire to pull back from the controversies generated by the *Merryman* opinion. Despite protestations to the contrary, the Supreme Court is never completely above politics, and its members surely noted that in a time of war, many Americans believed the loyal thing to do was to back the Lincoln administration in its attempt to win a civil war and suppress the activities of dangerous pro-Confederate subversives like Clement Vallandigham. The Court did not want to meddle in military matters anyway, if it could possibly avoid it, all the more so during a time when it badly needed to restore some of its lost prestige.

About the same time it was returning Vallandigham to the mercies of military justice, the Supreme Court issued its most important ruling of the Civil War period. The case—or rather, series of cases—concerned what should be done with a shipload of tobacco, 600 barrels of flour, and a little over 5,000 bags of coffee.

On May 17, 1861, the cargo vessel *Crenshaw* was boarded by crewmen from a steamer called the *Star* at the mouth of the James

River, about sixty miles from Richmond, Virginia. The same day, a British bark, the *Hiawatha*, sailed from Richmond; it was captured three days later by the *Minnesota*. Later that summer another cargo ship, the *Amy Warwick*, was boarded and captured by the *Quaker City;* like the *Crenshaw* and the *Hiawatha*, the *Amy Warwick* had started its voyage in Richmond, the Confederacy's new capital city. A fourth vessel, the *Brilliante*, a Mexican schooner that hailed from New Orleans, was seized by two small boats with registries in Massachusetts and escorted to Key West, Florida. All of the captured vessels were suspected of doing business with the Confederacy, and their captors were ships and crew that acted under the authority of the Lincoln administration (Bernath 1970, chap. 1).

Three weeks before the *Crenshaw* was captured, Lincoln had imposed a blockade on the Confederacy. This was a truly enormous project. It involved choking off shipping to and from a dozen Southern port cities stretched along more than 3,500 miles of coastline, with a navy that in the spring of 1861 numbered only forty-two vessels. By the end of the war the Union would become fairly effective at strangling Confederate shipping; its fleet would number more than 600 vessels, and by 1865 a Confederate blockade runner stood only a fifty-fifty chance of reaching its destination. In the spring of 1861, however, all of that lay in the future, and the blockade seemed fraught with practical difficulties (McPherson 2000, 177–179).

For the blockade to be effective, Union vessels had to stop not only ships that flew Confederate flags but also those flying foreign flags; otherwise Southerners would simply shift their cargoes to vessels owned by Southern sympathizers from, say, Great Britain. This meant that American blockaders would be using force to seize foreign ships manned by foreign crews—a potentially dicey situation involving confrontations on the high seas that in some circumstances might lead to actual war. International law provided a way to avoid such problems, however. If one nation formally declared that it was imposing a blockade on another nation, then vessels were forewarned that they sailed to the blockaded ports at their own peril. Declaration of a blockade was more than a military move; it established a legal set of conditions, recognized by international law and custom, that allowed Union vessels to seize foreign ships without causing international incidents (Bernath 1970, 7–11).

As a former lawyer, Abraham Lincoln understood all of this quite well. When he proclaimed a blockade on the Confederacy, he carefully observed all of the conventions required by international law and custom. "A competent force will be posted so as to prevent entrance and exit of vessels from [Confederate] ports," the proclamation read, and if a vessel tried to "enter or leave the blockaded port, she will be captured and sent to the nearest convenient port, for such proceedings against her and her cargo as prize, as may be deemed advisable" (Basler 1953, 4: 339).

According to international law, however, such a blockade could be imposed only on a foreign nation. As seen in chapter 2, the Lincoln administration had to maintain the legal position that the Confederacy did not exist as a viable nation-state and that its citizens were not Confederates but Americans in rebellion against their rightful leaders in Washington, D.C. By its own admission, the U.S. government, when it imposed a blockade on the Confederacy, was blockading itself. This was a legal absurdity, as Confederate leaders were quick to point out. They demanded that the Lincoln administration either lift the blockade or extend the Confederacy formal status as a bona fide belligerent nation (McPherson 2000, 217–219).

If Lincoln lifted the blockade, he would seriously damage the Northern war effort. If he left it in place, he risked sparking international incidents and maybe even a war with a European nation. Lincoln chose the latter, and in the spring of 1861 Northern patrol vessels began stopping and seizing ships that had any connection to the Confederacy, among them the *Crenshaw,* the *Hiawatha,* the *Amy Warwick,* and the *Brilliante.* The ships' owners and captains all claimed that they did know of any blockade against the South and that the seizures were illegal in any event because the blockade had no standing under international law. "Blockade is a belligerent right," the shipowners and their attorneys asserted. "There must be war, before there can [be a] blockade in the international sense, giving jurisdiction in prize."

In the roundabout way that is sometimes typical of the law, the fate of these four ships forced the Supreme Court to grapple with the central legal dilemma of the Civil War: Just what sort of war was the North fighting? The Lincoln administration presented one set of answers: this was a civil war, an internal conflict among Americans. Circumstance, the Confederacy itself, and international law supplied a different answer: this was a war between belligerent nations. The effects would be far-reaching, whichever way the Supreme Court chose to rule.

In the end, the Court took a practical course: it ruled that, depending on circumstance and the exigencies of the war, the Lincoln administration could treat Confederates as either rebellious American citizens or de facto citizens of a foreign nation called the Confederacy. Speaking for the majority, Justice Robert C. Grier pointed out that international rules for war making were designed to "mitigate the cruelties and misery produced by the scourge of war. Hence the parties to a civil war usually concede to each other belligerent rights. They exchange prisoners, and adopt the other courtesies and rules common to public or national wars." Moreover, merely labeling their actions a "rebellion" and not a "war" should not insulate Southerners from the consequences of their actions, and still less should it tie the hands of the president. "It is not the less a civil war, with belligerent parties in hostile array, because it may be called an 'insurrection' by one side, and the insurgents be considered as rebels or traitors," Grier argued, and so "it is not necessary that the independence of the revolted province or State be acknowledged in order to constitute it a party belligerent in a war according to the law of nations."

This took care of the immediate legal needs of the federal government. The Lincoln administration could now proceed against the Confederates in whatever manner was best suited to procuring victory. "Whether the President in fulfilling his duties, as Commander in chief, in suppressing an insurrection, has met with . . . a civil war of such alarming proportions as will compel him to accord to them the character of belligerents, is a question to be decided by him, and this Court must be governed by the decisions and acts of the political department of the Government to which this power was entrusted," Grier declared. "The proclamation of blockade is itself official and conclusive evidence to the Court that a state of war existed which demanded and authorized a recourse to such a measure, under the circumstances peculiar to the case."

The *Prize Cases,* however, raised other matters that went beyond the scope of the blockade and the Civil War itself. In their desire to overturn the blockade, the lawyers for the captured vessels wanted the Court to constrict the president's war-making powers in the narrowest conceivable way, arguing that because Congress had never declared war against the Confederacy, there was no justification for the blockade. Only a declaration of war could allow Lincoln to pursue military action, they argued, and Congress had not seen fit to do so.

"It is not pretended that at the time of this so-called capture, Congress had declared that there should be war, or that war existed, or had in any manner dealt with the question of war," the plaintiffs pointed out.

As in *Martin v. Mott*, however, the Court was wary of boxing in the president by making all of his powers as commander in chief dependent on legislative action. It is true, Grier admitted, that "by the Constitution, Congress alone has the power to declare a national or foreign war." And it is also true that the president "has no power to initiate or declare a war either against a foreign nation or a domestic State." But he "is Commander in chief of the Army and Navy of the United States, and of the militia of the several States when called into the actual service of the United States . . . [and] he is authorized to call out the militia and use the military and naval forces of the United States in case of invasion by foreign nations, and to suppress insurrection against the government of a State or of the United States." Indeed, the Court argued, he is duty-bound to do so. "He does not initiate the war, but is bound to accept the challenge without waiting for any special legislative authority. And whether the hostile party be a foreign invader, or States organized in rebellion, it is none the less a war."

Not everyone agreed with this flexible reading of the president's war powers. In a strongly worded dissent, Justice Samuel Nelson spoke for three of his brethren in favor of limiting the legal initiation of war to the congressional sphere. "The President does not possess the power under the Constitution to declare war or recognize its existence within the meaning of the law of nations," Nelson wrote. "This power belongs exclusively to the Congress of the United States, and, consequently, . . . the President had no power to set on foot a blockade under the law of nations." As a minority opinion, Nelson's concerns did not carry the force of law, but he and the other dissenting justices spoke for a significant number of Americans who worried that expansion of the president's prerogatives as commander in chief might someday carry the nation into a war that had no congressional (or democratic) mandate.

Nevertheless, the majority opinion in the *Prize Cases* was consistent with the Supreme Court's general approach to the legal aspects of war: a combination of pragmatism, flexibility, and a generally hands-off attitude toward military matters in general. The ancient maxim that "in times of war the laws fall silent" gained no purchase in the United States; the Supreme Court would see to that by carefully monitoring the legal consequences of the federal government's wartime actions. Contrary to what was expected in some quarters, the Civil War's military machinery did not grind the Constitution into useless legal junk, but the Court did allow the president to flex the Union's military muscle, and it allowed the government's armed forces the freedom of movement necessary to win the war. The law certainly did not fall silent, but the law's chief defender, the Supreme Court, got out of the way and let the soldiers do their jobs.

Reconstruction and *ex parte Milligan*

In some ways the war had been a simple undertaking. The goals for the Union were relatively straightforward. Defeat the Confederacy and then go home. Give the Lincoln administration the wherewithal to produce a battlefield victory. Let the federal government expand and flex its potent war-making muscles enough so that the Constitution becomes an asset rather than an impediment. Fight the war on the battlefield more than in the courtroom.

Wartime deference to the prerogatives of the presidents and the needs of the armed forces has a long tradition in the United States. Americans rally around the flag and the president in times of crisis, especially wars. During the Civil War, the Lincoln administration had its critics, of course, who loudly proclaimed that the president wanted to make the war an excuse for establishing a presidential dictatorship (Neely 1992, 231–232). By and large, however, most Northerners thought Lincoln had pursued a wise and necessary course in punishing suspected rebel sympathizers, suppressing possibly dangerous forms of dissent, and combating the Confederacy as both a treasonous nonentity and a belligerent nation-state, as circumstances dictated. Loyal Americans generally supported Lincoln in all of this. So did the Supreme Court (Paludan 1994, 80–83; Hyman and Weicek 1982, 232–278).

By the summer of 1865, however, the war was over. The Confederacy was dead, and Americans almost immediately began to indulge a second venerable national tradition by dismantling their massive military machine. The Union army was the best fighting force on the planet, over a million men strong, but Americans do not like to maintain armies any longer than is absolutely necessary to secure victory. As soon as the shooting stops, the soldiers invariably want to go home. After a colossal "Grand Review" down Pennsylvania Avenue that lasted two days in May 1865, the government granted the homesick men their wish and began handing out discharges in droves. By the fall of 1866, the army had only 65,000 men left (McPherson 2000, 486).

The political landscape had drastically changed as well. The pressing national goal now was not battlefield victory but the far more messy challenge of winning the peace. Other pressing problems, many only indirectly related to the war, clamored for the nation's attention: the growing pains of a new industrializing economy, corruption and scandal among government officials, and the final conquest of the western frontier (McPherson 2000, chap. 32).

Taken together, these developments—a shrunken military, the murky prerogatives of reconstruction, the distractions of industrialization, corruption, and expansion—presaged a retreat by the Supreme Court from the expansive reading of the government's war powers it had made during the Civil War. This retreat occurred primarily in the areas of wartime civil liberties and the military justice system. *Ex parte Vallandigham* had linked these two areas by establishing the precedent that military tribunals could try civilians accused of impeding the war effort, even in civilian regions where the normal machinery of justice still functioned.

Probably most Americans felt that Clement Vallandigham got what he deserved, but the notion that soldiers could hand down sentences arrived at through a hardfisted military court system was bound to make some people nervous. It certainly made the Supreme Court nervous, or at least it did once the Confederacy was defeated. What had seemed acceptable and necessary during the war now seemed less justifiable in peacetime. Most Americans view war as a temporary condition, an aberration that might create a temporary need to expand government power and encroach on individual liberties, but that otherwise should leave few lasting effects. Now, though, some worried that powers given to the federal government to win the Civil War might be used to impose a harsh brand of peace on the conquered South. Many Northerners who had been willing to accept slavery's demise in the name of military necessity were less comfortable with measures that might upset the racial order in the postwar South (Foner 1988, chaps. 10–12).

The Supreme Court was not immune to such considerations; indeed, it may have been ahead of public opinion on this issue. Aside from infrequent bursts of reform-minded activity (the Warren Court during the 1960s, for example), the Court has generally been a conservative force in American legal and political life. As a rule, the justices don't much like laws and court cases that carry the potential for unexpected and unforeseeable change. Most justices have seen themselves as preservers, stabilizers, protectors of the law's status quo against wrenching and possibly dangerous change. Predictability is supposed to be a hallmark of any legal system, and the ancient tradition of *stare decisis*—that judges must anchor their decisions in the reasoning and precedents set by previous courts—usually militates against a courtroom's becoming an agent for radical alterations in the legal system.

This was particularly true of the post–Civil War Supreme Court, which tried to rein in the potential for sudden change—in American social conditions, federal-state relationships, and economic development—that the war had wrought. The potential was not imaginary. In 1865, the nation ratified the Thirteenth Amendment, which outlawed slavery, but it also forbade "involuntary servitude." There were some who thought that "involuntary servitude" should involve the federal government in policing all sorts of labor, business, and civil rights relationships (Hyman and Weicek 1982, 276–278). Two years later, Congress created the Fourteenth Amendment, which offered federal guarantees of due process and equal protection rights. For the first time in U.S. history, the central government in Washington, D.C., could reach past the various state governments and offer direct protection to individual citizens (Hyman and Weicek 1982, 386–438).

The Court worried that this sudden expansion of federal power could dramatically alter the balance of power between the states and the federal government. Perhaps most disturbing of all, white Southerners lived under occupation by the U.S. Army. Congress passed the Military Reconstruction Acts in 1867, which divided the South into districts administered by the army. Soldiers patrolled the streets of the South. Although many Americans believed, with good reason, that these patrols were necessary to protect newly freed African-Americans, many others thought their presence was an affront to the rights and the dignity of white Southerners. Members of the Supreme Court no doubt shared these concerns and worried that the broad powers given to the military to win the war might now be used to trample individual liberties (Foner 1988, 271–291).

All of these considerations were brought to bear when the Court heard the case of an Indiana man named Lamdin P. Milligan. During the war Milligan was suspected by Union army authorities of having joined the Order of American Knights, a secret organization of Confederate sympathizers that tried to free Confederate prisoners of war, encouraged Northerners to resist the draft, passed along military intelligence to rebel officials, and engaged in various other espionage activities. The army arrested Milligan on October 5, 1864. Two weeks later he was brought before a military tribunal and found guilty of multiple crimes—conspiracy, giving "aid and comfort" to the rebels, "inciting insurrection," "disloyal practices," and "violations of the laws of war." In May 1865, he was sentenced to be hanged. After a series of appeals (which eventually outlasted the war itself), Milligan's case ended up before the Supreme Court during its 1866 term (*ex parte Milligan*). The case attracted an impressive array of talent, on both sides. Future president James A. Garfield and former attorney general Jeremiah Sullivan Black represented Milligan, and former Union general and respected antislavery lawyer Benjamin Butler— nicknamed "the Beast" during the war by angry Southerners who believed he had insulted Southern ladies during his tenure as military governor of New Orleans—filed a brief on behalf of the government (Hyman and Weicek 1982, 382–383).

Milligan had been tried under the auspices of the Habeas Corpus Act of 1863, which allowed the Lincoln administration to suspend the writ and declare martial law in places where he deemed the public safety—or the war effort—required such stern measures. The act allowed suspected Confederate saboteurs like Milligan to be tried, convicted, and punished by soldiers, with little interference by civilian courts, but the act did require that the army furnish lists of the prisoners it had arrested to civilian grand juries. If the jurors could not bring an indictment against an individual, then the army had to let the person go (Neely 1992, 68–69).

Milligan believed that his trial was illegal, since a civilian grand jury had considered his case but failed to bring an indictment against him. That procedural violation alone, he argued, should have been enough to void the military tribunal's verdict. But Milligan's lawyer went further, declaring that the tribunal, even if it had followed the letter of the law, was still illegal. Since Milligan had never been a member of the Confederate armed forces, he could not be considered a prisoner of war and thus subject to the army's authority. Moreover, a military court could become the final arbiter of justice in an area far behind the front lines, where civilian courts were open and operating normally. "Let it also be remembered, that Indiana, at the time of this trial, was a peaceful State," they pointed out, "the courts were all open; their processes had not been interrupted; the laws had their full sway." Soldiers had no business passing judgment—a death sentence, no less—on civilians under such circumstances.

Butler and the other attorneys for the United States responded by arguing that wartime of necessity gives military commanders sweeping authority to punish possibly dangerous persons within their purview. They dismissed Milligan's argument that he was a civilian living far away from a battlefield and hence was not subject to military justice. "Neither residence nor propinquity to the field of actual hostilities is the test to determine who is or who is not subject to martial law, even in a time of foreign war, and certainly not in a time of civil insurrection," they argued. Soldiers pursuing victory against a strong and devious foe had the right to restrain their enemies. "The commander-in-chief has full power to make an effectual use of his forces," they declared. "He must, therefore, have power to arrest and punish one who arms men to join the enemy in the field against him; one who holds correspondence with that enemy; one who is an officer of an armed force organized to oppose him; one who is preparing to seize arsenals and release prisoners of war taken in battle and confined within his military lines."

Here was a sweeping assertion of military authority, but the government's lawyers went further and offered an astonishingly broad reading of the president's war-making powers. Granted, they admitted, Congress has the sole power to declare war, but "after war is initiated . . . all the means and appliances by which the war is to be carried on by civilized nations, is given to the president." The president decided what was necessary and what was just on the battlefield. "He is the sole judge of the exigencies, necessities, and duties of the occasion," they argued, and "during the war his powers must be without limit, because, if defending, the means of offence may be nearly illimitable."

Why did the lawyers stake out such a position? It was their answer to Milligan's habeas corpus argument. The precise wording of the 1863 law called for lists to be presented to the grand juries of those "state or political prisoners" it had taken into custody, but this did not apply to Milligan. He was not a political detainee; he was not a

Clement Vallandigham, a man giving speeches and running for office. Lamdin Milligan was a military saboteur. He was "as much a prisoner of war as if he had been taken in action with arms in his hands." And, as such, he fell under the direct control of the commander in chief, the president, who could do with him what the hard exigencies of a civil war required.

Garfield and Milligan's other attorneys were taken aback by this approach. "Is it true, that the moment a declaration of war is made, the executive department of this government, without an act of Congress, becomes absolute master of our liberties and our lives?" they asked. "Are we, then, subject to martial rule, administered by the President upon his own sense of the exigency, with nobody to control him, and with every magistrate and every authority in the land subject to his will alone?" Surely not. "If the President has this awful power, whence does he derive it?" they wondered. Nothing in the Constitution, they argued, conferred on the president the sole authority to run a military court system.

If the war had still been on, the justices might have been less sympathetic to such arguments. If the case had been tried in 1861, when it seemed entirely possible that a "peaceful State" like Indiana could become a battleground, the Court might have felt that Milligan's trial was justified, but what seemed necessary in 1861 looked excessive in 1866, and the Court came down firmly on Milligan's side. It swept aside the government's claim that no violation of the Habeas Corpus Act of 1863 had occurred because of Milligan's prisoner-of-war status. The Court also held that military tribunals had no power to try civilians in areas where the civil courts were operating. Speaking for the majority, Chief Justice David Davis pointed out that "in Indiana the Federal authority was always unopposed, and its courts always open to hear criminal accusations and redress grievances; and no usage of war could sanction a military trial there for any offence whatever of a citizen in civil life." Davis could see no justification for submitting Milligan's case to a civil court. "Why was he not delivered to the Circuit Court of Indiana to be proceeded against according to law? No reason of necessity could be urged against it," he argued.

These procedural matters were important, of course, but there was a more general, more fundamental matter, and Justice Davis put his finger squarely on it: the times had changed. "During the late wicked Rebellion, the temper of the times did not allow that calmness in deliberation and discussion so necessary to a correct conclusion of a purely judicial question," he declared. "Then, considerations of safety were mingled with the exercise of power; and feelings and interests prevailed which are happily terminated. Now that the public safety is assured, this question, as well as all others, can be discussed and decided without passion or the admixture of any element not required to form a legal judgment." In the calmness of peace, Davis declared, it was possible to see that the framers of the Constitution wanted the trial rights guaranteed in the Bill of Rights to protect Americans from their government, during war as well as in peacetime. "The Constitution of the United States is a law for rulers and people, equally in war and in peace, and covers with the shield of its protection all classes of men, at all times, and under all circumstances," the Court declared. "No doctrine, involving more pernicious consequences, was ever invented by the wit of man than that any of its provisions can be suspended during any of the great exigencies of government. Such a doctrine leads directly to anarchy or despotism, but the theory of necessity on which it is based is false."

Davis likewise dismissed the government's robust reading of the president's war powers. "If this position is sound to the extent claimed, then when war exists . . . [a military commander] can, if he chooses . . . substitute military force for and to the exclusion of the laws, and punish all persons, as he thinks right and proper, without fixed or certain rules." The Court found this prospect disturbing. If it were true, then "martial law, established on such a basis, destroys every guarantee of the Constitution. . . . Civil liberty and this kind of martial law cannot endure together; the antagonism is irreconcilable; and, in the conflict, one or the other must perish."

This was no reflection on Abraham Lincoln, Davis hastened to add (probably with personal as well as political motives: Davis and Lincoln had been old friends). On the whole, Lincoln had exercised the powers of his office with care and had carefully avoided serious abuses of his ability to suspend habeas corpus and declare martial law. The nation, though, "has no right to expect that it will always have wise and humane rulers, sincerely attached to the principles of the Constitution. Wicked men, ambitious of power, with hatred of liberty and contempt of law, may fill the place once occupied by Washington and Lincoln; and if this right is conceded, and the calamities of war again befall us, the dangers to human liberty are frightful to contemplate."

That said, the Court was not willing to completely eviscerate the government's internal security powers during a war. The Constitution explicitly allowed the government to suspend habeas corpus, and rightly so, for "in every war, there are men of previously good character, wicked enough to counsel their fellow-citizens to resist the measures deemed necessary by a good government to sustain its just authority and overthrow its enemies." Moreover, the Court did not want to be seen as limiting the government's ability to declare martial law in war zones where it might well be necessary for soldiers to take over the machinery of justice. The mere threat of invasion, however, was not enough to justify a state's taking extreme measures: "The necessity must be actual and present [and] the invasion real." No such necessity existed in Indiana to the point that Milligan was subject to military authority, and so his conviction was overturned.

Some people hailed *ex parte Milligan* as a milestone for the protection of American civil liberties (Rehnquist 2000, 137). They had a point. The Supreme Court had now made it a matter of law that even in times of dire emergency, military justice—with its less stringent safeguards for defendants' rights—could not suddenly become the norm and shunt fully functional civil courts aside. Civil law, the Constitution, and the Bill of Rights were the norm, the center of gravity for the American criminal justice system, and war was the exception, the periphery—not vice versa. Justice Davis was entirely correct when he pointed out that Americans would do well not to count too heavily on the benevolence of a Washington or a Lincoln to exercise the potent powers of commander in chief responsibly, particularly during a war.

But if in this way *Milligan* was a victory, in another it was a stinging defeat. Radical Republicans counted on the army to be the enforcement arm of their Reconstruction policies, which were designed to remake Southern society and afford millions of newly freed slaves some measure of protection from their white neighbors. African-Americans needed the soldiers, but now there was serious doubt about how far the army could go in protecting their interests. The freedmen and the Radicals wanted martial law, suspensions of habeas corpus, and other tools of military justice to be used as a club to hold over the heads of recalcitrant white supremacists in the South. *Milligan* did not directly address this issue—in fact, it hardly mentioned the South at all—but the assumptions underlying the decision threw into doubt a variety of army-based Reconstruction measures, and

they may well have given some congressmen pause before consider-
ing using the army to secure and support civil rights (Hyman and
Weicek 1982, 382–383; Foner 1988, 272).

For better or worse, *ex parte Milligan* highlighted the Supreme
Court's discomfort with war. When the fighting began, the Court
tried to give the government what it needed to win, but the Court
also realized that war had the potential to dilute and perhaps even
eradicate some of the principles of the legal system held most dear by
Americans. The seesaw from wartime necessity to peacetime scruples
between the Civil War and Reconstruction illustrated either the
Supreme Court's flexibility or its inconsistency, depending on one's
point of view. But whatever the case may be, the Court found,
whether it wanted to or not, that it did have a role to play at the intersection of law and war.

World War I and Justice Holmes's Conscience

The Court was not given a chance to play that role for a long time.
During the half century between Robert E. Lee's surrender and the
U.S. entry into World War I, matters of law and war faded into the
background. The nation was involved in a variety of military conflicts during that time, ranging from the relatively large Spanish-
American War to smaller, isolated conflicts such as the U.S. incur-
sions into Cuba, Panama, Nicaragua, and Mexico (Boot 2002, chap.
6). Because of their short duration or their small scale, they generated
no prominent cases for the Supreme Court to consider.

Meanwhile, memories of the Civil War slowly faded. By 1900, gray-
bearded veterans of the Union and the Confederate armies clasped
hands and traded war stories during reunions held on ground that had
once been stained dark with their comrades' blood. Northerners and
Southerners alike erected scores of marble monuments on battlefields
across the country, monuments whose very grandeur seemed to belie
the violence, pain, and death that lay at the heart of the things they
commemorated. Americans gradually forgot about how dangerous
and hard-hearted war could be, or they made of the war's pain an en-
nobling experience of valor and sacrifice (Blight 2001, chaps. 4–6).

Probably no one better personified this process than Supreme
Court Justice Oliver Wendell Holmes Jr. As a young Union army officer, Holmes had certainly seen the dark side of combat. At the Battle of Ball's Bluff in October 1861 (the disaster that helped persuade

Congress to form the Joint Committee on the Conduct of the War), Holmes was shot in the chest. Coughing up blood and thinking he might die, he was dragged to a field hospital, where a mixture of whiskey, laudanum, and his own strong constitution helped him recover. Eleven months later he was wounded again, this time during the bloodbath at Antietam. A bullet entered the back of his neck, narrowly missing his spine, and exited from his neck's left side. "I suppose I should be dead or paralyzed or something," he wrote his family. This time careful medical attention from physicians and his family saved his life. The following spring a Confederate artillery shell left a chunk of shrapnel in his heel; the doctors managed to save his foot, but he was hobbled and on crutches for a long while afterward and was told to keep the wound free from infection by plugging it with, of all things, a piece of carrot. By July 1864, Holmes had enough, and he resigned from the army, battered, exhausted, and relieved to be done with "the butcher's bill" of war (Baker 1991, 117–119, 132–133, 143–144, 152).

One might have thought that, for a man like Holmes, memories of the war's brutality would linger and that he would have been reluctant to romanticize combat. Holmes didn't sentimentalize battle exactly, but in the decades following the war he came to think of it as a rite of passage, a difficult but necessary and, in the end, life-affirming experience that he believed made his generation better and stronger. In his famous 1884 Memorial Day address, "The Soldier's Faith," Holmes rhapsodized to a gathering of Harvard students that the Civil War generation had been fortunate to endure the hardships of battle. "We have shared the incommunicable experience of war; we have felt, we still feel, the passion of life to its top," he exclaimed, and he told his audience that if "you have known the vicissitudes of terror and of triumph in war . . . you know that man has in him that unspeakable something that makes him . . . able to face annihilation for blind belief" (White 1993, 81).

Holmes was far removed from the soldier's life when he spoke those words. After the Civil War he earned a law degree from Harvard, and in 1882 he became a member of the Harvard Law School's faculty. He rose rapidly through the ranks of legal academia, editing the *American Law Review* and a new edition of James Kent's famous *Commentaries on American Law*. In 1881, he wrote *The Common Law,* a landmark legal treatise that brought him fame and respect in legal circles. Eighteen years later he was appointed to the Massachusetts Supreme Court, and in 1902 President Theodore Roosevelt appointed him to the U.S. Supreme Court, where he would remain for more than three decades, until his death in 1934 (Baker 1991, chaps. 9–16).

By the time he reached the nation's highest bench, Holmes's worldview had matured into a hardfisted pragmatism with no illusions about human nature or the often cruel requirements society might impose on its citizens. The sacrifice of so many young men's lives during the Civil War—a sacrifice that Holmes wholeheartedly supported, at least after 1865—taught him that the individual's life was ultimately subordinate to the needs of the community, the society, and the nation. This philosophy could lead him down some strange and even chilling paths; after all, if the individual is truly subordinate to society, then cannot society, pleading necessity and the health of the national organism, legally and morally justify all sorts of intrusions into individual rights? Holmes thought so. Hence his infamous support of Virginia's eugenics law in the 1927 case *Buck v. Bell.* In upholding the state's right to sterilize mentally ill citizens, Holmes had the Civil War's body count in the back of his mind when he wrote, "We have seen more than once that the public welfare may call upon the best citizens for their lives. It would be strange if it could not call upon those who already sap the strength of the State for these lesser sacrifices . . . it is better for all the world, if instead of waiting to execute degenerate offspring for crime, or let them starve for their imbecility, society can prevent those who are manifestly unfit from continuing their kind . . . three generations of imbeciles are enough."

But the same judicial philosophy that led Holmes to justify sterilization could also make him a harsh critic of those on the bench who sought to use the law to justify the groaning inequities of early-twentieth-century industrial America. By rejecting the abstract notions of justice and fairness that animated other judges, he could be keenly sensitive to the ways in which those abstractions were often used to paper over a judge's own biases and obscure the social consequences of legal decision making. Probably the most famous example of this was Holmes's dissenting opinion in *Lochner v. New York,* a 1905 case in which a majority of the Court struck down laws regulating the working hours of bakers as an unwarranted intrusion on the bakers' Fourteenth Amendment rights to freely enter into contracts with their employers. Of course, *Lochner*'s effect had little to do with a baker's abstract right to negotiate the terms of his employment. In the real world, the Supreme Court had simply reinforced the power of businessmen to exploit their laborers by forcing them to work under harsh conditions; the "right" to work a sixteen-hour day or else starve was no right at all. Holmes clearly saw this, and in his dissent he blasted the Court majority for its disingenuous reinforcement of business interests under the false guise of guarding workers' rights. "General propositions do not decide concrete cases," he wrote, and he excoriated the Court for basing its judgment "upon an economic theory which a large part of the country does not entertain."

Oliver Wendell Holmes was a curious sort, a brilliant and learned academic who sneered at almost any form of idealism, a judge who insisted that experience does (and perhaps should) trump principle, a man who could with flinty indifference countenance eugenics and yet with equal aplomb issue arguments that might benefit the nation's working poor at the expense of corporations. And lying underneath it all was the war and what he thought it had taught him about bravery, sacrifice, and suffering. The Civil War never quite left him. Men with his military pedigree were few and far between on the Supreme Court; it would be anyone's guess as to how he might react if the Court was someday placed in the position of addressing matters of both law and war.

In 1917, the nation placed the Supreme Court in exactly that position. As seen in chapter 2, the U.S. entry into World War I sparked a tremendous expansion of federal authority, and, as it had fifty years before during Lincoln's day, the Supreme Court largely acquiesced in these developments. In the *Selective Draft Law Cases* in 1918, it unanimously backed the federal government's measures to conscript an army, commenting that "compelled military service is neither repugnant to a free government nor in conflict with the constitutional guarantees of individual liberty." The Court also upheld in a series of decisions the various economic measures created by Congress to maintain the wartime economy, including price controls and federal administration of the nation's railroad system. In *Northern Pacific Railway Co. v. North Dakota*, the Court argued that war powers can transcend other regulatory powers of the federal government and that the government's power to wage war is "complete and undivided." The Court even went so far as to back war-making measures created after the war was over. It argued in the war prohibition cases that the War-Time Prohibition Act of 1919 was constitutional, despite the fact that the armistice had been signed in 1918 (Kelly, Harbison, and Belz 1991, 435–436).

At first, Holmes behaved about as one might expect; he helped lead the Court's prowar charge. An opportunity to do so came with the arrest of Charles Schenck, the general secretary of the American Socialist Party, and several of his comrades. They were charged with violating the Espionage Act by arranging for the publication of an antiwar pamphlet that called on Americans to resist the draft and suggested that conscripts were treated like convicted felons. The government called this seditious; the defenders argued that the content of the pamphlet was constitutionally protected speech. In *Schenck v. United States* (1919), Holmes was assigned the task of writing the opinion of a unanimous Court upholding Schenck's conviction and the validity of the Espionage Act.

Holmes's opinion revealed his disdain for abstract notions of justice. There was no such thing as a pristine right to freedom of speech, he believed. The relevant question before the Court was not whether speech could be curtailed, but when and under what circumstances. Holmes believed that war was such a circumstance. "We admit that in many places and in ordinary times the defendants in saying all that was said in the circular would have been within their constitutional rights," Holmes wrote. But war was not an ordinary time, and "the character of every act depends upon the circumstances in which it was done." Holmes then employed a famous metaphor. "The most stringent protection of free speech would not protect a man in falsely shouting fire in a theater and causing a panic." Likewise in a time of war, when presumably the nation's security was in peril, citizens could not "shout fire" by resisting legal military measures such as the draft, and thus risk defeat and the collapse of the entire national edifice.

But what exactly might be the words that could bring about such a collapse? That was the central problem posed by restricting speech during a war. Federal authorities did not fear Schenck's words so much as the actions those words might inspire. After reading Schenck's pamphlet, men might choose to not show up at the recruiting depots. The army's ranks might thin as a result, and the army might in turn lose battles. The authors of the Espionage Act worried that antiwar words could lead to antiwar deeds and, eventually, to defeat. So did Holmes. "When a nation is at war many things that might be said in time of peace are such a hindrance to its effort that their utterance will not be endured," he wrote.

So what was the legal test of unendurable wartime words? "The question in every case is whether the words used are used in such circumstances and are of such a nature as to create clear and present danger that they will bring about the substantive evils that Congress has a right to prevent," Holmes argued. "It is a question of proximity and degree." Here, then, was the "clear and present danger" doctrine, the first real attempt by the Supreme Court to establish a clear rule for measuring free speech rights during wartime. "Clear and present danger" is now one of the most famous phrases in American history. Many people think of it as an expression of First Amendment protection for freedom of speech. In fact, the opposite is true. Holmes coined the phrase as a way to justify the government's preemptive attempt to nip dissent in the bud before it turned into dangerous antiwar behavior. Holmes wanted to expand government prerogatives at the expense of free speech rights, not the other way around. He did not want to make the government wait until Schenck's words produced bona fide draft evasion. "We perceive no ground for saying that success alone warrants making an act a crime," he wrote.

The *Schenck* opinion was entirely in character for a crusty old Civil War veteran and hard-hearted cynic like Holmes, and it was consistent with the tenor of the Court, which in a series of cases similar to *Schenck* repeatedly supported government arrests of antiwar activists (Kelly, Harbison, and Belz 1991, 510–513). Holmes concurred with his brethren in several of these cases, for example, joining the majority in upholding the arrest of labor activist Eugene Debs, whose socialist rhetoric was deemed a threat to national security (Rehnquist 2000, 179–180). But he could be an unpredictable sort, and on some level he relished (and cultivated) a certain amount of capriciousness. He was also steadily coming under the spell of young Progressives such as fellow Supreme Court Justice Louis Brandeis, whose libertarian proclivities may have rubbed off a bit and given him pause. Whatever the reason, in another landmark case Holmes backed off from his *Schenck* opinion, and in so doing produced a landmark defense of free speech rights in wartime.

The circumstances of this second case were similar to those in *Schenck*. During the war, a New Yorker named Jacob Abrams and four others published in Abrams's basement a pamphlet calling on Americans to resist their government's anticommunist activities in Russia. "Workers in the ammunition factories, you are producing bullets, bayonets [and] cannon, to murder not only Germans, but also your dearest, best, who are in Russia fighting for freedom," Abrams's pamphlet claimed. It also called for a general strike, whose "open challenge only will let the Government know that not only the Russian Worker fights for freedom, but also here in America lives the spirit of the revolution."

Abrams's little communist cell was not a very competent one. Some of the pamphlets were in Yiddish (which surely limited their impact), and its authors distributed many of them by haphazardly tossing handfuls out of an upper-story window (Rehnquist 2000, 180–181). The "clear and present danger" of damage to the war effort was virtually nil. Nevertheless, federal officials arrested Abrams and his comrades for violating the Sedition Act in their call for a strike that might "incite and advocate curtailment of things . . . essential to the prosecution of the war." A majority on the Supreme Court predictably upheld the arrests.

But not Holmes. Joined by Brandeis in dissent in *Abrams v. United States* (1919), he belittled the notion that Jacob Abrams posed a credible threat to the nation's military apparatus. Abrams criticized the American armed forces and the way they were being used, but so what? "A patriot might think that we were wasting money on aeroplanes, or making more cannon of a certain kind than we needed," he pointed out, yet "no one would hold such conduct a crime." Abrams's conduct was only words. Holmes admitted that the pamphlet did indeed call for a nationwide strike that, if carried out, would cripple the war effort. But "nobody can suppose that the surreptitious publishing of a silly leaflet by an unknown man, without more, would present any immediate danger that its opinions would hinder the success of the government arms or have any appreciable tendency to do so."

The distance between word and deed was the crux of the matter for Holmes. Punish activities that present a "clear and present danger" during war, he told the government, but show restraint and common sense in deciding what is dangerous and what is not. "It is only the present danger of immediate evil or an intent to bring it about that warrants Congress in setting a limit to the expression of opinion where private rights are concerned," he declared. Otherwise, the best interests of the nation are served by letting different ideas fight it out in the public square. "The best test of truth is the power of the thought to get itself accepted in the competition of the market," he wrote. "I think that we should be eternally vigilant against attempts to check the expression of opinions that we loathe and believe to be fraught with death, unless they so imminently threaten immediate interference with the lawful and pressing purposes of the law that an immediate check is required to save the country." Clearly, for Holmes, the mere fact that there was a war on did not in and of itself meet this standard.

In the final analysis, Holmes's legacy in the area of wartime civil liberties is one of ambivalence. His *Abrams* dissent is a quintessential statement of free speech rights, and his "clear and present danger" doctrine offers a justification for the curtailment of those same rights during a time of national emergency. But this ambivalence is not Holmes's alone. It reflects the greater ambivalence and complexity faced by the Supreme Court as it addressed free speech issues during times of war. In normal times the Court has generally been wary of measures that muzzle the American people, particularly in the exercise of political expression and criticisms of public policy. But the Court has also long been aware that war is not a normal time and that the government, acting under the genuine exigencies of national security, can be justified in restricting First Amendment freedoms to a greater degree than might be acceptable during peacetime. The precise line marking acceptable and unacceptable speech in war is difficult to locate; the *Schenck* and *Abrams* cases, and Justice Holmes's own rather contradictory impulses, indicate just how difficult a task this might prove to be.

World War II

Holmes died in 1935, two years after Adolf Hitler came to power in Germany and six years before the United States found itself again at war in the wake of the Japanese assault on Pearl Harbor. By 1941, the Supreme Court's wartime demeanor was well established. The judges would generally support the war effort, allow a degree of legal flexibility for government institutions engaged in mobilizing the country and suppressing dissent, and defer to the discretion of Congress and the president unless offered a compelling reason to do otherwise.

The Court's institutional reluctance to become directly involved in military matters was reinforced by the unprecedented complexity and scale of modern war itself. Fighting a world war in 1941 was an immense undertaking, requiring mobilization of the nation's resources on a scale never before imagined. Millions of men and women were placed in military uniforms, backed by millions more civilian defense workers and a multibillion-dollar wartime economy designed to fulfill the demanding technological needs of mid-twentieth-century combat.

The Court had no desire to involve itself in managing this enterprise, and it was ill equipped for it, so it usually deferred to the judgment of Congress and President Franklin Roosevelt. When questions concerning federal economic management came before the Court in 1944, for example, it allowed extensive price controls (*L. P. Steuart and Brothers v. Bowles* and *Bowles v. Willingham*) and upheld the creation of powerful new federal regulatory agencies (*Yakus v. United States*). Aside from Justice Owen J. Roberts's chairmanship of the government investigation into the Pearl Harbor assault, the Court generally stayed out of the day-to-day operations of the largest war effort in American history. But while the Court did not want to involve itself too directly in the military sphere, it was not willing to become a rubber stamp for government policies. World War II generated a considerable amount of war-related litigation—more than any previous war—and although the Supreme Court continued its tradition of support for most of the government's war-making policies, it proved less deferential than had been the case during the Civil War and World War I.

Like those other two major wars, World War II raised difficult legal issues of civil liberties; this was the area of law and war to which the Court devoted most of its attention. As during World War I, there were considerations regarding the loyalty and security of a large German-American population. Added to this were widespread suspicions concerning the loyalties of Japanese-Americans, suspicions that were greatly exacerbated by society's pervasive racism. There were also problems related to the rights of religious minorities who objected to war in any form. Pacifism was nothing new, of course, but World War II brought some of their heretofore largely invisible concerns into the public light.

In some respects, the Court reversed its dismal World War I record and acted as a bulwark of the individual's right to dissent, at a time when enormous social and political pressures required conformity to wartime ideals of national unity and patriotism. In the summer of 1943, the justices heard a case involving a West Virginia law requiring schoolchildren to salute the American flag. This requirement was odious to member's of the Jehovah's Witness faith, who took very seriously the biblical passage in Exodus 20:4–5, which states, "Thou shalt not make unto thee any graven image, or any likeness of anything that is in heaven above." Jehovah's Witnesses were reluctant to salute an "image" like the American flag, and in 1943 Jehovah's Witness William Barnette sued to have the West Virginia law revoked. One might have thought that the Court would subsume this case under the Establishment Clause of the First Amendment and deal with Barnette's claim as a matter of religious freedom. The justices instead viewed it as a matter of political expression, and in a classic statement of free speech rights, struck down the West Virginia law as a violation of both the First and the Fourteenth Amendments. Representing a unanimous Court, Justice Robert Jackson had the passionately patriotic wartime atmosphere of America in mind when he wrote, in *West Virginia State Board of Education v. Barnette,* that "the very purpose of a Bill of Rights was to withdraw certain subjects from the vicissitudes of political controversy, to place them beyond the reach of majorities and officials and to establish them as legal principles to be applied by the courts." Jackson worried about what could happen to embattled minorities in war—hundreds of Jehovah's Witnesses had suffered beatings and abuse from outraged "patriotic" neighbors—and he declared that "one's right to life, liberty, and property, to free speech, a free press, freedom of worship and assembly, and other fundamental rights may not be submitted to vote; they depend on the outcome of no elections."

The Court's newfound concern for wartime free speech rights extended to persons of German descent as well. In *Baumgartner v. United States* in 1944, it thwarted an attempt by the federal government to revoke the citizenship rights of an admitted Nazi sympathizer. The Court also felt compelled to protect citizens' rights to criticize the draft, far more so than during World War I. A week after the D-Day landings in 1944, in *Hartzel v. United States,* the Court rescinded the conviction of a man under the old Espionage Act of 1917 for disseminating literature that might harm the war effort. The "literature" was a vile racist concoction calling for Americans to make common cause with Germany against the Jews, communists, and others to save the white race. The Court found these arguments repugnant, but not dangerous and of no threat to the war effort. A year later, in *Keegan v. United States,* the Court again ruled against the government in the case of several members of the German-American Bund who were arrested, tried, and convicted after counseling people to evade the draft "if they can." The government saw this as a conspiracy to thwart the war effort, but the judges did not. The Court required the government to show an intent on the part of the defendants to commit (or cause others to commit) "specific acts" leading toward such an effort. The mere suggestion that Americans of German descent might "if they can" evade the draft did not meet this requirement.

The Court also chose to narrowly restrict the Constitution's treason language. Article III, Section 3 declares that treason "shall consist only in levying War against [the United States], or in adhering to their Enemies, [or] giving them Aid and Comfort." The framers required the government to find "two witnesses to the same overt Act" of treason for a conviction. In the early nineteenth century, the Supreme Court had narrowly construed the language of the treason provision, making it very difficult for the government to secure a conviction. Throughout American history, government lawyers had in fact avoided the Constitution's treason language because of the difficulty in attaining a conviction. As a result, treason was a relatively new issue for the Supreme Court (Kelly, Harbison, and Belz 1991, 175–177, 301–305).

In 1942, a man named Anthony Cramer met with two Germans in New York City. Cramer's profile was enough to raise eyebrows: he was a naturalized German who had served in the kaiser's army during World War I. But the two Germans he met were genuine Nazi espionage agents who had landed on American shores via submarine to engage in various acts of sabotage against American industries. Witnesses saw Cramer "engaged long and earnestly in conversation" with the spies at a hotel and a cafeteria, but no one really knew what they talked about or whether Cramer was part of the conspiracy to engage in acts of sabotage. Nevertheless, the federal government arrested Cramer and charged him with treason under Article III of the Constitution. A federal circuit court found him guilty and sentenced him to death.

In reviewing, and ultimately reversing, the conviction, the Supreme Court focused on the lack of specific information. The witnesses saw Cramer talking to the Germans and sharing meals and alcohol (Cramer even paid for the drinks), but could that really rise to the constitutional standard of an "overt act" of treason? The Court did not think so. "Cramer retained a strong affection for his fatherland," the Court admitted in *Cramer v. United States* in 1945, but this did not necessarily make him a saboteur. The Constitution's treason provisions were exceptionally strict in their evidentiary requirements, the Court believed, requiring more than mere inference and innuendo. "The very minimum function that an overt act must perform in a treason prosecution is that it show sufficient action by the accused, in its setting, to sustain a finding that the accused actually gave aid and comfort to the enemy," the Court declared, and "every act, movement, deed, and word of the defendant charged to constitute treason must be supported by the testimony of two witnesses."

The *Cramer* decision continued the long tradition of narrowly interpreting the phrase "overt act" in Article III as direct, treasonous behavior. But some of the justices thought *Cramer* was too narrow, particularly given the convincing evidence at trial of the defendant's ongoing and close cooperation with the two spies. Speaking for the four dissenting justices, Justice William O. Douglas wrote that "we do say that a meeting with the enemy is an act and may in its setting be an overt act of treason. We agree that overt acts innocent on their face should not be lightly transformed into incriminating acts. But so long as overt acts of treason need not manifest treason on their face, as the Court concedes, the sufficiency of the evidence to establish the treasonable character of the act, like the evidence of treasonable intent, depends on the quality of that evidence whatever the number of witnesses who supplied it." Douglas and his fellow dissenters worried that *Cramer* had destroyed the Constitution's treason provisions entirely. Indeed, two years later, in *Haupt v. United States,* the Court voted with only one dissent to uphold the conviction for treason of a man whose wartime aid to a group of saboteurs was much less direct or "overt" than had been the case for Cramer.

Thus, on what had been the hot-button issues of the World War I—draft evasion, freedom of speech, and the right to dissent—the nine Supreme Court justices proved more willing twenty-five years later to wrap a mantle of protection around those accused of antiwar and unpatriotic behavior. Theirs was an admirable stance, particularly during a war in which emotions ran high and otherwise admirable patriotic nationalism could—and sometimes did—lead to an oppressive conformity.

Still, the Court was not immune to the times, and its wartime record was not without controversy. It allowed the military to try foreign citizens in military courts without recourse to constitutional guarantees of their trial rights. In a decision harking back to the Civil

War's *ex parte Vallandigham*, the Court ruled in *ex parte Quirin* in 1942 that the government could try to convict seven accused German saboteurs in a military tribunal (which did not guarantee the defendants a jury trial) and that the tribunal's decisions did not fall within the purview of the Court. The Court also refused to hear appeals from the military trials of accused war criminals (*In re Yamashita*, 1946). After the war was over, the Court pulled back from this position a bit—again, as it had during the Civil War era in *ex parte Milligan*—and ruled in *Duncan v. Kahanamoku* in 1946 that the government did not have the power to arbitrarily replace civilian courts with military tribunals; in this case, the Court frowned on the army's trial of a civilian in a military court during its imposition of martial law in Hawaii. The Court apparently found it easier to honor the principle of civilian trials for civilian offenders only after the shooting had stopped.

By far the most disturbing blemish on the Court's record during World War II was its acquiescence in the government's repressive and shameful policies toward Japanese-Americans. These policies entailed the treatment of Americans with Japanese blood as a de facto security risk, forcible relocation of thousands of people like young George Takei from their homes on the West Coast, massive dispossession of their livelihoods and property, and prolonged incarceration in internment camps. Here surely was a situation that cried out for intervention from the judiciary, that branch of the federal government that supposedly speaks for the Bill of Rights and stands above the passions that sometimes rule the political fray.

But the Court turned a blind eye to the Japanese-Americans' plight. In June 1943, in *Hirabayashi v. United States,* the Court heard and rejected the challenge brought by a man named Gordon Hirabayashi against a curfew imposed upon him and other persons of Japanese descent in Seattle, Washington. The law required Hirabayashi and other Japanese-Americans to remain in their homes from 8:00 P.M. to 6:00 A.M., as a way of reducing the "security risk" these people allegedly represented. "There is support for the view that social, economic and political conditions which have prevailed since the close of the last century, when the Japanese began to come to this country in substantial numbers, have intensified their solidarity and have in large measure prevented their assimilation as an integral part of the white population," Justice Stone claimed in the Court's opinion; he cited the Japanese-American habit of having their children instructed in the Japanese language at special schools, some of which "are generally believed to be sources of Japanese nationalist propaganda." Along with the Japanese-Americans' propensity for congregating in separate neighborhoods, these conditions led Stone to conclude that the government was entirely reasonable in viewing the Japanese-American population as a serious threat to national security. Granted, actions that singled out a particular ethnic group for such special treatment would, in peacetime, have been "by their very nature odious to a free people whose institutions are founded on a doctrine of equality." But, Stone observed, in a time of war, things were different. "Because racial discriminations are in most circumstances irrelevant and therefore prohibited, it by no means follows that, in dealing with the perils of war, Congress and the Executive are wholly precluded from taking into account those facts and circumstances which are relevant to measures for our national defense and for successful prosecution of the war, which may in fact place citizens of one ancestry in a different category," according to Stone. The curfew therefore remained, and withstood a second challenge the following year, at which time the Court admitted that the treatment of Japanese-Americans had indeed created "hardship" but that "hardships are a part of war" (*Korematsu v. United States,* 1944).

The justices did believe that the hardships of war should not include a right to incarcerate Americans with no excuse at all. In December 1944, in *ex parte Endo,* they granted a writ of habeas corpus to Mitsuye Endo, a Japanese-American girl who had been imprisoned in the Tule Lake internment camp during the military's general security sweep of the West Coast. Endo asserted her loyalty to the United States, a point that the government's attorneys did not dispute. Instead, they argued that loyal citizens had been removed from their homes and imprisoned for their own safety. "But for such supervision," they claimed, "there might have been a dangerously disorderly migration of unwanted people to unprepared communities . . . unsupervised evacuation might have resulted in hardship and disorder." The Court did not buy this argument. "Whatever power the War Relocation Authority may have to detain other classes of citizens, it has no authority to subject citizens who are concededly loyal to its leave procedure."

The *Endo* decision explicitly avoided ruling on the propriety of the internment system itself. The brethren fell back on the time-honored position that they were not competent to pass judgment on military matters. How were they to know what was a reasonable detention during the extraordinary circumstances of war, and what was not? Maybe there was something to the military's insistence that a child such as George Takei posed a serious security risk. From the point of view of the generals, this deferential attitude toward the war-making branches of the government was appropriate, but for thousands of Japanese-American citizens, such institutional conservatism was a shameful abdication of the Court's authority.

After World War II: Traditions

By 1945, there were time-honored traditions embedded within the legal system concerning how America would wage war. Where war powers issues were concerned, the president was believed to have considerable war-making authority as commander in chief. He could initiate hostilities in either reacting to an immediate emergency or protecting U.S. interests abroad with a limited military response. But for any prolonged or extensive military action, most Americans agreed, the president must seek congressional approval and a formal declaration of war.

Where the other two major areas of law and war were concerned—civil liberties and military justice—Americans had proved to be pragmatic and flexible about the pressures of war on the legal system's normal operations. War is not "normal," in any sense, and Americans understood that in the pursuit of battlefield victory, personal liberties that were inviolate during peacetime could be curtailed when citizens entered the military or in civilian areas where problems of internal security prevailed. Most Americans understood that freedoms can and sometimes should be temporarily curtailed in war, but they understood there to be a heavy emphasis on the "temporary" part of that condition. Once the fighting ended, people expected a rapid return to normalcy.

The Supreme Court's role in these matters was also well established by 1945. The justices believed that the Court had only a limited role to play in wartime; the Constitution mandated no war-making responsibilities for the Court and gave it no means to compete with the powerful war-making tools assigned to the president and Congress. Most of the justices had not been military men either, and generally chose to defer to the professional soldiers and military policy makers, who were better equipped to assess the nation's wartime needs. This sometimes led to unfortunate circumstances—the Court's failure to protect ethnic minorities like Japanese-Americans, for example—but on the whole the justices were right more often than not when they chose to stay out of the military's way.

The Court and War in the Nuclear Age

The story of post–World War II America is the story of the nation's steady and gradually more intense exposure to what military thinkers call "asymmetrical warfare," meaning war waged against enemies whose level of technology is lower and who try to counteract this deficiency by using guerrilla and terror tactics. Of course, Americans before 1945 were familiar with such tactics; they were used by Native Americans, Confederate "bushwhackers," and Filipino nationalists, among others. But these "small wars" were always in the back of America's sense of itself as a military nation. Sherman's March was better than hunting down Confederate bushwhacker William Quantrill; Teddy Roosevelt's charge up San Juan Hill is much more famous than the "water cure" used against Filipino rebels; and Custer's Last Stand is so well remembered at least in part because his death occurred during one of the few "real," stand-up fights against the Plains Indians. Americans like to think that the American way of war is total war: big, blustering, and straightforward, against an enemy that fights on our terms. America wins those wars.

Unfortunately, the post-1945 world was not such a place. No one would seriously dispute that the United States emerged from World War II as the strongest nation on Earth, economically and militarily speaking. No bombs had ravaged U.S. cities; American casualty rates had been low compared with those of, say, Germany and Russia; and the war had fed a U.S. economic and technological boom unmatched in human history. No other nation could project its policies and its will on an equal footing with the United States, and although other "superpowers"—Russia and China—might hope to match American strength in some respects, other countries that opposed U.S. policies and interests found it necessary to develop tactics that did not require an unwinnable toe-to-toe slugging match with the United States. Shrewd and merciless foes such as Vietnam's Ho Chi Minh would later challenge American might on their own terms, using low-grade guerrilla warfare, terror and murder, and testing the U.S. civilian public's will to win as much as American soldiers' battlefield skills.

The result was uncertainty, controversy, and ambivalence for post–World War II Americans. The United States would come to know defeat at the hands of a foreign enemy, and it would live under a Damocles' sword of nuclear war while waging a difficult and costly "Cold War" against communism that sometimes threatened to undermine as well as reaffirm our most cherished ideals. There were disturbing developments, particularly in the war powers controversy, whereby presidents arrogated to themselves the authority to start and wage wars with little or no congressional input.

Youngstown and the "Imperial Presidency"

Seven years after the end of World War II, the Supreme Court did a most unusual thing: it reined in a sitting president's use of his war powers. It was a long time coming.

The presidency in general had ballooned in size and importance through most of the twentieth century. Franklin Roosevelt in particular had transformed the office into a powerhouse of political, legal, and cultural authority during the trying days of the Depression and World War II. The Cold War with Russia only served to reinforce these tendencies. For once, Americans did not gut their armed forces after winning a war. Large sums of taxpayer money were devoted to the development of new technologies such as the atomic bomb, the nuclear submarine, and the ballistic missile. The president now had a huge arsenal at his beck and call in peacetime, with enough bullets, bombs, and airplanes to be able to cause a great deal of damage to an enemy before having to ask Congress for more money or support. The technology wielded by these new Cold Warriors likewise fed presidential power. With his finger constantly poised over the nuclear button, a president could in a matter of minutes fight a war of apocalyptic dimensions without consulting anyone other than his cabinet and the Joint Chiefs of Staff.

The Supreme Court had little directly to do with these developments. The Court had laid the legal groundwork for much of the imperial presidency's power back in World War I, when it allowed Wilson a free rein in prosecuting the war effort, including massive federal regulation of the economy and onerous restrictions on Americans' civil liberties. The justices also were quite generous toward FDR's wartime policies.

But in 1952, a president finally went too far. In the spring of that year, Harry Truman confronted the specter of a nationwide strike in the steel industry that threatened to paralyze the nation. It also threatened to put a serious dent in the Korean War effort, then in its second year. Steel was vitally necessary for the tanks, guns, airplanes, and other military materiel being thrown at the North Korean forces, not to mention the nation's atomic energy and weapons programs, which seemed to be an indispensable deterrent against communist Russia.

Truman saw the strike as a threat to the nation's military machine, and he acted accordingly. In April, he issued an executive order authorizing federal officials to seize control of the nation's steel industry. There were several possible legal avenues for Truman to pursue here. He might have called on Congress to give him the necessary power via special legislation, or he might have used his powers under the Taft-Hartley Act to impose a "cooling-off" period on the strikers and management until a settlement could be reached. But Truman instead relied on his constitutional powers as commander in chief, arguing that the steel strike represented a grave threat to national security, in particular to the war effort in Korea (McCullough 1992, 895–903). Youngstown Sheet and Tube Company, one of the steel companies affected by the seizure, sued the Truman administration (specifically, the company sued Secretary of Commerce Charles Sawyer), and the case ended up before the Supreme Court.

Speaking for the Court's majority in *Youngstown Sheet and Tube Co. v. Sawyer,* Justice Hugo Black struck down Truman's order as an unwarranted extension of his executive powers. Black focused most of his attention on the fact that the order lacked statutory authority, but he also briefly addressed the military aspects of the case. "The order cannot properly be sustained as an exercise of the President's military power as Commander in Chief," Black argued. Truman's lawyers had drawn an analogy between the labor strikes and behavior in a theater of war, suggesting that because of the Korean conflict, the steel industry was in effect located in such a theater. Black dismissed this argument. Acknowledging that the new global realities of the mid–twentieth century were indeed stretching the definition of "theater of war," Black nevertheless thought that Truman had pushed the analogy past the breaking point. "We cannot with faithfulness to our constitutional system hold that the Commander in Chief of the

Armed Forces has the ultimate power as such to take possession of private property in order to keep labor disputes from stopping production."

The *Youngstown* decision was an embarrassing defeat for the Truman administration, although the president kept his sense of humor. "Hugo, I don't much care for your law, but, by golly, this bourbon is good," he told Black after the judge had poured him a drink at a party (McCullough 1992, 901). Where war powers issues were concerned, the decision signaled the Court's willingness to finally place some boundaries on the modern presidents' ever-expanding definition of their authority as commander in chief. Clearly, the Court was not willing to tolerate any and every use of the Article II military powers. But if there were boundaries, where exactly did those boundaries lie? The *Youngstown* decision rested on the fact that the Court did not interpret an impending steel strike as a wartime national emergency. But its criteria for doing so were not at all clear. And the Court did not want to be misconstrued as having intruded on the president's rightful powers as commander in chief. "I should indulge the widest latitude of interpretation to sustain his exclusive function to command the instruments of national force, at least when turned against the outside world for the security of our society," wrote Justice Douglas in a concurring opinion. And even if a majority of the justices thought a steel strike had crossed some sort of murky line between acceptable and unacceptable presidential behavior, a vocal minority did not. Justices Fred M. Vinson, Stanley F. Reed, and Sherman Minton wrote in their dissenting opinion that in times of war, the president must be given the broadest possible leeway in determining what was a threat to national security.

Youngstown was as close as the Court would come to directly addressing the war powers issue. In 1983, it indirectly voided part of the War Powers Act of 1973 by striking down the concept of a final legislative veto over executive authority, which had been provided for in the law (*INS v. Chadha*, 1983). Otherwise, the Court has left such questions well enough alone, refusing to hear cases brought by litigants who wanted the justices to declare, for example, that the Vietnam War was unconstitutional (*Mara v. McNamara*, 1967). Although some legal scholars argue that the Court has left open the possibility of future rulings on the constitutionality of undeclared, presidentially ordained wars, the Court has generally suggested that the war powers issue is a "political question" between the executive and legislative branches (Wormuth and Firmage 1989, 235–252; Kelly, Harbison, and Belz 1991, 661).

Expanding Wartime Dissent

The Court has been more active in the area of wartime civil liberties. The catalyst for much of its activity was the Vietnam War, which produced the most intense, sustained, and vocal antiwar movement in American history. From its beginnings at a small rally of 1,500 people in New York City in 1964, the antiwar movement grew rapidly, attracting hundreds of thousands of Americans within just a few years. Many were college students, who at the height of their power managed to shut down 500 campuses nationwide in 1970 to protest President Nixon's invasion of Cambodia. But this was more than a student movement; people from all walks of life marched against the war. There was even a strong organization of antiwar Vietnam veterans, who in one dramatic protest threw away their campaign ribbons and medals. America had never seen anything quite like it. Neither had the Supreme Court (Unger and Unger 1998, 282–286).

Before the Vietnam War, the Supreme Court had established for itself a consistent pattern on these issues. While hostilities were under way, the Court gave the benefit of the doubt to government officials who wanted to crack down on possibly dangerous forms of antiwar dissent, affording them a great deal of leeway. But such tolerance normally evaporated when the shooting stopped, and the Court had proved less likely to rubber-stamp government internal security measures once a war was over. These issues had normally only entered the nation's conscience during the "big wars," when military considerations dominated the public's attention, patriotism was intense, and the threat of military defeat by an enemy seemed palpable.

The Vietnam conflict presented a different dynamic from the world wars and the Civil War. Those wars involved relatively short, intense bursts of military activity, during which the justices—like everyone else—sensed the need for urgent internal security measures; they were probably swept up within the same burst of patriotism that enveloped most ordinary citizens, and they acted accordingly. Those wars also had easily identifiable goals—defeat the Confederacy, defeat the kaiser's Germany, occupy Tokyo and Berlin—which gave many government policies a temporary flavor. But Vietnam offered few moments of patriotic pride, it created little in the way of urgency, and many Americans doubted that Ho Chi Minh's government posed such a dire threat that security crackdowns were required. Also, during the 1960s, there seemed to be no end to the war in sight.

The Supreme Court therefore proved much less sensitive to the government's interests than it had previously, and there were other reasons for the Court's increased sympathies for wartime dissenters. When Chief Justice Earl Warren ascended to the bench in 1953, he ushered in a period of liberal activism that transformed the Supreme Court and the nation. The Warren Court handed down rulings that revolutionized civil rights, legislative apportionment, privacy rights, criminal procedures, freedom of expression, and church-state issues. In doing so, the Court displayed a libertarian bent that boded ill for any government attempts to silence antiwar opposition.

Accordingly, the Court moved in the 1960s and 1970s to protect the rights of antiwar Americans. A key case in this regard was *Brandenburg v. Ohio* in 1969. On the surface, the case had nothing directly to do with war. Brandenburg was an Ohio Ku Klux Klan leader whose inflammatory racist remarks at a 1969 rally got him arrested under a state law that banned "advocat[ing] the duty, necessity, or propriety of crime, sabotage, violence, or unlawful methods of terrorism as a means of accomplishing industrial or political reform." Brandenburg was recorded on film as threatening "revengeance" against the federal government, and the prosecution introduced evidence that he had in his possession several weapons, suggesting, they argued, that he intended to convert word into deed. The likelihood of words leading to actions was the essence of Justice Oliver Wendell Holmes's old "clear and present danger" doctrine: if the government could show a clear and present danger that someone's words would lead to dangerous deeds, then the government could restrict that person's ability to utter those words. The Supreme Court not only thought that Ohio failed to show such a likelihood, it also tossed out the "clear and present danger" doctrine entirely. "The 'clear and present danger' should have no place in the interpretation of the First Amendment," declared Justice Hugo Black. Citing Holmes's retreat from his own doctrine in the *Abrams* case, Black pointed out that the "clear and present danger" doctrine had been created during a time of war, and "whether the war power—the greatest leveler of them all—is adequate to sustain such a doctrine is debatable." From now on, the government would have to show a direct correlation between advocacy and action, and it would shoulder the burden of proof in doing so. "Action is often a method of expression and within the protection of the first amendment," Black believed.

When it jettisoned the "clear and present danger" doctrine, the Court undercut the foundation of modern wartime civil liberties law and substituted in its place a presumption in favor of citizens' First Amendment rights over government security interests. The decision also marked a departure from the Court's own ruling in *United States v. O'Brien* a year earlier, which held that a war protester's burning of his draft registration card was not protected free speech. "This Court's affirmance of that conviction was not, with all respect, consistent with the First Amendment," Black argued in *Brandenburg v. Ohio*. This new libertarian tolerance for antiwar demonstrations was further illustrated in 1971, when in *Cohen v. California* the Supreme Court overturned the conviction of a demonstrator who had appeared on the steps of a county courthouse sporting a jacket with the words "Fuck the Draft" emblazoned across the back. The justices saw this as a clear restriction of speech only, since there was no implied purpose to subvert the war effort by directly interfering with the draft. The case sent a clear message that government needed to tread carefully in the area of Vietnam War demonstrators' First Amendment rights—and, as later cases signaled, not only on courthouse steps but also in the schoolroom (*Tinker v. Des Moines Independent Community School District*, 1969) and on public streets in front of army bases (*Flower v. United States*, 1972).

Just how carefully government authorities needed to tread became apparent in *New York Times Co. v. United States*, a 1971 lawsuit involving that newspaper's publication of a series of top-secret Vietnam War documents, known ever since as the "Pentagon Papers." The documents showed clearly that the federal government was guilty of corruption, duplicity, and fraud in its attempts to justify the Vietnam War and to hide accurate casualty figures from the public. The Pentagon Papers were stolen from a secure Defense Department safe by an employee named Daniel Ellsberg, who leaked them to the press. A furious Nixon administration sued the newspaper, citing national security concerns that in another time might have persuaded the Court to suppress publication of such sensitive documents. The absence of a real sense of wartime urgency was decisive, however, and the Court allowed the documents to be published. In a troubled dissent, Justice Harry Blackmun worried that exposure of the documents to public

scrutiny might result in "the death of soldiers" and damage diplomatic negotiations to end the war, and others on the Court indicated
that if the Pentagon Papers had contained actual war plans, they
might have ruled differently. But the Court majority decided that at
worst the *New York Times* might embarrass the government, and
embarrassment, even during a war, was not enough to trump the
First Amendment.

The Court also opened the doors wider for Americans trying to
evade military service under "conscientious objector" status. In
1948, the army had created a set of guidelines for determining who
might be allowed conscientious objector status on the basis of "religious training and belief." Among other criteria, the army required
that a person's religious views include some notion of a "Supreme
Being" whose teachings involved a duty higher to that afforded human institutions (such as the army). In 1965, a Vietnam war draftee
named Seeger sought conscientious objector status, but when questioned about his belief in a Supreme Being, Seeger sounded evasive,
citing a "cosmic order" and a "creative intelligence." Army authorities did not think this signified a belief in a "Supreme Being," per se,
and denied Seeger conscientious objector status. Seeger sued, and
the Supreme Court sided with him. Speaking for the majority in
United States v. Seeger, Justice Clark told the army that it had no
right to hold potential conscientious objectors to such a rigid definition of terms. The only relevant consideration was "whether a given
belief that is sincere and meaningful occupies a place in the life of its
possessor equal to that filled by the orthodox belief in God." If military authorities found this standard to be somewhat vague, they
must have been truly nonplussed four years later when the Court
awarded conscientious objector status to a draftee who forthrightly
stated that his objections to the war weren't really "religious" in nature (*Welsh v. United States,* 1971) but based on a general moral
judgment about the evil of killing another human being. The Court
thought this was sufficient to grant him a deferment. This is not to
say that the justices were willing to make of the conscientious objector status a loophole through which any American could escape
the draft—in 1970 they ruled in *Gillette v. United States* that opposition to the Vietnam War did not by itself confer protected objector
status—but they did greatly expand the definition of acceptable
moral opposition to war in ways that would have been unthinkable
to previous generations.

Reining in Military Justice: The Military Court of Appeals and the My Lai Atrocities

The Court also began to dip its toes into the previously untested waters of military justice. Whereas in previous years the Court was extremely reluctant to involve itself directly in such matters, it proved more willing during the Vietnam conflict to examine just how America's soldiers were treated by the military courts. The generally liberalizing tendencies of the Warren Court meant that the justices were partial to an expansive reading of the Bill of Rights and its applicability to all American citizens, regardless of their station or circumstances. Congress had also begun to take note of the possible shortcomings inherent in the military justice system. In 1950, it authorized the creation of the U.S. Army Boards of Review (later the U.S. Army Court of Criminal Appeals), which gave court-martial defendants an appellate option. Congress held hearings in 1962 on the subject of military justice and in 1968 passed the Military Justice Act, which extended certain basic legal rights to court-martial defendants. Clearly the days when Congress fulfilled its Article I duty of making "Rules for the Government and Regulation of the land and naval forces" by simply passing the matter on to the soldiers were over (Generous 1973, 1–5).

The Supreme Court tried to place boundaries on how far the military could go in policing the behavior of servicemen without guaranteeing them basic constitutional rights. In 1955, the Court stopped the air force from trying by court-martial a discharged serviceman who had committed a murder in Korea five months before he was discharged *(Toth v. Quarles)*. Two years later, the Court ruled in *Reid v. Covert* that the wife of a serviceman could not be tried and convicted for murder by a military tribunal. The two cases together established the principle that military justice should be applied only to military personnel who were engaged in military duties *(Reid v. Covert)*.

In 1969, the Court agreed to hear an appeal from a seven-year-old case involving an army sergeant named O'Callahan, who, after getting himself thoroughly drunk one evening, left his post at Fort Shafter in Hawaii and assaulted a girl in her hotel room. Once the local police discovered he was a soldier (O'Callahan wore civilian clothes), they turned him over to the military police, who after a long interrogation wrung a confession from him. O'Callahan was then court-martialed and convicted under the Uniform Code of Military Justice for housebreaking, assault, and attempted rape. When he appealed the ruling to the Supreme Court, a majority of the justices agreed that he was unfairly deprived of his basic constitutional right to a jury trial. Military rules possess no such guarantees, but according to the Court, O'Callahan should never have been tried in a military matter: he was off his post at the time of the crime and during his arrest, and he was wearing civilian clothes. This made him, in the eyes of the law, a civilian entitled to all the rights guaranteed by the Constitution. Speaking for the majority in *O'Callahan v. Parker*, Justice William O. Douglas conceded that, for a military force to be effective on the battlefield, a disciplinary system was necessary that sometimes did not provide civilian guarantees of fairness. "That a system of specialized military courts, proceeding by practices different from the regular courts and in general less favorable to the defendants is necessary to an effective military establishment, few would deny," he wrote, "but the justification for such a system rests on the special needs of the military, and history teaches that expansion of military discipline beyond its proper domain carries with it a threat to liberty." Douglas also voiced the Court's general disdain for military justice, stating that "courts-martial as an institution are singularly inept in dealing with the nice subtleties of constitutional law."

But there were definite limits to the extent to which the justices were willing to go in this area. The Court was still not comfortable trying to proscribe military rules about discipline and appropriate behavior. This became clear in 1974, when an army doctor named Howard Levy found himself in trouble with his superiors for having encouraged African-American soldiers not to go to Vietnam even if ordered to do so, refusing to train Special Forces personnel, and referring to Special Forces soldiers as "liars and thieves," "killers of peasants," and "murderers of women and children." The army saw Levy's statements to the black soldiers and his refusal to administer training as direct disobedience of orders, and it subsumed his remarks under the catchall heading of "conduct unbecoming an officer and a gentleman." Levy argued that this last provision was so vague as to create a violation of his due process rights under the Fifth Amendment. The Supreme Court felt otherwise, however, and refused to overturn Levy's conviction. In the majority opinion in *Parker v. Levy*, Justice William Rehnquist argued that the military's rules were of a special nature that set them apart from ordinary civilian proceedings. "To maintain the discipline essential to perform its mission effectively, the military has developed what 'may not unfitly be called the customary military law' or 'general usage of the military service,'" Rehnquist wrote. The articles of military justice that punished Levy for his behavior, he indicated, were part of well-established military custom.

The majority justices in *Parker v. Levy* were on familiar turf, for the Court's deference to military decision makers had a long pedigree. By 1974, the Court was also taking a more conservative turn; Earl Warren had retired in 1969, and Nixon appointee Warren E. Burger had become chief justice. But several justices dissented in the *Parker* decision, and in so doing articulated the modern Court's understanding that military justice must be constructed as narrowly as possible so as to afford Americans in uniform basic constitutional rights.

Most of these decisions involving military justice took place far below the public's radar screen. Indeed, military justice has a long history of isolation and irrelevance to civilian concerns. Soldiers generally discipline their own, and both soldiers and civilians like it that way. But in 1969, military justice suddenly became front-page news in America because of the actions of a platoon led by an army lieutenant named William Calley in a small village in southern Vietnam called My Lai.

On the morning of March 16, 1968, Calley led his platoon into My Lai as part of a general sweep of the area by Charlie Company, Twentieth U.S. Infantry. The village was rumored to be an enemy stronghold, but when the Americans stormed into the village, they found almost no Vietcong, just hundreds of wide-eyed, terrified civilians. The precise reasons for what happened next are unclear: Calley later testified that he was told by his commanding officer to take no prisoners, and other GIs claimed to have seen weapons and other suspicious activities in the village. Whatever the case may be, the operation turned into a full-scale bloodbath, with Calley and his men rampaging through My Lai and indiscriminately murdering civilian men, women, and children. More than 500 people died at the hands of American soldiers, who calmly executed women, children, and the elderly and piled their bodies in heaps or stacked them in roadside ditches. One witness observed a group of soldiers quietly eating lunch in front of a ghastly pile of bodies, some still twitching. Others saw acts of sexual assault, thievery, and destruction of a type that few thought civilized men were capable of committing. "I cut their throats, cut off their hands, cut out their tongue[s], their hair, scalped them. I did it. A lot of people were doing it," a GI later recounted. One Charlie Company soldier later observed laconically, "I guess you could say the men were out of control" (Belknap 2002, 64–65).

What followed next was a record of neglect, indifference, and cover-up by army authorities that was nearly as shameful as the massacre itself. A few of the men present that morning in My Lai were horrified by the spectacle, and there were some members of Charlie Company who had refused to participate in the slaughter. One American soldier shot himself in the foot, saying that he had to "get out of there"; another threatened to turn his guns on his own troops. Taken together, these men might have been willing to become the catalysts of an official military investigation, but the few attempts that were made to start such a project were quickly silenced or redirected into channels where incriminating evidence would never see the light of day.

There matters might have remained, buried deep and forgotten within a pile of army paperwork and red tape. But rumors of a questionable operation in the My Lai area persisted, and several soldiers who had witnessed or heard about the shootings began pressuring their superiors and their congressmen for some sort of official army investigation. Lieutenant Calley became a lightning rod for controversy, since he was reported to have been personally responsible for more than 100 civilian deaths in My Lai. Eyewitnesses saw him shove Vietnamese civilians into a shallow ditch before turning his gun on them. He was also reported to have executed an elderly Buddhist monk who was begging for his life. "Lieutenant Calley took his rifle at point blank and just pulled the trigger," recalled a GI; the monk's head "was just blown off" (Belknap 2002, 72–74).

After investigations were conducted by a special congressional subcommittee and the army, Calley was court-martialed in November 1970 for committing mass murder. At the end of a lengthy trial (one of the longest court-martial proceedings in army history), Calley was convicted on March 31, 1971, and sentenced to life in prison. Public sympathy for the army lieutenant was strong, however; many Americans felt that he had been wrongly scapegoated for the army's shortcomings and that he was little more than the victim of a disastrous war that had tarnished everybody caught in its grasp. Telegrams poured into the White House, running 100 to 1 in favor of Nixon's granting Calley clemency (Reeves 2001, 307). Nixon was reluctant to go quite that far, but he reduced the sentence to what amounted to house arrest. In 1974, Calley was granted release and a dishonorable discharge from the army by a federal district court, having been "imprisoned" for less than three years (Bourke 1999, 163).

The Supreme Court never became directly involved in the Calley court-martial (although its 1955 ruling in *Toth v. Quarles* compelled prosecutors to bring their charges against Calley with haste, lest he be discharged from the army before they could try him). Army prosecutors planned an appeal to the nation's highest court after Calley's release by the district court, but by the time the Supreme Court denied the appeal, Calley was already a free man (Belknap 2002, 248–250).

The My Lai affair is more interesting for what it reveals about the problems that can occur when military justice and politics intersect. If the Calley trial is an example of what happens when the presidency and Congress become directly involved in the process of military justice, then the results are not encouraging. Calley's congressional sympathizers actually tried to hinder the investigation of My Lai, and the hearings conducted by a special House Armed Services subcommittee "generated more heat than light," in the words of historian Michael Belknap (Belknap 2002, 138–142). Nixon's involvement was even more dubious. The president saw the My Lai affair as nothing less than a referendum on his handling of the war, and he defended Lieutenant Calley (which included, among other things, pressuring Congress and the army to soft-pedal the whole affair) as a political ploy to further his own ends (Reeves 2001, 306–308). Calley's court-martial for the My Lai massacre was one of the most politically charged legal proceedings in American history.

Law and War: Whither the Supreme Court?

The framers of the Constitution appear to have envisioned little if any role for the Supreme Court in the nation's wars. Two centuries later, it can be seen that they were only partially successful in this regard, for the Court has indeed been a player in military matters.

Before 1945, the Court had established a certain amount of continuity in all of these matters. By long-established custom, dating back to the presidency of Thomas Jefferson, presidents were to be allowed a small amount of leeway in waging small wars without Congress's direct approval, as long as those wars were short, involved small numbers of professional soldiers, and served a legitimate policy goal. Anything larger required congressional approval. The Court was only peripherally involved in this process, which seemed to have been worked out between the legislative and executive branches to everyone's satisfaction. Where civil liberties were concerned, beginning with the Civil War the Court established the precedent that it would allow the president and Congress a great deal of flexibility in addressing internal security issues, but it would do so only during times of pressing national emergency; once the fighting stopped, the Court would generally cast a suspicious eye on government's attempts to suppress dissent. In the area of military justice, the Supreme Court applied a hands-off approach, allowing the soldiers to police their own ranks with a minimal amount of civilian interference.

After World War II, however, the consensus and continuity the Court had created or accepted on these issues was permanently disrupted. Harry Truman's unilateral exercise of war-making power in Korea and then Lyndon Johnson's disastrous policies during the Vietnam War dismantled the long-standing arrangement between the executive and legislative branches; now presidents simply asserted their prerogative as commander in chief to start and maintain wars whenever, however, and for whatever duration they saw fit to do so, without a formal declaration from Congress. Congress fought back with the War Powers Act of 1973, a law whose validity has rarely been formally recognized by subsequent presidents. The lines between "making" and "declaring" war are murkier than ever, and yet the Court has not seen fit to involve itself directly in this issue. There is no coherent Supreme Court philosophy for the war powers issue, which the justices see as a "political question" only, a fight between Congress and the president.

In the area of civil liberties, the Supreme Court's traditional perspective seems likewise outdated. Before 1945, the Court could safely assume that the federal government would make overt moves to suppress dissent only during the brief, intense circumstances of a major war, during which temporary breaches of Americans' liberties could be tolerated. But Vietnam was an entirely different scenario, a low-intensity, long-range, undeclared war that aroused intense opposition that made government officials nervous. The Court's response was to significantly restrict government's suppression powers during a war, something it had never really done before.

The Court also found itself moving to place narrower, better-defined boundaries on the operations of the military justice system. The catalysts were the Warren Court's newfound commitment to civil rights during the 1960s and Congress's creation of a military appeals system. The Court continued to allow soldiers a wide sphere of responsibility within the purview of direct military justice, but it signaled a new willingness to guard the rights of civilians on the fringes of the military community who found themselves swept up in its operations.

The consequences of the Court's war-making decisions—or, in the case of the war powers issue, its lack of decision making—are unclear. As the nation enters the twenty-first century and faces the radical new demands of the post–September 11 world and pursues its attendant war on terror, it will find both new and old legal and constitutional problems. How the legal system will respond, and what the Supreme Court's role will be in that response, will surely play an important role in how events unfold.

References and Further Reading

Baker, Liva. 1991. *The Justice from Beacon Hill: The Life and Times of Oliver Wendell Holmes.* New York: HarperCollins.

Basler, Roy P., ed. 1953. *The Collected Works of Abraham Lincoln.* 8 vols. New Brunswick, NJ: Rutgers University Press.

Belknap, Michael. 2002. *The Vietnam War on Trial: The My Lai Massacre and the Court-Martial of Lieutenant Calley.* Lawrence: University Press of Kansas.

Bernath, Stuart L. 1970. *Squall across the Atlantic: American Civil War Prize Cases and Diplomacy.* Berkeley: University of California Press.

Blight, David W. 2001. *Race and Reunion: The Civil War in American Memory.* Cambridge, MA: Belknap.

Boot, Max. 2002. *The Savage Wars of Peace: Small Wars and the Rise of American Power.* New York: Basic.

Bourke, Joanna. 1999. *An Intimate History of Killing.* New York: Basic.

Fehrenbacher, Don E. 2001. *The Dred Scott Case: Its Significance in Law and Politics.* New York: Oxford University Press.

Foner, Eric S. 1988. *Reconstruction: America's Unfinished Revolution, 1863–1877.* New York: Harper and Row.

Generous, William T., Jr. 1973. *Swords and Scales: The Development of the Uniform Code of Military Justice.* Port Washington, NY: Kennikat.

Hyman, Harold M., and William Weicek. 1982. *Equal Justice under Law: Constitutional Development, 1835–1875.* New York: HarperCollins.

Kelly, Alfred H., Winfred A. Harbison, and Herman Belz. 1991. *The American Constitution: Its Origins and Development.* Vol. 1. New York: W. W. Norton.

Lurie, Jonathan. 1992. *Arming Military Justice: The Origins of the United States Military Court of Appeals, 1775–1950.* Vol. 1. Princeton: Princeton University Press.

McCullough, David. 1992. *Truman.* New York: Simon and Schuster.

McKitrick, Eric, and Stanley Elkins. 1994. *The Age of Federalism.* New York: Oxford University Press.

McPherson, James M. 2000. *Ordeal by Fire: The Civil War and Reconstruction.* New York: McGraw-Hill.

Miller, Allan R., and Peter Maslowski, eds. 1994. *For the Common Defense: A Military History of the United States.* New York: Free Press.

Neely, Mark E., Jr. 1992. *The Fate of Liberty: Abraham Lincoln and Civil Liberties.* New York: Oxford University Press.

Newmyer, R. Kent. 1986. *The Supreme Court under Marshall and Taney.* New York: Harlan Davidson.

Paludan, Philip S. 1994. *The Presidency of Abraham Lincoln.* Lawrence: University Press of Kansas.

Reeves, Richard. 2001. *President Nixon: Alone in the White House.* New York: Simon and Schuster.

Rehnquist, William H. 2000. *All the Laws but One: Civil Liberties in War.* New York: Vintage.

Rossiter, Clinton, ed. 1999. *The Federalist Papers.* New York: Mentor.

Shy, John. 1990. *A People Numerous and Armed: Reflections on the Military Struggle for Independence.* Ann Arbor: University of Michigan Press.

Unger, Debi, and Irwin Unger. 1998. *The Times Were a Changin': The Sixties Reader.* New York: Three Rivers.

U.S. Government. 1880–1901. *War of the Rebellion: A Compilation of the Official Records of the Union and Confederate Armies.* 127 vols. Washington, DC: Government Printing Office.

White, G. Edward. 1993. *Justice Oliver Wendell Holmes: Law and the Inner Self.* New York: Oxford University Press.

Wormuth, Francis D., and Edwin B. Firmage. 1989. *To Chain the Dog of War: The War Power of Congress in History and War.* Urbana: University of Illinois Press.

4

Impact and Legacy

Met on a Battlefield, of Sorts

The United States observed the first anniversary of the World Trade Center attack just as this book was nearing completion. Americans are good at ceremonies, and September 11, 2002, was no exception. New Yorkers observed silence between 8:46 and 9:03 A.M., the precise moments when the two hijacked jets crashed into the World Trade Center towers. Over 13,000 people attended a ceremony at the Pentagon in Washington, D.C., to remember the Americans who died when a third jet destroyed part of that massive office complex. Family members of those killed on United Airlines Flight 93 as it was en route to an unknown target gathered at the crash site in a field near Shanksville, Pennsylvania, to hear President Bush and other dignitaries speak of Americans "coming to terms with the difficult knowledge that our nation has determined enemies, and that we are not invulnerable to their attacks" (*Atlanta Journal Constitution,* September 12, 2002, 1A; *New York Times,* September 12, 2002, B24; *Washington Post,* September 12, 2002, A25).

Everyone speaks of September 11 as the day America changed—and indeed, these are different times. The government is pursuing its "war on terrorism," and to this end the nation of Afghanistan has been liberated from the Taliban's regime of Islamic fundamentalism. Much of the al Qaeda terror network was once headquartered in Afghanistan, and now the network is broken and its remaining members are in hiding. Rumors of Osama bin Laden's whereabouts, or his death, abound. Some say he was killed by American missiles during the fighting in Afghanistan; others say he is hiding in the caves along the border between that country and Pakistan. The United States periodically convulses with rumors of an impending terrorist plot—against the Golden State Bridge, the Super Bowl, nuclear power plants, the postal system, computers, or food supply.

"In a sense, we meet on a battlefield," Secretary of Defense Donald Rumsfeld observed at the Pentagon memorial ceremony. Jerlynn Roche, whose sister-in-law died in the attack, agreed. "It's a hard war. And it's not just for our president to fight. It's for all of us" (*Washington Post,* September 12, 2002, A25). But the structure of the war on terrorism is unlike anything Americans have experienced. Bush administration experts warned the American people that they should not expect it to have the dynamic of "big wars" like the Civil War or World War II, and it doesn't. On the other hand, the war on terrorism doesn't look very much like previous "small wars" either. Rather, it seems to combine elements of both. The empty space where the World Trade Center stood is a strong reminder that this is not one of those wars whose reasons are obscure and whose policy goals are morally ambivalent. "Ground Zero" has a Pearl Harbor– like intensity of justification that was missing in, say, Vietnam or the Spanish-American War. But the daily grind of the war on terrorism bears faint resemblance to the mixture of patriotism, sacrifice, and easily measurable progress that ennobled World War II as "the Good War" for so many Americans. Business as usual has crept back into post–September 11 America, whether we like it or not. This between-big-and-small-war quality has played havoc on national perceptions, a fact that should be of some concern to the government. When a democracy goes to war, perception is everything.

Perception is likewise an important factor when it comes to the law and war in America. Members of Congress and presidents see military action in different ways, a fact that has enlivened the ongoing war powers debate for some time, particularly in the last fifty years. Americans from all walks of life—rich and poor, northerner and southerner, conservative and liberal—have a wide range of attitudes about whether a war should be fought and whether they should participate. The nation's legal system has tried—with varying degrees of success—to walk a fine line between a prudent containment of internal security threats and a permissive allowance of democratic debate and dissent. One person's patriotism is another's treason, given the circumstances, the times, and the judgments of those in authority.

Perception has also played a key role in how the Supreme Court addresses these matters of law and war. The justices usually don't like to be reminded of this. Perception is a relative thing, and most justices have long tried to maintain the pretense that their decisions are grounded in a dispassionate rendering of law's objective truths. The men and women who sit on the nation's highest tribunal are perceptive, however, of the prevailing winds of public opinion, no less so than Congress and the president, and during times of war those winds blow very hard. Judges hear the voices of Americans who demand conformity in the name of patriotism, they understand the president's need to be able to act quickly and forcibly in times of national emergency, and they perceive the wisdom of letting soldiers and sailors write their own rules of conduct whenever possible.

The process, however, cuts both ways. Remove the threat of immediate invasion or battlefield disaster, and Americans usually like to cut military budgets, ignore potential foreign threats, neglect internal security problems, and allow room for dissent in the public square. In much the same vein, judges are less willing to give government the benefit of the doubt after victory has been declared or when combat seems far away. This is as it should be. Democracies are usually better off with a short memory when it comes to war. True, America is often unprepared when real danger does arise, but the alternative—a peacetime paranoia about enemies real and perceived that could fuel unjustifiable repression—is surely the greater evil.

September 11 has changed none of this. The dynamics of waging war within America's legal and constitutional framework remain much the same. The law faces the same old questions: Who starts a war? Who is allowed to oppose a war, and in what ways and under what circumstances? How does the law balance the legitimate internal security needs of the government with the right to criticize and dissent? How much civilian control is needed over the operations of the military justice system? September 11, 2001, may seem to be the day America changed, but in many ways the questions posed at the intersection of law and war have not.

The War Powers Issue: Who's in Charge?

As noted, before 1950 there was a remarkable degree of continuity in the way the three branches of the federal government approached the war powers issue. Presidents could initiate military action without a congressional declaration of war, as long as that action remained brief and low key with few casualties and a minimal impact on American society. However, congressional approval was needed for anything large enough to require significant funding, a long-term military commitment, or drastic measures such as conscription. Presidents recognized this fact and asked for declarations of war when needed, or got congressional approval after the fact as soon as possible. This tacit arrangement worked quite well, and the Supreme Court approved it, first by acknowledging in *Bas v. Tingy* that a war could legally exist without a formal congressional declaration, and second by avoiding an active role in the war powers conversation and leaving well enough alone.

In 1950, however, everything changed. In that year, President Harry S. Truman asserted unilateral executive authority to send troops into Korea, on a scale that would previously have called for direct congressional action. In fairness to Truman, he faced an entirely new diplomatic situation. There was now a United Nations, whose mandates created security obligations that the United States, as the reigning superpower, felt compelled to meet. Truman justified the undeclared war in Korea by citing a UN pledge to aid South Korea if attacked, so he had at least some legal basis for his actions.

Things have not been the same since. Presidents now often see UN resolutions as a way of circumventing the need for congressional action. When it comes to Congress, presidents see war powers issues through an almost exclusively political lens, shorn of any sense of constitutional obligation. They may seek congressional approval for an impending war, but they are careful to explain that this in no way implies recognition that they are required by law to do so: the opinion polls just make it seem like a good idea to get Congress on their side. "The president has the authority to undertake this kind of operation without the approval of the Congress," George H. W. Bush's defense secretary, Richard Cheney, claimed in 1991 in the wake of the Gulf War. "We had a big debate about it [in the administration]. I argued that it was not necessary" (*U.S. News and World Report*, April 15, 1991, 31). For Cheney and many other Americans, Article II's title of "commander in chief" provides presidents with a blanket legal justification for nearly any military excursion. This position is not contingent on party or ideology: it has been commonplace among the Republicans and Democrats, conservatives and liberals alike who have sat in the Oval Office since 1950.

Congress's record after 1950 has not been particularly encouraging either. "There was a brief reflective moment near the end of the war in Indochina when Congress looked itself in the mirror and saw it wasn't there," wrote historian John Hart Ely. "It had been dodging its constitutional duty to make the decision whether to commit troops to combat. Instead, it had been laying back, neither disapproving presidential military ventures or forthrightly approving them" (Ely 1993, 48). The result of this reflective moment was the War Powers Act of 1973, in which Congress tried to restore a degree of balance in military decision making. However well intentioned, the act has garnered its share of critics on both sides of the issue. Supporters of presidential authority see it as an unconstitutional intrusion into the president's war-making powers, and congressional supporters think it doesn't go far enough in limiting presidential action, as it gives him a ninety-day window of opportunity to do what he wishes before he is obliged to seek congressional approval (Hall 1992, 911–912). As a statement of Congress's desire to make its voice heard in war-making matters, the War Powers Act has been at least somewhat effective, but as a legally binding check on the presidency's ever-expanding powers, it has been much less so.

Instead, modern presidents and Congress have an uneasy, generally strained relationship in the realm of war-making authority, one that tends to inflate the president's power and diminish Congress's, all without clear constitutional lines of authority. In this ongoing tug-of-war, Congress nearly always finds itself at a disadvantage. Modern presidents possess very powerful tools with which to motivate the public, so by the time debate over a military action actually reaches the floor of Congress, the president is usually firmly in the driver's seat of public opinion. Most members of Congress are loath to pay the heavy political price required for stopping a war started by a president who will invariably have already rallied Americans around the flag. During the Gulf War in 1991, for example, Congress heatedly debated the impending assault on Iraq while thousands of American troops were already deploying in the Middle East. Small wonder that a majority of Americans supported the Gulf War before

Congress had made up its mind, and equally small wonder that Congress, bowing to presidentially defined public pressures, gave its stamp of approval to Desert Shield and Desert Storm in what at least one expert called a "jury-rigged" conclusion (Glennon 1991, 84).

The war on terrorism may drive the War Powers Act further along toward irrelevance. Some observers wonder whether a congressional power to oversee military operations in an era of attacks such as that on the World Trade Center might be obsolete, a relic of a safer time before terrorists could kill thousands of people in a matter of seconds (Turner 2002, 519). At the same time, the war is likely to further enhance the power of the presidency. The Patriot Act created in the wake of the September 11 attacks further augments the president's authority during times of emergency, giving him expanded internal security and public surveillance powers with minimal or, some argue, no judicial and congressional oversight (Matthews 2002, 455).

In laying plans for a second military operation against Iraq, President Bush initially expressed his desire to act unilaterally, without congressional consent. Like his father before him, however, he found that the political costs might be too high, and he requested a war resolution from Congress. However (again, like his father), President Bush did not in doing so imply that he needed a formal declaration of war or Congress's explicit permission to invade Iraq.

Bush also articulated a relatively novel concept in the history of American war making: the preemptive war. In formulating a new national security strategy for the war on terrorism, Bush declared in the summer of 2002 that if the United States found convincing evidence that a foreign country possesses biological, chemical, or nuclear weapons, and also displays a propensity to use those weapons—or, worse, has demonstrable ties to terrorist organizations—he would not wait for an overt act; rather, he would launch direct military action against that country to preempt future destruction and loss of life. President Bush obviously had Iraq primarily in mind, but his language was general enough that preemptive warfare now became a possibility for any nation the administration deemed a threat to U.S. interests. The idea of the United States waging a preemptive war set off tremors throughout Europe, with critics arguing that the U.S. rationale for a preemptive strike could surely also be used by other nations—Russia, China, even Iraq itself—to justify their own preemptive wars, which could use prevention of terrorism as a pretext for all sorts of aggressive policies. "In the end, the basic issue is whether you trust America to act more-or-less wisely, or whether you think it (or Mr. Bush personally) is in fact a Wild West cowboy," pointed out one British writer (*Economist*, September 28, 2002, 2).

From a foreign policy perspective, preemptive war could be either defensible or unthinkable, depending on a variety of circumstances; one could certainly make a plausible case that such a policy is an unfortunate necessity in the new post–September 11 world. From the perspective of American constitutionalism, however, the matter is considerably more disturbing. The framers clearly did not intend to give the president the authority to launch, on his own, U.S. military action against foreign foes that had not yet committed any overt act of aggression. The notes from the 1787 convention indicate that the word "declare" was substituted for "make" in Article I, in the words of James Madison and Elbridge Gerry, to leave "to the Executive the power to repel sudden attacks" (Madison 1987, 476). As a matter of practical policy making, President Bush's preemptive war rationale may be sound. There is nearly a universal consensus that the world would be better off without Saddam Hussein, and effecting this end may very well require an invasion of Iraq. Effective countermeasures against terrorism may also require an expansive definition of justifiable military action, making an imminent terrorist attack reason enough to use force. In the process, however, are the war powers provisions of the Constitution being stretched past their breaking point? Combined with the fifty-year-old de facto moratorium on congressional declarations of war, Bush's preemptive war doctrine, however reasonable and well intentioned, may entirely remove the legislative branch from meaningful decision making on whether the nation goes to war, diminishing the democratic process and scuttling the framer's intentions.

Flying solo on war making could also prove to have political liabilities for the president. If President Bush is reluctant to share the power of waging war, he might also find it difficult to share the responsibility if the war goes awry. Acting unilaterally, the president also leaves himself more vulnerable to charges—however ill founded—that military assaults are a thinly disguised effort to divert national attention from pressing domestic problems. Conservatives leveled this charge at President Bill Clinton in 1998 when he launched cruise missiles against a chemical plant in Sudan that his administration claimed was a site (financed by the then relatively obscure Osama bin Laden) for weapons development. Critics claimed (with little actual proof) that the attack was a smoke screen to cover Clinton's extramarital affairs (*U.S. News and World Report,* December 28, 1998, 78). In a similar vein, some liberals have charged that George Bush's impending assault on Iraq is really a way to distract Americans from Bush's economic problems. One of the president's more vociferous critics, *New York Times* columnist Paul Krugman, wrote that "It's hard not to suspect that the Bush doctrine is also a diversion—a diversion from the real issues of dysfunctional security agencies, a sinking economy, a devastated budget and a tattered relationship with our allies" (*New York Times,* September 24, 2002 sec. 4, 17). Fair or not, such charges seem to be an almost natural byproduct of the tendency exhibited by recent presidents to make military decisions alone.

On a political level, then, presidents in the post–September 11 world might do well to reconsider their increasingly solo approach to war. On a constitutional level, however, the current of public opinion and policy making seems to be very much with them and bids fair to further exclude Congress from meaningful war-making decisions. Members of Congress have few tools at their disposal that would allow them to bring a president to heel, short of denying money and supplies for soldiers in the field. These are measures fraught with political peril in any period, but all the more so when a president can point to the smoking ruins of the World Trade Center as a powerful, visceral justification for unimpeded military action.

The Supreme Court meanwhile has continued to steer clear of this particular fight. But surely all of these unresolved questions will come knocking at the Court's door again, as they did during Vietnam, in the form of lawsuits brought by antiwar Americans. The justices may well emulate their predecessors and invoke the "political questions" doctrine to avoid ruling on these cases, particularly if the Court retains its current right-of-center ideological makeup, and if the war on terrorism appears to enjoy widespread public support. On the other hand, if a future president makes rash decisions on his own with little congressional input, and if those decisions get Americans killed or seem to exacerbate the threat of terrorism, public clamor for some sort of judicial decision that restores the Constitution's war-making balance may prove overwhelming. Then the political questions doctrine may become a luxury the Court—or the nation—can no longer afford.

Wartime Civil Liberties and Military Justice

Whatever the Supreme Court decides to do about war powers issues, it will almost certainly be unable to avoid a showdown with the president on the matter of civil liberties.

Immediately in the wake of the September 11 assault, the Bush administration asserted extraordinary legal authority in dealing with suspected terrorists, in the United States and abroad. These new powers are astonishingly broad. On November 13, 2001, President Bush signed an executive order allowing the Justice Department to bypass the civilian court system and try suspected terrorists in military courts. "Given the danger to the safety of the United States and the nature of international terrorism . . . it is not practicable to apply in military commissions under this order the principles of law and rules of evidence generally recognized in the trial of criminal cases in the United States district courts," read the order (*New York Times,* November 14, 2001, B8). This meant that military tribunals could operate behind closed doors and hand down death sentences and that appeals would be limited to the president or the secretary of defense. Bush also asserted his administration's right to hold suspects indefinitely without showing cause and to eavesdrop on conversations between suspects and their attorneys. The order was aimed directly at al Qaeda, but in truth it could be used against any noncitizen the administration chose to define as terrorist or enemy of the United States.

Administration officials have been quick to point out that defendants in the military tribunals will have basic constitutional rights, such as the presumption of innocence, protection against self-incrimination and double jeopardy, and the right to be present in court and cross-examine witnesses. Few doubt that the government faces an enormously difficult, sensitive task in trying to ferret out an enemy whose tactics are unique, immoral, and chilling in their effectiveness. The Bush administration feels that there are legitimate security risks in allowing suspected terrorists to be tried in a civilian courtroom. Still, the rules of military justice will not afford defendants a jury trial, they will allow hearsay evidence to be introduced into the proceedings, and they will not allow civilian review or direct congressional input. Worst of all, they are secret proceedings. "The war on terror is supposed to be a unified effort," observed columnist William

Safire. "Why go it contemptuously alone in setting up an extraordinary military judiciary?" (*New York Times,* March 21, 2002, A37).

These measures have been the most controversial pursued by the Bush administration so far in the war on terrorism. Civil libertarians worry about the potential for abuse contained in the administration's sweeping power to try people in secret without the usual constitutional protections for their rights. "It is the broadest move in American history to sweep aside constitutional protections," declared columnist Anthony Lewis, and "people do not understand the [executive] order's dangerous breadth" (*New York Times,* November 30, 2001, A27). Another observer claimed that the United States was embarking "on an incredible witch hunt, fueled, as witch hunts always are, by incredible fear" (*New York Times,* December 3, 2001, A19). Some of the reactions abroad were even more pointed. "Stalin would have approved of Bush's plan for military tribunals," said one Canadian observer (*Ottawa Citizen,* November 20, 2001, A16). Others argue that secret military trials would violate international legal agreements regarding the treatment of prisoners of war (*New York Times,* December 26, 2001, B1).

But the Bush security plan has had plenty of defenders as well. Some argue that terrorists do not deserve bona fide prisoner-of-war status, having made a deliberate decision to wage war on noncombatants (*New York Times,* December 31, 2001, A19). Others believe that the use of military tribunals greatly reduces the risk of al Qaeda detainees using a public forum to air their views or perhaps even communicate with one another via coded signals. Such a forum would also allow government lawyers to use classified information without the threat of compromising national security. More to the point, they argue, there is a war on. "The clerks want to file protests," sneered conservative columnist William Buckley, while "the soldiers [want] to go to war" (*National Review,* November 30, 2001, http://www. nationalreview.com/buckley/buckley113001.shtml). The *Wall Street Journal* characterized the critics of Bush's policies as "couch potato civil libertarians" (*Washington Times,* December 3, 2001, A20). One expert pointed out that "circumstances in a war zone often make it impossible to meet the authentication requirements for documents in a civilian court, yet documents from an al Qaeda safe house in Kabul [Afghanistan] might be essential to accurately determine the guilt of al Qaeda cell members hiding in the West" (*New York Times,* November 30, 2001, 1B). Another observer worries that a civilian trial before a civilian jury would be unacceptable, given the highly emotional atmosphere such proceedings would create, and the fact that the jurors "would have good reason to fear for their and their families' safety if they [are] convicted" (*National Review,* December 17, 2001, http://www.nationalreview.com/17dec01/bork121701.shtml).

Even the Bush administration's critics admit that the new security measures have so far failed to spark much debate or real concern among the American people, most of whom are worried enough about a new terrorist attack to countenance extraordinary measures. "Right now the country wants very much to be supportive of the war on terrorism, and is finding it hard to summon up much outrage over military tribunals, secret detentions or the possible mistreatment of immigrants from the Mideast," conceded one observer (*New York Times,* December 2, 2001, sec. 4, 14). Another critic lamented that "terrorized Americans [are] willing to subvert our Constitution to hold Soviet-style secret military trials" (*New York Times,* December 6, 2001, A31). Democratic Party leaders also seem unable to find consistency or clarity on war-related issues: some castigate the Bush administration for what they see as his internal security excesses, while others criticize the administration for not doing enough to protect the nation from future attacks. Antiadministration remarks by former Vice President Al Gore, for example, garnered a mixture of praise and criticism from members of his own party. Quite a few rank-and-file Democrats are dismayed by the party's lack of a truly potent antiwar stance, particularly regarding Bush administration plans for an invasion of Iraq. There is a sense among some observers that party leaders are unwilling to risk a popular backlash to any antiwar stance that might harm the party at the voting booth. "The Democratic leaders in Congress, in both the House and the Senate, largely have abandoned principle and long-term strategy for the short-term tactics they think will help them in this November's election," charged columnist David Broder (*Washington Post,* September 21, 2002, A37).

Nevertheless, some lower court judges have already expressed discomfort with the Bush security measures. In August 2002, District Court Judge Robert G. Doumar blasted the administration's war policies. The case involved Yaser Esam Hamdi, one of the al Qaeda suspects detained by the government at Guantánamo Bay, Cuba. The government asserted that Hamdi was an "enemy combatant" and therefore ineligible for prisoner-of-war or civilian detainee status, and so could not contact a defense attorney. Hamdi's father brought a lawsuit to get his son a lawyer. Judge Doumar twice granted his wish, but on both occasions military authorities prevented the attorney from meeting with Hamdi. An appeals court instructed Doumar to reconsider, in light of the government's security concerns and the president's war-making powers. Doumar held a hearing on the matter and again voiced his displeasure with the Bush administration. "Can the military do anything they want [to Hamdi], without a tribunal?" Doumar asked the government's lawyer, and noted that it was all too easy for the government to hold anyone as a suspected enemy combatant. "If the man next door to you is an unlawful combatant, maybe [the government] could say you're an enemy combatant," he argued (*Washington Post*, June 19, A17; and August 13, 2002, A11).

In addition to the Afghanistan detainees, the government rounded up more than 1,200 people nationwide whom it suspected of having ties to the September 11 terrorists. In some cases, the individuals detained were accused of immigration violations, and, in a new post–September 11 twist, their hearings were held in secret. Others were held as witnesses in the government's antiterrorist investigations and argued that they should not be compelled to give grand jury testimony. The *New York Times* characterized the resulting maze of lawsuits as "a sprawling legal battle, now being waged in federal courthouses around the country" (*New York Times*, August 4, 2002, sec. 1, 1).

Where these lawsuits are ultimately going is difficult to say. Judges, like Doumar, have been very reluctant to grant the government's requests for extraordinary powers to detain terrorist suspects, and they have been backed by a host of civil libertarians, legal academics, and human rights advocates. "Secret arrests are a concept odious to a democratic society," declared U.S. District Court Judge Gladys Kessler as she opened several deportation hearings to public scrutiny. Other judges, however, feel the government is justified by the unprecedented nature of the terrorist assault and the dangers posed by undetected al Qaeda operatives still waiting to strike (ibid.). As of this writing, the Bush administration has not yet attempted to try terrorist suspects with the military tribunals outlined in his August 13, 2002, executive order, so no judgments on that matter have been offered.

Ultimately, these issues will end up on the Supreme Court's docket. What the Court will do is unclear. There are precedents for the use of military tribunals to try civilians: *ex parte Milligan* comes immediately to mind, as do the military tribunals convened to render judgment on Japanese and German citizens accused of war crimes. Bush administration supporters have been quick to cite these precedents as incontrovertible support for the government plan's legality.

As noted, though, the Court's overall record reflects more ambivalence than these few isolated cases suggest. Once the emergencies of war have faded, the justices are far more reluctant to grant the government unusual leeway in prosecuting and punishing potential enemies and dissenters. As always, the answers will ultimately lie in the circumstances of the time and the perceptions of the justices concerning whether or not the nation faces such a dangerous situation that extraordinary measures are necessary. President Bush seems to well understand the need to sell the idea of a long-term war against a dangerous enemy to the American people, and for the most part he has done an admirable job of communicating to the public the dangers the United States faces in the post–September 11 world. He has been less successful in his pitch to Congress, his Democratic opponents, and the world at large, and so far he does not seem particularly cognizant of the need to sell the idea of a protracted war to the Supreme Court. Yet if history is any guide, the future of his internal security initiatives rides on whether or not the Court feels an immediate, palpable sense of wartime emergency of the type that motivated justices on past Courts to curb civil liberties and remove impediments to government action.

The Pending War with Iraq

In his January 19, 2002, State of the Union Address to Congress, President Bush sounded an expansive tone for the new war on terrorism. "Thousands of dangerous killers, schooled in the methods of murder, often supported by outlaw regimes, are now spread throughout the world like ticking time bombs," he declared. He informed Americans that the war in Afghanistan was progressing nicely, and indeed, by early 2002 even those pessimistic observers who predicted that ousting the Taliban and al Qaeda would be a long and bloody affair were beginning to breathe easier. President Bush saw victory in Afghanistan not as an end, but a beginning. "Tens of thousands of trained terrorists are still at large," he pointed out. "These enemies view the entire world as a battlefield, and we must pursue them wherever they are. . . . Our war on terror is well begun, but it is only begun."

Bush singled out three nations in particular that had abetted terrorism and destabilized international peace and security. "North Korea is a regime arming with missiles and weapons of mass destruction, while starving its citizens," Bush argued, and "Iran aggressively pursues these weapons and exports terror." He also singled out Iraq, declaring that Saddam Hussein "continues to flaunt his hostility toward America and to support terror." Bush offered a list of Iraqi threats and abuses. Hussein "plotted to develop anthrax, and nerve gas, and nuclear weapons, for over a decade," he claimed, and had "already used poison gas to murder thousands of its own citizens—leaving the bodies of mothers huddled over their dead children. This is a regime that agreed to international inspections—then kicked out the inspectors. This is a regime that has something to hide from the civilized world." Bush then wrapped his indictment of North Korea, Iran, and Iraq in a memorable phrase that has since resonated throughout the nation and the world: "States like these, and their terrorist allies, constitute an axis of evil, arming to threaten the peace of the world," he declared, and in defeating them "America will do what is necessary to ensure our nation's security" (http://www.whitehouse.gov).

There were those who applauded Bush's extraordinary moral clarity by declaiming against the "axis of evil." Others—some of America's European allies in particular—were concerned that President Bush's moral clarity might in fact be a clarion call for a renewed sense of American imperialism and an unwanted and dangerous exercise of American military and economic power. Former secretary of state Madeleine Albright declared that Bush's comments were "a big mistake" (BBC News, February 2, 2002).

Whatever the case may be, the president's message carried as much ambiguity as clarity. Osama bin Laden, al Qaeda, and the Taliban were obvious enemies requiring hard American action, and the fight against these terrorists would necessarily carry American troops into the terrorist stronghold of Afghanistan. There were those who protested even this extension of American military power, but the goal was at least clear: clean out al Qaeda by conquering its primary (and most readily identifiable) bases of operations in the Afghan mountains.

What's next? How far does the United States advance along the "axis of evil"? North Korea and Iran each present problems as future targets. North Korea's regime was suspected of developing a nuclear weapons program—a suspicion confirmed by that nation's leaders in October 2002—and any American military action could trigger a nuclear nightmare, with America's hard-won ally South Korea as the first likely target. An assault on North Korea would also sabotage South Korea's recent peace overtures to its northern neighbor, probably fatally (*Newsweek Online*, January 30, 2002). Iran has a history of antagonism with the United States dating back to the hostage crisis of 1978–1981, but in recent years there have been signs of liberalization of the regime and the possibility of a corresponding thaw in Iranian-U.S. relations. An assault on Iran might well push that nation back into the arms of Islamist extremists, frustrating the hopes of more tolerant, democratic elements in the Middle East and destabilizing the entire region.

Then there is Iraq. Ten years after the Gulf War, Saddam Hussein's nation is, for many Americans, like an old wound, scabbed over and crusted, but still there and still sore. American and United Nations coalition aircraft continue to enforce "no-fly zones" over portions of Iraq in an attempt to protect ethnic Kurdish minorities from Hussein's wrath. Periodically over the past few years Iraqi antiaircraft installations have attacked American aircraft over the no-fly zones (usually by "painting" the planes with radar, a first step in locking missiles on target), and American pilots have responded by bombing the installations. For his part, Hussein stonewalled United Nations inspectors trying to ascertain the type and extent of the weapons programs he is developing. In June 1993, the Iraqi dictator tried to engineer the assassination of former president George H. W. Bush; President Bill Clinton responded by leveling an Iraqi army intelligence plant in Baghdad. Meanwhile, United Nations economic sanctions, designed to bring down the Hussein regime, have instead produced severe misery for the Iraqi population, as Hussein has hoarded supplies and resources while simply transferring the heavy burden of sanctions onto the backs of ordinary Iraqis.

There has been a feeling in some quarters that President Bush's father left unfinished business by failing to remove Hussein entirely from power during the Gulf War victory of 1991. Perhaps. It may also be true that George W. Bush feels a personal sense of obligation to finally eradicate the threat of a man he calls a mass murderer and a bully. Whatever the case may be, the younger President Bush began laying plans for an assault on Iraq in the summer of 2002. He placed these plans firmly within the larger context of the war on terrorism, citing Hussein's numerous human rights violations, his predilection for violence and weapons of mass destruction, and possible connections between the Iraqi intelligence community and terrorists. "Eleven years ago, as a condition for ending the Persian Gulf War, the Iraqi regime was required to destroy its weapons of mass destruction, to cease all development of such weapons, and to stop all support for terrorist groups," Bush noted in a speech in Cincinnati, but it "has violated all of those obligations. It possesses and produces biological and chemical weapons. It is seeking nuclear weapons. It has given shelter and support to terrorism, and practices terror against its own people" (http://www.whitehouse.gov).

Bush supporters have for the most part backed the plans for a second war on Iraq. Still, even some Republicans have wondered whether such a war is necessary. The plans have met opposition at some American universities (many of which have never exactly been a bastion of Republican strength) and of course among many Democrats. The plan's reception at the United Nations has also been lukewarm, particularly among European member nations such as France, Germany, and Russia. The American public as a rule supports the war on terrorism and the president—Bush's approval ratings routinely register in the 60–70 percent range—and think that something needs to be done about Iraq. But support among the American people for a military assault, while present, seems soft and circumstantial, and unlikely to last if the assault on Iraq proves too costly in men and materiel (*U.S. News and World Report,* October 21, 2002, 30).

The ambivalent nature of the public's support for a new war against Iraq led President Bush (again following in his father's footsteps) to seek a resolution of support from Congress. Like his predecessors, the president has been careful to point out that this does not imply executive acquiescence in the age-old war powers debates between the presidency and Congress. Bush is no more willing to legitimate the War Powers Act of 1973 than his predecessors, believing rather that a congressional resolution would be useful in diplomacy and in domestic politics. In the end, he got what he wanted: an open-ended congressional resolution of support for a new war against Iraq. As is usually the case, even antiwar members of Congress felt enormous pressure to adapt to events already initiated by the White House. "The Democrats can't stand up to Bush on Iraq because they're afraid of looking soft on terrorism and Saddam Hussein," complained one critic (Pollitt 2002). In such an atmosphere—particularly with September 11 still vividly etched in the national memory—congressional oversight of war making is essentially a chimera. There were voices of doubt, to be sure—Senator Robert Byrd, of West Virginia, voted for the Tonkin Gulf Resolution in 1964 but voted against the Iraqi resolution, declaring, "I will not make that mistake again"—but not even Democratic Party leaders felt confident in resisting a tide of war that the president has created (*U.S. News and World Report*, October 21, 2002, 32). Americans "have accepted the Bush line that Iraq represents phase two of the war against terror," a London observer pointed out, and so, "short of a coup against Saddam, war this winter is inevitable" (*The Independent* [London], October 26, 2002, 18). Congress has proved entirely unable to prevent this and has again demonstrated that formal declarations of war may be a thing of the past.

Law and War in the Terrorism Era: Old Wine in New Bottles?

September 11, 2001, is certainly the day America changed, in many ways. Before those airplanes slammed into the World Trade Center towers, the Pentagon, and a Pennsylvania field, Americans could reasonably conclude that the very idea of a direct attack on our soil was unthinkable, a relic from the distant past when redcoats burned the capital, Civil War soldiers slugged it out on their native soil, and Japanese kamikazes bombed an island so far away that many people barely perceived it to be American territory. It had been so long since anyone had really done damage to us in this fashion that the dominant metaphor for national reaction was stark disbelief. "The legacy of September 11, 2001, must be nothing less than a new sense of the possible," observed a writer in *The New Republic*, because "when those planes flew into those buildings, America's luck ran out" (*The New Republic*, September 24, 2001, 10). Since then, Americans have repeatedly expressed a strong sense that America has passed a watershed moment in its history.

The war on terrorism is likewise a very different sort of war. There is no easily identifiable enemy territory, no clear boundary between winning and losing, and the targets lie coiled in the shadows of society, patiently waiting for their chance to strike. The terrorists by their very nature have chosen to blur the lines between combatant and noncombatant, legitimate and illegitimate targets, moral and immoral warfare, in ways Americans have never seen before. There is a newfound desperate edge to the war as well, a sense that this time failure will mean more than simply a failure of abstract policy making or loss of national prestige. The stakes are high. "We have been, we and our leaders emphatically agree, savagely thrust into a new kind of war that we have no choice but to win," declared one observer (*National Review,* September 18, 2001, http://www.nationalreview.com/comment/comment-berkowitz091801.shtml).

So yes, September 11, 2001, was the day America changed. Perhaps, though, there is danger in focusing so much on this notion of a radical break with the past. The very idea of newness could all too easily fuel unprecedented measures that suddenly and sharply break with an American past that has traditionally valued freedom and liberty. The pull of American history, the nation's center of gravity, is liberty, determination, and the right to dissent. It is traditionally believed that the burden of proof must lie with those who would curtail, not defend, freedoms. Of course, there have been unfortunate moments when this was not the case, and the coercive power of government was used to silence unpopular or inconvenient voices. On the whole, however, Americans can justly be proud of their track record on civil liberties, particularly in times of war.

Now, after September 11, 2001, America is voyaging in truly perilous waters. The legal and constitutional system, over two centuries old, remains strong and (perhaps even more remarkable) relevant to the needs of the times. The framers knew what they were doing when they vested war-making powers equally with Congress and the president, and subsequent generations of Americans have—again, with some lamentable exceptions—applied the laws of war equitably and well. But fear and anxiety stalk the land. Working hand in hand with a grim determination to punish the perpetrators of the September 11 attacks, fear may work great evil, motivating Americans to upset the already lopsided war-making balance between the president and Congress and between acceptable measures in peace and in war. If that happens, the terrorists' work is being done for them.

References and Further Reading

Ely, John Hart. 1993. *War and Responsibility: Constitutional Lessons of Vietnam and Its Aftermath.* Princeton: Princeton University Press.

Glennon, Michael J. 1991. "The Gulf War and the Constitution." *Foreign Affairs* (Spring): 84–101.

Hall, Kermit. 1992. *The Oxford Companion to the Supreme Court.* New York: Oxford University Press.

Madison, James. 1987. *Notes of Debates in the Federal Convention of 1787.* New York: W. W. Norton.

Matthews, Melissa K. 2002. "Restoring the Imperial Presidency: An Examination of President Bush's New Emergency Powers." *Hamline Journal of Public Law and Policy* 23, no. 455 (Spring): 455–487.

Pollitt, Catherine. 2002. "Dems Roll Over, Film at 11." *The Nation Online,* October 10. Available online at http://www.thenation.com/doc.mhtml?i=20021028&s=pollitt. Accessed March 5, 2003.

Turner, Robert F. 2002. "The War on Terrorism and the Modern Relevance of the Congressional Power to 'Declare War.'" *Harvard Journal of Law and Public Policy* 25, no. 519 (Spring): 519–545.

Part Two

Documents

Constitutional Language about War

In a sense, the entire Constitution is a war-related document, in that all of its major components—separation of powers, federal/state relations, civil liberties, federal economic regulations—can come into play when a war begins. The most directly relevant war-making sections can be found in the Article I and Article II allocations of war-making and military authority and in the document's treason provisions, and the preamble sets defense as a top national priority. The Constitution, however, also leaves a host of unanswered questions about what a "war" is, who gets to start one, and under what circumstances a national war effort is to be either maintained or terminated.

Preamble

We the People of the United States, in Order to form a more perfect Union, establish Justice, insure domestic Tranquility, provide for the common defence, promote the general Welfare, and secure the Blessings of Liberty to ourselves and our Posterity, do ordain and establish this Constitution for the United States of America.

Article I

Section 8: The Congress shall have Power To lay and collect Taxes, Duties, Imposts and Excises, to pay the Debts and provide for the common Defence and general Welfare of the United States; but all Duties, Imposts and Excises shall be uniform throughout the United States. . . . To declare War, grant Letters of Marque and Reprisal, and make Rules concerning Captures on Land and Water; To raise and

155

support Armies, but no Appropriation of Money to that Use shall be for a longer Term than two Years; To provide and maintain a Navy; To make Rules for the Government and Regulation of the land and naval Forces; To provide for calling forth the Militia to execute the Laws of the Union, suppress Insurrections and repel Invasions; To provide for organizing, arming, and disciplining the Militia, and for governing such Part of them as may be employed in the Service of the United States, reserving to the States respectively, the Appointment of the Officers, and the Authority of training the Militia according to the discipline prescribed by Congress ... to exercise like Authority over all Places purchased by the Consent of the Legislature of the State in which the Same shall be, for the Erection of Forts, Magazines, Arsenals, dock-Yards, and other needful Buildings; And To make all Laws which shall be necessary and proper for carrying into Execution the foregoing Powers, and all other Powers vested by this Constitution in the Government of the United States, or in any Department or Officer thereof.

Section 9: The Privilege of the Writ of Habeas Corpus shall not be suspended, unless when in Cases of Rebellion or Invasion the public Safety may require it.

Section 10: No State shall, without the Consent of Congress, lay any Duty of Tonnage, keep Troops, or Ships of War in time of Peace, enter into any Agreement or Compact with another State, or with a foreign Power, or engage in War, unless actually invaded, or in such imminent Danger as will not admit of delay.

Article II

Section 2: The President shall be Commander in Chief of the Army and Navy of the United States, and of the Militia of the several States, when called into the actual Service of the United States.

Article III

Section 3: Treason against the United States shall consist only in levying War against them, or in adhering to their Enemies, giving them Aid and Comfort. No Person shall be convicted of Treason unless on the Testimony of two Witnesses to the same overt Act, or on Confession in open Court.

Article IV

Section 4: The United States shall guarantee to every State in this Union a Republican Form of Government, and shall protect each of them against Invasion. ...

Second Amendment

A well regulated Militia, being necessary to the security of a free State, the right of the people to keep and bear Arms, shall not be infringed.

Third Amendment

No Soldier shall, in time of peace be quartered in any house, without the consent of the Owner, nor in time of war, but in a manner to be prescribed by law.

What Is a "War"?

Bas v. Tingy 4 U.S. (4 Dall.) 37 (1800)

Defining what sort of situation constitutes a "war" in the legal and constitutional sense has long been a key issue for American policy makers. Can a legal state of war exist only with formal congressional action? Or can the president, or circumstances in general, create a legal war without an explicit congressional declaration of war? This issue first surfaced in 1800 when Americans were involved in a quasi war with France, and Congress had created a complicated set of rules for awarding compensation to privately owned American ships that rescued other American ships from the clutches of the French Navy. In Bas v. Tingy, one shipowner tried to wriggle out of these provisions by claiming that the hostilities with France could not be legally described as a "war" without a formal congressional declaration of war. Here for the first time the Supreme Court grappled with the legal nature of warfare under the new U.S. constitutional system. The multiple opinions by the various justices reflect the difficulty they faced in arriving at a consensus on the issue.

OPINION BY JUSTICE MOORE. [It is argued] that the word "enemy" cannot be applied to the French; because the section in which it is used, is confined to such a state of war, as would authorise a re-capture of property belonging to a nation in amity with the United States, and such a state of war, it is said, does not exist between America and France. A number of books have been cited to furnish a glossary on the word enemy; yet, our situation is so extraordinary, that I doubt whether a parallel case can be traced in the history of nations. But, if words are the representatives of ideas, let me ask, by what other word the idea of the relative situation of America and France could be communicated, than by that of hostility, or war? And how can the characters of the parties engaged in hostility or war, be otherwise described than by the denomination of enemies? It is for the honour and dignity of both nations, therefore, that they should be called enemies; for, it is by that description alone, that either could justify or excuse, the scene of bloodshed, depredation and confiscation, which has unhappily occurred. . . .

OPINION BY JUSTICE WASHINGTON. It may, I believe, be safely laid down, that every contention by force between two nations, in external matters, under the authority of their respective governments, is not only war, but public war. If it be declared in form, it is called solemn, and is of the perfect kind; because one whole nation is at war with another whole nation; and all the members of the nation declaring war, are authorised to commit hostilities against all the members of the other, in every place, and under every circumstance. In such a war all the members act under a general authority, and all the rights and consequences of war attach to their condition.

But hostilities may subsist between two nations more confined in its nature and extent; being limited as to places, persons, and things; and this is more properly termed imperfect war; because not solemn, and because those who are authorised to commit hostilities, act under special authority, and can go no farther than to the extent of their commission. Still, however, it is public war, because it is an external contention by force, between some of the members of the two nations, authorised by the legitimate powers. It is a war between the two nations, though all the members are not authorised to commit hostilities such as in a solemn war, where the government restrain the general power.

OPINION BY JUSTICE CHASE. Congress is empowered to declare a general war, or congress may wage a limited war; limited in place, in objects and in time. If a general war is declared, its extent and operations are only restricted and regulated by the jus belli, forming a part of the law of nations; but if a partial war is waged, its extent and operation depend on our municipal laws.

What, then, is the nature of the contest subsisting between America and France? In my judgment, it is a limited, partial, war. Congress has not declared war in general terms; but Congress has authorised hostilities on the high seas by certain persons in certain cases. There is no authority given to commit hostilities on land; to capture unarmed French vessels, nor even to capture French armed vessels lying in a

French port; and the authority is not given, indiscriminately, to every citizen of America, against every citizen of France; but only to citizens appointed by commissions, or exposed to immediate outrage and violence. So far it is, unquestionably, a partial war; but, nevertheless, it is a public war, on account of the public authority from which it emanates.

Martin v. Mott 25 U.S. (12 Wheat.) 19 (1827)

Once the nation is at war, what authority does the president have over the various state militia units? For early Americans, this was more than a simple matter of logistics. They saw the militias as a bulwark of liberty, proof that professional soldiers—the dreaded "standing army"—were not really needed in a democracy where citizen-soldiers were fully capable of defending hearth and home. Some people felt that the militiamen had a right to refuse orders from the U.S. Army if for some reason they believed those orders were a violation of their liberties. The matter was first tested in the following case, when a New York militiaman named Jacob Mott refused to obey the president's orders to prepare for an imminent British invasion of his state.

OPINION BY JUSTICE STORY. [T]he power to provide for repelling invasions includes the power to provide against the attempt and danger of invasion, as the necessary and proper means to effectuate the object. One of the best means to repeal invasion is to provide the requisite force for action before the invader himself has reached the soil.

The power thus confided by Congress to the President, is, doubtless, of a very high and delicate nature. A free people are naturally jealous of the exercise of military power; and the power to call the militia into actual service is certainly felt to be one of no ordinary magnitude. But it is not a power which can be executed without a correspondent responsibility. It is, in its terms, a limited power, confined to cases of actual invasion, or of imminent danger of invasion. If it be a limited power, the question arises, by whom is the exigency to be judged of and decided? Is the President the sole and exclusive judge whether the exigency has arisen, or is it to be considered as an open question, upon which every officer to whom the orders of the President are addressed, may decide for himself, and equally open to be contested by every militia-man who shall refuse to obey the orders of the President?

We are all of opinion, that the authority to decide whether the exigency has arisen, belongs exclusively to the President, and that his decision is conclusive upon all other persons. . . . A prompt and unhesitating obedience to orders is indispensable to the complete attainment of the object. The service is a military service, and the command of a military nature; and in such cases, every delay, and every obstacle to an efficient and immediate compliance, necessarily tend to jeopardize the public interests. While subordinate officers or soldiers are pausing to consider whether they ought to obey, or are scrupulously weighing the evidence of the facts upon which the commander in chief exercises the right to demand their services, the hostile enterprise may be accomplished without the means of resistance. If "the power of regulating the militia, and of commanding its services in times of insurrection and invasion, are (as it has been emphatically said they are) natural incidents to the duties of superintending the common defence, and of watching over the internal peace of the confederacy," these powers must be so construed as to the modes of their exercise as not to defeat the great end in view. . . . Besides, in many instances, the evidence upon which the President might decide that there is imminent danger of invasion, might be of a nature not constituting strict technical proof, or the disclosure of the evidence might reveal important secrets of state, which the public interest, and even safety, might imperiously demand to be kept in concealment.

Dynes v. Hoover 61 U.S. (20 How.) 65 (1858)

During the nation's first decades, the Supreme Court largely stayed out of the army and navy's way when it came to administering military justice. In Dynes v. Hoover, *a sailor convicted by a military tribunal of "attempting to desert" found a way to get the Supreme Court's attention—by suing the Washington, D.C., marshal. When he actually had his day in (civilian) court, however, the results were not encouraging.*

COURT OPINION BY JUSTICE WAYNE. The charge by the Secretary of the Navy was desertion, with this specification: "that on or about the twelfth day of September, in the year of our Lord one thousand eight hundred and fifty-four, Frank Dynes deserted from the United States ship Independence, at New York." He pleaded not guilty. After hearing the evidence, the court declared, "We do find the accused, Frank Dynes, seaman of the United States navy, as follows: Of the specification of the charge, guilty of attempting to desert; of the charge, not guilty of deserting, but guilty of attempting to desert; and the court do thereupon sentence the said Frank Dynes, a seaman of the United States navy, to be confined in the penitentiary of the District of Columbia, at hard labor, without pay, for the term of six months from the date of the approval of this sentence, and not to be again enlisted in the naval service." . . .

[T]he court, instead of finding Dynes guilty of the high offence of desertion, which authorizes the punishment of death, convicted him of attempting to desert, and sentenced him to imprisonment for six months at hard labor in the penitentiary of the District of Columbia, it is argued that the court had no jurisdiction or authority to pass such a sentence. . . .

[The decision of a proper military court-martial] is altogether beyond the jurisdiction or inquiry of any civil tribunal whatever, unless it shall be in a case in which the court had not jurisdiction over the subject-matter or charge, or one in which, having jurisdiction over the subject-matter, it has failed to observe the rules prescribed by the statute for its exercise. . . .

With the sentences of courts-martial . . . civil courts have nothing to do, nor are they in any way alterable by them. If it were otherwise, the civil courts would virtually administer the rules and articles of war, irrespective of those to whom that duty and obligation has been confided by the laws of the United States, from whose decisions no appeal or jurisdiction of any kind has been given to the civil magistrate or civil courts. [If] a court-martial has no jurisdiction over the subject-matter of the charge it has been convened to try, or shall inflict a punishment forbidden by the law, though its sentence shall be approved by the officers having a revisory power of it, civil courts may, on an action by a party aggrieved by it, inquire into the want of the court's jurisdiction, and give him redress. . . .

In this case, all of us think that the court which tried Dynes had jurisdiction over the subject-matter of the charge against him; that the sentence of the court against him was not forbidden by law. . . .

Ex parte Merryman 17 Fed. Cas. 144 (No. 9487) (1961)

When Abraham Lincoln declared martial law and suspended the writ of habeas corpus in the troubled winter of 1861, he saw himself as having acted boldly to save the Union from the potentially fatal danger of Maryland going Confederate (and necessarily taking the capital city of Washington, D.C., with it). Others felt differently, however, especially Chief Justice Roger B. Taney, who thought the president's actions—taken without the approval of a Congress that was then in recess—were the hallmarks of tyranny. He therefore went looking for a way to rein in the president, and he found it in the plight of accused Confederate sympathizer John Merryman. Was the resulting opinion a hallmark statement of individual liberty or the hardheaded obstructionism of a slaveholder and Southern sympathizer?

OPINION BY JUSTICE TANEY. [Merryman] presents the following case: [he] resides in Maryland, in Baltimore county; while peaceably in his own house, with his family, it was at two o'clock on the morning of the 25th of May 1861, entered by an armed force, professing to act under military orders; he was then compelled to rise from his bed, taken into custody, and conveyed to Fort McHenry, where he is imprisoned by the commanding officer, without warrant from any lawful authority.

The commander of the fort, General George Cadwalader . . . states that the prisoner was . . . conducted . . . to Fort McHenry . . . and placed in his (General Cadwalader's) custody, to be there detained by him as a prisoner.

A copy of the warrant or order under which the prisoner was arrested was demanded by his counsel, and refused: and it is not alleged in the return, that any specific act, constituting any offence against the laws of the United States, has been charged against him upon oath, but he appears to have been arrested upon general charges of treason and rebellion, without proof, and without giving the names of the witnesses, or specifying the acts which, in the judgment of the military officer, constituted these crimes. Having the prisoner thus in custody upon these vague and unsupported accusations, [General Cadwalader] refuses to obey the writ of habeas corpus, upon the ground that he is duly authorized by the president to suspend it.

The case, then, is simply this: a military officer . . . issues an order to arrest a citizen of Maryland, upon vague and indefinite charges, without any proof, so far as appears; under this order, his house is entered in the night, he is seized as a prisoner, and conveyed to Fort McHenry, and there kept in close confinement; and when a habeas corpus is served on the commanding officer, requiring him to produce the prisoner before a justice of the supreme court, in order that he may examine into the legality of the imprisonment, the answer of the officer, is that he is authorized by the president to suspend the writ of habeas corpus at his discretion, and in the exercise of that discretion, suspends it in this case, and on that ground refuses obedience to the writ.

As the case comes before me, therefore, I understand that the president not only claims the right to suspend the writ of habeas corpus himself, at his discretion, but to delegate that discretionary power to a military officer, and to leave it to him to determine whether he will or will not obey judicial process that may be served upon him. No official notice has been given to the courts of justice, or to the public, by proclamation or otherwise, that the president claimed this power, and had exercised it in the manner stated in the return. And I certainly listened to it with some surprise, for I had supposed it to be one of those points of constitutional law upon which there was no difference of opinion, and that it was admitted on all hands, that the privilege of the writ could not be suspended, except by act of congress. . . .

[B]elieving, as I do, that the president has exercised a power which he does not possess under the constitution, a proper respect for the high office he fills, requires me to state plainly and fully the grounds of my opinion, in order to show that I have not ventured to question the legality of his act, without a careful and deliberate examination of the whole subject.

The clause of the constitution, which authorizes the suspension of the privilege of the writ of habeas corpus, is in the 9th section of the first article. This article is devoted to the legislative department of the United States, and has not the slightest reference to the executive department. . . .

The great importance which the framers of the constitution attached to the privilege of the writ of habeas corpus, to protect the liberty of the citizen, is proved by the fact, that its suspension, except in cases of invasion or rebellion, is first in the list of prohibited powers; and even in these cases the power is denied, and its exercise prohibited, unless the public safety shall require it. . . .

It is the second article of the constitution that provides for the organization of the executive department, enumerates the powers conferred on it, and prescribes its duties. And if the high power over the liberty of the citizen now claimed, was intended to be conferred on the president, it would undoubtedly be found in plain words in this article; but there is not a word in it that can furnish the slightest ground to justify the exercise of the power. . . .

Even if the privilege of the writ of habeas corpus were suspended by act of congress, and a party not subject to the rules and articles of war were afterwards arrested and imprisoned by regular judicial process, he could not be detained in prison, or brought to trial before a military tribunal, for the [Sixth Amendment] . . . provides, that "in all criminal prosecutions, the accused shall enjoy the right to a speedy and public trial by an impartial jury of the state and district wherein the crime shall have been committed, which district shall have been previously ascertained by law; and to be informed of the nature and cause of the accusation; to be confronted with the witnesses against him; to have compulsory process for obtaining witnesses in his favor; and to have the assistance of counsel for his defence." . . .

With such provisions in the constitution, expressed in language too clear to be misunderstood by any one, I can see no ground whatever for supposing that the president, in any emergency, or in any state of things, can authorize the suspension of the privileges of the writ of habeas corpus, or the arrest of a citizen, except in aid of the judicial power. He certainly does not faithfully execute the laws, if he takes upon himself legislative power, by suspending the writ of habeas corpus, and the judicial power also, by arresting and imprisoning a person without due process of law.

Nor can any argument be drawn from the nature of sovereignty, or the necessity of government, for self-defence in times of tumult and danger. The government of the United States is one of delegated and limited powers; it derives its existence and authority altogether from the constitution, and neither of its branches, executive, legislative or judicial, can exercise any of the powers of government beyond those specified and granted. . . .

[T]he documents before me show, that the military authority in this case has gone far beyond the mere suspension of the privilege of the writ of habeas corpus. It has, by force of arms, thrust aside the judicial authorities and officers to whom the constitution has confided the power and duty of interpreting and administering the laws, and substituted a military government in its place, to be administered and executed by military officers. . . . There was no danger of any obstruction or resistance to the action of the civil authorities, and therefore no reason whatever for the interposition of the military. . . .

Such is the case now before me, and I can only say that if the authority which the constitution has confided to the judiciary department and judicial officers, may thus, upon any pretext or under any circumstances, be usurped by the military power, at its discretion, the people of the United States are no longer living under a government of laws, but every citizen holds life, liberty and property at the will and pleasure of the army officer in whose military district he may happen to be found. . . .

In such a case, my duty was too plain to be mistaken. I have exercised all the power which the constitution and laws confer upon me, but that power has been resisted by a force too strong for me to overcome. It is possible that the officer who has incurred this grave responsibility may have misunderstood his instructions, and exceeded the authority intended to be given him; I shall, therefore, order all the proceedings in this case, with my opinion, to be filed and recorded in the circuit court of the United States for the district of Maryland, and direct the clerk to transmit a copy, under seal, to the president of the United States. It will then remain for that high officer, in fulfilment of his constitutional obligation to "take care that the laws be faithfully executed," to determine what measures he will take to cause the civil process of the United States to be respected and enforced.

Ex parte Vallandigham 68 U.S. (1 Wall.) 243 (1864)

During the Civil War, the Supreme Court found itself again addressing issues of personal liberty and dissent. By 1863, the context of these questions was different from that of the Merryman matter. Now Justice Roger Taney was near death, and the Court seemed little inclined to follow his lead. In this case, the Court considered and rejected the petition of Clement Vallandigham, a notorious Confederate sympathizer from Ohio, who had been exiled to the South by the federal government.

COURT OPINION BY JUSTICE WAYNE. The appellate powers of the Supreme Court, as granted by the Constitution, are limited and regulated by the acts of Congress, and must be exercised subject to the exceptions and regulations made by Congress. In other words, the petition before us we think not to be within the letter or spirit of the grants of appellate jurisdiction to the Supreme Court. It is not in law or equity within the meaning of those terms as used in the 3d article of the Constitution. Nor is a military commission a court within the meaning of the 14th section of the Judiciary Act of 1789. . . .

Whatever may be the force of Vallandigham's protest, that he was not triable by a court of military commission, it is certain that his petition cannot be brought within the 14th section of the act; and further, that the court cannot, without disregarding its frequent decisions and interpretation of the Constitution in respect to its judicial power, originate a writ of certiorari to review or pronounce any opinion upon the proceedings of a military commission. . . .

For the reasons given, our judgment is, that the writ of certiorari prayed for to revise and review the proceedings of the military commission, by which Clement L. Vallandigham was tried, sentenced, and imprisoned, must be denied, and so do we order accordingly.

Prize Cases 67 U.S. (2BL) 635 (1863)

The most important Supreme Court decision made during the Civil War involved the disposition of four vessels accused of running the Union blockade for the Confederacy. At issue was the basic legal definition of the Confederate nation: Was it a "nation," per se, or a collection of American citizens engaged in armed rebellion against America's rightful government? Either answer created difficulties for the Lincoln administration and the war effort in general. If the Confederacy was a legally constituted nation, then the entire moral foundation of the Union war effort might be endangered, and the Confederacy might be legally entitled to recognition by foreign powers. If, on the other hand, the Confederates were merely traitorous Americans, then under international law they could not be subjected to a blockade. In the end, the Court took a pragmatic approach, allowing the government to define the Confederacy as either a belligerent nation or collection of traitors, as circumstances required. At the same time, the argument presented on behalf of the plaintiff and the dissenting opinion by Justice Grier constitute classic arguments for limiting the president's war-making powers.

COURT OPINION BY JUSTICE GRIER. To legitimate the capture of a neutral vessel or property on the high seas, a war must exist de facto, and the neutral must have a knowledge or notice of the intention of one of the parties belligerent to use this mode of coercion against a port, city, or territory, in possession of the other.

Let us enquire whether, at the time this blockade was instituted, a state of war existed which would justify a resort to these means of subduing the hostile force.

War has been well defined to be, "That state in which a nation prosecutes its right by force."

The parties belligerent in a public war are independent nations. But it is not necessary to constitute war, that both parties should be acknowledged as independent nations or sovereign States. A war may exist where one of the belligerents claims sovereign rights as against the other.

Insurrection against a government may or may not culminate in an organized rebellion, but a civil war always begins by insurrection against the lawful authority of the Government. A civil war is never solemnly declared; it becomes such by its accidents—the number, power, and organization of the persons who originate and carry it on. When the party in rebellion occupy and hold in a hostile manner a certain portion of territory; have declared their independence; have cast off their allegiance; have organized armies; have commenced hostilities against their former sovereign, the world acknowledges them as belligerents, and the contest a war. They claim to be in arms to establish their liberty and independence, in order to become a sovereign State, while the sovereign party treats them as insurgents and rebels who owe allegiance, and who should be punished with death for their treason.

The laws of war, as established among nations, have their foundation in reason, and all tend to mitigate the cruelties and misery produced by the scourge of war. Hence the parties to a civil war usually concede to each other belligerent rights. They exchange prisoners, and adopt the other courtesies and rules common to public or national wars. . . .

Those two parties, therefore, must necessarily be considered as constituting, at least for a time, two separate bodies, two distinct societies. Having no common superior to judge between them, they stand in precisely the same predicament as two nations who engage in a contest and have recourse to arms. . . .

As a civil war is never publicly proclaimed . . . eo nomine against insurgents, its actual existence is a fact in our domestic history which the Court is bound to notice and to know. . . .

If a war be made by invasion of a foreign nation, the President is not only authorized but bound to resist force by force. He does not initiate the war, but is bound to accept the challenge without waiting for any special legislative authority. And whether the hostile party be a foreign invader, or States organized in rebellion, it is none the less a war, although the declaration of it be "unilateral." . . .

This greatest of civil wars was not gradually developed by popular commotion, tumultuous assemblies, or local unorganized insurrections. However long may have been its previous conception, it nevertheless sprung forth suddenly from the parent brain, a Minerva in the full panoply of war. The President was bound to meet it in the shape it presented itself, without waiting for Congress to baptize it with a name; and no name given to it by him or them could change the fact.

It is not the less a civil war, with belligerent parties in hostile array, because it may be called an "insurrection" by one side, and the insurgents be considered as rebels or traitors. It is not necessary that the independence of the revolted province or State be acknowledged in order to constitute it a party belligerent in a war according to the law of nations. Foreign nations acknowledge it as war by a declaration of neutrality. . . .

[A] citizen of a foreign State is estopped to deny the existence of a war with all its consequences as regards neutrals. They cannot ask a Court to affect a technical ignorance of the existence of a war, which all the world acknowledges to be the greatest civil war known in the history of the human race, and thus cripple the arm of the Government and paralyze its power by subtle definitions and ingenious sophisms. . . .

Whether the President in fulfilling his duties, as Commander in chief, in suppressing an insurrection, has met with such armed hostile resistance, and a civil war of such alarming proportions as will compel him to accord to them the character of belligerents, is a question to be decided by him, and this Court must be governed by the decisions and acts of the political department of the Government to which this power was entrusted. "He must determine what degree of force the crisis demands." The proclamation of blockade is itself official and conclusive evidence to the Court that a state of war existed which demanded and authorized a recourse to such a measure, under the circumstances peculiar to the case. . . .

If it were necessary to the technical existence of a war, that it should have a legislative sanction, we find it in almost every act passed at the extraordinary session of the Legislature of 1861, which was wholly employed in enacting laws to enable the Government to prosecute the war with vigor and efficiency. . . .

[T]herefore we are of the opinion that the President had a right . . . to institute a blockade of ports in possession of the States in rebellion, which neutrals are bound to regard. . . .

The appellants contend that the term "enemy" is properly applicable to those only who are subjects or citizens of a foreign State at war with our own. They quote from the pages of the common law, which say, "that persons who wage war against the King may be of two kinds, subjects or citizens. The former are not proper enemies, but rebels and traitors; the latter are those that come properly under the name of enemies." . . .

They contend, also, that insurrection is the act of individuals and not of a government or sovereignty; that the individuals engaged are subjects of law. . . .

This argument rests on the assumption of two propositions, each of which is without foundation on the established law of nations. It assumes that where a civil war exists, the party belligerent claiming to be sovereign, cannot, for some unknown reason, exercise the rights of belligerents, although the revolutionary party may. Being sovereign, he can exercise only sovereign rights over the other party. The insurgent may be killed on the battle-field or by the executioner; his property on land may be confiscated under the municipal law; but the commerce on the ocean, which supplies the rebels with means to support the war, cannot be made the subject of capture under the laws of war, because it is "unconstitutional!!!" Now, it is a proposition never doubted, that the belligerent party who claims to be sovereign, may exercise both belligerent and sovereign rights. . . .

[I]n organizing this rebellion, [the Rebels] have acted as States claiming to be sovereign over all persons and property within their respective limits. . . . Several of these States have combined to form a new confederacy, claiming to be acknowledged by the world as a sovereign State. Their right to do so is now being decided by wager of battle. The ports and territory of each of these States are held in hostility to the General Government. It is no loose, unorganized insurrection, having no defined boundary or possession. It has a boundary marked by lines of bayonets, and which can be crossed only by force—south of this line is enemies' territory, because it is claimed and held in possession by an organized, hostile and belligerent power.

All persons residing within this territory whose property may be used to increase the revenues of the hostile power are, in this contest, liable to be treated as enemies, though not foreigners. They have cast off their allegiance and made war on their Government, and are none the less enemies because they are traitors. . . .

DISSENTING OPINION BY JUSTICE NELSON. [The plaintiffs argue] that there was no existing war between the United States and the States in insurrection within the meaning of the law of nations, which drew after it the consequences of a public or civil war. A contest by force between independent sovereign States is called a public war; and, when duly commenced by proclamation or otherwise, it entitles both of the belligerent parties to all the rights of war against each other, and as respects neutral nations. . . .

It is not to be denied, therefore, that if a civil war existed between that portion of the people in organized insurrection to overthrow this Government at the time this vessel and cargo were seized, and if she was guilty of a violation of the blockade, she would be lawful prize of war. But before this insurrection against the established Government can be dealt with on the footing of a civil war, within the meaning of the law of nations and the Constitution of the United States, and which will draw after it belligerent rights, it must be recognized or declared by the war-making power of the Government. No power short of this can change the legal status of the Government or the relations of its citizens from that of peace to a state of war, or bring into existence all those duties and obligations to neutral third parties growing out of a state of war. The war power of the Government must be exercised before this changed condition of the Government and people and of neutral third parties can be admitted. . . .

An idea seemed to be entertained that all that was necessary to constitute a war was organized hostility in the district of country in a state of rebellion. . . .

Now, in one sense, no doubt this is war, and may be a war of the most extensive and threatening dimensions and effects, but it is a statement simply of its existence in a material sense, and has no relevancy or weight when the question is what constitutes war in a legal sense, in the sense of the law of nations, and of the Constitution of the United States? For it must be a war in this sense to attach to it all the consequences that belong to belligerent rights. Instead, therefore, of inquiring after armies and navies, and victories lost and won, or organized rebellion against the general Government, the inquiry should be into the law of nations and into the municipal fundamental laws of the Government. . . .

Congress alone can determine whether war exists or should be declared; and until they have acted, no citizen of the State can be punished in his person or property, unless he had committed some offence against a law of Congress passed before the act was committed, which made it a crime, and defined the punishment. . . .

[The question before us is] whether the President can recognize or declare a civil war, under the Constitution, with all its belligerent rights, between his own Government and a portion of its citizens in a state of insurrection. That power, as we have seen, belongs to Congress. We agree when such a war is recognized or declared to exist by the war-making power, but not otherwise, it is the duty of the Courts to follow the decision of the political power of the Government. . . .

Upon the whole, after the most careful consideration of this case which the pressure of other duties has admitted, I am compelled to the conclusion that no civil war existed between this Government and the States in insurrection till recognized by the Act of Congress 13th of July, 1861; that the President does not possess the power under the Constitution to declare war or recognize its existence within the meaning of the law of nations, which carries with it belligerent rights, and thus change the country and all its citizens from a state of peace to a state of war; that this power belongs exclusively to the Congress of the United States, and, consequently, that the President had no power to set on foot a blockade under the law of nations, and that the capture of the vessel and cargo in this case, and in all cases before us in which the capture occurred before the 13th of July, 1861, for breach of blockade, or as enemies' property, are illegal and void, and that the decrees of condemnation should be reversed and the vessel and cargo restored.

Ex parte Milligan 71 U.S. (4 Wall.) 2 (1866)

By the time the case of suspected Confederate sympathizer Lamdin Milligan arrived on the Supreme Court's docket, the Civil War had been over for more than a year—and that made all the difference. Now the Court was much less disposed to give the government a free hand in suppressing dissenting opinions. This case deserves extended examination, for it was the first significant commentary by the Court on the subject of trying civilians in a military court. The arguments by

lawyers on both sides are also excerpted at length here, for they offer
an unusually concise and cogent examination of the issues involved in
allowing the government a free rein in prosecuting a war.

Lamdin P. Milligan, a citizen of the United States, and a resident and
citizen of the State of Indiana, was arrested on the 5th day of October,
1864, at his home in the said State, by the order of Brevet Major-
General Hovey, military commandant of the District of Indiana, and
by the same authority confined in a military prison, at or near Indianapolis, the capital of the State. On the 21st day of the same month,
he was placed on trial before a "military commission," convened at Indianapolis, by order of the said General, upon the following charges;
preferred by Major Burnett, Judge Advocate of the Northwestern
Military Department, namely:

1. "Conspiracy against the Government of the United States";
2. "Affording aid and comfort to rebels against the authority of the
United States";
3. "Inciting insurrection";
4. "Disloyal practices"; and
5. "Violation of the laws of war." . . .

An objection by him to the authority of the commission to try him
being overruled, Milligan was found guilty on all the charges, and sentenced to suffer death by hanging; and this sentence, having been approved, he was ordered to be executed on Friday, the 19th of May,
1865.

On the 10th of that same May, 1865, Milligan filed his petition in
the Circuit Court of the United States for the District of Indiana, by
which, or by the documents appended to which as exhibits, the above
facts appeared. These exhibits consisted of the order for the commission; the charges and specifications; the findings and sentence of the
court, with a statement of the fact that the sentence was approved by
the President of the United States, who directed that it should "be carried into execution without delay"; all "by order of the Secretary of
War."

The petition set forth the additional fact, that while the petitioner
was held and detained, as already mentioned, in military custody (and
more than twenty days after his arrest), a grand jury of the Circuit
Court of the United States for the District of Indiana was convened at
Indianapolis, his said place of confinement, and duly empanelled,
charged, and sworn for said district, held its sittings, and finally ad-

journed without having found any bill of indictment, or made any presentment whatever against him. That at no time had he been in the military service of the United States, or in any way connected with the land or naval force, or the militia in actual service; nor within the limits of any State whose citizens were engaged in rebellion against the United States, at any time during the war; but during all the time aforesaid, and for twenty years last past, he had been an inhabitant, resident, and citizen of Indiana. And so, that it had been "wholly out of his power to have acquired belligerent rights, or to have placed himself in such relation to the government as to have enabled him to violate the laws of war." . . .

[Counsel for the government argued that] [t]he officer executing martial law is at the same time supreme legislator, supreme judge, and supreme executive. As necessity makes his will the law, he only can define and declare it; and whether or not it is infringed, and of the extent of the infraction, he alone can judge; and his sole order punishes or acquits the alleged offender. . . .

Hence arise military commissions, to investigate and determine, not offences against military law by soldiers and sailors, not breaches of the common laws of war by belligerents, but the quality of the acts which are the proper subject of restraint by martial law.

Martial law and its tribunals have thus come to be recognized in the military operations of all civilized warfare. . . .

[N]either residence nor propinquity to the field of actual hostilities is the test to determine who is or who is not subject to martial law, even in a time of foreign war, and certainly not in a time of civil insurrection. The commander-in-chief has full power to make an effectual use of his forces. He must, therefore, have power to arrest and punish one who arms men to join the enemy in the field against him; one who holds correspondence with that enemy; one who is an officer of an armed force organized to oppose him; one who is preparing to seize arsenals and release prisoners of war taken in battle and confined within his military lines. . . .

[T]he Constitution has delegated to Congress the power of originating war by declaration. . . . [But] after war is originated, whether by declaration, invasion, or insurrection, the whole power of conducting it . . . is given to the President. He is the sole judge of the exigencies, necessities, and duties of the occasion, their extent and duration. . . .

During the war his powers must be without limit, because, if defending, the means of offence may be nearly illimitable; or, if acting

offensively, his resources must be proportionate to the end in view,—
"to conquer a peace." New difficulties are constantly arising, and new
combinations are at once to be thwarted, which the slow movement of
legislative action cannot meet. . . .

By the Constitution, as originally adopted, no limitations were put
upon the war-making and war-conducting powers of Congress and
the President; and after discussion, and after the attention of the country was called to the subject, no other limitation by subsequent
amendment has been made, except by the Third Article, which prescribes that "no soldier shall be quartered in any house in time of
peace without consent of the owner, or in time of war, except in a
manner prescribed by law."

This, then, is the only expressed constitutional restraint upon the
President as to the manner of carrying on war. There would seem to be
no implied one; on the contrary, while carefully providing for the
privilege of the writ of habeas corpus in time of peace, the Constitution takes it for granted that it will be suspended "in case of rebellion
or invasion (i.e., in time of war), when the public safety requires it."

[Counsel for Milligan argued that] . . . [t]his is not a question of the
discipline of camps; it is not a question of the government of armies in
the field; it is not a question of respecting the power of a conqueror
over conquered armies or conquered states.

It is not a question of how far the legislative department of the government can deal with the question of martial rule. Whatever has been
done in these cases, has been done by the executive department alone.

Nor is it a question of the patriotism, or the character, or the services of the late chief magistrate, or of his constitutional advisers.

It is a question of the rights of the citizen in time of war.

Is it true, that the moment a declaration of war is made, the executive department of this government, without an act of Congress, becomes absolute master of our liberties and our lives? Are we, then,
subject to martial rule, administered by the President upon his own
sense of the exigency, with nobody to control him, and with every
magistrate and every authority in the land subject to his will alone?
These are the considerations which give to the case its greatest significance. . . .

Let it also be remembered, that Indiana, at the time of this trial, was
a peaceful State; the courts were all open; their processes had not been
interrupted; the laws had their full sway.

Then let it be remembered that the petitioners were simple citizens, not belonging to the army or navy; not in any official position; not connected in any manner with the public service. . . .

Bearing in mind, therefore, the nature of the charges, and the time of the trial and sentence; bearing in mind, also, the presence and undisputed authority of the civil tribunals and the civil condition of the petitioners, we ask by what authority they were withdrawn from their natural judges?

[Congress does] not confer upon military commissions jurisdiction over any persons other than those in the military service and spies. . . .

Has the President, in time of war, upon his own mere will and judgment, the power to bring before his military officers any person in the land, and subject him to trial and punishment, even to death? The proposition is stated in this form, because it really amounts to this.

If the President has this awful power, whence does he derive it? He can exercise no authority whatever but that which the Constitution of the country gives him. Our system knows no authority beyond or above the law. We may, therefore, dismiss from our minds every thought of the President's having any prerogative, as representative of the people, or as interpreter of the popular will. He is elected by the people to perform those functions, and those only, which the Constitution of his country, and the laws made pursuant to that Constitution, confer. . . .

The question, therefore, is narrowed down to this: Does the authority to command an army carry with it authority to arrest and try by court-martial civilians? . . . The question is easily answered. To command an army, whether in camp, or on the march, or in battle, requires the control of no other persons than the officers, soldiers, and camp followers. It can hardly be contended that, if Congress neglects to find subsistence, the commander-in-chief may lawfully take it from our own citizens. It cannot be supposed that, if Congress fails to provide the means of recruiting, the commander-in-chief may lawfully force the citizens into the ranks. What is called the war power of the President, if indeed there be any such thing, is nothing more than the power of commanding the armies and fleets which Congress causes to be raised. To command them is to direct their operations.

[T]he powers of the President do not include the power to raise or support an army, or to provide or maintain a navy, or to call forth the militia, to repel an invasion, or to suppress an insurrection, or execute the laws, or even to govern such portions of the militia as are called into the service of the United States, or to make law for any of the forts, magazines, arsenals, or dock-yards. If the President could not, even in flagrant war, except as authorized by Congress, call forth the militia of Indiana to repel an invasion of that State, or, when called, govern them, it is absurd to say that he could nevertheless, under the same circumstances, govern the whole State and every person in it by martial rule. . . .

I submit, therefore, that upon the text of the original Constitution, as it stood when it was ratified, there is no color for the assumption that the President, without act of Congress, could create military commissions for the trial of persons not military, for any cause or under any circumstances whatever. . . .

[M]ilitary tribunals for civilians, or non-military persons, whether in war or peace, are inconsistent with the liberty of the citizen, and can have no place in constitutional government. . . .

COURT OPINION BY JUSTICE DAVIS. During the late wicked Rebellion, the temper of the times did not allow that calmness in deliberation and discussion so necessary to a correct conclusion of a purely judicial question. Then, considerations of safety were mingled with the exercise of power; and feelings and interests prevailed which are happily terminated. Now that the public safety is assured, this question, as well as all others, can be discussed and decided without passion or the admixture of any element not required to form a legal judgment. We approach the investigation of this case, fully sensible of the magnitude of the inquiry and the necessity of full and cautious deliberation. . . .

The Constitution of the United States is a law for rulers and people, equally in war and in peace, and covers with the shield of its protection all classes of men, at all times, and under all circumstances. No doctrine, involving more pernicious consequences, was ever invented by the wit of man than that any of its provisions can be suspended during any of the great exigencies of government. Such a doctrine leads directly to anarchy or despotism, but the theory of necessity on which it is based is false; for the government, within the Constitution, has all the powers granted to it, which are necessary to preserve its existence; as has been happily proved by the result of the great effort to throw off its just authority. . . .

Every trial involves the exercise of judicial power; and from what source did the military commission that tried him derive their authority? Certainly no part of the judicial power of the country was conferred on them; because the Constitution expressly vests it "in one supreme court and such inferior courts as the Congress may from time to time ordain and establish," and it is not pretended that the commission was a court ordained and established by Congress. They cannot justify on the mandate of the President; because he is controlled by law, and has his appropriate sphere of duty, which is to execute, not to make, the laws; and there is "no unwritten criminal code to which resort can be had as a source of jurisdiction."

But it is said that the jurisdiction is complete under the "laws and usages of war."

It can serve no useful purpose to inquire what those laws and usages are, whence they originated, where found, and on whom they operate; they can never be applied to citizens in states which have upheld the authority of the government, and where the courts are open and their process unobstructed. This court has judicial knowledge that in Indiana the Federal authority was always unopposed, and its courts always open to hear criminal accusations and redress grievances; and no usage of war could sanction a military trial there for any offence whatever of a citizen in civil life, in nowise connected with the military service. Congress could grant no such power; and to the honor of our national legislature be it said, it has never been provoked by the state of the country even to attempt its exercise. One of the plainest constitutional provisions was, therefore, infringed when Milligan was tried by a court not ordained and established by Congress, and not composed of judges appointed during good behavior.

Why was he not delivered to the Circuit Court of Indiana to be proceeded against according to law? No reason of necessity could be urged against it; because Congress had declared penalties against the offences charged, provided for their punishment, and directed that court to hear and determine them. And soon after this military tribunal was ended, the Circuit Court met, peacefully transacted its business, and adjourned. It needed no bayonets to protect it, and required no military aid to execute its judgments. It was held in a state, eminently distinguished for patriotism, by judges commissioned during the Rebellion, who were provided with juries, upright, intelligent, and selected by a marshal appointed by the President. The government had no right to conclude that Milligan, if guilty, would not receive in that court merited punishment; for its records disclose that it was constantly engaged in the trial of similar offences, and was never interrupted in its administration of criminal justice. If it was dangerous, in the distracted condition of affairs, to leave Milligan unrestrained of his liberty, because he "conspired against the government, afforded aid and comfort to rebels, and incited the people to insurrection," the law said arrest him, confine him closely, render him powerless to do further mischief; and then present his case to the grand jury of the district, with proofs of his guilt, and, if indicted, try him according to the course of the common law. If this had been done, the Constitution would have been vindicated, the law of 1863 enforced, and the securities for personal liberty preserved and defended.

Another guarantee of freedom was broken when Milligan was denied a trial by jury. The great minds of the country have differed on the correct interpretation to be given to various provisions of the Federal Constitution; and judicial decision has been often invoked to settle their true meaning; but until recently no one ever doubted that the right of trial by jury was fortified in the organic law against the power of attack. It is now assailed; but if ideas can be expressed in words, and language has any meaning, this right—one of the most valuable in a free country—is preserved to every one accused of crime who is not attached to the army, or navy, or militia in actual service. . . .

The discipline necessary to the efficiency of the army and navy, required other and swifter modes of trial than are furnished by the common law courts; and, in pursuance of the power conferred by the Constitution, Congress has declared the kinds of trial, and the manner in which they shall be conducted, for offences committed while the party is in the military or naval service. Every one connected with these branches of the public service is amenable to the jurisdiction which Congress has created for their government, and, while thus serving, surrenders his right to be tried by the civil courts. All other persons, citizens of states where the courts are open, if charged with crime, are guaranteed the inestimable privilege of trial by jury. This privilege is a vital principle, underlying the whole administration of criminal justice; it is not held by sufferance, and cannot be frittered away on any plea of state or political necessity. When peace prevails, and the authority of the government is undisputed, there is no difficulty of preserving the safeguards of liberty; for the ordinary modes of trial are never neglected, and no one wishes it otherwise; but if society is disturbed by civil commotion— if the passions of men are aroused and the restraints of law weakened, if not disregarded—these safeguards need, and should receive, the watchful care of those intrusted with the guardianship of the Constitution and laws. In no other way can we transmit to posterity unimpaired the blessings of liberty, consecrated by the sacrifices of the Revolution.

It is claimed that martial law covers with its broad mantle the proceedings of this military commission. The proposition is this: that in a time of war the commander of an armed force (if in his opinion the exigencies of the country demand it, and of which he is to judge), has the power, within the lines of his military district, to suspend all civil rights and their remedies, and subject citizens as well as soldiers to the rule of his will; and in the exercise of his lawful authority cannot be restrained, except by his superior officer or the President of the United States.

If this position is sound to the extent claimed, then when war exists, foreign or domestic, and the country is subdivided into military departments for mere convenience, the commander of one of them can, if he chooses, within his limits, on the plea of necessity, with the approval of the Executive, substitute military force for and to the exclusion of the laws, and punish all persons, as he thinks right and proper, without fixed or certain rules. . . .

This nation, as experience has proved, cannot always remain at peace, and has no right to expect that it will always have wise and humane rulers, sincerely attached to the principles of the Constitution. Wicked men, ambitious of power, with hatred of liberty and contempt of law, may fill the place once occupied by Washington and Lincoln; and if this right is conceded, and the calamities of war again befall us, the dangers to human liberty are frightful to contemplate. If our fathers had failed to provide for just such a contingency, they would have been false to the trust reposed in them. They knew—the history of the world told them—the nation they were founding, be its existence short or long, would be involved in war; how often or how long continued, human foresight could not tell; and that unlimited power, wherever lodged at such a time, was especially hazardous to freemen. For this, and other equally weighty reasons, they secured the inheritance they had fought to maintain, by incorporating in a written constitution the safeguards which time had proved were essential to its preservation. Not one of these safeguards can the President, or Congress, or the Judiciary disturb, except the one concerning the writ of habeas corpus.

It is essential to the safety of every government that, in a great crisis, like the one we have just passed through, there should be a power somewhere of suspending the writ of habeas corpus. In every war, there are men of previously good character, wicked enough to counsel their fellow-citizens to resist the measures deemed necessary by a good government to sustain its just authority and overthrow its enemies; and their influence may lead to dangerous combinations. In the emergency of the times, an immediate public investigation according to law may not be possible; and yet, the peril to the country may be too imminent to suffer such persons to go at large. Unquestionably, there is then an exigency which demands that the government, if it should see fit in the exercise of a proper discretion to make arrests, should not be required to produce the persons arrested in answer to a writ of habeas corpus. The Constitution goes no further. It does not say after a writ of habeas corpus is denied a citizen, that he shall be tried otherwise than by the course of the common law; if it had intended this result, it was easy by the use of direct words to have accomplished it. . . .

It will be borne in mind that this is not a question of the power to proclaim martial law, when war exists in a community and the courts and civil authorities are overthrown. Nor is it a question what rule a military commander, at the head of his army, can impose on states in rebellion to cripple their resources and quell the insurrection. The jurisdiction claimed is much more extensive. The necessities of the service, during the late Rebellion, required that the loyal states should be placed within the limits of certain military districts and commanders appointed in them; and, it is urged, that this, in a military sense, constituted them the theatre of military operations; and, as in this case, Indiana had been and was again threatened with invasion by the enemy, the occasion was furnished to establish martial law. The conclusion does not follow from the premises. If armies were collected in Indiana, they were to be employed in another locality, where the laws were obstructed and the national authority disputed. On her soil there was no hostile foot; if once invaded, that invasion was at an end, and with it all pretext for martial law. Martial law cannot arise from a threatened invasion. The necessity must be actual and present; the invasion real, such as effectually closes the courts and deposes the civil administration.

It is difficult to see how the safety of the country required martial law in Indiana. If any of her citizens were plotting treason, the power of arrest could secure them, until the government was prepared for their trial, when the courts were open and ready to try them. It was as easy to protect witnesses before a civil as a military tribunal; and as there could be no wish to convict, except on sufficient legal evidence, surely an ordained and established court was better able to judge of this than a military tribunal composed of gentlemen not trained to the profession of the law. . . .

Controlling the Wartime Economy

Northern Pacific Railway Co. v. North Dakota
236 U.S. 585 (1915)

Modern warfare has a tremendous impact on a national economy, and in fact wars can be won or lost through the management (or misman-agement) of economic resources. During World War I, the Wilson ad-ministration and Congress placed many regulatory powers at the fed-eral government's disposal, including those of setting wages and price ceilings and of managing vital defense-related industries. The question of the constitutionality of these measures came before the Supreme Court in the spring of 1919. The Court's task was to examine whether the exigencies of war allowed the government to control the nation's railroads in ways that would be unimaginable during peacetime.

COURT OPINION BY JUSTICE WHITE. In taking over the rail-roads from private ownership to its control and operation, was the re-sulting power of the United States to fix the rates to be charged for the transportation services to be by it rendered subordinated to the as-serted authority of the several States to regulate the rates for all local or intrastate business, is the issue raised on this record. . . .

Congress gave the President power "in time of war . . . to take pos-session and assume control of any system or systems of transportation, or any part thereof, and to utilize the same, to the exclusion as far as may be necessary of all other traffic thereon, for the transfer or trans-portation of troops, war material and equipment, or for such other pur-poses connected with the emergency as may be needful or desirable." War with Germany was declared in April, 1917, and with Austria on December 7th of the same year. On December 26, 1917, the President, referring to the existing state of war and the power with which he had been invested by Congress in August, 1916, proclaimed that:

"Under and by virtue of the powers vested in me by the foregoing resolutions and statute, and by virtue of all other powers thereto me enabling, [I] do hereby . . . take possession and assume control at 12 o'clock noon on the twenty-eighth day of December, 1917, of each and every system of transportation and the appurtenances thereof located wholly or in part within the boundaries of the continental United States." ...

By the proclamation a Director General of Railroads was appointed with full authority to take possession and control of the systems embraced by the proclamation and to operate and administer the same. ...

On May 25, 1918, the Director General made an order establishing a schedule of rates for all roads under his control and covering all classes of service, intrastate as well as interstate. The order made these rates effective on designated dates in the month of June and they were continuously enforced during a period of about eight months up to the 14th of February, 1919, when the bill in this case was filed by the State Utilities Commission for mandamus against the Director General and the officers of the Northern Pacific Railway, asserting the want of power in the United States over intrastate rates and the exclusive right of the State of North Dakota to fix such rates for all intrastate business done in that State. ...

The complete and undivided character of the war power of the United States is not disputable. ... On the face of the statutes it is manifest that they were in terms based upon the war power, since the authority they gave arose only because of the existence of war, and the right to exert such authority was to cease upon the war's termination. To interpret, therefore, the exercise of the power by a presumption of the continuance of a state power limiting and controlling the national authority was but to deny its existence. It was akin to the contention that the supreme right to raise armies and use them in case of war did not extend to directing where and when they should be used. ...

Hamilton v. Kentucky Distilleries Co;
Dryfoos v. Edwards (The War Prohibition Cases)
251 U.S. 146 (1919)

Generally speaking, Americans have assumed that extraordinary war-related measures, such as a draft or price controls, will last only as long as the war lasts. Once peace is declared, Americans believe, life should return to normal. In the following case, however, the Supreme Court interpreted a wartime power—in this case, the right to regulate distilleries—so broadly that they allowed the power to extend past the date of Germany's surrender in 1918.

[Counsel for the distilleries argued that] [i]n order to guard and promote the health, welfare and efficiency of the men composing the army and navy, and to increase the efficiency of the workers in the production of arms, munitions, ships, food and clothing for them, Congress has the right temporarily to regulate the sale of liquor, and, if reasonably necessary to accomplish such objects, to forbid its sale. . . .

[But] [t]he War-Time Prohibition Act has, by its own terms, ceased to be operative. The evil sought to be remedied was the danger of intoxication of soldiers, sailors and war workers during the war and during the subsequent period of demobilization. . . . The demobilization process has continued steadily until the strength of both the army and navy has been reduced to less than the authorized peace quota. The production of war munitions has stopped, all existing contracts have been canceled and the Government is actively disposing of its surplus war supplies of arms, munitions, food and clothing, etc. . . .

A foreign war may not be terminated in respect of various considerations arising under international law and yet be concluded in respect of the rights and duties of citizens of the United States under the Federal Constitution; and it does not follow that because a technical state of war still prevails between the United States, Germany and Austria, notwithstanding the complete demobilization of our army and navy, the constitutional rights of the citizens of the United States are to be tested as if war actually existed. It is not necessary that there should ever be a definite treaty of peace. History presents many instances where there has been a "conclusion of war" without any treaty of peace. Whether or not war has been terminated is, after all, a question of fact to be determined in each case by the situation presented.

The War-time Prohibition Act has become obsolete with the passing of the emergency. . . .

COURT OPINION BY JUSTICE BRANDEIS. Did the act become void by the passing of the war emergency before the commencement of these suits? It is conceded that the mere cessation of hostilities under the armistice did not abridge or suspend the power of Congress to resort to prohibition of the liquor traffic as a means of increasing our war efficiency; that the support and care of the army and navy during demobilization was within the war emergency; and that, hence, the act was valid when passed. The contention is that between the date of its enactment and the commencement of these suits it had become evident that hostilities would not be resumed; that demobilization had been effected; that thereby the war emergency was removed; and that when the emergency ceased the statute became void.

To establish that the emergency has passed, statements and acts of the President and of other executive officers are adduced; some of them antedating the enactment of the statute here in question. There are statements of the President to the effect that the war has ended and peace has come; that certain war agencies and activities should be discontinued; that our enemies are impotent to renew hostilities and that the objects of the act here in question have been satisfied in the demobilization of the army and navy. It is shown that many war-time activities have been suspended; that vast quantities of war materials have been disposed of; that trade with Germany has been resumed; and that the censorship of postal, telegraphic and wire communications has been removed. But we have also the fact that since these statements were made and these acts were done, Congress . . . [has treated] the war as continuing and demobilization as incomplete. . . .

The present contention may be stated thus: That notwithstanding the act was a proper exercise of the war power of Congress at the date of its approval and contains its own period of limitation—"until the conclusion of the present war and thereafter until the termination of demobilization,"—the progress of events since that time had produced so great a change of conditions and there now is so clearly a want of necessity for conserving the man power of the nation, for increased efficiency in the production of arms, munitions and supplies, that the prohibition of the sale of distilled spirits for beverage purposes can no longer be enforced, because it would be beyond the constitutional authority of Congress in the exercise of the war power to impose such a prohibition under present circumstances. . . .

Conceding, then, for the purposes of the present case, that the question of the continued validity of the war prohibition act under the changed circumstances depends upon whether it appears that there is no longer any necessity for the prohibition of the sale of distilled spirits for beverage purposes, it remains to be said that on obvious grounds every reasonable intendment must be made in favor of its continuing validity, the prescribed period of limitation not having arrived; that to Congress in the exercise of its powers, not least the war power upon which the very life of the nation depends, a wide latitude of discretion must be accorded; and that it would require a clear case to justify a court in declaring that such an act, passed for such a purpose, had ceased to have force because the power of Congress no longer continued. In view of facts of public knowledge, some of which have been referred to, that the treaty of peace has not yet been concluded, that the railways are still under national control by virtue of the war powers, that other war activities have not been brought to a close, and that it can not even be said that the man power of the nation has been restored to a peace footing, we are unable to conclude that the act has ceased to be valid.

Clear and Present Danger: *Schenck v. United States*

In 1919, Justice Oliver Wendell Holmes Jr. introduced into the American lexicon the famous phrase "clear and present danger" to describe a state of affairs that could justify government restriction of civil liberties. Here Holmes articulated a sweeping rationale for government censorship in limiting the right of an American to oppose the draft.

Schenck v. United States and *Baer v. United States* 249 U.S. 47 (1919)

COURT OPINION BY JUSTICE HOLMES. This is an indictment in three counts. The first charges a conspiracy to violate the Espionage Act of June 15, 1917, c. 30, § 3, 40 Stat. 217, 219, by causing and attempting to cause insubordination, &c., in the military and naval forces of the United States, and to obstruct the recruiting and enlistment service of the United States, when the United States was at war with the German Empire, to wit, that the defendants wilfully conspired to have printed and circulated to men who had been called and accepted for military service under the Act of May 18, 1917, a document set forth and alleged to be calculated to cause such insubordination and obstruction. The count alleges overt acts in pursuance of the conspiracy, ending in the distribution of the document set forth. The second count alleges a conspiracy to commit an offence against the United States, to wit, to use the mails for the transmission of matter declared to be non-mailable by Title XII, § 2 of the Act of June 15, 1917, to wit, the above mentioned document, with an averment of the same overt acts. The third count charges an unlawful use of the mails for the transmission of the same matter and otherwise as above. The defendants were found guilty on all the counts. They set up the First Amendment to the Constitution forbidding Congress to make any law abridging the freedom of speech, or of the press, and bringing the case here on that ground have argued some other points also of which we must dispose.

It is argued that the evidence, if admissible, was not sufficient to prove that the defendant Schenck was concerned in sending the documents. According to the testimony Schenck said he was general secretary of the Socialist party and had charge of the Socialist headquarters from which the documents were sent. He identified a book found there as the minutes of the Executive Committee of the party. The book showed a resolution of August 13, 1917, that 15,000 leaflets should be printed on the other side of one of them in use, to be mailed to men who had passed exemption boards, and for distribution. Schenck personally attended to the printing. On August 20 the general secretary's report said "Obtained new leaflets from printer and started work addressing envelopes" &c.; and there was a resolve that Comrade Schenck be allowed $125 for sending leaflets through the mail. He said that he had about fifteen or sixteen thousand printed. There were files of the circular in question in the inner office which he said were printed on the other side of the one sided circular and were there for distribution. Other copies were proved to have been sent through the mails to drafted men. Without going into confirmatory details that were proved, no reasonable man could doubt that the defendant Schenck was largely instrumental in sending the circulars about. As to the defendant Baer there was evidence that she was a member of the Executive Board and that the minutes of its transactions were hers. The argument as to the sufficiency of the evidence that the defendants conspired to send the documents only impairs the seriousness of the real defence. . . .

The document in question upon its first printed side recited the first section of the Thirteenth Amendment, said that the idea embodied in it was violated by the Conscription Act and that a conscript is little better than a convict. In impassioned language it intimated that conscription was despotism in its worst form and a monstrous wrong against humanity in the interest of Wall Street's chosen few. It said "Do not submit to intimidation," but in form at least confined itself to peaceful measures such as a petition for the repeal of the act. The other and later printed side of the sheet was headed "Assert Your Rights." It stated reasons for alleging that any one violated the Constitution when he refused to recognize "your right to assert your opposition to the draft," and went on "If you do not assert and support your rights, you are helping to deny or disparage rights which it is the solemn duty of all citizens and residents of the United States to retain." It described the arguments on the other side as coming from cunning politicians and a mercenary capitalist press, and even silent consent to the conscription law as helping to support an infamous conspiracy. It denied the power to send our citizens away to foreign shores to shoot up the people of other lands, and added that words could not express the condemnation such cold-blooded ruthlessness deserves, &c., &c., winding up "You must do your share to maintain, support and uphold the rights of the people of this country." Of course the documents would not have been sent unless it had been intended to have some effect, and we do not see what effect it could be expected to have upon persons subject to the draft except to influence them to obstruct the carrying of it out. The defendants do not deny that the jury might find against them on this point.

But it is said, suppose that that was the tendency of this circular, it is protected by the First Amendment to the Constitution. Two of the strongest expressions are said to be quoted respectively from well-known public men. It well may be that the prohibition of laws abridging the freedom of speech is not confined to previous restraints, although to prevent them may have been the main purpose. . . . We admit that in many places and in ordinary times the defendants in saying all that was said in the circular would have been within their constitutional rights. But the character of every act depends upon the circumstances in which it is done. . . . The most stringent protection of free speech would not protect a man in falsely shouting fire in a theatre and causing a panic. It does not even protect a man from an injunction against uttering words that may have all the effect of force. . . . The question in every case is whether the words used are used in such circumstances and are of such a nature as to create a clear and present danger that they will bring about the substantive evils that Congress has a right to prevent. It is a question of proximity and degree. When a nation is at war many things that might be said in time of peace are such a hindrance to its effort that their utterance will not be endured so long as men fight and that no Court could regard them as protected by any constitutional right. It seems to be admitted that if an actual obstruction of the recruiting service were proved, liability for words that produced that effect might be enforced.... If the act (speaking, or circulating a paper), its tendency and the intent with which it is done are the same, we perceive no ground for saying that success alone warrants making the act a crime....

Frohwerk v. United States 249 U.S. 204 (1919)

In Frohwerk, *a case similar to the Schenck affair, the Court affirmed the wide latitude it had given to suppress wartime dissent. Here the justices argue that mere words alone, without direct action, can trigger government suppression, thereby stretching the "clear and present danger" doctrine to the breaking point by suggesting in effect that words are actions. Again the target was a person of German descent, and again Holmes delivered the majority's opinion.*

COURT OPINION BY JUSTICE HOLMES. [The indictment] alleges a conspiracy between [Frohwerk] and one Carl Gleeser, they then being engaged in the preparation and publication of a newspaper, the Missouri Staats Zeitung, to violate the Espionage Act of June 15, 1917.... It alleges as overt acts the preparation and circulation of twelve articles, &c. in the said newspaper at different dates from July 6, 1917, to December 7 of the same year. The other counts allege attempts to cause disloyalty, mutiny and refusal of duty in the military and naval forces of the United States, by the same publications.... There was a trial and Frohwerk was ... sentenced to a fine and to ten years imprisonment....

[W]e think it necessary to add to what has been said in *Schenck v. United States* ... only that the First Amendment while prohibiting legislation against free speech as such cannot have been, and obviously was not, intended to give immunity for every possible use of language.... We venture to believe that neither Hamilton nor Madison, nor any other competent person then or later, ever supposed that to make criminal the counselling of a murder within the jurisdiction of Congress would be an unconstitutional interference with free speech.

[A] person may be convicted of a conspiracy to obstruct recruiting by words of persuasion....

It may be that [Frohwerk's antidraft remarks] might be said or written even in time of war in circumstances that would not make it a crime. We do not lose our right to condemn either measures or men because the Country is at war. It does not appear that there was any special effort to reach men who were subject to the draft. . . . [It] is impossible to say that it might not have been found that the circulation of the paper was in quarters where a little breath would be enough to kindle a flame and that the fact was known and relied upon by those who sent the paper out.

Debs v. United States 249 U.S. 211 (1919)

During the war, government authorities habitually conflated antiwar extremism with labor radicalism and socialism. By engaging in labor agitation, the argument went, union radicals must by definition be interested in wrecking the country's war effort. In fact, many labor activists were highly critical of the Wilson administration and the draft, particularly Eugene V. Debs, president of the American Railway Union. In 1918, Debs was arrested for delivering an antiadministration and antiwar speech in Canton, Ohio, on charges of violating the Espionage Act. The Court, predictably, upheld Debs's arrest and conviction.

COURT OPINION BY JUSTICE HOLMES. This is an indictment under the Espionage Act of June 15, 1917 . . . [alleging that] the defendant caused and incited and attempted to cause and incite insubordination, disloyalty, mutiny and refusal of duty in the military and naval forces of the United States and with intent so to do delivered, to an assembly of people, a public speech, set forth. [It also] alleges that he obstructed and attempted to obstruct the recruiting and enlistment service of the United States and to that end and with that intent delivered the same speech, again set forth. . . .

The main theme of the speech was socialism, its growth, and a prophecy of its ultimate success. With that we have nothing to do, but if a part of the manifest intent of the more general utterances was to encourage those present to obstruct the recruiting service and if in passages such encouragement was directly given, the immunity of the general theme may not be enough to protect the speech. . . .

The chief defences upon which the defendant seemed willing to rely were the denial that we have dealt with and that based upon the First Amendment to the Constitution, disposed of in *Schenck v. United States.* . . .

The Retreat from *Schenck: Abrams v. United States*

The Court continued to follow the line of thinking Holmes had laid out in the Schenck *case, giving the government wide latitude in punishing wartime dissenters, and when a case involving more draft resisters came before the Court later in 1919, a majority ruled much as Holmes had indicated with his "clear and present danger" test. Holmes himself had begun to back away from his earlier argument, however, and in* Abrams *offered a dissent that many view as classic defense of civil liberties in wartime.*

Abrams v. United States 250 U.S. 616 (1919)

OPINION BY JUSTICE CLARKE. On a single indictment, containing four counts, the five plaintiffs in error, hereinafter designated the defendants, were convicted of conspiring to violate provisions to the Espionage Act of Congress. . . .

Each of the first three counts charged the defendants with conspiring, when the United States was at war with the Imperial Government of Germany, to unlawfully utter, print, write and publish: In the first count, "disloyal, scurrilous and abusive language about the form of Government of the United States"; in the second count, language "intended to bring the form of Government of the United States into contempt, scorn, contumely and disrepute"; and in the third count, language "intended to incite, provoke and encourage resistance to the United States in said war." The charge in the fourth count was that the defendants conspired "when the United States was at war with the Imperial German Government, . . . unlawfully and wilfully, by utterance, writing, printing and publication, to urge, incite and advocate curtailment of production of things and products, to wit, ordnance and ammunition, necessary and essential to the prosecution of the war." The offenses were charged in the language of the act of Congress.

It was charged in each count of the indictment that it was a part of the conspiracy that the defendants would attempt to accomplish their unlawful purpose by printing, writing and distributing in the City of New York many copies of a leaflet or circular, printed in the English language, and of another printed in the Yiddish language, copies of which, properly identified, were attached to the indictment.

All of the five defendants were born in Russia. They were intelligent, had considerable schooling, and at the time they were arrested they had lived in the United States terms varying from five to ten years, but none of them had applied for naturalization. Four of them testified as witnesses in their own behalf and of these, three frankly avowed that they were "rebels," "revolutionists," "anarchists," that they did not believe in government in any form, and they declared that they had no interest whatever in the Government of the United States. The fourth defendant testified that he was a "socialist" and believed in "a proper kind of government, not capitalistic," but in his classification the Government of the United States was "capitalistic."

It was admitted on the trial that the defendants had united to print and distribute the described circulars and that five thousand of them had been printed and distributed about the 22d day of August, 1918. The group had a meeting place in New York City, in rooms rented by defendant Abrams, under an assumed name, and there the subject of printing the circulars was discussed about two weeks before the defendants were arrested. The defendant Abrams, although not a printer, on July 27, 1918, purchased the printing outfit with which the circulars were printed and installed it in a basement room where the work was done at night. The circulars were distributed some by throwing them from a window of a building where one of the defendants was employed and others secretly, in New York City.

The defendants pleaded "not guilty," and the case of the Government consisted in showing the facts we have stated, and in introducing in evidence copies of the two printed circulars attached to the indictment, a sheet entitled "Revolutionists Unite for Action," written by the defendant Lipman, and found on him when he was arrested, and another paper, found at the headquarters of the group, and for which Abrams assumed responsibility.

Thus the conspiracy and the doing of the overt acts charged were largely admitted and were fully established. . . .

[The pamphlets published by the defendants were] not an attempt to bring about a change of administration by candid discussion, for no matter what may have incited the outbreak on the part of the defendant anarchists, the manifest purpose of such a publication was to create an attempt to defeat the war plans of the Government of the United States, by bringing upon the country the paralysis of a general strike, thereby arresting the production of all munitions and other things essential to the conduct of the war. . . .

That the interpretation we have put upon these articles, circulated in the greatest port of our land, from which great numbers of soldiers were at the time taking ship daily, and in which great quantities of war supplies of every kind were at the time being manufactured for transportation overseas, is not only the fair interpretation of them, but that it is the meaning which their authors consciously intended should be conveyed by them to others is further shown by the additional writings found in the meeting place of the defendant group and on the person of one of them. One of these circulars is headed: "Revolutionists! Unite for Action!"

[Excerpts from the pamphlets] sufficiently show, that while the immediate occasion for this particular outbreak of lawlessness, on the part of the defendant alien anarchists, may have been resentment caused by our Government sending troops into Russia as a strategic operation against the Germans on the eastern battle front, yet the plain purpose of their propaganda was to excite, at the supreme crisis of the war, disaffection, sedition, riots, and, as they hoped, revolution, in this country for the purpose of embarrassing and if possible defeating the military plans of the Government in Europe. A technical distinction may perhaps be taken between disloyal and abusive language applied to the form of our government or language intended to bring the form of our government into contempt and disrepute, and language of like character and intended to produce like results directed against the President and Congress, the agencies through which that form of government must function in time of war. But it is not necessary to a decision of this case to consider whether such distinction is vital or merely formal, for the language of these circulars was obviously intended to provoke and to encourage resistance to the United States in the war, as the third count runs, and, the defendants, in terms, plainly urged and advocated a resort to a general strike of workers in ammunition factories for the purpose of curtailing the production of ordnance and munitions necessary and essential to the prosecution of the war as is charged in the fourth count. Thus it is clear not only that some evidence but that much persuasive evidence was before the jury tending to prove that the defendants were guilty as charged in both the third and fourth counts of the indictment and under the long established rule of law hereinbefore stated the judgment of the District Court must be Affirmed.

DISSENT BY JUSTICE HOLMES. This indictment is founded wholly upon the publication of two leaflets which I shall describe in a moment. The first count charges a conspiracy pending the war with Germany to publish abusive language about the form of government of the United States, laying the preparation and publishing of the first leaflet as overt acts. The second count charges a conspiracy pending the war to publish language intended to bring the form of government into contempt, laying the preparation and publishing of the two leaflets as overt acts. The third count alleges a conspiracy to encourage resistance to the United States in the same war and to attempt to effectuate the purpose by publishing the same leaflets. The fourth count lays a conspiracy to incite curtailment of production of things necessary to the prosecution of the war and to attempt to accomplish it by publishing the second leaflet to which I have referred.

The first of these leaflets says that the President's cowardly silence about the intervention in Russia reveals the hypocrisy of the plutocratic gang in Washington. It intimates that "German militarism combined with allied capitalism to crush the Russian revolution"—goes on that the tyrants of the world fight each other until they see a common enemy—working class enlightenment, when they combine to crush it; and that now militarism and capitalism combined, though not openly, to crush the Russian revolution. It says that there is only one enemy of the workers of the world and that is capitalism; that it is a crime for workers of America, &c., to fight the workers' republic of Russia, and ends "Awake! Awake, you Workers of the World! Revolutionists." A note adds "It is absurd to call us pro-German. We hate and despise German militarism more than do you hypocritical tyrants. We have more reasons for denouncing German militarism than has the coward of the White House."

The other leaflet, headed "Workers—Wake Up," with abusive language says that America together with the Allies will march for Russia to help the Czecho-Slovaks in their struggle against the Bolsheviki, and that this time the hypocrites shall not fool the Russian emigrants and friends of Russia in America. It tells the Russian emigrants that they now must spit in the face of the false military propaganda by which their sympathy and help to the prosecution of the war have been called forth and says that with the money they have lent or are going to lend "they will make bullets not only for the Germans but also for the Workers Soviets of Russia," and further, "Workers in the ammunition factories, you are producing bullets, bayonets, cannon, to murder not only the Germans, but also your dearest, best, who are in Russia and are fighting for freedom." It then appeals to the same Russian emigrants at some length not to consent to the "inquisitionary expedition to Russia," and says that the destruction of the Russian revolution is "the politics of the march to Russia." The leaflet winds up by saying "Workers, our reply to this barbaric intervention has to be a general strike!," and after a few words on the spirit of revolution, exhortations not to be afraid, and some usual tall talk ends "Woe unto those who will be in the way of progress. Let solidarity live! The Rebels."

No argument seems to me necessary to show that these pronunciamentos in no way attack the form of government of the United States, or that they do not support either of the first two counts. What little I have to say about the third count may be postponed until I have considered the fourth. With regard to that it seems too plain to be denied that the suggestion to workers in the ammunition factories that they are producing bullets to murder their dearest, and the further advocacy of a general strike, both in the second leaflet, do urge curtailment of production of things necessary to the prosecution of the war within the meaning of the Act of May 16, 1918, c. 75, 40 Stat. 553, amending § 3 of the earlier Act of 1917. But to make the conduct criminal that statute requires that it should be "with intent by such curtailment to cripple or hinder the United States in the prosecution of the war." It seems to me that no such intent is proved.

I am aware of course that the word intent as vaguely used in ordinary legal discussion means no more than knowledge at the time of the act that the consequences said to be intended will ensue. Even less than that will satisfy the general principle of civil and criminal liability. A man may have to pay damages, may be sent to prison, at common law might be hanged, if at the time of his act he knew facts from which common experience showed that the consequences would follow, whether he individually could foresee them or not. But, when words are used exactly, a deed is not done with intent to produce a consequence unless that consequence is the aim of the deed. It may be obvious, and obvious to the actor, that the consequence will follow, and he may be liable for it even if he regrets it, but he does not do the act with intent to produce it unless the aim to produce it is the proximate motive of the specific act, although there may be some deeper motive behind.

It seems to me that this statute must be taken to use its words in a strict and accurate sense. They would be absurd in any other. A patriot might think that we were wasting money on aeroplanes, or making more cannon of a certain kind than we needed, and might advocate curtailment with success, yet even if it turned out that the curtailment hindered and was thought by other minds to have been obviously likely to hinder the United States in the prosecution of the war, no one would hold such conduct a crime. I admit that my illustration does not answer all that might be said but it is enough to show what I think and to let me pass to a more important aspect of the case. I refer to the First Amendment to the Constitution that Congress shall make no law abridging the freedom of speech.

I never have seen any reason to doubt that the questions of law that alone were before this Court ... were rightly decided. I do not doubt for a moment that by the same reasoning that would justify punishing persuasion to murder, the United States constitutionally may punish speech that produces or is intended to produce a clear and imminent danger that it will bring about forthwith certain substantive evils that the United States constitutionally may seek to prevent. The power undoubtedly is greater in time of war than in time of peace because war opens dangers that do not exist at other times.

But as against dangers peculiar to war, as against others, the principle of the right to free speech is always the same. It is only the present danger of immediate evil or an intent to bring it about that warrants Congress in setting a limit to the expression of opinion where private rights are not concerned. Congress certainly cannot forbid all effort to change the mind of the country. Now nobody can suppose that the surreptitious publishing of a silly leaflet by an unknown man, without more, would present any immediate danger that its opinions would hinder the success of the government arms or have any appreciable tendency to do so. Publishing those opinions for the very purpose of obstructing, however, might indicate a greater danger and at any rate would have the quality of an attempt. So I assume that the second leaflet if published for the purposes alleged in the fourth count might be punishable. But it seems pretty clear to me that nothing less than that would bring these papers within the scope of this law. An actual intent in the sense that I have explained is necessary to constitute an attempt, where a further act of the same individual is required to complete the substantive crime. ... It is necessary where the success of the attempt depends upon others because if that intent is not present the actor's aim may be accomplished without bringing about the evils sought to be checked. An intent to prevent interference with the revolution in Russia might have been satisfied without any hindrance to carrying on the war in which we were engaged.

I do not see how anyone can find the intent required by the statute in any of the defendants' words. The second leaflet is the only one that affords even a foundation for the charge, and there, without invoking the hatred of German militarism expressed in the former one, it is evident from the beginning to the end that the only object of the paper is to help Russia and stop American intervention there against the popular government—not to impede the United States in the war that it was carrying on. To say that two phrases taken literally might import a suggestion of conduct that would have interference with the war as an indirect and probably undesired effect seems to me by no means enough to show an attempt to produce that effect.

I return for a moment to the third count. That charges an intent to provoke resistance to the United States in its war with Germany. Taking the clause in the statute that deals with that in connection with the other elaborate provisions of the act, I think that resistance to the United States means some forcible act of opposition to some proceeding of the United States in pursuance of the war. I think the intent must be the specific intent that I have described and for the reasons that I have given I think that no such intent was proved or existed in fact. I also think that there is no hint at resistance to the United States as I construe the phrase.

In this case sentences of twenty years imprisonment have been imposed for the publishing of two leaflets that I believe the defendants had as much right to publish as the Government has to publish the Constitution of the United States now vainly invoked by them. Even if I am technically wrong and enough can be squeezed from these poor and puny anonymities to turn the color of legal litmus paper; I will add, even if what I think the necessary intent were shown; the most nominal punishment seems to me all that possibly could be inflicted, unless the defendants are to be made to suffer not for what the indictment alleges but for the creed that they avow—a creed that I believe to be the creed of ignorance and immaturity when honestly held, as I see no reason to doubt that it was held here, but which, although made the subject of examination at the trial, no one has a right even to consider in dealing with the charges before the Court.

Persecution for the expression of opinions seems to me perfectly logical. If you have no doubt of your premises or your power and want a certain result with all your heart you naturally express your wishes in law and sweep away all opposition. To allow opposition by speech seems to indicate that you think the speech impotent, as when a man says that he has squared the circle, or that you do not care whole-heartedly for the result, or that you doubt either your power or your premises. But when men have realized that time has upset many fighting faiths, they may come to believe even more than they believe the very foundations of their own conduct that the ultimate good desired is better reached by free trade in ideas—that the best test of truth is the power of the thought to get itself accepted in the competition of the market, and that truth is the only ground upon which their wishes safely can be carried out. That at any rate is the theory of our Constitution. It is an experiment, as all life is an experiment. Every year if not every day we have to wager our salvation upon some prophecy based upon imperfect knowledge. While that experiment is part of our system I think that we should be eternally vigilant against attempts to check the expression of opinions that we loathe and believe to be fraught with death, unless they so imminently threaten immediate interference with the lawful and pressing purposes of the law that an immediate check is required to save the country.... Of course I am speaking only of expressions of opinion and exhortations, which were all that were uttered here, but I regret that I cannot put into more impressive words my belief that in their conviction upon this indictment the defendants were deprived of their rights under the Constitution of the United States.

West Virginia State Board of Education v. Barnette 319 U.S. 624 (1943)

After the Japanese attack on Pearl Harbor, Americans were subjected to enormous social, cultural, and political pressure to conform to the prowar, patriotic mainstream. Some communities enlisted the law's aid to achieve uniformity, requiring their schoolchildren to demonstrate patriotism by saluting the flag and reciting the pledge of allegiance. Members of some religious minorities refused to do so because of their pacifism and their belief that oaths taken before any entity other than God are inherently blasphemous. One such case that reached the Supreme Court involved West Virginia's attempt to force patriotic conformity on Jehovah's Witnesses. The case is worth citing at length, because both the minority and dissenting opinions eloquently laid bare the problems involved in attempting to use the law to enforce wartime homogeneity of thought and feeling.

COURT OPINION BY JUSTICE JACKSON. [T]he West Virginia legislature amended its statutes to require all schools therein to conduct courses of instruction in history, civics, and in the Constitutions of the United States and of the State "for the purpose of teaching, fostering and perpetuating the ideals, principles and spirit of Americanism, and increasing the knowledge of the organization and machinery of the government." Appellant Board of Education was directed, with advice of the State Superintendent of Schools, to "prescribe the courses of study covering these subjects" for public schools. The Act made it the duty of private, parochial and denominational schools to prescribe courses of study "similar to those required for the public schools." . . .

The Board of Education on January 9, 1942, adopted a resolution containing recitals taken largely from the Court's *Gobitis* opinion and ordering that the salute to the flag become "a regular part of the program of activities in the public schools," that all teachers and pupils "shall be required to participate in the salute honoring the Nation represented by the Flag; provided, however, that refusal to salute the Flag be regarded as an act of insubordination, and shall be dealt with accordingly."

Failure to conform is "insubordination" dealt with by expulsion. Readmission is denied by statute until compliance. Meanwhile the expelled child is "unlawfully absent" and may be proceeded against as a delinquent. His parents or guardians are liable to prosecution, and if convicted are subject to fine not exceeding $50 and jail term not exceeding thirty days.

Appellees, citizens of the United States and of West Virginia, brought suit in the United States District Court for themselves and others similarly situated asking its injunction to restrain enforcement of these laws and regulations against Jehovah's Witnesses. The Witnesses are an unincorporated body teaching that the obligation imposed by law of God is superior to that of laws enacted by temporal government. Their religious beliefs include a literal version of Exodus, Chapter 20, verses 4 and 5, which says: "Thou shalt not make unto thee any graven image, or any likeness of anything that is in heaven above, or that is in the earth beneath, or that is in the water under the earth; thou shalt not bow down thyself to them nor serve them." They consider that the flag is an "image" within this command. For this reason they refuse to salute it.

Children of this faith have been expelled from school and are threatened with exclusion for no other cause. Officials threaten to send them to reformatories maintained for criminally inclined juveniles. Parents of such children have been prosecuted and are threatened with prosecutions for causing delinquency.

The Board of Education moved to dismiss the complaint setting forth these facts and alleging that the law and regulations are an unconstitutional denial of religious freedom, and of freedom of speech, and are invalid under the "due process" and "equal protection" clauses of the Fourteenth Amendment to the Federal Constitution. The cause was submitted on the pleadings to a District Court of three judges. It restrained enforcement as to the plaintiffs and those of that class. The Board of Education brought the case here by direct appeal. . . .

The freedom asserted by these appellees does not bring them into collision with rights asserted by any other individual. It is such conflicts which most frequently require intervention of the State to determine where the rights of one end and those of another begin. But the refusal of these persons to participate in the ceremony does not interfere with or deny rights of others to do so. Nor is there any question in this case that their behavior is peaceable and orderly. The sole conflict is between authority and rights of the individual. The State asserts power to condition access to public education on making a prescribed sign and profession and at the same time to coerce attendance by punishing both parent and child. The latter stand on a right of self-determination in matters that touch individual opinion and personal attitude.

Here . . . we are dealing with a compulsion of students to declare a belief. They are not merely made acquainted with the flag salute so that they may be informed as to what it is or even what it means. The issue here is whether this slow and easily neglected route to aroused loyalties constitutionally may be short-cut by substituting a compulsory salute and slogan. . . .

There is no doubt that, in connection with the pledges, the flag salute is a form of utterance. Symbolism is a primitive but effective way of communicating ideas. The use of an emblem or flag to symbolize some system, idea, institution, or personality, is a short cut from mind to mind. Causes and nations, political parties, lodges and ecclesiastical groups seek to knit the loyalty of their followings to a flag or banner, a color or design. The State announces rank, function, and authority through crowns and maces, uniforms and black robes; the church speaks through the Cross, the Crucifix, the altar and shrine, and clerical raiment. Symbols of State often convey political ideas just as religious symbols come to convey theological ones.

Associated with many of these symbols are appropriate gestures of acceptance or respect: a salute, a bowed or bared head, a bended knee. A person gets from a symbol the meaning he puts into it, and what is one man's comfort and inspiration is another's jest and scorn. . . .

It is also to be noted that the compulsory flag salute and pledge requires affirmation of a belief and an attitude of mind. It is not clear whether the regulation contemplates that pupils forgo any contrary convictions of their own and become unwilling converts to the prescribed ceremony or whether it will be acceptable if they simulate assent by words without belief and by a gesture barren of meaning. It is now a commonplace that censorship or suppression of expression of opinion is tolerated by our Constitution only when the expression presents a clear and present danger of action of a kind the State is empowered to prevent and punish. It would seem that involuntary affirmation could be commanded only on even more immediate and urgent grounds than silence. But here the power of compulsion is invoked without any allegation that remaining passive during a flag salute ritual creates a clear and present danger that would justify an effort even to muffle expression. To sustain the compulsory flag salute we are required to say that a Bill of Rights which guards the individual's right to speak his own mind, left it open to public authorities to compel him to utter what is not in his mind.

Whether the First Amendment to the Constitution will permit officials to order observance of ritual of this nature does not depend upon whether as a voluntary exercise we would think it to be good, bad or merely innocuous. Any credo of nationalism is likely to include what some disapprove or to omit what others think essential, and to give off different overtones as it takes on different accents or interpretations. If official power exists to coerce acceptance of any patriotic creed, what it shall contain cannot be decided by courts, but must be largely discretionary with the ordaining authority, whose power to prescribe would no doubt include power to amend. Hence validity of the asserted power to force an American citizen publicly to profess any statement of belief or to engage in any ceremony of assent to one, presents questions of power that must be considered independently of any idea we may have as to the utility of the ceremony in question.

Nor does the issue as we see it turn on one's possession of particular religious views or the sincerity with which they are held. While religion supplies appellees' motive for enduring the discomforts of making the issue in this case, many citizens who do not share these religious views hold such a compulsory rite to infringe constitutional liberty of the individual. It is not necessary to inquire whether nonconformist beliefs will exempt from the duty to salute unless we first find power to make the salute a legal duty. . . .

Free public education, if faithful to the ideal of secular instruction and political neutrality, will not be partisan or enemy of any class, creed, party, or faction. If it is to impose any ideological discipline, however, each party or denomination must seek to control, or failing that, to weaken the influence of the educational system. Observance of the limitations of the Constitution will not weaken government in the field appropriate for its exercise. . . .

The Fourteenth Amendment, as now applied to the States, protects the citizen against the State itself and all of its creatures—Boards of Education not excepted. These have, of course, important, delicate, and highly discretionary functions, but none that they may not perform within the limits of the Bill of Rights. That they are educating the young for citizenship is reason for scrupulous protection of Constitutional freedoms of the individual, if we are not to strangle the free mind at its source and teach youth to discount important principles of our government as mere platitudes.

Such Boards are numerous and their territorial jurisdiction often small. But small and local authority may feel less sense of responsibility to the Constitution, and agencies of publicity may be less vigilant in calling it to account. The action of Congress in making flag observance voluntary and respecting the conscience of the objector in a matter so vital as raising the Army contrasts sharply with these local regulations in matters relatively trivial to the welfare of the nation. There are village tyrants as well as village Hampdens, but none who acts under color of law is beyond reach of the Constitution. . . .

The very purpose of a Bill of Rights was to withdraw certain subjects from the vicissitudes of political controversy, to place them beyond the reach of majorities and officials and to establish them as legal principles to be applied by the courts. One's right to life, liberty, and property, to free speech, a free press, freedom of worship and assembly, and other fundamental rights may not be submitted to vote; they depend on the outcome of no elections. . . .

National unity as an end which officials may foster by persuasion and example is not in question. The problem is whether under our Constitution compulsion as here employed is a permissible means for its achievement.

Struggles to coerce uniformity of sentiment in support of some end thought essential to their time and country have been waged by many good as well as by evil men. Nationalism is a relatively recent phenomenon but at other times and places the ends have been racial or territorial security, support of a dynasty or regime, and particular plans for saving souls. As first and moderate methods to attain unity have failed, those bent on its accomplishment must resort to an ever-increasing severity. As governmental pressure toward unity becomes greater, so strife becomes more bitter as to whose unity it shall be. Probably no deeper division of our people could proceed from any provocation than from finding it necessary to choose what doctrine and whose program public educational officials shall compel youth to unite in embracing. Ultimate futility of such attempts to compel coherence is the lesson of every such effort from the Roman drive to stamp out Christianity as a disturber of its pagan unity, the Inquisition, as a means to religious and dynastic unity, the Siberian exiles as a means to Russian unity, down to the fast failing efforts of our present totalitarian enemies. Those who begin coercive elimination of dissent soon find themselves exterminating dissenters. Compulsory unification of opinion achieves only the unanimity of the graveyard. . . .

The case is made difficult not because the principles of its decision are obscure but because the flag involved is our own. Nevertheless, we apply the limitations of the Constitution with no fear that freedom to be intellectually and spiritually diverse or even contrary will disintegrate the social organization. To believe that patriotism will not flourish if patriotic ceremonies are voluntary and spontaneous instead of a compulsory routine is to make an unflattering estimate of the appeal of our institutions to free minds. We can have intellectual individualism and the rich cultural diversities that we owe to exceptional minds only at the price of occasional eccentricity and abnormal attitudes. When they are so harmless to others or to the State as those we deal with here, the price is not too great. But freedom to differ is not limited to things that do not matter much. That would be a mere shadow of freedom. The test of its substance is the right to differ as to things that touch the heart of the existing order.

If there is any fixed star in our constitutional constellation, it is that no official, high or petty, can prescribe what shall be orthodox in politics, nationalism, religion, or other matters of opinion or force citizens to confess by word or act their faith therein. If there are any circumstances which permit an exception, they do not now occur to us.

We think the action of the local authorities in compelling the flag salute and pledge transcends constitutional limitations on their power and invades the sphere of intellect and spirit which it is the purpose of the First Amendment to our Constitution to reserve from all official control.

MR. JUSTICE BLACK and MR. JUSTICE DOUGLAS, concurring: We are substantially in agreement with the opinion just read. . . . The statute requires the appellees to participate in a ceremony aimed at inculcating respect for the flag and for this country. The Jehovah's Witnesses, without any desire to show disrespect for either the flag or the country, interpret the Bible as commanding, at the risk of God's displeasure, that they not go through the form of a pledge of allegiance to any flag. The devoutness of their belief is evidenced by their willingness to suffer persecution and punishment, rather than make the pledge.

No well-ordered society can leave to the individuals an absolute right to make final decisions, unassailable by the State, as to everything they will or will not do. The First Amendment does not go so far. Religious faiths, honestly held, do not free individuals from responsibility to conduct themselves obediently to laws which are either imperatively necessary to protect society as a whole from grave and pressingly imminent dangers or which, without any general prohibition, merely regulate time, place or manner of religious activity. . . .

[But] [w]ords uttered under coercion are proof of loyalty to nothing but self-interest. Love of country must spring from willing hearts and free minds, inspired by a fair administration of wise laws enacted by the people's elected representatives within the bounds of express constitutional prohibitions. These laws must, to be consistent with the First Amendment, permit the widest toleration of conflicting viewpoints consistent with a society of free men.

Neither our domestic tranquillity in peace nor our martial effort in war depend on compelling little children to participate in a ceremony which ends in nothing for them but a fear of spiritual condemnation. If, as we think, their fears are groundless, time and reason are the proper antidotes for their errors. The ceremonial, when enforced against conscientious objectors, more likely to defeat than to serve its high purpose, is a handy implement for disguised religious persecution. As such, it is inconsistent with our Constitution's plan and purpose.

MR. JUSTICE MURPHY, concurring: I am unable to agree that the benefits that may accrue to society from the compulsory flag salute are sufficiently definite and tangible to justify the invasion of freedom and privacy that is entailed or to compensate for a restraint on the freedom of the individual to be vocal or silent according to his conscience or personal inclination. The trenchant words in the preamble to the Virginia Statute for Religious Freedom remain unanswerable: " . . . all attempts to influence [the mind] by temporal punishments, or burdens, or by civil incapacitations, tend only to beget habits of hypocrisy and meanness. . . ." Any spark of love for country which may be generated in a child or his associates by forcing him to make what is to him an empty gesture and recite words wrung from him contrary to his religious beliefs is overshadowed by the desirability of preserving freedom of conscience to the full. It is in that freedom and the example of persuasion, not in force and compulsion, that the real unity of America lies.

MR. JUSTICE FRANKFURTER, dissenting: One who belongs to the most vilified and persecuted minority in history is not likely to be insensible to the freedoms guaranteed by our Constitution. Were my purely personal attitude relevant I should wholeheartedly associate myself with the general libertarian views in the Court's opinion, representing as they do the thought and action of a lifetime. But as judges we are neither Jew nor Gentile, neither Catholic nor agnostic. We owe equal attachment to the Constitution and are equally bound by our judicial obligations whether we derive our citizenship from the earliest or the latest immigrants to these shores. As a member of this Court I am not justified in writing my private notions of policy into the Constitution, no matter how deeply I may cherish them or how mischievous I may deem their disregard. . . . Most unwillingly, therefore, I must differ from my brethren with regard to legislation like this. I cannot bring my mind to believe that the "liberty" secured by the Due Process Clause gives this Court authority to deny to the State of West Virginia the attainment of that which we all recognize as a legitimate legislative end, namely, the promotion of good citizenship, by employment of the means here chosen. . . .

Of course patriotism can not be enforced by the flag salute. But neither can the liberal spirit be enforced by judicial invalidation of illiberal legislation. Our constant preoccupation with the constitutionality of legislation rather than with its wisdom tends to preoccupation of the American mind with a false value.

Baumgartner v. United States 322 U.S. 665 (1944)

As was the case twenty years earlier, Americans during World War II looked with suspicion upon neighbors who had overt ties to Germany. The government tried to crack down on what it thought was the more egregious cases by revoking their naturalization status. The Supreme Court, as we see in this case, looked upon these policies with skepticism.

COURT OPINION BY JUSTICE FRANKFURTER. On September 26, 1932, the United States District Court for the Western District of Missouri entered its order admitting Baumgartner to citizenship and issued a certificate of naturalization to him. . . .

As a condition to receiving his American citizenship, Baumgartner, like every other alien applying for that great gift, was required to declare on oath that he renounced his former allegiance, in this case to the German Reich, and that he would "support and defend the Constitution and laws of the United States of America against all enemies, foreign and domestic," and that he would "bear true faith and allegiance to the same." That he did not truly and fully renounce his allegiance to Germany and that he did not in fact intend to support the Constitution and laws of the United States and to give them true faith and allegiance, are the charges of fraud and illegality on which his citizenship is claimed forfeit. . . .

There was testimony that Baumgartner justified the German invasions in the late 1930s, and announced, when Dunkerque fell, that "Today I am rejoicing." One witness testified that Baumgartner told him that he "belonged to an order called the so-called 'Bund'," and the diary which Baumgartner kept from December 1, 1938, to the summer of 1941 reveals that he attended a meeting of the German Vocational League where the German national anthem was sung and "everyone naturally arose and assumed the usual German stance with the arm extended to give the National Socialist greeting." Other diary entries reflect violent anti-Semitism, impatience at the lack of pro-German militancy of German-Americans, and approval of Germans who have not "been Americanized, that is, ruined." . . .

We cannot escape the conviction that the case made out by the Government lacks that solidity of proof which leaves no troubling doubt in deciding a question of such gravity as is implied in an attempt to reduce a person to the status of alien from that of citizen. . . .

The gravamen of the Government's complaint and of the findings and opinions below is that Baumgartner consciously withheld allegiance to the United States and its Constitution and laws; in short, that Baumgartner was guilty of fraud. To prove such intentional misrepresentation evidence calculated to establish only the objective falsity of Baumgartner's oath was adduced. Nothing else was offered to show that Baumgartner was aware of a conflict between his views and the new political allegiance he assumed. . . . [I]t is our view that the evidence does not measure up to the standard of proof which must be applied to this case. . . .

American citizenship is the right to criticize public men and measures—and that means not only informed and responsible criticism but the freedom to speak foolishly and without moderation. Our trust in the good sense of the people on deliberate reflection goes deep. For such is the contradictoriness of the human mind that the expression of views which may collide with cherished American ideals does not necessarily prove want of devotion to the Nation. It would be foolish to deny that even blatant intolerance toward some of the presuppositions of the democratic faith may not imply rooted disbelief in our system of government. . . .

The insufficiency of the evidence to show that Baumgartner did not renounce his allegiance to Germany in 1932 need not be labored. Whatever German political leanings Baumgartner had in 1932, they were to Hitler and Hitlerism, certainly not to the Weimar Republic. Hitler did not come to power until after Baumgartner forswore his allegiance to the then German nation. . . .

And so we conclude that the evidence as to Baumgartner's attitude after 1932 affords insufficient proof that in 1932 he had knowing reservations in forswearing his allegiance to the Weimar Republic and embracing allegiance to this country so as to warrant the infliction of the grave consequences involved in making an alien out of a man ten years after he was admitted to citizenship. The evidence in the record before us is not sufficiently compelling to require that we penalize a naturalized citizen for the expression of silly or even sinister-sounding views which native-born citizens utter with impunity. The judgment must accordingly be reversed and the case remanded to the District Court for further proceedings not inconsistent with this opinion. . . .

Hartzel v. United States 322 U.S. 680 (1944)

The old Espionage Act of 1917 remained in force during World War II and could serve as an effective means by which the government could silence antiwar dissenters. During World War I, the Supreme Court had given the government a fairly free rein in using this potentially powerful internal security tool. By 1944, however, the justices on the Supreme Court were more wary of possible abuses and held government authorities to a high evidentiary standard.

COURT OPINION BY JUSTICE MURPHY. For the first time during the course of the present war we are confronted with a prosecution under the Espionage Act of 1917. The narrow issue is whether there was sufficient evidence to support the jury's determination that petitioner violated the Act in that, in time of war, he willfully attempted to cause insubordination, disloyalty, mutiny and refusal of duty in the armed forces and willfully obstructed the recruiting and enlistment service of the United States.

Petitioner and two others were charged in a seven-count indictment with violations of the second and third clauses n2 of § 3 of the Act, together with a violation of § 4. It was alleged that in time of war they published and disseminated three pamphlets to numerous persons and organizations, among whom were individuals available and eligible for recruitment and enlistment in the military and naval forces of the United States as well as individuals already members of the armed forces. . . . Petitioner was found guilty on all counts and was sentenced generally to five years in prison.

No question is here raised as to the constitutionality of [the Espionage Act]. . . . But such legislation, being penal in nature and restricting the right to speak and write freely, must be construed narrowly. . . .

There is nothing on the face of the three pamphlets in question to indicate that petitioner intended specifically to cause insubordination, disloyalty, mutiny or refusal of duty in the military forces or to obstruct the recruiting and enlistment service. No direct or affirmative appeals are made to that effect and no mention is made of military personnel or of persons registered under the Selective Training and Service Act. They contain, instead, vicious and unreasoning attacks on one of our military allies, flagrant appeals to false and sinister racial theories and gross libels of the President. Few ideas are more odious to the majority of the American people or more destructive of national unity in time of war. But while such iniquitous doctrines may be used under certain circumstances as vehicles for the purposeful undermining of the morale and loyalty of the armed forces and those persons of draft age, they cannot by themselves be taken as proof beyond a reasonable doubt that petitioner had the narrow intent requisite to a violation of this statute. . . .

We are not unmindful of the fact that the United States is now engaged in a total war for national survival and that total war of the modern variety cannot be won by a doubtful, disunited nation in which any appreciable sector is disloyal. For that reason our enemies have developed psychological warfare to a high degree in an effort to cause unrest and disloyalty. Much of this type of warfare takes the form of insidious propaganda in the manner and tenor displayed by petitioner's three pamphlets. Crude appeals to overthrow the government or to discard our arms in open mutiny are seldom made. Emphasis is laid, rather, on such matters as the futility of our war aims, the vices of our allies and the inadequacy of our leadership. But the mere fact that such ideas are enunciated by a citizen is not enough by itself to warrant a finding of a criminal intent to violate § 3 of the Espionage Act. Unless there is sufficient evidence from which a jury could infer beyond a reasonable doubt that he intended to bring about the specific consequences prohibited by the Act, an American citizen has the right to discuss these matters either by temperate reasoning or by immoderate and vicious invective without running afoul of the Espionage Act of 1917. Such evidence was not present in this case.

DISSENT BY JUSTICE REED. The First Amendment to the Constitution preserves freedom of speech and of the press in war as well as in peace. The right to criticize the Government and the handling of the war is not questioned. Congress has not sought, directly or indirectly, to abridge the right of anyone to present his views on the conduct of the war or the making of the peace. The legislation under which Hartzel was tried and convicted was aimed at those who, in time of war, "shall willfully cause or attempt to cause insubordination, disloyalty, or refusal of duty, in the military or naval forces of the United States." It is only when the requisite intent to produce those results is present that criticism may cross over the line of prohibited conduct. The constitutional power of Congress so to protect the national interest is beyond question. . . .

[W]e think that enough facts revealing the requisite intent were presented to justify the verdict. Other similar articles circulated prior to the declaration of war tended to show a continuing intention. The articles which were the basis of the indictment were sent to military officers including those of the highest rank. This circumstance is brought forward by petitioner as indicative of a lack of intention to undermine the military forces. This was doubtless weighed by the jury, but certainly it cannot be said that circulation of propaganda among officers shows less intention to proselyte than to circulate among the enlisted personnel. Copies were sent to the Infantry Journal, a publication circulating largely in the armed forces. Nothing appears as to any motive, other than interference with discipline, that the petitioner might have in distributing this type of pamphlet to professional military officers. The jury was entitled to weigh the fact that the articles were sent anonymously. The jury was also entitled to weigh the fact that those to whom the articles were sent were hand-picked and composed a select group. These actions speak as loud as words. . . .

These pamphlets were distributed in 1942. The military situation was then nothing like so strong as now nor confidence in our strategy so uniform. A large segment of public opinion desired to concentrate against Japan, rather than Germany and Italy, a viewpoint which doubtless had advocates among the members of the armed forces. It was an opportune time from the viewpoint of the German enemy to put pamphlets such as these in circulation which taught suspicion of Britain, vilified Jews and promoted lack of confidence in the President. On the question of intention, the circumstances under which the pamphlets were distributed were important and entitled to weight. Petitioner played precisely upon those prejudices from which at that time insubordination or disloyalty was most likely to develop.

Keegan v. United States 325 U.S. 478 (1945)

During World War I, attempts by antiwar Americans to evade—or persuade others to evade—the draft had been a primary trigger for the government's internal security programs. Government lawyers argued that attempts to subvert the draft were by definition direct threats to the war effort and could therefore be suppressed. The Supreme Court in 1918 had agreed, but in 1945 the justices were less likely to do so.

COURT OPINION BY JUSTICE ROBERTS. The conspiracy charged was to counsel diverse persons to *evade, resist,* and *refuse service* in the land and naval forces of the United States in violation of § 11 of the Selective Training and Service Act of 1940, 50 U.S.C. App. 311....

The 25 defendants [members of the German-American Bund] were tried together.... The Government correctly states that the evidence offered by the prosecutor falls into two classes: (1) that touching the German-American Bund and its purposes, which was offered to indicate the motives and purposes for the defendants' statements and actions; and (2) evidence touching specific actions, conduct, and statements tending to show the existence of a conspiracy and the steps taken pursuant to it. The evidence in the first category is overwhelmingly greater in volume than that in the second. Indeed a question arises whether it was not an abuse of discretion to permit the Government to go, at such inordinate length, into evidence concerning the Bund and its predecessor, the Friends of New Germany, during a period of seven years prior to the inception of the alleged conspiracy; and concerning Bund uniforms and paraphernalia, and pictures and literature in the possession of various defendants....

The professed purpose of the Bund was to keep alive the German spirit among persons of German blood in the United States. Speeches and literature justify the inference that the Bund endorsed the Nazi movement in Germany and, if it did not actually advocate some such form of government in this country, at least essayed to create public opinion favorable to the Hitler regime and to the German National Socialist State. The Bund was also anti-British and opposed our entering the war on the side of the British; its aim was to keep us neutral and friendly to the new Germany....

The Bund desired this country to maintain neutrality by not having our soldiers go to foreign shores. These views were then shared by many loyal citizens, and some of them were enacted into law by Congress....

Bund Command No. 37 on October 1, 1940 [stated that] ... "EVERY MAN, if he can, will REFUSE *to do military duty until this law and all other laws of the country or the states which confine the citizenship rights of Bund members* ARE REVOKED!" ...

[T]he Government's case is really pitched on this command, which it construes as a counsel to *evade* military service....

Now the surest way of rendering oneself incapable of evading military service, of slipping away or escaping it, is to register. And the

Bund command which is at the core of the Government's case enjoins registration in the strongest terms. That accomplished, a refusal to serve may follow when the registrant is to be inducted. But to counsel merely refusal is not made criminal by the Act. . . .

[W]e are of opinion, first, that the promulgation and communication of Bund Command No. 37 was not in itself a counsel to evade; second, that the evidence of the general disposition of the petitioners either towards the Government of the United States or towards the Selective Service Act did not make the Command such; third, that the evidence and oral statements of the various petitioners at committee meetings and unit meetings of the Bund did not supply the basis for a finding, beyond a reasonable doubt, of counselling, or intending to counsel, or conspiring to counsel, evasion of military service within the meaning of § 11 of the statute. We are of the view, therefore, that, on the case made by the Government, the defendants were entitled to the direction of acquittal, for which they moved.

Cramer v. United States 325 U.S. 1 (1945)

Charges of treason against wartime dissenters are relatively frequent in politics and social intercourse. Where the law is concerned, however, treason is an uncommon accusation, and very difficult to prove. The Constitution places strict limitations on treason proceedings, requiring two witnesses to an overt act. Early in the nation's history, the Supreme Court made certain that these provisions would be rigidly enforced, so that treason could not be used as a political weapon. Treason cases were subsequently rare, and during World War II government officials discovered that the justices fully intended to uphold tradition by making treason charges difficult to sustain.

COURT OPINION BY JUSTICE JACKSON. Anthony Cramer, the petitioner, stands convicted of violating Section 1 of the Criminal Code, which provides: "Whoever, owing allegiance to the United States, levies war against them or adheres to their enemies, giving them aid and comfort within the United States or elsewhere, is guilty of treason."

Cramer owed allegiance to the United States. A German by birth, he had been a resident of the United States since 1925 and was naturalized in 1936. Prosecution resulted from his association with two of the German saboteurs who in June 1942 landed on our shores from enemy submarines to disrupt industry in the United States. . . .

There was no evidence, and the Government makes no claim, that he had foreknowledge that the saboteurs were coming to this country or that he came into association with them by prearrangement. Cramer, however, had known intimately the saboteur Werner Thiel while the latter lived in this country. They had worked together, roomed together, and jointly had ventured in a small and luckless delicatessen enterprise. Thiel early and frankly avowed adherence to the National Socialist movement in Germany; he foresaw the war and returned in 1941 for the purpose of helping Germany. Cramer did not do so. How much he sympathized with the doctrines of the Nazi Party is not clear. . . .

Coming down to the time of the alleged treason, the main facts, as related on the witness stand by Cramer, are not seriously in dispute. He was living in New York; and in response to a cryptic note left under his door, which did not mention Thiel, he went to the Grand Central Station. There Thiel appeared. Cramer had supposed that Thiel was in Germany, knowing that he had left the United States shortly before the war to go there. Together they went to public places and had some drinks. Cramer denies that Thiel revealed his mission of sabotage. Cramer said to Thiel that he must have come to America by submarine, but Thiel refused to confirm it, although his attitude increased Cramer's suspicion. Thiel promised to tell later how he came to this country. Thiel asked about a girl who was a mutual acquaintance and whom Thiel had engaged to marry previous to his going to Germany. Cramer knew where she was, and offered to and did write to her to come to New York, without disclosing in the letter that Thiel had arrived. Thiel said that he had in his possession about $3,600, but did not disclose that it was provided by the German Government, saying only that one could get money in Germany if he had the right connections. Thiel owed Cramer an old debt of $200. He gave Cramer his money belt containing some $3,600, from which Cramer was to be paid. Cramer agreed to and did place the rest in his own safe-deposit box, except a sum which he kept in his room in case Thiel should want it quickly.

After the second of these meetings Thiel and Kerling, who was present briefly at one meeting, were arrested. Cramer's expectation of meeting Thiel later and of bringing him and his fiancée together was foiled. Shortly thereafter Cramer was arrested, tried, and found guilty....

Cramer's case raises questions as to application of the constitutional provision that "Treason against the United States shall consist only in levying War against them, or in adhering to their Enemies, giving them Aid and Comfort. No person shall be convicted of Treason unless on the Testimony of two Witnesses to the same overt Act, or on Confession in open Court." ...

When our forefathers took up the task of forming an independent political organization for New World society, no one of them appears to have doubted that to bring into being a new government would originate a new allegiance for its citizens and inhabitants. Nor were they reluctant to punish as treason any genuine breach of allegiance, as every government time out of mind had done....

However, their experience with treason accusations had been many-sided. More than a few of them were descendants of those who had fled from measures against sedition and its ecclesiastic counterpart, heresy. Now the treason offense was under revision by a Convention whose members almost to a man had themselves been guilty of treason under any interpretation of British law....

The temper and attitude of the [1787 Constitutional] Convention toward treason prosecutions is unmistakable. It adopted every limitation that the practice of governments had evolved or that politico-legal philosophy to that time had advanced....

Distrust of treason prosecutions was not just a transient mood of the Revolutionists. In the century and a half of our national existence not one execution on a federal treason conviction has taken place. Never before has this Court had occasion to review a conviction....

Thus the crime of treason consists of two elements: adherence to the enemy; and rendering him aid and comfort. A citizen intellectually or emotionally may favor the enemy and harbor sympathies or convictions disloyal to this country's policy or interest, but so long as he commits no act of aid and comfort to the enemy, there is no treason. On the other hand, a citizen may take actions which do aid and comfort the enemy—making a speech critical of the government or opposing its measures, profiteering, striking in defense plants or essential work, and the hundred other things which impair our cohesion and diminish our strength—but if there is no adherence to the enemy in this, if there is no intent to betray, there is no treason....

Since intent must be inferred from conduct of some sort, we think it is permissible to draw usual reasonable inferences as to intent from the overt acts. The law of treason, like the law of lesser crimes, assumes every man to intend the natural consequences which one standing in his circumstances and possessing his knowledge would reasonably expect to result from his acts. Proof that a citizen did give aid and comfort to an enemy may well be in the circumstances sufficient evidence that he adhered to that enemy and intended and purposed to strike at his own country. It may be doubted whether it would be what the founders intended, or whether it would well serve any of the ends they cherished, to hold the treason offense available to punish only those who make their treacherous intentions more evident than may be done by rendering aid and comfort to an enemy. Treason—insidious and dangerous treason—is the work of the shrewd and crafty more often than of the simple and impulsive. . . .

The very minimum function that an overt act must perform in a treason prosecution is that it show sufficient action by the accused, in its setting, to sustain a finding that the accused actually gave aid and comfort to the enemy. Every act, movement, deed, and word of the defendant charged to constitute treason must be supported by the testimony of two witnesses. The two-witness principle is to interdict imputation of *incriminating acts* to the accused by circumstantial evidence or by the testimony of a single witness. The prosecution cannot rely on evidence which does not meet the constitutional test for overt acts to create any inference that the accused did other acts or did something more than was shown in the overt act, in order to make a giving of aid and comfort to the enemy. The words of the Constitution were chosen, not to make it hard to prove merely routine and everyday acts, but to make the proof of acts that convict of treason as sure as trial processes may. When the prosecution's case is thus established, the Constitution does not prevent presentation of corroborative or cumulative evidence of any admissible character either to strengthen a direct case or to rebut the testimony or inferences on behalf of defendant. The Government is not prevented from making a strong case; it is denied a conviction on a weak one. . . .

We proceed to consider the application of these principles to Cramer's case. . . .

The Government contends that outside of the overt acts, and by lesser degree of proof, it has shown a treasonable intent on Cramer's part in meeting and talking with Thiel and Kerling. But if it showed him disposed to betray, and showed that he had opportunity to do so, it still has not proved in the manner required that he did any acts submitted to the jury as a basis for conviction which had the effect of betraying by giving aid and comfort. To take the intent for the deed would carry us back to constructive treasons. . . .

The Government has urged that our initial interpretation of the treason clause should be less exacting, lest treason be too hard to prove and the Government disabled from adequately combating the techniques of modern warfare. But the treason offense is not the only nor can it well serve as the principal legal weapon to vindicate our national cohesion and security. . . .

The framers' effort to compress into two sentences the law of one of the most intricate of crimes gives a superficial appearance of clarity and simplicity which proves illusory when it is put to practical application. There are few subjects on which the temptation to utter abstract interpretative generalizations is greater or on which they are more to be distrusted. The little clause is packed with controversy and difficulty. The offense is one of subtlety, and it is easy to demonstrate lack of logic in almost any interpretation by hypothetical cases, to which real treasons rarely will conform. The protection of the two-witness requirement, limited as it is to overt acts, may be wholly unrelated to the real controversial factors in a case. We would be understood as speaking only in the light of the facts and of the issues raised in the case under consideration, although that leaves many undetermined grounds of dispute which, after the method of the common law, we may defer until they are presented by facts which may throw greater light on their significance. . . .

Certainly the treason rule, whether wisely or not, is severely restrictive. . . . Time has not made the accusation of treachery less poisonous, nor the task of judging one charged with betraying the country, including his triers, less susceptible to the influence of suspicion and rancor. The innovations made by the forefathers in the law of treason were conceived in a faith such as [Revolutionary-era writer Thomas] Paine put in the maxim that "He that would make his own liberty secure must guard even his enemy from oppression; for if he violates this duty he establishes a precedent that will reach himself." We still put trust in it.

We hold that overt acts 1 and 2 are insufficient as proved to support the judgment of conviction, which accordingly is *Reversed.*

Haupt v. United States 330 U.S. 631 (1947)

In the Cramer *case, the Court was terribly worried about how treason accusations could be used (or abused) to suppress dissent—so much so that some observers felt the Court had gutted the treason laws altogether, making convictions practically impossible. Apparently some on the Court worried they had gone too far as well. Two years later, the Court upheld a treason conviction of another accused German saboteur. Compare this case with the* Cramer *opinion: How did they differ? How were they alike? Is the Court contradicting its earlier ruling?*

COURT OPINION BY JUSTICE JACKSON. Petitioner, Hans Max Haupt was indicted for treason, convicted and sentenced to life imprisonment and to pay a fine of $10,000. . . .

Petitioner is the father of Herbert Haupt, one of the eight saboteurs convicted by a military tribunal. . . . Sheltering his son, assisting him in getting a job, and in acquiring an automobile, all alleged to be with knowledge of the son's mission, involved defendant in the treason charge.

The background facts are not in dispute. The defendant is a naturalized citizen, born in Germany. He came to this country in 1923 and lived in or near Chicago. In 1939 the son, Herbert, who had also been born in Germany, worked for the Simpson Optical Company in Chicago which manufactured lenses for instruments, including parts for the Norden bomb sight. In the spring of 1941 Herbert went to Mexico and, with the aid of the German Consul, from there to Japan and thence to Germany where he entered the employ of the German Government and was trained in sabotage work.

On the 17th of June 1942, Herbert returned to the United States by submarine. His mission was to act as a secret agent, spy and saboteur for the German Reich. He was instructed to proceed to Chicago, to procure an automobile for the use of himself and his confederates in their work of sabotage and espionage, to obtain reemployment with the Simpson Optical Company where he was to gather information, particularly as to the vital parts and bottlenecks of the plant, to be communicated to his coconspirators to guide their attack. He came with various other instructions, equipped with large sums of money, and went to Chicago.

After some six days there, Herbert was arrested on June 27, 1942, having been under surveillance by Government agents during his entire stay in Chicago. This petitioner was thereafter taken into custody and was arraigned on July 21, 1942. He later asked to talk to an F.B.I. agent, two of whom were summoned, and he appears to have volunteered considerable information and to have given more in answer to their questions. He blamed certain others for the predicament of his son and wanted to testify against them. For this purpose, he disclosed that he had been present when Herbert had told the complete story of his trip to Mexico, Japan, his return to the United States by submarine, and his bringing large sums of money with him. During his confinement in the Cook County jail, he also talked with two fellow prisoners concerning his case and they testified as to damaging admissions made to them.

The indictment alleged twenty-nine overt acts of treason. Its sufficiency was challenged by demurrer which was overruled and by a motion to quash which was denied. The defendant, at the close of the Government's case and again at the close of all the evidence, made motions for a directed verdict generally and also specifically as to each overt act charged, all of which were denied. Seventeen of the overt acts were withdrawn before submission and twelve were submitted to the jury. Generally stated, the overt acts submitted fall into three groups of charges: First, the charge that this defendant accompanied his son to assist him in obtaining employment in a plant engaged in manufacturing the Norden bomb sight; second, the charge of harboring and sheltering Herbert Haupt; and third, the charge of accompanying Herbert to an automobile sales agency, arranging, making payment for and purchasing an automobile for Herbert. Each of these was alleged to be in aid of Herbert's known purpose of sabotage.

The defendant argues here that the overt acts submitted do not constitute acts of treason, but that each is commonplace, insignificant and colorless, and not sufficient, even if properly proved, to support a conviction. We have held that the minimum function of the overt act in a treason prosecution is that it show action by the accused which really was aid and comfort to the enemy. *Cramer v. United States,* 325 U.S. 1, 34. This is a separate inquiry from that as to whether the acts were done because of adherence to the enemy, for acts helpful to the enemy may nevertheless be innocent of treasonable character.

Cramer's case held that what must be proved by the testimony of two witnesses is a "sufficient" overt act. There the only proof by two witnesses of two of the three overt acts submitted to the jury was that the defendant had met and talked with enemy agents. We did not set aside Cramer's conviction because two witnesses did not testify to the treasonable character of his meeting with the enemy agents. It was reversed because the Court found that the act which two witnesses saw could not on their testimony be said to have given assistance or comfort to anyone, whether it was done treacherously or not. To make a sufficient overt act, the Court thought it would have been necessary to assume that the meeting or talk was of assistance to the enemy, or to rely on other than two-witness proof. Here, on the contrary, such assumption or reliance is unnecessary—there can be no question that sheltering, or helping to buy a car, or helping to get employment is helpful to an enemy agent, that they were of aid and comfort to Herbert Haupt in his mission of sabotage. They have the unmistakable quality which was found lacking in the *Cramer* case of forwarding the saboteur in his mission. We pointed out that Cramer furnished no shelter, sustenance or supplies. The overt acts charged here, on the contrary, may be generalized as furnishing harbor and shelter for a period of six days, assisting in obtaining employment in the lens plant and helping to buy an automobile. No matter whether young Haupt's mission was benign or traitorous, known or unknown to defendant, these acts were aid and comfort to him. In the light of his mission and his instructions, they were more than casually useful; they were aid in steps essential to his design for treason. If proof be added that the defendant knew of his son's instructions, preparation and plans, the purpose to aid and comfort the enemy becomes clear. All of this, of course, assumes that the prosecution's evidence properly in the case is credited, as the jury had a right to do. We hold, therefore, that the overt acts laid in the indictment and submitted to the jury do perform the functions assigned to overt acts in treason cases and are sufficient to support the indictment and to sustain the conviction if they were proved with the exactitude required by the Constitution.

OPINION BY JUSTICE DOUGLAS. There is a close parallel between this case and *Cramer v. United States*, 325 U.S. 1.

Two witnesses saw Cramer talking with an enemy agent. So far as they knew, the conversation may have been wholly innocent, as they did not overhear it. But Cramer, by his own testimony at the trial, explained what took place: he knew or had reason to believe that the agent was here on a mission for the enemy and arranged, among other things, to conceal the funds brought here to promote the project. Thus there was the most credible evidence that Cramer was guilty of "adhering" to the enemy, giving him "aid and comfort." Article III, § 3 of the Constitution. And the overt act which joined him with the enemy agent was proved by two witnesses. Cramer's conviction, however, was set aside because two witnesses did not testify to the treasonable character of Cramer's meeting with the enemy agent.

Two witnesses saw the son enter Haupt's apartment house at night and leave in the morning. That act, without more, was as innocent as Cramer's conversation with the agent. For nothing would be more natural and normal, or more "commonplace" (325 U.S. p. 34), or less suspicious, or less "incriminating" (325 U.S. p. 35), than the act of a father opening the family door to a son. That act raised, therefore, no more implication that the father was giving his son aid and comfort in a treasonable project than did the meeting of the defendant with the enemy agent in the *Cramer* case. But that act, wholly innocent on its face, was shown to be of a treasonable character, not by the two witnesses, but by other evidence: that Haupt was sympathetic with the Nazi cause, that he knew the nature of his son's mission to this country. Haupt's conviction is sustained, though the conversion of an innocent appearing act into a treasonable act is not made by two witnesses. . . .

As the *Cramer* case makes plain, the overt act and the intent with which it is done are separate and distinct elements of the crime. Intent need not be proved by two witnesses but may be inferred from all the circumstances surrounding the overt act. But if two witnesses are not required to prove treasonable intent, two witnesses need not be required to show the treasonable character of the overt act. For proof of treasonable intent in the doing of the overt act necessarily involves proof that the accused committed the overt act with the knowledge or understanding of its treasonable character.

The requirement of an overt act is to make certain a treasonable project has moved from the realm of thought into the realm of action. That requirement is undeniably met in the present case, as it was in the case of *Cramer*.

The *Cramer* case departed from those rules when it held that "The two-witness principle is to interdict imputation of *incriminating acts* to the accused by circumstantial evidence or by the testimony of a single witness." 325 U.S. p. 35. The present decision is truer to the constitutional definition of treason when it forsakes that test and holds that an act, quite innocent on its face, does not need two witnesses to be transformed into an incriminating one.

DISSENT BY JUSTICE MURPHY. Petitioner was charged with having committed three general types of overt acts of treason: (1) harboring and sheltering his son; (2) assisting his son in obtaining reemployment; (3) accompanying and assisting his son in the purchase of an automobile. All of these alleged overt acts were contained in a single count of the indictment and the jury's verdict was a general one. The Court indicates that a fatal deficiency as to any of the alleged overt acts under such circumstances invalidates the conviction. Since the acts relating to the harboring and sheltering of petitioner's son did not, in my opinion, amount to overt acts of treason, I would accordingly reverse the judgment below, regardless of the sufficiency of the other acts.

The high crime of treason, as I understand it, consists of an act rendering aid and comfort to the enemy by one who adheres to the enemy's cause. *Cramer v. United States,* 325 U.S. 1. The act may be one which extends material aid; or it may be one which merely lends comfort and encouragement. The act may appear to be innocent on its face, yet prove to be treasonable in nature when examined in light of its purpose and context.

It does not follow, however, that every act that gives aid and comfort to an enemy agent constitutes an overt act of treason, even though the agent's status is known. The touch of one who aids is not Midas-like, giving a treasonable hue to every move. An act of assistance may be of the type which springs from the well of human kindness, from the natural devotion to family and friends, or from a practical application of religious tenets. Such acts are not treasonous, however else they may be described. They are not treasonous even though, in a sense, they help in the effectuation of the unlawful purpose. To rise to the status of an overt act of treason, an act of assistance must be utterly incompatible with any of the foregoing sources of action. It must be an act which is consistent only with a treasonable intention and with the accomplishment of the treasonable plan, giving due consideration to all the relevant surrounding circumstances. Thus an act of supplying a military map to a saboteur for use in the execution of his nefarious plot is an overt act of treason since it excludes all possibility of having been motivated by non-treasonable considerations. But an act of providing a meal to an enemy agent who is also one's son retains the possibility of having a non-treasonable basis even when performed in a treasonable setting; accordingly, it cannot qualify as an overt act of treason.

It is true that reasonable doubts may be raised as to whether or not the prime motive for an act was treasonous. Yet the nature of some acts is such that a non-treasonous motive cannot be completely dismissed as a possibility. An overt act of treason, however, should rest upon something more substantial than a reasonable doubt. Treason is different from ordinary crimes, possessing unique and difficult standards of proof which confine it within narrow spheres. It has such serious connotations that its substance cannot be left to conjecture. Only when the alleged overt act manifests treason beyond all reasonable doubt can we be certain that the traitor's stigma will be limited to those whose actions constitute a real threat to the safety of the nation.

Tested by that standard, the conviction in the instant case cannot be sustained. . . .

Ex parte Quirin 317 U.S. 1 (1942)

For various reasons, government officials in time of war prefer trying accused spies and saboteurs by military commission, if possible. To their way of thinking, military trials are less risky because, lacking a civilian jury, military tribunals run by soldiers are less likely to acquit. Also, the rules of evidence are less stringent, the proceedings are held in secret (thereby safeguarding any sensitive security information that might be exposed during the trial), and guarding prisoners from outside contact with their compatriots is much easier. Of course, civil libertarians deplore such trials as subversive of personal liberties. Early in World War II, the Supreme Court confronted the question of whether or not military trials for several accused German saboteurs were permissible. The justices felt this matter was so urgent that they took the unusual step of setting aside a special term of the Court devoted only to the arguments on both sides of the case.

COURT OPINION BY JUSTICE STONE. The question for decision is whether the detention of petitioners by respondent for trial by Military Commission, appointed by Order of the President of July 2, 1942, on charges preferred against them purporting to set out their violations of the law of war and of the Articles of War, is in conformity to the laws and Constitution of the United States.

After denial of their applications by the District Court, 47 F. Supp. 431, petitioners asked leave to file petitions for habeas corpus in this Court. In view of the public importance of the questions raised by their petitions and of the duty which rests on the courts, in time of war as well as in time of peace, to preserve unimpaired the constitutional safeguards of civil liberty, and because in our opinion the public interest required that we consider and decide those questions without any avoidable delay, we directed that petitioners' applications be set down for full oral argument at a special term of this Court, convened on July 29, 1942. . . .

The following facts appear from the petitions or are stipulated. Except as noted they are undisputed.

All the petitioners were born in Germany; all have lived in the United States. . . .

After the declaration of war between the United States and the German Reich, petitioners received training at a sabotage school near Berlin, Germany, where they were instructed in the use of explosives and in methods of secret writing. Thereafter petitioners, with a German citizen, Dasch, proceeded from Germany to a seaport in Occupied France, where petitioners Burger, Heinck and Quirin, together with Dasch, boarded a German submarine which proceeded across the Atlantic to Amagansett Beach on Long Island, New York. The four were there landed from the submarine in the hours of darkness, on or about June 13, 1942, carrying with them a supply of explosives, fuses, and incendiary and timing devices. While landing they wore German Marine Infantry uniforms or parts of uniforms. Immediately after landing they buried their uniforms and the other articles mentioned, and proceeded in civilian dress to New York City.

The remaining four petitioners at the same French port boarded another German submarine, which carried them across the Atlantic to Ponte Vedra Beach, Florida. On or about June 17, 1942, they came ashore during the hours of darkness, wearing caps of the German Marine Infantry and carrying with them a supply of explosives, fuses, and incendiary and timing devices. They immediately buried their caps and the other articles mentioned, and proceeded in civilian dress to Jacksonville, Florida, and thence to various points in the United States. All were taken into custody in New York or Chicago by agents of the Federal Bureau of Investigation. All had received instructions in Germany from an officer of the German High Command to destroy war industries and war facilities in the United States, for which they or their relatives in Germany were to receive salary payments from the German Government. . . .

The President, as President and Commander in Chief of the Army and Navy, by Order of July 2, 1942, appointed a Military Commission and directed it to try petitioners for offenses against the law of war and the Articles of War, and prescribed regulations for the procedure on the trial and for review of the record of the trial and of any judgment or sentence of the Commission. On the same day, by Proclamation, the President declared that "all persons who are subjects, citizens or residents of any nation at war with the United States or who give obedience to or act under the direction of any such nation, and who during time of war enter or attempt to enter the United States . . . through coastal or boundary defenses, and are charged with committing or attempting or preparing to commit sabotage, espionage, hostile or warlike acts, or violations of the law of war, shall be subject to the law of war and to the jurisdiction of military tribunals." . . .

Petitioners' main contention is that the President is without any statutory or constitutional authority to order the petitioners to be tried by military tribunal for offenses with which they are charged; that in consequence they are entitled to be tried in the civil courts with the safeguards, including trial by jury, which the Fifth and Sixth Amendments guarantee to all persons charged in such courts with criminal offenses. . . .

The Government challenges each of these propositions. But regardless of their merits, it also insists that petitioners must be denied access to the courts, both because they are enemy aliens or have entered our territory as enemy belligerents, and because the President's Proclamation undertakes in terms to deny such access to the class of persons defined by the Proclamation, which aptly describes the character and conduct of petitioners. . . .

We are not here concerned with any question of the guilt or innocence of petitioners. Constitutional safeguards for the protection of all who are charged with offenses are not to be disregarded in order to inflict merited punishment on some who are guilty. . . . But the detention and trial of petitioners—ordered by the President in the declared exercise of his powers as Commander in Chief of the Army in time of war and of grave public danger—are not to be set aside by the courts without the clear conviction that they are in conflict with the Constitution or laws of Congress constitutionally enacted. . . .

An important incident to the conduct of war is the adoption of measures by the military command not only to repel and defeat the enemy, but to seize and subject to disciplinary measures those enemies who in their attempt to thwart or impede our military effort have violated the law of war. It is unnecessary for present purposes to determine to what extent the President as Commander in Chief has constitutional power to create military commissions without the support of Congressional legislation. For here Congress has authorized trial of offenses against the law of war before such commissions. We are concerned only with the question whether it is within the constitutional power of the National Government to place petitioners upon trial before a military commission for the offenses with which they are charged. We must therefore first inquire whether any of the acts charged is an offense against the law of war cognizable before a military tribunal, and if so whether the Constitution prohibits the trial. . . . [T]hese petitioners were charged with an offense against the law of war which the Constitution does not require to be tried by jury.

By universal agreement and practice, the law of war draws a distinction between the armed forces and the peaceful populations of belligerent nations and also between those who are lawful and unlawful combatants. Lawful combatants are subject to capture and detention as prisoners of war by opposing military forces. Unlawful combatants are likewise subject to capture and detention, but in addition they are subject to trial and punishment by military tribunals for acts which render their belligerency unlawful. The spy who secretly and without uniform passes the military lines of a belligerent in time of war, seeking to gather military information and communicate it to the enemy, or an enemy combatant who without uniform comes secretly through the lines for the purpose of waging war by destruction of life or property, are familiar examples of belligerents who are generally deemed not to be entitled to the status of prisoners of war, but to be offenders against the law of war subject to trial and punishment by military tribunals. . . .

Our Government, by thus defining lawful belligerents entitled to be treated as prisoners of war, has recognized that there is a class of unlawful belligerents not entitled to that privilege, including those who, though combatants, do not wear "fixed and distinctive emblems." And by Article 15 of the Articles of War Congress has made provision for their trial and punishment by military commission, according to "the law of war."

By a long course of practical administrative construction by its military authorities, our Government has likewise recognized that those who during time of war pass surreptitiously from enemy territory into our own, discarding their uniforms upon entry, for the commission of hostile acts involving destruction of life or property, have the status of unlawful combatants punishable as such by military commission. . . .

As we have seen, entry upon our territory in time of war by enemy belligerents, including those acting under the direction of the armed forces of the enemy, for the purpose of destroying property used or useful in prosecuting the war, is a hostile and warlike act. It subjects those who participate in it without uniform to the punishment prescribed by the law of war for unlawful belligerents. It is without significance that petitioners were not alleged to have borne conventional weapons or that their proposed hostile acts did not necessarily contemplate collision with the Armed Forces of the United States. Paragraphs 351 and 352 of the Rules of Land Warfare, already referred to, plainly contemplate that the hostile acts and purposes for which unlawful belligerents may be punished are not limited to assaults on the Armed Forces of the United States. Modern warfare is directed at the destruction of enemy war supplies and the implements of their production and transportation, quite as much as at the armed forces. Every consideration which makes the unlawful belligerent punishable is equally applicable whether his objective is the one or the other. The law of war cannot rightly treat those agents of enemy armies who enter our territory, armed with explosives intended for the destruction of war industries and supplies, as any the less belligerent enemies than are agents similarly entering for the purpose of destroying fortified places or our Armed Forces. By passing our boundaries for such purposes without uniform or other emblem signifying their belligerent status, or by discarding that means of identification after entry, such enemies become unlawful belligerents subject to trial and punishment.

Citizenship in the United States of an enemy belligerent does not relieve him from the consequences of a belligerency which is unlawful because in violation of the law of war. Citizens who associate themselves with the military arm of the enemy government, and with its aid, guidance and direction enter this country bent on hostile acts, are enemy belligerents within the meaning of the Hague Convention and the law of war. . . .

Nor are petitioners any the less belligerents if, as they argue, they have not actually committed or attempted to commit any act of depredation or entered the theatre or zone of active military operations. . . .

But petitioners insist that, even if the offenses with which they are charged are offenses against the law of war, their trial is subject to the requirement of the Fifth Amendment that no person shall be held to answer for a capital or otherwise infamous crime unless on a presentment or indictment of a grand jury, and that such trials by Article III,

§ 2, and the Sixth Amendment must be by jury in a civil court. Before the Amendments, § 2 of Article III, the Judiciary Article, had provided, "The Trial of all Crimes, except in Cases of Impeachment, shall be by Jury," and had directed that "such Trial shall be held in the State where the said Crimes shall have been committed." . . .

[W]e must conclude that § 2 of Article III and the Fifth and Sixth Amendments cannot be taken to have extended the right to demand a jury to trials by military commission, or to have required that offenses against the law of war not triable by jury at common law be tried only in the civil courts. . . .

We cannot say that Congress in preparing the Fifth and Sixth Amendments intended to extend trial by jury to the cases of alien or citizen offenders against the law of war otherwise triable by military commission, while withholding it from members of our own armed forces charged with infractions of the Articles of War punishable by death. It is equally inadmissible to construe the Amendments—whose primary purpose was to continue unimpaired presentment by grand jury and trial by petit jury in all those cases in which they had been customary—as either abolishing all trials by military tribunals, save those of the personnel of our own armed forces, or, what in effect comes to the same thing, as imposing on all such tribunals the necessity of proceeding against unlawful enemy belligerents only on presentment and trial by jury. We conclude that the Fifth and Sixth Amendments did not restrict whatever authority was conferred by the Constitution to try offenses against the law of war by military commission, and that petitioners, charged with such an offense not required to be tried by jury at common law, were lawfully placed on trial by the Commission without a jury.

In re Yamashita 327 U.S. 1 (1946)

World War II witnessed the worst atrocities in human history, with millions of dead people in German concentration camps, the grisly genocide of the Holocaust, and wartime atrocities like the Rape of Nanking and the Bataan death march. When the war was over, the allies faced the difficult task of formulating appropriate trials and punishments for enemy personnel accused of committing these atrocities. The case of Japanese General Yamashita Tomoyuki posed particularly complex problems. Soldiers under his command had in 1942 perpetrated the infamous Bataan death march, during which thou-

*sands of American prisoners of war were bayoneted, shot, or starved
to death. When Yamashita surrendered himself to U.S. authorities in
1945, he was placed on trial in a military court for failing to prevent
his men from carrying out the death march atrocities. He was found
guilty and sentenced to be executed; he appealed his case to the
Supreme Court.*

*The Court declined to hear his case, thereby suggesting that a
purely military trial in such circumstances was appropriate and just.
In the majority opinion, Justice Stone offers important reasons for doing so. Note also the lengthy and eloquent dissent by Justice Murphy,
who raised interesting and troubling issues of how the laws of war
could be fairly applied to judge defeated enemies fairly.*

COURT OPINION BY JUSTICE STONE. [P]rior to September 3,
1945, petitioner was the Commanding General of the Fourteenth
Army Group of the Imperial Japanese Army in the Philippine Islands.
On that date he surrendered to and became a prisoner of war of the
United States Army Forces in Baguio, Philippine Islands.... On October 8, 1945, petitioner, after pleading not guilty to the charge, was
held for trial before a military commission of five Army officers appointed by order of General Styer. The order appointed six Army officers, all lawyers, as defense counsel. Throughout the proceedings
which followed, including those before this Court, defense counsel
have demonstrated their professional skill and resourcefulness and
their proper zeal for the defense with which they were charged.

On the same date a bill of particulars was filed by the prosecution,
and the commission heard a motion made in petitioner's behalf to dismiss the charge on the ground that it failed to state a violation of the
law of war. On October 29th the commission was reconvened, a sup-
plemental bill of particulars was filed, and the motion to dismiss was
denied. The trial then proceeded until its conclusion on December 7,
1945, the commission hearing two hundred and eighty-six witnesses,
who gave over three thousand pages of testimony. On that date petitioner was found guilty of the offense as charged and sentenced to
death by hanging....

Congress, in the exercise of the power conferred upon it by Article
I, § 8, Cl. 10 of the Constitution to "define and punish ... Offences
against the Law of Nations ...," of which the law of war is a part, had
by the Articles of War (10 U.S.C. §§ 1471–1593) recognized the "military commission" appointed by military command, as it had previ-

ously existed in United States Army practice, as an appropriate tribunal for the trial and punishment of offenses against the law of war. . . .

[B]y sanctioning trial of enemy combatants for violations of the law of war by military commission, [Congress] had not attempted to codify the law of war or to mark its precise boundaries. Instead, by Article 15 it had incorporated, by reference, as within the preexisting jurisdiction of military commissions created by appropriate military command, all offenses which are defined as such by the law of war, and which may constitutionally be included within that jurisdiction. It thus adopted the system of military common law applied by military tribunals so far as it should be recognized and deemed applicable by the courts, and as further defined and supplemented by the Hague Convention, to which the United States and the Axis powers were parties.

[W]e are not concerned with the guilt or innocence of the petitioners. We consider here only the lawful power of the commission to try the petitioner for the offense charged. In the present cases it must be recognized throughout that the military tribunals which Congress has sanctioned by the Articles of War are not courts whose rulings and judgments are made subject to review by this Court. . . .

[T]he order creating the commission for the trial of petitioner was authorized by military command, and was in complete conformity to the Act of Congress sanctioning the creation of such tribunals for the trial of offenses against the law of war committed by enemy combatants. And we turn to the question of whether the authority to create the commission and direct the trial by military order continued after the cessation of hostilities.

An important incident to the conduct of war is the adoption of measures by the military commander, not only to repel and defeat the enemy, but to seize and subject to disciplinary measures those enemies who, in their attempt to thwart or impede our military effort, have violated the law of war. . . . The trial and punishment of enemy combatants who have committed violations of the law of war is thus not only a part of the conduct of war operating as a preventive measure against such violations, but is an exercise of the authority sanctioned by Congress to administer the system of military justice recognized by the law of war. That sanction is without qualification as to the exercise of this authority so long as a state of war exists—from its declaration until peace is proclaimed. . . . The war power, from which the commission derives its existence, is not limited to victories in the field, but carries with it the inherent power to guard against the immediate renewal of the conflict, and to remedy, at least in ways Congress has recognized, the evils which the military operations have produced. . . .

We cannot say that there is no authority to convene a commission after hostilities have ended to try violations of the law of war committed before their cessation, at least until peace has been officially recognized by treaty or proclamation of the political branch of the Government. In fact, in most instances the practical administration of the system of military justice under the law of war would fail if such authority were thought to end with the cessation of hostilities. For only after their cessation could the greater number of offenders and the principal ones be apprehended and subjected to trial. . . .

It is evident that the conduct of military operations by troops whose excesses are unrestrained by the orders or efforts of their commander would almost certainly result in violations which it is the purpose of the law of war to prevent. Its purpose to protect civilian populations and prisoners of war from brutality would largely be defeated if the commander of an invading army could with impunity neglect to take reasonable measures for their protection. Hence the law of war presupposes that its violation is to be avoided through the control of the operations of war by commanders who are to some extent responsible for their subordinates.

These provisions [of international law] plainly imposed on petitioner, who at the time specified was military governor of the Philippines, as well as commander of the Japanese forces, an affirmative duty to take such measures as were within his power and appropriate in the circumstances to protect prisoners of war and the civilian population.

DISSENT BY JUSTICE MURPHY. The significance of the issue facing the Court today cannot be overemphasized. An American military commission has been established to try a fallen military commander of a conquered nation for an alleged war crime. The authority for such action grows out of the exercise of the power conferred upon Congress by Article I, § 8, Cl. 10 of the Constitution to "define and punish . . . Offences against the Law of Nations. . . ." The grave issue raised by this case is whether a military commission so established and so authorized may disregard the procedural rights of an accused person as guaranteed by the Constitution, especially by the due process clause of the Fifth Amendment.

The answer is plain. The Fifth Amendment guarantee of due process of law applies to "any person" who is accused of a crime by the

Federal Government or any of its agencies. No exception is made as to those who are accused of war crimes or as to those who possess the status of an enemy belligerent. Indeed, such an exception would be contrary to the whole philosophy of human rights which makes the Constitution the great living document that it is. The immutable rights of the individual, including those secured by the due process clause of the Fifth Amendment, belong not alone to the members of those nations that excel on the battlefield or that subscribe to the democratic ideology. They belong to every person in the world, victor or vanquished, whatever may be his race, color or beliefs. They rise above any status of belligerency or outlawry. They survive any popular passion or frenzy of the moment. No court or legislature or executive, not even the mightiest army in the world, can ever destroy them. Such is the universal and indestructible nature of the rights which the due process clause of the Fifth Amendment recognizes and protects when life or liberty is threatened by virtue of the authority of the United States.

The existence of these rights, unfortunately, is not always respected. They are often trampled under by those who are motivated by hatred, aggression or fear. But in this nation individual rights are recognized and protected, at least in regard to governmental action. They cannot be ignored by any branch of the Government, even the military, except under the most extreme and urgent circumstances.

The failure of the military commission to obey the dictates of the due process requirements of the Fifth Amendment is apparent in this case. The petitioner was the commander of an army totally destroyed by the superior power of this nation. While under heavy and destructive attack by our forces, his troops committed many brutal atrocities and other high crimes. Hostilities ceased and he voluntarily surrendered. At that point he was entitled, as an individual protected by the due process clause of the Fifth Amendment, to be treated fairly and justly according to the accepted rules of law and procedure. He was also entitled to a fair trial as to any alleged crimes and to be free from charges of legally unrecognized crimes that would serve only to permit his accusers to satisfy their desires for revenge.

A military commission was appointed to try the petitioner for an alleged war crime. The trial was ordered to be held in territory over which the United States has complete sovereignty. No military necessity or other emergency demanded the suspension of the safeguards of due process. Yet petitioner was rushed to trial under an improper charge, given insufficient time to prepare an adequate defense, deprived of the benefits of some of the most elementary rules of evidence and summarily sentenced to be hanged. In all this needless and unseemly haste there was no serious attempt to charge or to prove that he committed a recognized violation of the laws of war. He was not charged with personally participating in the acts of atrocity or with ordering or condoning their commission. Not even knowledge of these crimes was attributed to him. It was simply alleged that he unlawfully disregarded and failed to discharge his duty as commander to control the operations of the members of his command, permitting them to commit the acts of atrocity. The recorded annals of warfare and the established principles of international law afford not the slightest precedent for such a charge. This indictment in effect permitted the military commission to make the crime whatever it willed, dependent upon its biased view as to petitioner's duties and his disregard thereof, a practice reminiscent of that pursued in certain less respected nations in recent years.

In my opinion, such a procedure is unworthy of the traditions of our people or of the immense sacrifices that they have made to advance the common ideals of mankind. The high feelings of the moment doubtless will be satisfied. But in the sober afterglow will come the realization of the boundless and dangerous implications of the procedure sanctioned today. No one in a position of command in an army, from sergeant to general, can escape those implications. Indeed, the fate of some future President of the United States and his chiefs of staff and military advisers may well have been sealed by this decision. But even more significant will be the hatred and ill-will growing out of the application of this unprecedented procedure. That has been the inevitable effect of every method of punishment disregarding the element of personal culpability. The effect in this instance, unfortunately, will be magnified infinitely, for here we are dealing with the rights of man on an international level. To subject an enemy belligerent to an unfair trial, to charge him with an unrecognized crime, or to vent on him our retributive emotions only antagonizes the enemy nation and hinders the reconciliation necessary to a peaceful world.

That there were brutal atrocities inflicted upon the helpless Filipino people, to whom tyranny is no stranger, by Japanese armed forces under the petitioner's command is undeniable. Starvation, execution or massacre without trial, torture, rape, murder and wanton destruction of property were foremost among the outright violations of the laws of war and of the conscience of a civilized world. That just punishment should be meted out to all those responsible for criminal acts of this nature is also beyond dispute. But these factors do not answer the problem in this case. They do not justify the abandonment of our devotion to justice in dealing with a fallen enemy commander. To conclude otherwise is to admit that the enemy has lost the battle but has destroyed our ideals.

War breeds atrocities. From the earliest conflicts of recorded history to the global struggles of modern times inhumanities, lust and pillage have been the inevitable by-products of man's resort to force and arms. Unfortunately, such despicable acts have a dangerous tendency to call forth primitive impulses of vengeance and retaliation among the victimized peoples. The satisfaction of such impulses in turn breeds resentment and fresh tension. Thus does the spiral of cruelty and hatred grow.

If we are ever to develop an orderly international community based upon a recognition of human dignity it is of the utmost importance that the necessary punishment of those guilty of atrocities be as free as possible from the ugly stigma of revenge and vindictiveness. Justice must be tempered by compassion rather than by vengeance. In this, the first case involving this momentous problem ever to reach this Court, our responsibility is both lofty and difficult. We must insist, within the confines of our proper jurisdiction, that the highest standards of justice be applied in this trial of an enemy commander conducted under the authority of the United States. Otherwise stark retribution will be free to masquerade in a cloak of false legalism. And the hatred and cynicism engendered by that retribution will supplant the great ideals to which this nation is dedicated. . . .

The determination of the extent of review of war trials calls for judicial statesmanship of the highest order. The ultimate nature and scope of the writ of habeas corpus are within the discretion of the judiciary unless validly circumscribed by Congress. Here we are confronted with a use of the writ under circumstances novel in the history of the Court. For my own part, I do not feel that we should be confined by the traditional lines of review drawn in connection with the use of the writ by ordinary criminals who have direct access to the judiciary in the first instance. Those held by the military lack any such access; consequently the judicial review available by habeas corpus must be wider than usual in order that proper standards of justice may be enforceable.

The Court, in my judgment, demonstrates conclusively that the military commission was lawfully created in this instance and that petitioner could not object to its power to try him for a recognized war crime. . . . [H]owever, I find it impossible to agree that the charge against the petitioner stated a recognized violation of the laws of war.

The findings of the military commission bear out this absence of any direct personal charge against the petitioner. The commission merely found that atrocities and other high crimes "have been committed by members of the Japanese armed forces under your command . . . that they were not sporadic in nature but in many cases were methodically supervised by Japanese officers and noncommissioned officers. . . . That during the period in question you failed to provide effective control of your troops as was required by the circumstances."

In other words, read against the background of military events in the Philippines subsequent to October 9, 1944, these charges amount to this: "We, the victorious American forces, have done everything possible to destroy and disorganize your lines of communication, your effective control of your personnel, your ability to wage war. In those respects we have succeeded. We have defeated and crushed your forces. And now we charge and condemn you for having been inefficient in maintaining control of your troops during the period when we were so effectively besieging and eliminating your forces and blocking your ability to maintain effective control. Many terrible atrocities were committed by your disorganized troops. Because these atrocities were so widespread we will not bother to charge or prove that you committed, ordered or condoned any of them. We will assume that they must have resulted from your inefficiency and negligence as a commander. In short, we charge you with the crime of inefficiency in controlling your troops. We will judge the discharge of your duties by the disorganization which we ourselves created in large part. Our standards of judgment are whatever we wish to make them."

Nothing in all history or in international law, at least as far as I am aware, justifies such a charge against a fallen commander of a defeated force. To use the very inefficiency and disorganization created by the victorious forces as the primary basis for condemning officers of the defeated armies bears no resemblance to justice or to military reality.

International law makes no attempt to define the duties of a commander of an army under constant and overwhelming assault; nor does it impose liability under such circumstances for failure to meet the ordinary responsibilities of command. The omission is understandable. Duties, as well as ability to control troops, vary according to the nature and intensity of the particular battle. To find an unlawful deviation from duty under battle conditions requires difficult and speculative calculations. Such calculations become highly untrustworthy when they are made by the victor in relation to the actions of a vanquished commander. Objective and realistic norms of conduct are then extremely unlikely to be used in forming a judgment as to deviations from duty. The probability that vengeance will form the major part of the victor's judgment is an unfortunate but inescapable fact. So great is that probability that international law refuses to recognize such a judgment as a basis for a war crime, however fair the judgment may be in a particular instance. It is this consideration that undermines the charge against the petitioner in this case. The indictment permits, indeed compels, the military commission of a victorious nation to sit in judgment upon the military strategy and actions of the defeated enemy and to use its conclusions to determine the criminal liability of an enemy commander. Life and liberty are made to depend upon the biased will of the victor rather than upon objective standards of conduct. . . .

Even the laws of war heretofore recognized by this nation fail to impute responsibility to a fallen commander for excesses committed by his disorganized troops while under attack. . . .

The only conclusion I can draw is that the charge made against the petitioner is clearly without precedent in international law or in the annals of recorded military history. This is not to say that enemy commanders may escape punishment for clear and unlawful failures to prevent atrocities. But that punishment should be based upon charges fairly drawn in light of established rules of international law and recognized concepts of justice. . . .

At a time like this when emotions are understandably high it is difficult to adopt a dispassionate attitude toward a case of this nature. Yet now is precisely the time when that attitude is most essential. While peoples in other lands may not share our beliefs as to due process and the dignity of the individual, we are not free to give effect to our emotions in reckless disregard of the rights of others. We live under the Constitution, which is the embodiment of all the high hopes and aspirations of the new world. And it is applicable in both war and peace. We must act accordingly. Indeed, an uncurbed spirit of revenge and retribution, masked in formal legal procedure for purposes of dealing with a fallen enemy commander, can do more lasting harm than all of the atrocities giving rise to that spirit. The people's faith in the fairness and objectiveness of the law can be seriously undercut by that spirit. The fires of nationalism can be further kindled. And the hearts of all mankind can be embittered and filled with hatred, leaving forlorn and impoverished the noble ideal of malice toward none and charity to all. These are the reasons that lead me to dissent in these terms.

Duncan v. Kahanamoku 327 U.S. 304 (1946)

This case again raised the issue broached in the Milligan *case of trying civilians in a military court when civilian courts continued to function normally. In* Milligan, *the Supreme Court found that civilians could not be subjected to military justice when civilian courts were available. In the aftermath of World War II, the Court's rulings remained consistent with this precedent. The case offers an interesting and detailed window into the operations of the military justice system under martial law. Note also the Court's discussion of the vagaries and difficulties implied in defining the legal state of "martial law." Also, the dissent offered by Justice Burton should have a familiar ring to Americans living in the post–September 11 age, for he poses questions we are asking today: What exactly is a "battlefield" during a modern war? When the enemy forgos the ordinary rules of war, how should the nation's legal institutions respond? Do the ends of victory justify the means of military rule and martial law?*

COURT OPINION BY JUSTICE BLACK. The petitioners in these cases were sentenced to prison by military tribunals in Hawaii. Both are civilians. The question before us is whether the military tribunals had power to do this. The United States district court for Hawaii in habeas corpus proceedings held that the military tribunals had no such power and ordered that they be set free. The circuit court of appeals reversed, and ordered that the petitioners be returned to prison. 146 F.2d 576. Both cases thus involve the rights of individuals charged with crime and not connected with the armed forces to have their guilt or innocence determined in courts of law which provide established procedural safeguards, rather than by military tribunals which fail to afford many of these safeguards. . . .

The following events led to the military tribunals' exercise of jurisdiction over the petitioners. On December 7, 1941, immediately following the surprise air attack by the Japanese on Pearl Harbor, the Governor of Hawaii by proclamation undertook to suspend the privilege of the writ of habeas corpus and to place the Territory under "martial law." . . .

The Commanding General established military tribunals to take the place of the courts. These were to try civilians charged with violating the laws of the United States and of the Territory, and rules, regulations, orders or policies of the Military Government. Rules of evidence and procedure of courts of law were not to control the military trials. In imposing penalties the military tribunals were to be "guided by, but not limited to the penalties authorized by the courts martial manual, the laws of the United States, the Territory of Hawaii, the District of Columbia, and the customs of war in like cases." . . . Thus the military authorities took over the government of Hawaii. They could and did, by simply promulgating orders, govern the day to day activities of civilians who lived, worked, or were merely passing through there. The military tribunals interpreted the very orders promulgated by the military authorities and proceeded to punish violators. The sentences imposed were not subject to direct appellate court review, since it had long been established that military tribunals are not part of our judicial system. . . . The military undoubtedly assumed that its rule was not subject to any judicial control whatever, for by orders issued on August 25, 1943, it prohibited even accepting of a petition for writ of habeas corpus by a judge or judicial employee or the filing of such a petition by a prisoner or his attorney. Military tribunals could punish violators of these orders by fine, imprisonment or death.

White, the petitioner in No. 15, was a stockbroker in Honolulu. Neither he nor his business was connected with the armed forces. On August 20, 1942, more than eight months after the Pearl Harbor attack, the military police arrested him. The charge against him was embezzling stock belonging to another civilian in violation of Chapter 183 of the Revised Laws of Hawaii. . . . On August 22nd, White was brought before a military tribunal designated as a "Provost Court." The "Court" orally informed him of the charge. He objected to the tribunal's jurisdiction but the objection was overruled. He demanded to be tried by a jury. This request was denied. His attorney asked for additional time to prepare the case. This was refused. On August 25th he was tried and convicted. The tribunal sentenced him to five years imprisonment. Later the sentence was reduced to four years.

Duncan, the petitioner in No. 14, was a civilian shipfitter employed in the Navy Yard at Honolulu. On February 24, 1944, more than two years and two months after the Pearl Harbor attack, he engaged in a brawl with two armed Marine sentries at the yard. He was arrested by the military authorities. By the time of his arrest the military had to some extent eased the stringency of military rule. Schools, bars and motion picture theatres had been reopened. Courts had been authorized to "exercise their normal jurisdiction." They were once more summoning jurors and witnesses and conducting criminal trials. There were important exceptions, however. One of these was that only military tribunals were to try "Criminal prosecutions for violations of military orders." As the record shows, these military orders still covered a wide range of day to day civilian conduct. Duncan was charged with violating one of these orders, paragraph 8.01, Title 8, of General Order No. 2, which prohibited assault on military or naval personnel with intent to resist or hinder them in the discharge of their duty. He was, therefore, tried by a military tribunal rather than the territorial court, although the general laws of Hawaii made assault a crime. Revised L. H. 1935, ch. 166. A conviction followed and Duncan was sentenced to six months imprisonment. . . .

Congress did intend the Governor of Hawaii, with the approval of the President, to invoke military aid under certain circumstances. But Congress did not specifically state to what extent the army could be used or what power it could exercise. It certainly did not explicitly declare that the Governor in conjunction with the military could for days, months or years close all the courts and supplant them with military tribunals. . . . If a power thus to obliterate the judicial system of Hawaii can be found at all in the Organic Act, it must be inferred from § 67's provision for placing the Territory under "martial law." But the term "martial law" carries no precise meaning. The Constitution does not refer to "martial law" at all and no Act of Congress has defined the term. It has been employed in various ways by different people and at different times. By some it has been identified as "military law" limited to members of, and those connected with, the armed forces. Others have said that the term does not imply a system of established rules but denotes simply some kind of day to day expression of a general's will dictated by what he considers the imperious necessity of the moment. . . .

Since the Act's language does not provide a satisfactory answer, we look to the legislative history for possible further aid in interpreting the term "martial law" as used in the statute. The Government contends that the legislative history shows that Congress intended to give the armed forces extraordinarily broad powers to try civilians before military tribunals. . . .

Congress did not intend the Constitution to have a limited application to Hawaii. . . . It follows that civilians in Hawaii are entitled to the constitutional guarantee of a fair trial to the same extent as those who live in any other part of our country. We are aware that conditions peculiar to Hawaii might imperatively demand extraordinarily speedy and effective measures in the event of actual or threatened invasion. But this also holds true for other parts of the United States. Extraordinary measures in Hawaii, however necessary, are not supportable on the mistaken premise that Hawaiian inhabitants are less entitled to constitutional protection than others. . . .

Have the principles and practices developed during the birth and growth of our political institutions been such as to persuade us that Congress intended that loyal civilians in loyal territory should have their daily conduct governed by military orders substituted for criminal laws, and that such civilians should be tried and punished by military tribunals? . . .

Our system of government clearly is the antithesis of total military rule and the founders of this country are not likely to have contemplated complete military dominance within the limits of a territory made part of this country and not recently taken from an enemy. They were opposed to governments that placed in the hands of one man the power to make, interpret and enforce the laws. Their philosophy has been the people's throughout our history. For that reason we have maintained legislatures chosen by citizens or their representatives and courts and juries to try those who violate legislative enactments. We have always been especially concerned about the potential evils of summary criminal trials and have guarded against them by provisions embodied in the Constitution itself. . . .

Military tribunals have no such standing. . . .

We believe that when Congress passed the Hawaiian Organic Act and authorized the establishment of "martial law" it had in mind and did not wish to exceed the boundaries between military and civilian power, in which our people have always believed, which responsible military and executive officers had heeded, and which had become part of our political philosophy and institutions prior to the time Congress passed the Organic Act. The phrase "martial law" as em-

ployed in that Act, therefore, while intended to authorize the military
to act vigorously for the maintenance of an orderly civil government
and for the defense of the Islands against actual or threatened rebellion
or invasion, was not intended to authorize the supplanting of courts
by military tribunals. Yet the Government seeks to justify the punishment of both White and Duncan on the ground of such supposed congressional authorization. We hold that both petitioners are now entitled to be released from custody.

DISSENT BY JUSTICE BURTON. With the rest of this Court I
subscribe unreservedly to the Bill of Rights. I recognize the importance of the civil courts in protecting individual rights guaranteed by
the Constitution. I prefer civil to military control of civilian life and I
agree that in war our Constitution contemplates the preservation of
the individual rights of all of our people in accordance with a plan of
constitutional procedure fitted to the needs of a self-governing republic at war.

Our Constitution expressly provides for waging war, and it is with
the constitutional instruments for the successful conduct of war that I
am concerned. I recognize here, as elsewhere, the constitutional direction that our respective branches of the Government do not exceed
their allotted shares of authority. The courts, as well as our other agencies of the Government, accordingly owe a constitutional obligation
not to invade the fields reserved either to the people, the States, or the
other coordinate branches of the Government. The courts have an
obligation to help define and protect the discretion with which the
people have invested their legislative and executive representatives.
Within their proper spheres, the robust strength and freedom of action
allowed to the policy making and policy executing agencies of our
Government are as vital to the success of our great experiment in securing "the Blessings of Liberty to ourselves and our Posterity" as are
the checks and balances which have been imposed upon our representatives. It is in the application of these views to the cases before us that
I am obliged to dissent from the majority of this Court and to sound
a note of warning against the dangers of overexpansion of judicial control into the fields allotted by the Constitution to agencies of legislative and executive action. . . .

The complete disregard of international law evidenced by the first
attack [on Pearl Harbor] and the possible presence on the Islands of
many Japanese collaborators gave warning that the enemy's next move
might take the form of disastrous sabotage and terrorism among civil-

ians. The extraordinary breach of international law evidenced by the attack made it essential to take extraordinary steps to protect the Islands against subversive action that might spring from deeply laid plans as secret, well aimed, and destructive as the original attack.

On December 7 and in the period immediately following, every inch of the Territory of Hawaii was like a frontier stockade under savage attack with notice that such attack would not be restrained by the laws of civilized nations. Measures of defense had to be taken on the basis that anything could happen. The relation of the Constitution of the United States to such a situation is important. Of course, the Constitution is not put aside. It was written by a generation fresh from war. The people established a more perfect union, in part, so that they might the better defend themselves from military attack. In doing so they centralized far more military power and responsibility in the Chief Executive than previously had been done. The Constitution was built for rough as well as smooth roads. In time of war the nation simply changes gears and takes the harder going under the same power. . . .

The conduct of war under the Constitution is largely an executive function. Within the field of military action in time of war, the executive is allowed wide discretion. While, even in the conduct of war, there are many lines of jurisdiction to draw between the proper spheres of legislative, executive and judicial action, it seems clear that at least on an active battle field, the executive discretion to determine policy is there intended by the Constitution to be supreme. The question then arises: What is a battle field and how long does it remain one after the first barrage?

It is well that the outer limits of the jurisdiction of our military authorities is subject to review by our courts even under such extreme circumstances as those of the battle field. This, however, requires the courts to put themselves as nearly as possible in the place of those who had the constitutional responsibility for immediate executive action. For a court to recreate a complete picture of the emergency is impossible. That impossibility demonstrates the need for a zone of executive discretion within which courts must guard themselves with special care against judging past military action too closely by the inapplicable standards of judicial, or even military, hindsight. . . .

For this Court to intrude its judgment into spheres of constitutional discretion that are reserved either to the Congress or to the Chief Executive, is to invite disregard of that judgment by the

Congress or by executive agencies under a claim of constitutional right to do so. On the other hand, this Court can contribute much to the orderly conduct of government, if it will outline reasonable boundaries for the discretion of the respective departments of the Government, with full regard for the limitations and also for the responsibilities imposed upon them by the Constitution.

It is important to approach the present cases with a full appreciation of the responsibility of the executive branch of the Government in Hawaii under the invasion which occurred on December 7, 1941. The question is not shall the Constitution apply under such circumstances? The question is with what authority has the Constitution and laws of this country vested the official representatives of the people upon whom are placed the responsibilities of leadership under those extraordinary circumstances?

The vital distinction is between conditions in "the theatre of actual military operations" and outside of that theatre. In this case Hawaii was not only in the theatre of operations, it was under fire. If the Territory of Hawaii, on that date and during the immediately succeeding period, is recognized as the battle field it was, then under such circumstances of invasion and threat of immediate further invasion, the actions taken by the Governor of Hawaii and by the Commanding General of the Hawaiian Department, supported by the President of the United States, in suspending the writ of habeas corpus, declaring martial law and vesting in such Commanding General for those first several days the powers normally exercised by the Governor and by the judicial officers and employees of the Territory (at least to the extent that would be involved in the present cases if they had arisen at that time), were within the executive discretion of the officials who authorized the action. The actual presence of battle in a community creates a substantially different condition from that which exists in other parts of a nation at war. That conditions of war and the means of meeting its emergencies were within the contemplation of the Constitution of the United States is shown by the broad authority vested in the President of the United States as Chief Executive and as Commander in Chief of the Army and Navy and in the war powers of the Congress and the Chief Executive to preserve the safety of the nation in time of war. The present cases arose in a Territory of the United States, directly under the care and jurisdiction of the Federal Government. . . .

Starting with the propriety of that battle field regulation in the presence of disastrous invasion, the question resolves itself solely to one of when and to what extent the constitutional executive discretion to continue these orders can or should be held by this Court to have been exceeded. Once the Islands are visualized as a battle field under actual invasion, threatened with further invasion, and invaluable to the enemy as a base from which to attack the continental United States, the situation is completely changed from that of an ordinary civilian community. Under conditions likely to disregard even the laws of civilized warfare, the island population was threatened with immediate destruction. It thus became necessary to organize and protect that population against imminent danger from bombing, fire, disruption of water and food supply, disease and all the other incidents of modern warfare. The limited area, limited garrison and great isolation of the Islands put a premium on the efficiency of its civilian defense and on the integration of it with the military defense. All activity was subordinated to executive control as the best constitutional safeguard of the civilian as well as the military life.

That in such a case there must be restoration of civilian control is clear. It is equally clear that there must be limits to the extent to which the executive discretion constitutionally may delay such restoration. In the first instance, however, there is a period, bearing a reasonable relation to the original emergency, during which it must be within the discretion of the executive agencies of the Government to decide when and how to restore the battle field to its peace time controls.

In view of the responsibility placed upon the executive branch of the Government and especially upon its armed forces in time of invasion and threatened invasion, it is essential that that branch of the Government have freedom of action equal to its needs. At the center of invasion, military control is the proper control to be applied, subject to provisions of the Constitution, treaties and laws of the United States applicable to a battle field. On December 7, 1941, I believe that the facts of the invasion and threatened further invasion amply established such a condition and justified at the time the military control established on that basis throughout the Islands.

Whether or not from the vantage post of the present this Court may disagree with the judgment exercised by the military authorities in their schedule of relaxation of control is not material unless this Court finds that the schedule was so delayed as to exceed the range of discretion which such conditions properly vest in the military authorities. . . .

Now that the war has been won and the safety of the Islands has been again assured, there is opportunity, in the calm light of peace, for the readjustment of sentences imposed upon civilians and military personnel during the emergency of war and which have not yet expired. It is important, however, that in reviewing the constitutionality of the conduct of our agencies of government in time of war, invasion and threatened invasion, we do not now make precedents which in other emergencies may handicap the executive branch of the Government in the performance of duties allotted to it by the Constitution and by the exercise of which it successfully defended the nation against the greatest attack ever made upon it. . . .

In order to have the benefit of the full strength of our Constitution, both in time of peace and in time of war, it is necessary to protect the authority of our legislative and executive officials, as well as that of our courts, in the performance of their respective obligations to help to "establish Justice, insure domestic Tranquility, provide for the common defence, promote the general Welfare, and secure the Blessings of Liberty to ourselves and our Posterity."

Hirabayashi v. United States 320 U.S. 81 (1942)

One of the darkest episodes in America's history of war making occurred during World War II, when Americans confronted the supposed internal security issues posed by thousands of Japanese-Americans. As we saw in chapter 2, persons of Japanese descent were subjected to extraordinary internal security measures, including curfews and relocation to internment camps.

Given the caution Supreme Court justices exhibited when approaching internal security measures aimed at Germans and German-Americans, Japanese-Americans had reason for hope. As we see in Hirabayashi, *however, those hopes were ill founded. Perhaps the Court saw the Japanese as a greater threat to national security than the Germans. Perhaps the Court's innate reluctance to involve itself in military matters drove its judgment on the issue of Japanese-Americans. Or perhaps the justices simply proved that they were not immune to the racial biases American society as a whole had against Americans of Asian descent. Whatever the reasons, the Supreme Court upheld what amounted to a caste distinction in wartime and justified it both as a matter of military necessity and as a response to alleged failures of Japanese-Americans to fully assimilate into American society. This was not a proud moment in the Court's history. On the other hand, Justice Murphy's opinion, while concurring with the majority, reveals the sometimes agonized legal contortions the Court felt compelled to use in upholding the Japanese-American exclusionary rules.*

COURT OPINION BY JUSTICE STONE. Appellant, an American citizen of Japanese ancestry, was convicted in the district court of violating the Act of Congress of March 21, 1942, 56 Stat. 173, which makes it a misdemeanor knowingly to disregard restrictions made applicable by a military commander to persons in a military area prescribed by him as such, all as authorized by an Executive Order of the President.

The questions for our decision are whether the particular restriction violated, namely that all persons of Japanese ancestry residing in such an area be within their place of residence daily between the hours of 8:00 P.M. and 6:00 A.M., was adopted by the military commander in the exercise of an unconstitutional delegation by Congress of its legislative power, and whether the restriction unconstitutionally discriminated between citizens of Japanese ancestry and those of other ancestries in violation of the Fifth Amendment.

The indictment is in two counts. The second charges that appellant, being a person of Japanese ancestry, had on a specified date, contrary to a restriction promulgated by the military commander of the Western Defense Command, Fourth Army, failed to remain in his place of residence in the designated military area between the hours of 8:00 o'clock P.M. and 6:00 A.M. The first count charges that appellant, on May 11 and 12, 1942, had, contrary to a Civilian Exclusion Order issued by the military commander, failed to report to the Civil Control Station within the designated area, it appearing that appellant's required presence there was a preliminary step to the exclusion from that area of persons of Japanese ancestry.

[A]ppellant asserted that the indictment should be dismissed because he was an American citizen who had never been a subject of and had never borne allegiance to the Empire of Japan, and also because the Act of March 21, 1942, was an unconstitutional delegation of Congressional power. On the trial to a jury it appeared that appellant was born in Seattle in 1918, of Japanese parents who had come from Japan to the United States, and who had never afterward returned to Japan; that he was educated in the Washington public schools and at the time of his arrest was a senior in the University of Washington; that he had never been in Japan or had any association with Japanese residing there.

The evidence showed that appellant had failed to report to the Civil Control Station on May 11 or May 12, 1942, as directed, to register for evacuation from the military area. He admitted failure to do so, and stated it had at all times been his belief that he would be waiving his rights as an American citizen by so doing. The evidence also showed that for like reason he was away from his place of residence after 8:00 P.M. on May 9, 1942. The jury returned a verdict of guilty on both counts and appellant was sentenced to imprisonment for a term of three months on each, the sentences to run concurrently. . . .

Appellant does not deny that he knowingly failed to obey the curfew order as charged in the second count of the indictment, or that the order was authorized by the terms of Executive Order No. 9066, or that the challenged Act of Congress purports to punish with criminal penalties disobedience of such an order. His contentions are only that Congress unconstitutionally delegated its legislative power to the military commander by authorizing him to impose the challenged regulation, and that, even if the regulation were in other respects lawfully authorized, the Fifth Amendment prohibits the discrimination made between citizens of Japanese descent and those of other ancestry. . . .

[S]o far as it lawfully could, Congress authorized and implemented such curfew orders as the commanding officer should promulgate pursuant to the Executive Order of the President. The question then is not one of Congressional power to delegate to the President the promulgation of the Executive Order, but whether, acting in cooperation, Congress and the Executive have constitutional authority to impose the curfew restriction here complained of. We must consider also whether, acting together, Congress and the Executive could leave it to the designated military commander to appraise the relevant conditions and on the basis of that appraisal to say whether, under the circumstances, the time and place were appropriate for the promulgation of the curfew order and whether the order itself was an appropriate means of carrying out the Executive Order for the "protection against espionage and against sabotage" to national defense materials, premises and utilities. For reasons presently to be stated, we conclude that it was within the constitutional power of Congress and the executive arm of the Government to prescribe this curfew order for the period under consideration and that its promulgation by the military commander involved no unlawful delegation of legislative power. . . .

The war power of the national government is "the power to wage war successfully." . . . It extends to every matter and activity so related to war as substantially to affect its conduct and progress. The power is not restricted to the winning of victories in the field and the repulse of enemy forces. It embraces every phase of the national defense, including the protection of war materials and the members of the armed forces from injury and from the dangers which attend the rise, prosecution and progress of war. . . . Since the Constitution commits to the Executive and to Congress the exercise of the war power in all the vicissitudes and conditions of warfare, it has necessarily given them wide scope for the exercise of judgment and discretion in determining the nature and extent of the threatened injury or danger and in the selection of the means for resisting it. . . . Where, as they did here, the conditions call for the exercise of judgment and discretion and for the choice of means by those branches of the Government on which the Constitution has placed the responsibility of war-making, it is not for any court to sit in review of the wisdom of their action or substitute its judgment for theirs. . . .

Although the results of the attack on Pearl Harbor were not fully disclosed until much later, it was known that the damage was extensive, and that the Japanese by their successes had gained a naval superiority over our forces in the Pacific which might enable them to seize Pearl Harbor, our largest naval base and the last stronghold of defense lying between Japan and the west coast. That reasonably prudent men charged with the responsibility of our national defense had ample ground for concluding that they must face the danger of invasion, take measures against it, and in making the choice of measures consider our internal situation, cannot be doubted.

The challenged orders were defense measures for the avowed purpose of safeguarding the military area in question, at a time of threatened air raids and invasion by the Japanese forces, from the danger of sabotage and espionage. As the curfew was made applicable to citizens residing in the area only if they were of Japanese ancestry, our inquiry must be whether in the light of all the facts and circumstances there was any substantial basis for the conclusion, in which Congress and the military commander united, that the curfew as applied was a protective measure necessary to meet the threat of sabotage and espionage which would substantially affect the war effort and which might reasonably be expected to aid a threatened enemy invasion. The alternative which appellant insists must be accepted is for the military authorities to impose the curfew on all citizens within the military area, or on none. In a case of threatened danger requiring prompt action, it is a choice between inflicting obviously needless hardship on the many, or sitting passive and unresisting in the presence of the threat. We think that constitutional government, in time of war, is not so powerless and does not compel so hard a choice if those charged with the responsibility of our national defense have reasonable ground for believing that the threat is real. . . .

At a time of threatened Japanese attack upon this country, the nature of our inhabitants' attachments to the Japanese enemy was consequently a matter of grave concern. Of the 126,000 persons of Japanese descent in the United States, citizens and non-citizens, approximately 112,000 resided in California, Oregon and Washington at the time of the adoption of the military regulations. Of these approximately two-thirds are citizens because born in the United States. Not only did the great majority of such persons reside within the Pacific Coast states but they were concentrated in or near three of the large cities, Seattle, Portland and Los Angeles, all in Military Area No. 1. . . .

There is support for the view that social, economic and political conditions which have prevailed since the close of the last century, when the Japanese began to come to this country in substantial numbers, have intensified their solidarity and have in large measure prevented their assimilation as an integral part of the white population. In addition, large numbers of children of Japanese parentage are sent to Japanese language schools outside the regular hours of public schools in the locality. Some of these schools are generally believed to be sources of Japanese nationalistic propaganda, cultivating allegiance to Japan. Considerable numbers, estimated to be approximately 10,000, of American-born children of Japanese parentage have been sent to Japan for all or a part of their education.

Congress and the Executive, including the military commander, could have attributed special significance, in its bearing on the loyalties of persons of Japanese descent, to the maintenance by Japan of its system of dual citizenship. Children born in the United States of Japanese alien parents, and especially those children born before December 1, 1924, are under many circumstances deemed, by Japanese law, to be citizens of Japan. No official census of those whom Japan regards as having thus retained Japanese citizenship is available, but there is ground for the belief that the number is large.

The large number of resident alien Japanese, approximately one-third of all Japanese inhabitants of the country, are of mature years and occupy positions of influence in Japanese communities. The association of influential Japanese residents with Japanese Consulates has been deemed a ready means for the dissemination of propaganda and for the maintenance of the influence of the Japanese Government with the Japanese population in this country.

As a result of all these conditions affecting the life of the Japanese, both aliens and citizens, in the Pacific Coast area, there has been relatively little social intercourse between them and the white population. The restrictions, both practical and legal, affecting the privileges and opportunities afforded to persons of Japanese extraction residing in the United States, have been sources of irritation and may well have tended to increase their isolation, and in many instances their attachments to Japan and its institutions.

Viewing these data in all their aspects, Congress and the Executive could reasonably have concluded that these conditions have encouraged the continued attachment of members of this group to Japan and Japanese institutions. These are only some of the many considerations which those charged with the responsibility for the national defense could take into account in determining the nature and extent of the danger of espionage and sabotage, in the event of invasion or air raid attack. The extent of that danger could be definitely known only after the event and after it was too late to meet it. Whatever views we may entertain regarding the loyalty to this country of the citizens of Japanese ancestry, we cannot reject as unfounded the judgment of the military authorities and of Congress that there were disloyal members of that population, whose number and strength could not be precisely and quickly ascertained. We cannot say that the war-making branches of the Government did not have ground for believing that in a critical hour such persons could not readily be isolated and separately dealt with, and constituted a menace to the national defense and safety, which demanded that prompt and adequate measures be taken to guard against it.

Appellant does not deny that, given the danger, a curfew was an appropriate measure against sabotage. It is an obvious protection against the perpetration of sabotage most readily committed during the hours of darkness. If it was an appropriate exercise of the war power its validity is not impaired because it has restricted the citizen's liberty. Like every military control of the population of a dangerous zone in war time, it necessarily involves some infringement of individual liberty, just as does the police establishment of fire lines during a fire, or the confinement of people to their houses during an air raid alarm—

neither of which could be thought to be an infringement of constitutional right. Like them, the validity of the restraints of the curfew order depends on all the conditions which obtain at the time the curfew is imposed and which support the order imposing it.

But appellant insists that the exercise of the power is inappropriate and unconstitutional because it discriminates against citizens of Japanese ancestry, in violation of the Fifth Amendment. The Fifth Amendment contains no equal protection clause and it restrains only such discriminatory legislation by Congress as amounts to a denial of due process. . . . Congress may hit at a particular danger where it is seen, without providing for others which are not so evident or so urgent. . . .

Distinctions between citizens solely because of their ancestry are by their very nature odious to a free people whose institutions are founded upon the doctrine of equality. For that reason, legislative classification or discrimination based on race alone has often been held to be a denial of equal protection. . . . We may assume that these considerations would be controlling here were it not for the fact that the danger of espionage and sabotage, in time of war and of threatened invasion, calls upon the military authorities to scrutinize every relevant fact bearing on the loyalty of populations in the danger areas. Because racial discriminations are in most circumstances irrelevant and therefore prohibited, it by no means follows that, in dealing with the perils of war, Congress and the Executive are wholly precluded from taking into account those facts and circumstances which are relevant to measures for our national defense and for the successful prosecution of the war, and which may in fact place citizens of one ancestry in a different category from others. . . . The adoption by Government, in the crisis of war and of threatened invasion, of measures for the public safety, based upon the recognition of facts and circumstances which indicate that a group of one national extraction may menace that safety more than others, is not wholly beyond the limits of the Constitution and is not to be condemned merely because in other and in most circumstances racial distinctions are irrelevant. . . .

Here the aim of Congress and the Executive was the protection against sabotage of war materials and utilities in areas thought to be in danger of Japanese invasion and air attack. We have stated in detail facts and circumstances with respect to the American citizens of Japanese ancestry residing on the Pacific Coast which support the judgment of the war-waging branches of the Government that some restrictive measure was urgent. We cannot say that these facts and cir-cumstances, considered in the particular war setting, could afford no ground for differentiating citizens of Japanese ancestry from other groups in the United States. The fact alone that attack on our shores was threatened by Japan rather than another enemy power set these citizens apart from others who have no particular associations with Japan.

Our investigation here does not go beyond the inquiry whether, in the light of all the relevant circumstances preceding and attending their promulgation, the challenged orders and statute afforded a reasonable basis for the action taken in imposing the curfew. We cannot close our eyes to the fact, demonstrated by experience, that in time of war resi-dents having ethnic affiliations with an invading enemy may be a greater source of danger than those of a different ancestry. Nor can we deny that Congress, and the military authorities acting with its autho-rization, have constitutional power to appraise the danger in the light of facts of public notoriety. We need not now attempt to define the ul-timate boundaries of the war power. We decide only the issue as we have defined it—we decide only that the curfew order as applied, and at the time it was applied, was within the boundaries of the war power. In this case it is enough that circumstances within the knowledge of those charged with the responsibility for maintaining the national de-fense afforded a rational basis for the decision which they made. Whether we would have made it is irrelevant. . . .

The military commander's appraisal of facts in the light of the au-thorized standard, and the inferences which he drew from those facts, involved the exercise of his informed judgment. But as we have seen, those facts, and the inferences which could be rationally drawn from them, support the judgment of the military commander, that the dan-ger of espionage and sabotage to our military resources was imminent, and that the curfew order was an appropriate measure to meet it.

CONCURRING OPINION BY JUSTICE MURPHY. Distinc-tions based on color and ancestry are utterly inconsistent with our tra-ditions and ideals. They are at variance with the principles for which we are now waging war. We cannot close our eyes to the fact that for centuries the Old World has been torn by racial and religious conflicts and has suffered the worst kind of anguish because of inequality of treatment for different groups. There was one law for one and a dif-ferent law for another. Nothing is written more firmly into our law than the compact of the Plymouth voyagers to have just and equal laws. To say that any group cannot be assimilated is to admit that the great American experiment has failed, that our way of life has failed when confronted with the normal attachment of certain groups to the lands of their forefathers. As a nation we embrace many groups, some of them among the oldest settlements in our midst, which have isolated themselves for religious and cultural reasons.

Today is the first time, so far as I am aware, that we have sustained a substantial restriction of the personal liberty of citizens of the United States based upon the accident of race or ancestry. Under the curfew order here challenged no less than 70,000 American citizens have been placed under a special ban and deprived of their liberty because of their particular racial inheritance. In this sense it bears a melancholy resemblance to the treatment accorded to members of the Jewish race in Germany and in other parts of Europe. The result is the creation in this country of two classes of citizens for the purposes of a critical and perilous hour—to sanction discrimination between groups of United States citizens on the basis of ancestry. In my opinion this goes to the very brink of constitutional power.

Except under conditions of great emergency a regulation of this kind applicable solely to citizens of a particular racial extraction would not be regarded as in accord with the requirement of due process of law contained in the Fifth Amendment. We have consistently held that attempts to apply regulatory action to particular groups solely on the basis of racial distinction or classification is not in accordance with due process of law as prescribed by the Fifth and Fourteenth Amendments. . . . It is true that the Fifth Amendment, unlike the Fourteenth, contains no guarantee of equal protection of the laws. . . . It is also true that even the guaranty of equal protection of the laws allows a measure of reasonable classification. It by no means follows, however, that there may not be discrimination of such an injurious character in the application of laws as to amount to a denial of due process of law as that term is used in the Fifth Amendment. I think that point is dangerously approached when we have one law for the majority of our citizens and another for those of a particular racial heritage.

For instance, if persons of an accused's race were systematically excluded from a jury in a federal court, any conviction undoubtedly would be considered a violation of the requirement of due process of law, even though the ground commonly stated for setting aside convictions so obtained in state courts is denial of equal protection of the laws. . . .

In view, however, of the critical military situation which prevailed on the Pacific Coast area in the spring of 1942, and the urgent necessity of taking prompt and effective action to secure defense installations and military operations against the risk of sabotage and espionage, the military authorities should not be required to conform to standards of regulatory action appropriate to normal times. Because of the damage wrought by the Japanese at Pearl Harbor and the availability of new weapons and new techniques with greater capacity for speed and deception in offensive operations, the immediate possibility of an attempt at invasion somewhere along the Pacific Coast had to be reckoned with. However desirable such a procedure might have been, the military authorities could have reasonably concluded at the time that determinations as to the loyalty and dependability of individual members of the large and widely scattered group of persons of Japanese extraction on the West Coast could not be made without delay that might have had tragic consequences. Modern war does not always wait for the observance of procedural requirements that are considered essential and appropriate under normal conditions. Accordingly I think that the military arm, confronted with the peril of imminent enemy attack and acting under the authority conferred by the Congress, made an allowable judgment at the time the curfew restriction was imposed. Whether such a restriction is valid today is another matter.

In voting for affirmance of the judgment I do not wish to be understood as intimating that the military authorities in time of war are subject to no restraints whatsoever, or that they are free to impose any restrictions they may choose on the rights and liberties of individual citizens or groups of citizens in those places which may be designated as "military areas." While this Court sits, it has the inescapable duty of seeing that the mandates of the Constitution are obeyed. That duty exists in time of war as well as in time of peace, and in its performance we must not forget that few indeed have been the invasions upon essential liberties which have not been accompanied by pleas of urgent necessity advanced in good faith by responsible men. . . .

Nor do I mean to intimate that citizens of a particular racial group whose freedom may be curtailed within an area threatened with attack should be generally prevented from leaving the area and going at large in other areas that are not in danger of attack and where special precautions are not needed. Their status as citizens, though subject to requirements of national security and military necessity, should at all times be accorded the fullest consideration and respect. When the danger is past, the restrictions imposed on them should be promptly removed and their freedom of action fully restored.

Korematsu v. United States 323 U.S. 214 (1944)

Two years later, the Supreme Court again had reason to review the Japanese-American situation, and it again upheld the government's internal security measures. Doubts seem to have crept into the justices' reasoning—they openly acknowledged the hardships posed by the curfew and relocation orders—and the presence of dissenting opinions suggest that the Court had grown uncomfortable with the matter.

COURT OPINION BY JUSTICE BLACK. The petitioner, an American citizen of Japanese descent, was convicted in a federal district court for remaining in San Leandro, California, a "Military Area," contrary to Civilian Exclusion Order No. 34 of the Commanding General of the Western Command, U.S. Army, which directed that after May 9, 1942, all persons of Japanese ancestry should be excluded from that area. No question was raised as to petitioner's loyalty to the United States. . . .

It should be noted, to begin with, that all legal restrictions which curtail the civil rights of a single racial group are immediately suspect. That is not to say that all such restrictions are unconstitutional. It is to say that courts must subject them to the most rigid scrutiny. Pressing public necessity may sometimes justify the existence of such restrictions; racial antagonism never can. . . .

Exclusion Order No. 34, which the petitioner knowingly and admittedly violated, was one of a number of military orders and proclamations, all of which were substantially based upon Executive Order No. 9066, 7 Fed. Reg. 1407. That order, issued after we were at war with Japan, declared that "the successful prosecution of the war requires every possible protection against espionage and against sabotage to national-defense material, national-defense premises, and national-defense utilities. . . ."

One of the series of orders and proclamations, a curfew order, which like the exclusion order here was promulgated pursuant to Executive Order 9066, subjected all persons of Japanese ancestry in prescribed West Coast military areas to remain in their residences from 8 P.M. to 6 A.M. As is the case with the exclusion order here, that prior curfew order was designed as a "protection against espionage and against sabotage." In *Hirabayashi v. United States,* 320 U.S. 81, we sustained a conviction obtained for violation of the curfew order. The Hirabayashi conviction and this one thus rest on the same 1942 Congressional Act and the same basic executive and military orders, all of which orders were aimed at the twin dangers of espionage and sabotage.

The 1942 Act was attacked in the *Hirabayashi* case as an unconstitutional delegation of power; it was contended that the curfew order and other orders on which it rested were beyond the war powers of the Congress, the military authorities and of the President, as Commander in Chief of the Army; and finally that to apply the curfew order against none but citizens of Japanese ancestry amounted to a constitutionally prohibited discrimination solely on account of race. To these questions, we gave the serious consideration which their importance justified. We upheld the curfew order as an exercise of the power of the government to take steps necessary to prevent espionage and sabotage in an area threatened by Japanese attack.

In the light of the principles we announced in the *Hirabayashi* case, we are unable to conclude that it was beyond the war power of Congress and the Executive to exclude those of Japanese ancestry from the West Coast war area at the time they did. True, exclusion from the area in which one's home is located is a far greater deprivation than constant confinement to the home from 8 P.M. to 6 A.M. Nothing short of apprehension by the proper military authorities of the gravest imminent danger to the public safety can constitutionally justify either. But exclusion from a threatened area, no less than curfew, has a definite and close relationship to the prevention of espionage and sabotage. The military authorities, charged with the primary responsibility of defending our shores, concluded that curfew provided inadequate protection and ordered exclusion. They did so, as pointed out in our *Hirabayashi* opinion, in accordance with Congressional authority to the military to say who should, and who should not, remain in the threatened areas.

In this case the petitioner challenges the assumptions upon which we rested our conclusions in the *Hirabayashi* case. He also urges that by May 1942, when Order No. 34 was promulgated, all danger of Japanese invasion of the West Coast had disappeared. After careful consideration of these contentions we are compelled to reject them. . . .

Like curfew, exclusion of those of Japanese origin was deemed necessary because of the presence of an unascertained number of disloyal
members of the group, most of whom we have no doubt were loyal to
this country. It was because we could not reject the finding of the military authorities that it was impossible to bring about an immediate
segregation of the disloyal from the loyal that we sustained the validity of the curfew order as applying to the whole group. In the instant
case, temporary exclusion of the entire group was rested by the military on the same ground. The judgment that exclusion of the whole
group was for the same reason a military imperative answers the contention that the exclusion was in the nature of group punishment
based on antagonism to those of Japanese origin. That there were
members of the group who retained loyalties to Japan has been confirmed by investigations made subsequent to the exclusion. Approximately five thousand American citizens of Japanese ancestry refused
to swear unqualified allegiance to the United States and to renounce
allegiance to the Japanese Emperor, and several thousand evacuees requested repatriation to Japan.

We uphold the exclusion order as of the time it was made and when
the petitioner violated it. . . . In doing so, we are not unmindful of the
hardships imposed by it upon a large group of American citizens. . . .
But hardships are part of war, and war is an aggregation of hardships.
All citizens alike, both in and out of uniform, feel the impact of war in
greater or lesser measure. Citizenship has its responsibilities as well as
its privileges, and in time of war the burden is always heavier. Compulsory exclusion of large groups of citizens from their homes, except
under circumstances of direst emergency and peril, is inconsistent
with our basic governmental institutions. But when under conditions
of modern warfare our shores are threatened by hostile forces, the
power to protect must be commensurate with the threatened danger. . . .

It is said that we are dealing here with the case of imprisonment of
a citizen in a concentration camp solely because of his ancestry, without evidence or inquiry concerning his loyalty and good disposition
towards the United States. Our task would be simple, our duty clear,
were this a case involving the imprisonment of a loyal citizen in a concentration camp because of racial prejudice. Regardless of the true nature of the assembly and relocation centers—and we deem it unjustifiable to call them concentration camps with all the ugly connotations
that term implies—we are dealing specifically with nothing but an

exclusion order. To cast this case into outlines of racial prejudice, without reference to the real military dangers which were presented, merely confuses the issue. Korematsu was not excluded from the Military Area because of hostility to him or his race. He *was* excluded because we are at war with the Japanese Empire, because the properly constituted military authorities feared an invasion of our West Coast and felt constrained to take proper security measures, because they decided that the military urgency of the situation demanded that all citizens of Japanese ancestry be segregated from the West Coast temporarily, and finally, because Congress, reposing its confidence in this time of war in our military leaders—as inevitably it must—determined that they should have the power to do just this. There was evidence of disloyalty on the part of some, the military authorities considered that the need for action was great, and time was short. We cannot—by availing ourselves of the calm perspective of hindsight—now say that at that time these actions were unjustified.

DISSENT BY JUSTICE ROBERTS. I dissent, because I think the indisputable facts exhibit a clear violation of Constitutional rights.

This is not a case of keeping people off the streets at night as was *Hirabayashi v. United States*, 320 U.S. 81, nor a case of temporary exclusion of a citizen from an area for his own safety or that of the community, nor a case of offering him an opportunity to go temporarily out of an area where his presence might cause danger to himself or to his fellows. On the contrary, it is the case of convicting a citizen as a punishment for not submitting to imprisonment in a concentration camp, based on his ancestry, and solely because of his ancestry, without evidence or inquiry concerning his loyalty and good disposition towards the United States. If this be a correct statement of the facts disclosed by this record, and facts of which we take judicial notice, I need hardly labor the conclusion that Constitutional rights have been violated.

The Government's argument, and the opinion of the court, in my judgment, erroneously divide that which is single and indivisible and thus make the case appear as if the petitioner violated a Military Order, sanctioned by Act of Congress, which excluded him from his home, by refusing voluntarily to leave and, so, knowingly and intentionally, defying the order and the Act of Congress.

The petitioner, a resident of San Leandro, Alameda County, California, is a native of the United States of Japanese ancestry who, according to the uncontradicted evidence, is a loyal citizen of the nation. . . .

The predicament in which the petitioner thus found himself was this: He was forbidden, by Military Order, to leave the zone in which he lived; he was forbidden, by Military Order, after a date fixed, to be found within that zone unless he were in an Assembly Center located in that zone. General DeWitt's report to the Secretary of War concerning the programme of evacuation and relocation of Japanese makes it entirely clear, if it were necessary to refer to that document,—and, in the light of the above recitation, I think it is not,—that an Assembly Center was a euphemism for a prison. No person within such a center was permitted to leave except by Military Order. . . .

DISSENT BY JUSTICE MURPHY. This exclusion of "all persons of Japanese ancestry, both alien and non-alien," from the Pacific Coast area on a plea of military necessity in the absence of martial law ought not to be approved. Such exclusion goes over "the very brink of constitutional power" and falls into the ugly abyss of racism.

In dealing with matters relating to the prosecution and progress of a war, we must accord great respect and consideration to the judgments of the military authorities who are on the scene and who have full knowledge of the military facts. The scope of their discretion must, as a matter of necessity and common sense, be wide. And their judgments ought not to be overruled lightly by those whose training and duties ill-equip them to deal intelligently with matters so vital to the physical security of the nation.

At the same time, however, it is essential that there be definite limits to military discretion, especially where martial law has not been declared. Individuals must not be left impoverished of their constitutional rights on a plea of military necessity that has neither substance nor support. Thus, like other claims conflicting with the asserted constitutional rights of the individual, the military claim must subject itself to the judicial process of having its reasonableness determined and its conflicts with other interests reconciled. . . .

The judicial test of whether the Government, on a plea of military necessity, can validly deprive an individual of any of his constitutional rights is whether the deprivation is reasonably related to a public danger that is so "immediate, imminent, and impending" as not to admit of delay and not to permit the intervention of ordinary constitutional processes to alleviate the danger. . . . Civilian Exclusion Order No. 34, banishing from a prescribed area of the Pacific Coast "all persons of Japanese ancestry, both alien and non-alien," clearly does not meet that test. Being an obvious racial discrimination, the order deprives all those within its scope of the equal protection of the laws as guaranteed by the Fifth Amendment. It further deprives these individuals of their constitutional rights to live and work where they will, to establish a home where they choose and to move about freely. In excommunicating them without benefit of hearings, this order also deprives them of all their constitutional rights to procedural due process. Yet no reasonable relation to an "immediate, imminent, and impending" public danger is evident to support this racial restriction which is one of the most sweeping and complete deprivations of constitutional rights in the history of this nation in the absence of martial law.

It must be conceded that the military and naval situation in the spring of 1942 was such as to generate a very real fear of invasion of the Pacific Coast, accompanied by fears of sabotage and espionage in that area. The military command was therefore justified in adopting all reasonable means necessary to combat these dangers. In adjudging the military action taken in light of the then apparent dangers, we must not erect too high or too meticulous standards; it is necessary only that the action have some reasonable relation to the removal of the dangers of invasion, sabotage and espionage. But the exclusion, either temporarily or permanently, of all persons with Japanese blood in their veins has no such reasonable relation. And that relation is lacking because the exclusion order necessarily must rely for its reasonableness upon the assumption that *all* persons of Japanese ancestry may have a dangerous tendency to commit sabotage and espionage and to aid our Japanese enemy in other ways. It is difficult to believe that reason, logic or experience could be marshalled in support of such an assumption.

That this forced exclusion was the result in good measure of this erroneous assumption of racial guilt rather than bona fide military necessity is evidenced by the Commanding General's Final Report on the evacuation from the Pacific Coast area. In it he refers to all individuals of Japanese descent as "subversive," as belonging to "an enemy race" whose "racial strains are undiluted," and as constituting "over 112,000 potential enemies . . . at large today" along the Pacific Coast. In support of this blanket condemnation of all persons of Japanese descent, however, no reliable evidence is cited to show that such individuals were generally disloyal, or had generally so conducted themselves in this area as to constitute a special menace to defense installations or war industries, or had otherwise by their behavior furnished reasonable ground for their exclusion as a group. . . .

The main reasons relied upon by those responsible for the forced evacuation, therefore, do not prove a reasonable relation between the group characteristics of Japanese Americans and the dangers of invasion, sabotage and espionage. The reasons appear, instead, to be largely an accumulation of much of the misinformation, half-truths and insinuations that for years have been directed against Japanese Americans by people with racial and economic prejudices—the same people who have been among the foremost advocates of the evacuation. A military judgment based upon such racial and sociological considerations is not entitled to the great weight ordinarily given the judgments based upon strictly military considerations. Especially is this so when every charge relative to race, religion, culture, geographical location, and legal and economic status has been substantially discredited by independent studies made by experts in these matters. . . .

The military necessity which is essential to the validity of the evacuation order thus resolves itself into a few intimations that certain individuals actively aided the enemy, from which it is inferred that the entire group of Japanese Americans could not be trusted to be or remain loyal to the United States. No one denies, of course, that there were some disloyal persons of Japanese descent on the Pacific Coast who did all in their power to aid their ancestral land. Similar disloyal activities have been engaged in by many persons of German, Italian and even more pioneer stock in our country. But to infer that examples of individual disloyalty prove group disloyalty and justify discriminatory action against the entire group is to deny that under our system of law individual guilt is the sole basis for deprivation of rights. Moreover, this inference, which is at the very heart of the evacuation orders, has been used in support of the abhorrent and despicable treatment of minority groups by the dictatorial tyrannies which this nation is now pledged to destroy. To give constitutional sanction to that inference in this case, however well-intentioned may have been the military command on the Pacific Coast, is to adopt one of the cruelest of the rationales used by our enemies to destroy the dignity of the individual and to encourage and open the door to discriminatory actions against other minority groups in the passions of tomorrow.

No adequate reason is given for the failure to treat these Japanese Americans on an individual basis by holding investigations and hearings to separate the loyal from the disloyal, as was done in the case of persons of German and Italian ancestry. . . . It is asserted merely that the loyalties of this group "were unknown and time was of the essence." Yet nearly four months elapsed after Pearl Harbor before the first exclusion order was issued; nearly eight months went by until the last order was issued; and the last of these "subversive" persons was not actually removed until almost eleven months had elapsed. Leisure and deliberation seem to have been more of the essence than speed. And the fact that conditions were not such as to warrant a declaration of martial law adds strength to the belief that the factors of time and military necessity were not as urgent as they have been represented to be. . . .

I dissent, therefore, from this legalization of racism. Racial discrimination in any form and in any degree has no justifiable part whatever in our democratic way of life. It is unattractive in any setting but it is utterly revolting among a free people who have embraced the principles set forth in the Constitution of the United States. All residents of this nation are kin in some way by blood or culture to a foreign land. Yet they are primarily and necessarily a part of the new and distinct civilization of the United States. They must accordingly be treated at all times as the heirs of the American experiment and as entitled to all the rights and freedoms guaranteed by the Constitution.

DISSENT BY JUSTICE JACKSON. Korematsu was born on our soil, of parents born in Japan. The Constitution makes him a citizen of the United States by nativity and a citizen of California by residence. No claim is made that he is not loyal to this country. There is no suggestion that apart from the matter involved here he is not law-abiding and well disposed. Korematsu, however, has been convicted of an act not commonly a crime. It consists merely of being present in the state whereof he is a citizen, near the place where he was born, and where all his life he has lived.

Even more unusual is the series of military orders which made this conduct a crime. They forbid such a one to remain, and they also forbid him to leave. They were so drawn that the only way Korematsu could avoid violation was to give himself up to the military authority. This meant submission to custody, examination, and transportation out of the territory, to be followed by indeterminate confinement in detention camps.

A citizen's presence in the locality, however, was made a crime only if his parents were of Japanese birth. Had Korematsu been one of four—the others being, say, a German alien enemy, an Italian alien enemy, and a citizen of American-born ancestors, convicted of treason but out on parole—only Korematsu's presence would have violated the order. The difference between their innocence and his crime would result, not from anything he did, said, or thought, different than they, but only in that he was born of different racial stock.

Now, if any fundamental assumption underlies our system, it is that guilt is personal and not inheritable. Even if all of one's antecedents had been convicted of treason, the Constitution forbids its penalties to be visited upon him, for it provides that "no attainder of treason shall work corruption of blood, or forfeiture except during the life of the person attainted." But here is an attempt to make an otherwise innocent act a crime merely because this prisoner is the son of parents as to whom he had no choice, and belongs to a race from which there is no way to resign. If Congress in peace-time legislation should enact such a criminal law, I should suppose this Court would refuse to enforce it.

But the "law" which this prisoner is convicted of disregarding is not found in an act of Congress, but in a military order. Neither the Act of Congress nor the Executive Order of the President, nor both together, would afford a basis for this conviction. It rests on the orders of General DeWitt. And it is said that if the military commander had reasonable military grounds for promulgating the orders, they are constitutional and become law, and the Court is required to enforce them. There are several reasons why I cannot subscribe to this doctrine.

It would be impracticable and dangerous idealism to expect or insist that each specific military command in an area of probable operations will conform to conventional tests of constitutionality. When an area is so beset that it must be put under military control at all, the paramount consideration is that its measures be successful, rather than legal. The armed services must protect a society, not merely its Constitution. The very essence of the military job is to marshal physical force, to remove every obstacle to its effectiveness, to give it every strategic advantage. Defense measures will not, and often should not, be held within the limits that bind civil authority in peace. No court can require such a commander in such circumstances to act as a reasonable man; he may be unreasonably cautious and exacting. Perhaps he should be. But a commander in temporarily focusing the life of a community on defense is carrying out a military program; he is not making law in the sense the courts know the term. He issues orders, and they may have a certain authority as military commands, although they may be very bad as constitutional law.

But if we cannot confine military expedients by the Constitution, neither would I distort the Constitution to approve all that the military may deem expedient. That is what the Court appears to be doing, whether consciously or not. I cannot say, from any evidence before me, that the orders of General DeWitt were not reasonably expedient military precautions, nor could I say that they were. But even if they were permissible military procedures, I deny that it follows that they are constitutional. If, as the Court holds, it does follow, then we may as well say that any military order will be constitutional and have done with it.

The limitation under which courts always will labor in examining the necessity for a military order are illustrated by this case. How does the Court know that these orders have a reasonable basis in necessity? No evidence whatever on that subject has been taken by this or any other court. There is sharp controversy as to the credibility of the DeWitt report. So the Court, having no real evidence before it, has no choice but to accept General DeWitt's own unsworn, self-serving statement, untested by any cross-examination, that what he did was reasonable. And thus it will always be when courts try to look into the reasonableness of a military order.

In the very nature of things, military decisions are not susceptible of intelligent judicial appraisal. They do not pretend to rest on evidence, but are made on information that often would not be admissible and on assumptions that could not be proved. Information in support of an order could not be disclosed to courts without danger that it would reach the enemy. Neither can courts act on communications made in confidence. Hence courts can never have any real alternative to accepting the mere declaration of the authority that issued the order that it was reasonably necessary from a military viewpoint.

Much is said of the danger to liberty from the Army program for deporting and detaining these citizens of Japanese extraction. But a judicial construction of the due process clause that will sustain this order is a far more subtle blow to liberty than the promulgation of the order itself. A military order, however unconstitutional, is not apt to last longer than the military emergency. Even during that period a succeeding commander may revoke it all. But once a judicial opinion rationalizes such an order to show that it conforms to the Constitution, or rather rationalizes the Constitution to show that the Constitution sanctions such an order, the Court for all time has validated the principle of racial discrimination in criminal procedure and of transplanting American citizens. The principle then lies about like a loaded weapon ready for the hand of any authority that can bring forward a plausible claim of an urgent need. Every repetition imbeds that principle more deeply in our law and thinking and expands it to new purposes. All who observe the work of courts are familiar with what Judge Cardozo described as "the tendency of a principle to expand itself to the limit of its logic." A military commander may overstep the bounds of constitutionality, and it is an incident. But if we review and approve, that passing incident becomes the doctrine of the Constitution. There it has a generative power of its own, and all that it creates will be in its own image. Nothing better illustrates this danger than does the Court's opinion in this case. . . .

My duties as a justice as I see them do not require me to make a military judgment as to whether General DeWitt's evacuation and detention program was a reasonable military necessity. I do not suggest that the courts should have attempted to interfere with the Army in carrying out its task. But I do not think they may be asked to execute a military expedient that has no place in law under the Constitution. I would reverse the judgment and discharge the prisoner.

Ex parte Endo 323 U.S. 284 (1944)

Fortunately, there were limits to the extent to which the Supreme Court was willing to go in supporting the military authorities' treatment of Japanese-Americans, as the case below indicates. Indeed, the contrast between the Court's permissive attitude in Hirabayashi *and this case is striking.*

COURT OPINION BY JUSTICE DOUGLAS. Mitsuye Endo, hereinafter designated as the appellant, is an American citizen of Japanese ancestry. She was evacuated from Sacramento, California, in 1942, pursuant to certain military orders which we will presently discuss, and was removed to the Tule Lake War Relocation Center located at Newell, Modoc County, California. In July, 1942, she filed a petition for a writ of habeas corpus in the District Court of the United States for the Northern District of California, asking that she be discharged and restored to liberty. That petition was denied by the District Court in July, 1943, and an appeal was perfected to the Circuit Court of Appeals in August, 1943. Shortly thereafter appellant was transferred from the Tule Lake Relocation Center to the Central Utah Relocation Center located at Topaz, Utah, where she is presently detained. . . .

Her petition for a writ of habeas corpus alleges that she is a loyal and law-abiding citizen of the United States, that no charge has been made against her, that she is being unlawfully detained, and that she is confined in the Relocation Center under armed guard and held there against her will.

It is conceded by the Department of Justice and by the War Relocation Authority that appellant is a loyal and law-abiding citizen. They make no claim that she is detained on any charge or that she is even suspected of disloyalty. Moreover, they do not contend that she may be held any longer in the Relocation Center. They concede that it is beyond the power of the War Relocation Authority to detain citizens against whom no charges of disloyalty or subversiveness have been made for a period longer than that necessary to separate the loyal from the disloyal and to provide the necessary guidance for relocation. But they maintain that detention for an additional period after leave clearance has been granted is an essential step in the evacuation program. . . .

It is argued that such a planned and orderly relocation was essential to the success of the evacuation program; that but for such supervision there might have been a dangerously disorderly migration of unwanted people to unprepared communities; that unsupervised evacuation might have resulted in hardship and disorder; that the success of the evacuation program was thought to require the knowledge that the federal government was maintaining control over the evacuated population except as the release of individuals could be effected consistently with their own peace and well-being and that of the nation; that although community hostility towards the evacuees has diminished, it has not disappeared and the continuing control of the Authority over the relocation process is essential to the success of the evacuation program. It is argued that supervised relocation, as the chosen method of terminating the evacuation, is the final step in the entire process and is a consequence of the first step taken. It is conceded that appellant's detention pending compliance with the leave regulations is not directly connected with the prevention of espionage and sabotage at the present time. But it is argued that Executive Order No. 9102 confers power to make regulations necessary and proper for controlling situations created by the exercise of the powers expressly conferred for protection against espionage and sabotage. The leave regulations are said to fall within that category.

We are of the view that Mitsuye Endo should be given her liberty. In reaching that conclusion we do not come to the underlying constitutional issues which have been argued. For we conclude that, whatever power the War Relocation Authority may have to detain other classes of citizens, it has no authority to subject citizens who are concededly loyal to its leave procedure. . . .

This Court has quite consistently given a narrower scope for the operation of the presumption of constitutionality when legislation appeared on its face to violate a specific prohibition of the Constitution. We have likewise favored that interpretation of legislation which gives it the greater chance of surviving the test of constitutionality. Those analogies are suggestive here. We must assume that the Chief Executive and members of Congress, as well as the courts, are sensitive to and respectful of the liberties of the citizen. In interpreting a wartime measure we must assume that their purpose was to allow for the greatest possible accommodation between those liberties and the exigencies of war. We must assume, when asked to find implied powers in a grant of legislative or executive authority, that the law makers intended to place no greater restraint on the citizen than was clearly and unmistakably indicated by the language they used. . . .

A citizen who is concededly loyal presents no problem of espionage or sabotage. Loyalty is a matter of the heart and mind, not of race, creed, or color. He who is loyal is by definition not a spy or a saboteur. When the power to detain is derived from the power to protect the war effort against espionage and sabotage, detention which has no relationship to that objective is unauthorized.

Nor may the power to detain an admittedly loyal citizen or to grant him a conditional release be implied as a useful or convenient step in the evacuation program, whatever authority might be implied in case of those whose loyalty was not conceded or established. If we assume (as we do) that the original evacuation was justified, its lawful character was derived from the fact that it was an espionage and sabotage measure, not that there was community hostility to this group of American citizens. The evacuation program rested explicitly on the former ground not on the latter as the underlying legislation shows. The authority to detain a citizen or to grant him a conditional release as protection against espionage or sabotage is exhausted at least when his loyalty is conceded. If we held that the authority to detain continued thereafter, we would transform an espionage or sabotage measure into something else. That was not done by Executive Order No. 9066 or by the Act of March 21, 1942, which ratified it. What they did not do we cannot do. Detention which furthered the campaign against espionage and sabotage would be one thing. But detention which has no relationship to that campaign is of a distinct character. Community hostility even to loyal evacuees may have been (and perhaps still is) a serious problem. . . .

Mitsuye Endo is entitled to an unconditional release by the War Relocation Authority.

CONCURRING OPINION BY JUSTICE MURPHY. I join in the opinion of the Court, but I am of the view that detention in Relocation Centers of persons of Japanese ancestry regardless of loyalty is not only unauthorized by Congress or the Executive but is another example of the unconstitutional resort to racism inherent in the entire evacuation program. . . . [R]acial discrimination of this nature bears no reasonable relation to military necessity and is utterly foreign to the ideals and traditions of the American people.

Slowing the Imperial Presidency: *Youngstown*

By the Cold War period, American presidents had come to dominate the nation's political landscape, and they were increasingly the dominant figure in foreign and military affairs. In 1952, Harry S. Truman became the first president to assert the legal right to involve the nation in a major war without prior congressional approval. The Supreme Court stayed out of this affair, but it did react when Truman tried to use such an expansive reading of his war powers to shut down a steel strike.

Youngstown Sheet and Tube Co. v. Sawyer 343 U.S. 579 (1952)

COURT OPINION BY JUSTICE BLACK. We are asked to decide whether the President was acting within his constitutional power when he issued an order directing the Secretary of Commerce to take possession of and operate most of the Nation's steel mills. The mill owners argue that the President's order amounts to lawmaking, a legislative function which the Constitution has expressly confided to the Congress and not to the President. The Government's position is that the order was made on findings of the President that his action was necessary to avert a national catastrophe which would inevitably result from a stoppage of steel production, and that in meeting this grave emergency the President was acting within the aggregate of his constitutional powers as the Nation's Chief Executive and the Commander in Chief of the Armed Forces of the United States. . . .

The contention is that presidential power should be implied from the aggregate of his powers under the Constitution. Particular reliance is placed on provisions in Article II which say that "The executive Power shall be vested in a President . . ."; that "he shall take Care that the Laws be faithfully executed"; and that he "shall be Commander in Chief of the Army and Navy of the United States."

The order cannot properly be sustained as an exercise of the President's military power as Commander in Chief of the Armed Forces. The Government attempts to do so by citing a number of cases upholding broad powers in military commanders engaged in day-to-day fighting in a theater of war. Such cases need not concern us here. Even though "theater of war" be an expanding concept, we cannot with faithfulness to our constitutional system hold that the Commander in Chief of the Armed Forces has the ultimate power as such to take possession of private property in order to keep labor disputes from stopping production. This is a job for the Nation's lawmakers, not for its military authorities.

CONCURRING OPINION BY JUSTICE FRANKFURTER. The power to seize has uniformly been given only for a limited period or for a defined emergency, or has been repealed after a short period. Its exercise has been restricted to particular circumstances such as "time of war or when war is imminent," the needs of "public safety" or of "national security or defense," or "urgent and impending need." . . .

The clause on which the Government . . . relies is that "The President shall be Commander in Chief of the Army and Navy of the United States. . . ." These cryptic words have given rise to some of the most persistent controversies in our constitutional history. Of course, they imply something more than an empty title. But just what authority goes with the name has plagued presidential advisers who would not waive or narrow it by nonassertion yet cannot say where it begins or ends. It undoubtedly puts the Nation's armed forces under presidential command. Hence, this loose appellation is sometimes advanced as support for any presidential action, internal or external, involving use of force, the idea being that it vests power to do anything, anywhere, that can be done with an army or navy.

That seems to be the logic of an argument tendered at our bar—that the President having, on his own responsibility, sent American troops abroad derives from that act "affirmative power" to seize the means of producing a supply of steel for them. To quote, "Perhaps the most forceful illustration of the scope of Presidential power in this connection is the fact that American troops in Korea, whose safety and effectiveness are so directly involved here, were sent to the field by an exercise of the President's constitutional powers." Thus, it is said, he has invested himself with "war powers."

I cannot foresee all that it might entail if the Court should indorse this argument. Nothing in our Constitution is plainer than that declaration of a war is entrusted only to Congress. Of course, a state of war may in fact exist without a formal declaration. But no doctrine that the Court could promulgate would seem to me more sinister and alarming than that a President whose conduct of foreign affairs is so largely uncontrolled, and often even is unknown, can vastly enlarge his mastery over the internal affairs of the country by his own commitment of the Nation's armed forces to some foreign venture. I do not, however, find it necessary or appropriate to consider the legal status of the Korean enterprise to discountenance argument based on it. . . .

Assuming that we are in a war *de facto*, whether it is or is not a war *de jure*, does that empower the Commander in Chief to seize industries he thinks necessary to supply our army? The Constitution expressly places in Congress power "to raise and *support* Armies" and "to *provide* and *maintain* a Navy." (Emphasis supplied.) This certainly lays upon Congress primary responsibility for supplying the armed forces. Congress alone controls the raising of revenues and their appropriation and may determine in what manner and by what means they shall be spent for military and naval procurement. I suppose no one would doubt that Congress can take over war supply as a Government enterprise. On the other hand, if Congress sees fit to rely on free private enterprise collectively bargaining with free labor for support and maintenance of our armed forces, can the Executive, because of lawful disagreements incidental to that process, seize the facility for operation upon Government-imposed terms?

There are indications that the Constitution did not contemplate that the title Commander in Chief *of the Army and Navy* will constitute him also Commander in Chief of the country, its industries and its inhabitants. He has no monopoly of "war powers," whatever they are. While Congress cannot deprive the President of the command of the army and navy, only Congress can provide him an army or navy to command. It is also empowered to make rules for the "Government and Regulation of land and naval Forces," by which it may to some unknown extent impinge upon even command functions. . . .

We should not use this occasion to circumscribe, much less to contract, the lawful role of the President as Commander in Chief. I should indulge the widest latitude of interpretation to sustain his exclusive function to command the instruments of national force, at least when turned against the outside world for the security of our society. But, when it is turned inward, not because of rebellion but because of a lawful economic struggle between industry and labor, it should have no such indulgence. His command power is not such an absolute as might be implied from that office in a militaristic system but is subject to limitations consistent with a constitutional Republic whose law and policy-making branch is a representative Congress. The purpose of lodging dual titles in one man was to insure that the civilian would control the military, not to enable the military to subordinate the presidential office. No penance would ever expiate the sin against free government of holding that a President can escape control of executive powers by law through assuming his military role. What the power of command may include I do not try to envision, but I think it is not a military prerogative, without support of law, to seize persons or property because they are important or even essential for the military and naval establishment.

Gulf of Tonkin Resolution (1964)

In response to an alleged assault by North Vietnamese torpedo boats on a U.S. destroyer in the Gulf of Tonkin, President Lyndon Johnson asked Congress for a resolution supporting an expanded American military role in the region. Angered by what was believed to have been an unprovoked assault on an American vessel in neutral waters, Congress responded with a resolution that practically gave Johnson a blank check to pursue whatever military measures he thought were necessary to secure victory in Vietnam. The result was a wholesale relinquishment to the president of Congress's oversight authority on matters of waging war.

Joint Resolution
  To promote the maintenance of international peace and security in southeast Asia.

Whereas naval units of the Communist regime in Vietnam, in violation of the principles of the Charter of the United Nations and of international law, have deliberately and repeatedly attacked United States naval vessels lawfully present in international waters; and have thereby created a serious threat to international peace; and

Whereas these attacks are part of a deliberate and systematic campaign of aggression that the Communist regime in North Vietnam has been waging against its neighbors and the nations joined with them in the collective defense of their freedom; and

Whereas the United States is assisting the peoples of southeast Asia to protect their freedom and has no territorial, military or political ambitions in that area, but desires only that these peoples should be left in peace to work out their own destinies in their own way: Now, therefore, be it

Resolved by the Senate and House of Representatives of the United States of America in Congress assembled, That the Congress approves and supports the determination of the President, as Commander in Chief, to take all necessary measures to repel any armed attack against the forces of the United States and to prevent further aggression.

Sec. 2. The United States regards as vital to its national interest and to world peace the maintenance of international peace and security in southeast Asia. Consonant with the Constitution of the United States and the Charter of the United Nations and in accordance with its obligations under the Southeast Asia Collective Defense Treaty, the United States is, therefore, prepared, as the President determines, to take all necessary steps, including the use of armed force, to assist any member or protocol state of the Southeast Asia Collective Treaty requesting assistance in defense of its freedom.

Sec. 3. This resolution shall expire when the President shall determine that the peace and security of the area is reasonably assured by international conditions created by action of the United Nations or otherwise, except that it may be terminated earlier by concurrent resolution of the Congress.

Approved August 10, 1964

War Powers Act (1973)

Dismayed by the willingness of President Johnson and then President Richard Nixon to plunge the nation deeper into the Vietnam quagmire with little or no congressional input, a contrite Congress repealed the Gulf of Tonkin Resolution in 1971. Two years later, Congress passed the War Powers Act of 1973, an attempt to restore the balance of constitutional authority for war-making decisions. The act tried to balance the legitimate need of a president to strike quickly in the case of a sudden military emergency with Congress's right to involve itself in decisions concerning long-term military commitments.

Joint Resolution Concerning the War Powers of Congress and the President.

Resolved by the Senate and House of Representatives of the United States of America in Congress assembled,

Short Title

Section 1. This joint resolution may be cited as the "War Powers Resolution."

Purpose and Policy

Sec. 2. (a) It is the purpose of this joint resolution to fulfill the intent of the framers of the Constitution of the United States and insure that the collective judgment of both the Congress and the President will apply to the introduction of United States Armed Forces into hostilities, or into situations where imminent involvement in hostilities is clearly indicated by the circumstances, and to the continued use of such forces in hostilities or in such situations.

(b) Under article I, section 8, of the Constitution, it is specifically provided that the Congress shall have the power to make all laws necessary and proper for carrying into execution, not only its own powers but also all other powers vested by the Constitution in the Government of the United States, or in any department or officer thereof.

(c) The constitutional powers of the President as Commander-in-Chief to introduce United States Armed Forces into hostilities, or into situations where imminent involvement in hostilities is clearly indicated by the circumstances, are exercised only pursuant to (1) a declaration of war, (2) specific statutory authorization, or (3) a national emergency created by attack upon the United States, its territories or possessions, or its armed forces.

Consultation

Sec. 3. The President in every possible instance shall consult with Congress before introducing United States Armed Forces into hostilities or into situations where imminent involvement in hostilities is clearly indicated by the circumstances, and after every such introduction shall consult regularly with the Congress until United States

Armed Forces are no longer engaged in hostilities or have been removed from such situations.

Reporting

Sec. 4. (a) In the absence of a declaration of war, in any case in which United States Armed Forces are introduced—

(1) into hostilities or into situations where imminent involvement in hostilities is clearly indicated by the circumstances;

(2) into the territory, airspace or waters of a foreign nation, while equipped for combat, except for deployments which relate solely to supply, replacement, repair, or training of such forces; or

(3) in numbers which substantially enlarge United States Armed Forces equipped for combat already located in a foreign nation; the President shall submit within 48 hours to the Speaker of the House of Representatives and to the President pro tempore of the Senate a report, in writing, setting forth—

(A) the circumstances necessitating the introduction of United States Armed Forces;

(B) the constitutional and legislative authority under which such introduction took place; and

(C) the estimated scope and duration of the hostilities or involvement.

(b) The President shall provide such other information as the Congress may request in the fulfillment of its constitutional responsibilities with respect to committing the Nation to war and to the use of United States Armed Forces abroad.

(c) Whenever United States Armed Forces are introduced into hostilities or into any situation described in subsection (a) of this section, the President shall, so long as such armed forces continue to be engaged in such hostilities or situation, report to the Congress periodically on the status of such hostilities or situations as well as on the scope and duration of such hostilities or situation, but in no event shall he report to the Congress less often than once very six months.

Congressional Action

Sec. 5. (a) Each report submitted pursuant to section 4(a)(1) shall be transmitted to the Speaker of the House of Representatives and to the President pro tempore of the Senate on the same calendar day. Each report so transmitted shall be referred to the Committee on Foreign Affairs on the House of Representatives and to the Committee on Foreign Relations of the Senate for appropriate action. If, when the report is transmitted, the Congress has adjourned sine die or has adjourned for any period in excess of three calendar days, the Speaker of the House of Representatives and the President pro tempore of the Senate, if they deem it advisable (or if petitioned by at least 30 percent of the membership of their respective Houses) shall jointly request the President to convene Congress in order that it may consider the report and take appropriate action pursuant to this section.

(b) Within sixty calendar days after a report is submitted or is required to be submitted pursuant to section 4(a)(1), whichever is earlier, the President shall terminate any use of United States Armed Forces with respect to which such report was submitted (or required to be submitted), unless the Congress (1) has declared war or has enacted a specific authorization for such use of United States Armed Forces, (2) has extended by law such sixty-day period, or (3) is physically unable to meet as a result of an armed attack upon the United States. Such sixty-day period shall be extended for not more than an additional thirty days if the President determines and certifies to the Congress in writing that unavoidable military necessity respecting the safety of United States Armed Forces requires the continued use of such armed forces in the course of bringing about a prompt removal of such forces.

(c) Notwithstanding subsection (b), at any time that United States Armed Forces are engaged in hostilities outside the territory of the United States, its possessions and territories without a declaration of war or specific statutory authorization, such forces shall be removed by the President if the Congress so directs by concurrent resolution.

Congressional Priority Procedures for Joint Resolution of Bill

Sec. 6. (a) Any joint resolution or bill introduced pursuant to section 5(b) at least thirty calendar days before the expiration of the sixty-day period specified in such section shall be referred to the Committee on Foreign Affairs of the House of Representatives or the Committee on Foreign Relations of the Senate, as the case may be, and such committee shall report one such joint resolution or bill, together with its recommendations, not later than twenty-four calendar days before the expiration of the sixty-day period specified in such section, unless such House shall otherwise determine by the yeas and nays.

(b) Any joint resolution or bill so reported shall become the pending business of the House in question (in the case of the Senate the time for debate shall be equally divided between the proponents and the opponents), and shall be voted on within three calendar days thereafter, unless such House shall otherwise determine by yeas and nays.

(c) Such a joint resolution or bill passed by one House shall be referred to the committee of the other House named in subsection (a) and shall be reported out not later than fourteen calendar days before the expiration of the sixty-day period specified in section 5(b). The joint resolution or bill so reported shall become the pending business of the House in question and shall be voted on within three calendar days after it has been reported, unless such House shall otherwise determine by yeas and nays.

(d) In the case of any disagreement between the two Houses of Congress with respect to a joint resolution or bill passed by both Houses, conferees shall be promptly appointed and the committee of conference shall make and file a report with respect to such resolution or bill not later than four calendar days before the expiration of the sixty-day period specified in section 5(b). In the event the conferees are unable to agree within 48 hours, they shall report back to their respective Houses in disagreement. Notwithstanding any rule in either House concerning the printing of conference reports in the Record or concerning any delay in the consideration of such reports, such report shall be acted on by both Houses not later than the expiration of such sixty-day period.

Congressional Priority Procedures for Concurrent Resolution

Sec. 7. (a) Any concurrent resolution introduced pursuant to section 5(c) shall be referred to the Committee on Foreign Affairs of the House of Representatives or the Committee on Foreign Relations of the Senate, as the case may be, and one such concurrent resolution shall be reported out by such committee together with its recommendations within fifteen calendar days, unless such House shall otherwise determine by the yeas and nays.

(b) Any concurrent resolution so reported shall become the pending business of the House in question (in the case of the Senate the time for debate shall be equally divided between the proponents and the opponents) and shall be voted on within three calendar days thereafter, unless such House shall otherwise determine by yeas and nays.

(c) Such a concurrent resolution passed by one House shall be referred to the committee of the other House named in subsection (a) and shall be reported out by such committee together with its recommendations within fifteen calendar days and shall thereupon become the pending business of such House and shall be voted upon within three calendar days, unless such House shall otherwise determine by yeas and nays.

(d) In the case of any disagreement between the two Houses of Congress with respect to a concurrent resolution passed by both Houses, conferees shall be promptly appointed and the committee of conference shall make and file a report with respect to such concurrent resolution within six calendar days after the legislation is referred to the committee of conference. Notwithstanding any rule in either House concerning the printing of conference reports in the Record or concerning any delay in the consideration of such reports, such report shall be acted on by both Houses not later than six calendar days after the conference report is filed. In the event the conferees are unable to agree within 48 hours, they shall report back to their respective Houses in disagreement.

Interpretation of Joint Resolution

Sec. 8. (a) Authority to introduce United States Armed Forces into hostilities or into situations wherein involvement in hostilities is clearly indicated by the circumstances shall not be inferred—

(1) from any provision of law (whether or not in effect before the date of the enactment of this joint resolution), including any provision contained in any appropriation Act, unless such provision specifically authorizes the introduction of United States Armed Forces into hostilities or into such situations and states that it is intended to constitute specific statutory authorization within the meaning of this joint resolution; or

(2) from any treaty heretofore or hereafter ratified unless such treaty is implemented by legislation specifically authorizing the introduction of United States Armed Forces into hostilities or into such situations and stating that it is intended to constitute specific statutory authorization within the meaning of this joint resolution.

(b) Nothing in this joint resolution shall be construed to require any further specific statutory authorization to permit members of United States Armed Forces to participate jointly with members of the armed forces of one or more foreign countries in the headquarters operations of high-level military commands which were established prior to the date of enactment of this joint resolution and pursuant to the United Nations Charter or any treaty ratified by the United States prior to such date.

(c) For purposes of this joint resolution, the term "introduction of United States Armed Forces" includes the assignment of members of such armed forces to command, coordinate, participate in the movement of, or accompany the regular or irregular military forces of any foreign country or government when such military forces are engaged, or there exists an imminent threat that such forces will become engaged, in hostilities.

(d) Nothing in this joint resolution—

(1) is intended to alter the constitutional authority of the Congress or of the President, or the provisions of existing treaties; or

(2) shall be construed as granting any authority to the President with respect to the introduction of United States Armed Forces into hostilities or into situations wherein involvement in hostilities is clearly indicated by the circumstances which authority he would not have had in the absence of this joint resolution.

Separability Clause

Sec. 9. If any provision of this joint resolution or the application thereof to any person or circumstance is held invalid, the remainder of the joint resolution and the application of such provision to any other person or circumstance shall not be affected thereby.

Effective Date

Sec. 10. This joint resolution shall take effect on the date of its enactment.

In the House of Representatives, U.S., November 7, 1973.

The House of Representatives having proceeded to reconsider the resolution (H.J. Res. 542) entitled "Joint resolution concerning the war powers of Congress and the President," returned by the President of the United States with his objections, to the House of Representatives, in which it originated, it was

Resolved, That the said resolution pass, two-thirds of the House of Representatives agreeing to pass the same.

Brandenburg v. Ohio 393 U.S. 948 (1969)

On the surface, the Brandenburg *case had little to do with war, involving instead an attempt by the state of Ohio to muzzle the racist pronouncements of a local Klansman. The Court's very libertarian reading of free speech rights in the* Brandenburg *case had an impact on the way Americans thought about free speech issues in general, however, and the Court explicitly repudiated the "clear and present danger" doctrine created by Justice Holmes in the* Schenck *case as a litmus test for wartime speech restrictions. The* Brandenburg *legacy has been to place the burden of proof on the government when it tries to curb free speech rights, in peacetime or in wartime.*

MR. JUSTICE BLACK, concurring [with the majority opinion, per curiam, and a concurring opinion by Justice Douglas]. I agree with the views expressed by MR. JUSTICE DOUGLAS in his concurring opinion in this case that the "clear and present danger" doctrine should have no place in the interpretation of the First Amendment. . . .

MR. JUSTICE DOUGLAS, concurring. [The World War I cases put] the gloss of "clear and present danger" on the First Amendment. Whether the war power—the greatest leveler of them all—is adequate to sustain that doctrine is debatable. . . . Though I doubt if the "clear and present danger" test is congenial to the First Amendment in time of a declared war, I am certain it is not reconcilable with the First Amendment in days of peace. . . .

I see no place in the regime of the First Amendment for any "clear and present danger" test, whether strict and tight as some would make it. . . .

When one reads the opinions closely and sees when and how the "clear and present danger" test has been applied, great misgivings are aroused. . . . [T]he threats were often loud but always puny and made serious only by judges so wedded to the *status quo* that critical analysis made them nervous. . . .

Suppose one tears up his own copy of the Constitution in eloquent protest to a decision of this Court. May he be indicted?

Suppose one rips his own Bible to shreds to celebrate his departure from one "faith" and his embrace of atheism. May he be indicted?

United States v. O'Brien 391 U.S. 367 (1968)

By 1968, the anti–Vietnam War movement in America was in full bloom, with thousands of activists—mainly college students—taking to the streets to engage in various forms of protest. One particularly egregious form, at least in the eyes of military authorities, was the illegal act of burning one's draft registration card as a symbolic protest of the war. The Supreme Court was eventually called upon to decide whether or not such activities were protected political speech. During the world wars, such an overt and dramatic attempt to subvert the draft would not likely have been met with much sympathy from the judges. In this case, the Court likewise decided that the government had a legitimate interest in protecting its power to register potential draftees. The times, however, would soon be changing.

COURT OPINION BY JUSTICE WARREN. On the morning of March 31, 1966, David Paul O'Brien and three companions burned their Selective Service registration certificates on the steps of the South Boston Courthouse. . . .

For this act, O'Brien was indicted, tried, convicted, and sentenced in the United States District Court for the District of Massachusetts. . . .

He was sentenced . . . to the custody of the Attorney General for a maximum period of six years for supervision and treatment. . . .

O'Brien argued that the [law] prohibiting the knowing destruction or mutilation of certificates was unconstitutional because it was enacted to abridge free speech, and because it served no legitimate legislative purpose. . . .

We cannot accept the view that an apparently limitless variety of conduct can be labeled "speech" whenever the person engaging in the conduct intends thereby to express an idea. However, even on the assumption that the alleged communicative element in O'Brien's conduct is sufficient to bring into play the First Amendment, it does not necessarily follow that the destruction of a registration certificate is constitutionally protected activity. . . . We think it clear that a government regulation is sufficiently justified if it is within the constitutional power of the Government; if it furthers an important or substantial governmental interest; if the governmental interest is unrelated to the suppression of free expression; and if the incidental restriction on alleged First Amendment freedoms is no greater than is essential to the furtherance of that interest. We find that the [law prohibiting destruction of draft cards] meets all of these requirements, and consequently that O'Brien can be constitutionally convicted for violating it.

The constitutional power of Congress to raise and support armies and to make all laws necessary and proper to that end is broad and sweeping. . . . Pursuant to this power, Congress may establish a system of registration for individuals liable for training and service, and may require such individuals within reason to cooperate in the registration system. The issuance of certificates indicating the registration and eligibility classification of individuals is a legitimate and substantial administrative aid in the functioning of this system. And legislation to insure the continuing availability of issued certificates serves a legitimate and substantial purpose in the system's administration.

Cohen v. California 403 U.S. 15 (1971)

Strictly speaking, the Cohen *case was not a direct reversal of the* O'Brien *ruling three years earlier. In that case, the Court saw the issue as a matter of one antiwar protester's actions, whereas in* Cohen *the issue is a matter of words—and the Court has always taken a dimmer view of government restrictions on the former. Also, the* Cohen *case does not address the matter of wartime dissent, per se; rather, it focuses on the general interests of the state in trying to abolish offensive speech, whether during times of war or of peace.* Cohen, *however, does signal a general underlying change in the philosophy of the Court, away from presumptions in favor of government's wartime interests to restrict dissent and more in favor of the right to express antiwar dissent.*

The defendant, while in the corridor of a county courthouse, was wearing a jacket bearing the plainly visible words "Fuck the Draft." On the basis of his having done this, he was convicted by a California municipal court for disturbing the peace by offensive conduct. . . .

COURT OPINION BY JUSTICE HARLAN. This case may seem at first blush too inconsequential to find its way into our books, but the issue it presents is of no small constitutional significance. . . .

Cohen consistently claimed that, as construed to apply to the facts of this case, the statute infringed his rights to freedom of expression guaranteed by the First and Fourteenth Amendments of the Federal Constitution. . . .

The conviction quite clearly rests upon the asserted offensiveness of the *words* Cohen used to convey his message to the public. The only "conduct" which the State sought to punish is the fact of communication. . . . Further, the State certainly lacks power to punish Cohen for the underlying content of the message the inscription conveyed. At least so long as there is no showing of an intent to incite disobedience to or disruption of the draft, Cohen could not, consistently with the First and Fourteenth Amendments, be punished for asserting the evident position on the inutility or immorality of the draft his jacket reflected. . . .

Appellant's conviction, then, rests squarely upon his exercise of the "freedom of speech" protected from arbitrary governmental interference by the Constitution and can be justified, if at all, only as a valid regulation of the manner in which he exercised that freedom, not as a permissible prohibition on the substantive message it conveys. . . .

The constitutional right of free expression is powerful medicine in a society as diverse and populous as ours. It is designed and intended to remove governmental restraints from the arena of public discussion, putting the decision as to what views shall be voiced largely into the hands of each of us, in the hope that use of such freedom will ultimately produce a more capable citizenry and more perfect polity and in the belief that no other approach would comport with the premise of individual dignity and choice upon which our political system rests. . . .

To many, the immediate consequence of this freedom may often appear to be only verbal tumult, discord, and even offensive utterance. These are, however, within established limits, in truth necessary side effects of the broader enduring values which the process of open debate permits us to achieve. That the air may at times seem filled with verbal cacophony is, in this sense not a sign of weakness but of strength. We cannot lose sight of the fact that, in what otherwise might seem a trifling and annoying instance of individual distasteful abuse of a privilege, these fundamental societal values are truly implicated. . . .

[W]e cannot indulge the facile assumption that one can forbid particular words without also running a substantial risk of suppressing ideas in the process. Indeed, governments might soon seize upon the censorship of particular words as a convenient guise for banning the expression of unpopular views. We have been able, as noted above, to discern little social benefit that might result from running the risk of opening the door to such grave results.

Tinker v. Des Moines Independent Community School District 393 U.S. 503 (1969)

This newfound presumption in favor of antiwar dissent can also be glimpsed in this case, which involved the right of schoolchildren to protest the Vietnam War. Again, the case did not directly address wartime dissent, per se, but the issues in question were anti–Vietnam War activism and First Amendment rights in public schools.

COURT OPINION BY JUSTICE FORTAS. In December 1965, a group of adults and students in Des Moines held a meeting at the Eckhardt home. The group determined to publicize their objections to the hostilities in Vietnam and their support for a truce by wearing black armbands during the holiday season and by fasting on December 16 and New Year's Eve. . . .

The principals of the Des Moines schools became aware of the plan to wear armbands. On December 14, 1965, they met and adopted a policy that any student wearing an armband to school would be asked to remove it, and if he refused he would be suspended until he returned without the armband. . . .

On December 16, Mary Beth and Christopher wore black armbands to their schools. John Tinker wore his armband the next day. They were all sent home and suspended from school until they would come back without their armbands. . . .

[T]he wearing of armbands in the circumstances of this case was entirely divorced from actually or potentially disruptive conduct by those participating in it. It was closely akin to "pure speech" which, we have repeatedly held, is entitled to comprehensive protection under the First Amendment. . . .

First Amendment rights, applied in light of the special characteristics of the school environment, are available to teachers and students. It can hardly be argued that either students or teachers shed their constitutional rights to freedom of speech or expression at the schoolhouse gate. . . .

The school officials banned and sought to punish petitioners for a silent, passive expression of opinion, unaccompanied by any disorder or disturbance on the part of petitioners. There is here no evidence whatever of petitioners' interference, actual or nascent, with the schools' work or of collision with the rights of other students to be secure and to be let alone. Accordingly, this case does not concern speech or action that intrudes upon the work of the schools or the rights of other students. . . .

[I]n our system, undifferentiated fear or apprehension of disturbance is not enough to overcome the right to freedom of expression. Any departure from absolute regimentation may cause trouble. Any variation from the majority's opinion may inspire fear. Any word spoken, in class, in the lunchroom, or on the campus, that deviates from the views of another person may start an argument or cause a disturbance. But our Constitution says we must take this risk. . . .

[O]ur independent examination of the record fails to yield evidence that the school authorities had reason to anticipate that the wearing of the armbands would substantially interfere with the work of the school or impinge upon the rights of other students. . . .

Moreover, the testimony of school authorities at trial indicates that it was not fear of disruption that motivated the regulation prohibiting the armbands; the regulation was directed against "the principle of the demonstration" itself. School authorities simply felt that "the schools are no place for demonstrations," and if the students "didn't like the way our elected officials were handling things, it should be handled with the ballot box and not in the halls of our public schools."

On the contrary, the action of the school authorities appears to have been based upon an urgent wish to avoid the controversy which might result from the expression, even by the silent symbol of armbands, of opposition to this Nation's part in the conflagration in Vietnam. . . .

It is also relevant that the school authorities did not purport to prohibit the wearing of all symbols of political or controversial significance. The record shows that students in some of the schools wore buttons relating to national political campaigns, and some even wore the Iron Cross, traditionally a symbol of Nazism. The order prohibiting the wearing of armbands did not extend to these. Instead, a particular symbol—black armbands worn to exhibit opposition to this Nation's involvement in Vietnam—was singled out for prohibition. Clearly, the prohibition of expression of one particular opinion, at least without evidence that it is necessary to avoid material and substantial interference with schoolwork or discipline, is not constitutionally permissible. . . .

Under our Constitution, free speech is not a right that is given only to be so circumscribed that it exists in principle but not in fact. Freedom of expression would not truly exist if the right could be exercised only in an area that a benevolent government has provided as a safe haven for crackpots. The Constitution says that Congress (and the States) may not abridge the right to free speech. This provision means what it says. We properly read it to permit reasonable regulation of speech-connected activities in carefully restricted circumstances. But we do not confine the permissible exercise of First Amendment rights to a telephone booth or the four corners of a pamphlet, or to supervised and ordained discussion in a school classroom.

Flower v. United States 407 U.S. 197 (1972)

By 1972, the Vietnam War was slowly winding down to its tragic end, and the Supreme Court had traveled far down the road of libertarian

interpretation of First Amendment rights. In this case, the Court up-
held the right of a Vietnam War protester to express his views within
the shadow of a major military installation.

COURT OPINION PER CURIAM. Petitioner John Thomas
Flower, a regional "Peace Education Secretary" of the American
Friends Service Committee and a civilian, was arrested by military police while quietly distributing leaflets on New Braunfels Avenue at a
point within the limits of Fort Sam Houston, San Antonio, Texas. . . .
[I]t was established that petitioner had previously been barred from
the post by order of the deputy commander because of alleged participation in an attempt to distribute "unauthorized" leaflets. The District Court . . . sentenced petitioner to six months in prison. . . .

We reverse. Whatever power the authorities may have to restrict
general access to a military facility . . . here the fort commander chose
not to exclude the public from the street where petitioner was arrested. . . .

Under such circumstances the military has abandoned any claim
that it has special interests in who walks, talks, or distributes leaflets
on the avenue. The base commandant can no more order petitioner off
this public street because he was distributing leaflets than could the
city police order any leafleteer off any public street. . . .

New York Times Co. v. United States 403 U.S. 713 (1971)

In 1971, a Defense Department employee named Daniel Ellsberg
leaked classified Pentagon documents about the Vietnam War to the
press, touching off a firestorm of controversy. The "Pentagon Papers"
documented years of lies, half-truths, and errors committed by the
Kennedy and Johnson administrations relating to Vietnam War poli-
cies. Even though the papers had little to do with him, President
Richard Nixon was furious at this security leak, and he tried to stop
the New York Times *and other newspapers from publishing the pa-*
pers. Nixon cited national security concerns, which in another time
might have had some effect on the justices. In 1971, however, the
Supreme Court was far less willing to give the executive branch the
benefit of the doubt when it asserted wartime security concerns as a
means to suppress First Amendment rights.

The litigation here was extremely complex, with several of the jus-
tices filing lengthy concurring and dissenting opinions from the brief

per curiam opinion allowing publication of the papers. The portions cited below are those that deal most directly with the issues of wartime dissent.

CONCURRING OPINION BY JUSTICE BLACK. I believe that every moment's continuance of the injunctions against these newspapers amounts to a flagrant, indefensible, and continuing violation of the First Amendment. . . .

[T]he Government argues in its brief that in spite of the First Amendment, "the authority of the Executive Department to protect the nation against publication of information whose disclosure would endanger the national security stems from two interrelated sources: the constitutional power of the President over the conduct of foreign affairs and his authority as Commander-in-Chief."

In other words, we are asked to hold that despite the First Amendment's emphatic command, the Executive Branch, the Congress, and the Judiciary can make laws enjoining publication of current news and abridging freedom of the press in the name of "national security." The Government does not even attempt to rely on any act of Congress. Instead it makes the bold and dangerously far-reaching contention that the courts should take it upon themselves to "make" a law abridging freedom of the press in the name of equity, presidential power and national security, even when the representatives of the people in Congress have adhered to the command of the First Amendment and refused to make such a law. . . . To find that the President has "inherent power" to halt the publication of news by resort to the courts would wipe out the First Amendment and destroy the fundamental liberty and security of the very people the Government hopes to make "secure." . . .

The word "security" is a broad, vague generality whose contours should not be invoked to abrogate the fundamental law embodied in the First Amendment. The guarding of military and diplomatic secrets at the expense of informed representative government provides no real security for our Republic. . . .

CONCURRING OPINION BY JUSTICE DOUGLAS. The power to wage war is "the power to wage war successfully." . . . But the war power stems from a declaration of war. The Constitution . . . gives Congress, not the President, power "to declare War." Nowhere are presidential wars authorized. We need not decide therefore what leveling effect the war power of Congress might have. . . .

Secrecy in government is fundamentally anti-democratic, perpetuating bureaucratic errors. Open debate and discussion of public issues are vital to our national health. On public questions there should be "uninhibited, robust, and wide-open" debate. . . .

CONCURRING OPINION BY JUSTICE BRENNAN. The entire thrust of the Government's claim throughout these cases has been that publication of the material sought to be enjoined "could," or "might," or "may" prejudice the national interest in various ways. But the First Amendment tolerates absolutely no prior judicial restraints of the press predicated upon surmise or conjecture that untoward consequences may result. Our cases, it is true, have indicated that there is a single, extremely narrow class of cases in which the First Amendment's ban on prior judicial restraint may be overridden. Our cases have thus far indicated that such cases may arise only when the Nation "is at war." . . . Even if the present world situation were assumed to be tantamount to a time of war, or if the power of presently available armaments would justify even in peacetime the suppression of information that would set in motion a nuclear holocaust, in neither of these actions has the Government presented or even alleged that publication of items from or based upon the material at issue would cause the happening of an event of that nature. . . .

CONCURRING OPINION BY JUSTICE STEWART. In the governmental structure created by our Constitution, the Executive is endowed with enormous power in the two related areas of national defense and international relations. This power, largely unchecked by the Legislative and Judicial branches, has been pressed to the very hilt since the advent of the nuclear missile age. For better or for worse, the simple fact is that a President of the United States possesses vastly greater constitutional independence in these two vital areas of power than does, say, a prime minister of a country with a parliamentary form of government. . . .

In the absence of the governmental checks and balances present in other areas of our national life, the only effective restraint upon executive policy and power in the areas of national defense and international affairs may lie in an enlightened citizenry—in an informed and critical public opinion which alone can here protect the values of democratic government. For this reason, it is perhaps here that a press that is alert, aware, and free most vitally serves the basic purpose of the First Amendment. For without an informed and free press there cannot be an enlightened people.

Yet it is elementary that the successful conduct of international diplomacy and the maintenance of an effective national defense require both confidentiality and secrecy. Other nations can hardly deal with this Nation in an atmosphere of mutual trust unless they can be assured that their confidences will be kept. And within our own executive departments, the development of considered and intelligent international policies would be impossible if those charged with their formulation could not communicate with each other freely, frankly, and in confidence. In the area of basic national defense the frequent need for absolute secrecy is, of course, self-evident.

I think there can be but one answer to this dilemma, if dilemma it be. The responsibility must be where the power is. If the Constitution gives the Executive a large degree of unshared power in the conduct of foreign affairs and the maintenance of our national defense, then under the Constitution the Executive must have the largely unshared duty to determine and preserve the degree of internal security necessary to exercise that power successfully. It is an awesome responsibility, requiring judgment and wisdom of a high order. I should suppose that moral, political, and practical considerations would dictate that a very first principle of that wisdom would be an insistence upon avoiding secrecy for its own sake. For when everything is classified, then nothing is classified, and the system becomes one to be disregarded by the cynical or the careless, and to be manipulated by those intent on self-protection or self-promotion. I should suppose, in short, that the hallmark of a truly effective internal security system would be the maximum possible disclosure, recognizing that secrecy can best be preserved only when credibility is truly maintained. But be that as it may, it is clear to me that it is the constitutional duty of the Executive—as a matter of sovereign prerogative and not as a matter of law as the courts know law—through the promulgation and enforcement of executive regulations, to protect the confidentiality necessary to carry out its responsibilities in the fields of international relations and national defense.

But in the cases before us we are [asked] to perform a function that the Constitution gave to the Executive, not the Judiciary. We are asked, quite simply, to prevent the publication by two newspapers of material that the Executive Branch insists should not, in the national interest, be published. I am convinced that the Executive is correct with respect to some of the documents involved. But I cannot say that disclosure of any of them will surely result in direct, immediate, and irreparable damage to our Nation or its people. That being so, there can under the First Amendment be but one judicial resolution of the issues before us. I join the judgments of the Court.

DISSENT BY JUSTICE BLACKMUN. The First Amendment, after all, is only one part of an entire Constitution. Article II of the great document vests in the Executive Branch primary power over the conduct of foreign affairs and places in that branch the responsibility for the Nation's safety. Each provision of the Constitution is important, and I cannot subscribe to a doctrine of unlimited absolutism for the First Amendment at the cost of downgrading other provisions. First Amendment absolutism has never commanded a majority of this Court.... What is needed here is a weighing, upon properly developed standards, of the broad right of the press to print and of the very narrow right of the Government to prevent. Such standards are not yet developed. The parties here are in disagreement as to what those standards should be. But even the newspapers concede that there are situations where restraint is in order and is constitutional....

I strongly urge, and sincerely hope, that these two newspapers [the *New York Times* and the *Washington Post*] will be fully aware of their ultimate responsibilities to the United States of America. Judge Wilkey, dissenting in the District of Columbia case, after a review of only the affidavits before his court (the basic papers had not then been made available by either party), concluded that there were a number of examples of documents that, if in the possession of the *Post*, and if published, "could clearly result in great harm to the nation," and he defined "harm" to mean "the death of soldiers, the destruction of alliances, the greatly increased difficulty of negotiation with our enemies, the inability of our diplomats to negotiate...." I, for one, have now been able to give at least some cursory study not only to the affidavits, but to the material itself. I regret to say that from this examination I fear that Judge Wilkey's statements have possible foundation. I therefore share his concern. I hope that damage has not already been done. If, however, damage has been done, and if, with the Court's action today, these newspapers proceed to publish the critical documents and there results therefrom "the death of soldiers, the destruction of alliances, the greatly increased difficulty of negotiation with our enemies, the inability of our diplomats to negotiate," to which list I might add the factors of prolongation of the war and of further delay in the freeing of United States prisoners, then the Nation's people will know where the responsibility for these sad consequences rests.

Modern Times: The Gulf War and the War on Terrorism

To date, the government's actions during the Gulf War and the war on terrorism have not been the subject of major litigation. Below are several key documents related to those issues. Congress's 1991 Gulf War resolution supporting the use of force by President George H. W. Bush in Desert Storm in 1991; President George W. Bush's address to Congress after the September 11, 2001, attacks; and the October 2002 congressional resolution supporting the use of force against Iraq.

Gulf War Resolution (1991)

Persian Gulf Resolution
"Authorization for Use of Military Force Against Iraq Resolution"
January 12, 1991
Joint Resolution
To authorize the use of United States Armed Forces Pursuant to United Nations Security Council resolution 678.

Whereas both the House of Representatives (in HJ Res. 658 of the 101st Congress) and the Senate (in S Con Res 147 of the 101st Congress) have condemned Iraq's invasion of Kuwait and declared their support for international action to reverse Iraq's aggression; and

Whereas, Iraq's conventional, chemical, biological, and nuclear weapons and ballistic missile programs and its demonstrated willingness to use weapons of mass destruction pose a grave threat to world peace; and

Whereas the international community has demanded that Iraq withdraw unconditionally and immediately from Kuwait and that Kuwait's independence and legitimate government be restored; and

Whereas the U.N. Security Council repeatedly affirmed the inherent right of individual or collective self-defense in response to armed attack by Iraq against Kuwait in accordance with Article 51 of the U.N. Charter; and

Whereas, in the absence of full compliance by Iraq with its resolutions, the U.N. Security Council in Resolution 678 has authorized member states of the United Nations to use all necessary means, after January 15, 1991, to uphold and implement all relevant Security Council resolutions and to restore international peace and security in the area; and

Whereas Iraq has persisted in its illegal occupation of, and brutal aggression against, Kuwait: Now, therefore be it

Resolved by the Senate and House of Representatives of the United States of America in Congress assembled,

Section 2. Authorization for Use of United States Armed Forces

(a) AUTHORIZATION.—The President is authorized, subject to subsection (b), to use United States Armed Forces pursuant to United Nations Security Council Resolution 678 (1990) in order to achieve implementation of Security Council Resolutions 660, 661, 662, 664, 665, 666, 667, 669, 670, 674, and 677.

(b) REQUIREMENT FOR DETERMINATION THAT USE OF MILITARY FORCE IS NECESSARY.—Before exercising the authority granted in subsection (a), the President shall make available to the Speaker of the House of Representatives and the President pro tempore of the Senate his determination that—

(1) the United States has used all appropriate diplomatic and other peaceful means to obtain compliance by Iraq with the United Nations Security Council resolutions cited in subsection (a); and

(2) that those efforts have not been successful in obtaining such compliance.

(c) WAR POWERS RESOLUTION REQUIREMENTS.—

(1) SPECIFIC STATUTORY AUTHORIZATION.—Consistent with section 8(a)(1) of the War Powers Resolution, the Congress declares that this section is intended to constitute specific statutory authorization within the meaning of section 5(b) of the War Powers Resolution.

(2) APPLICABILITY OF OTHER REQUIREMENTS.—Nothing in this resolution supersedes any requirement of the War Powers Resolution.

Section 3. REPORTS TO CONGRESS.

At least once every 60 days, the President shall submit to the Congress a summary on the status of efforts to obtain compliance by Iraq with the resolutions adopted by the United Nations Security Council in response to Iraq's aggression.

Address by President George W. Bush to Congress Concerning the September 11, 2001, Attacks

Mr. Speaker, Mr. President Pro Tempore, members of Congress, and fellow Americans:

In the normal course of events, Presidents come to this chamber to report on the state of the Union. Tonight, no such report is needed. It has already been delivered by the American people. . . .

My fellow citizens, for the last nine days, the entire world has seen for itself the state of our Union—and it is strong.

Tonight we are a country awakened to danger and called to defend freedom. Our grief has turned to anger, and anger to resolution. Whether we bring our enemies to justice, or bring justice to our enemies, justice will be done. . . .

On September the 11th, enemies of freedom committed an act of war against our country. Americans have known wars—but for the past 136 years, they have been wars on foreign soil, except for one Sunday in 1941. Americans have known the casualties of war—but not at the center of a great city on a peaceful morning. Americans have known surprise attacks—but never before on thousands of civilians. All of this was brought upon us in a single day—and night fell on a different world, a world where freedom itself is under attack.

Americans have many questions tonight. Americans are asking: Who attacked our country? The evidence we have gathered all points to a collection of loosely affiliated terrorist organizations known as al Qaeda. They are the same murderers indicted for bombing American embassies in Tanzania and Kenya, and responsible for bombing the USS *Cole*.

Al Qaeda is to terror what the mafia is to crime. But its goal is not making money; its goal is remaking the world—and imposing its radical beliefs on people everywhere.

The terrorists practice a fringe form of Islamic extremism that has been rejected by Muslim scholars and the vast majority of Muslim clerics—a fringe movement that perverts the peaceful teachings of Islam. The terrorists' directive commands them to kill Christians and Jews, to kill all Americans, and make no distinction among military and civilians, including women and children.

This group and its leader—a person named Osama bin Laden—are linked to many other organizations in different countries, including the Egyptian Islamic Jihad and the Islamic Movement of Uzbekistan. There are thousands of these terrorists in more than 60 countries. They are recruited from their own nations and neighborhoods and brought to camps in places like Afghanistan, where they are trained in the tactics of terror. They are sent back to their homes or sent to hide in countries around the world to plot evil and destruction.

The leadership of al Qaeda has great influence in Afghanistan and supports the Taliban regime in controlling most of that country. In Afghanistan, we see al Qaeda's vision for the world.

Afghanistan's people have been brutalized—many are starving and many have fled. Women are not allowed to attend school. You can be jailed for owning a television. Religion can be practiced only as their leaders dictate. A man can be jailed in Afghanistan if his beard is not long enough.

The United States respects the people of Afghanistan—after all, we are currently its largest source of humanitarian aid—but we condemn the Taliban regime. . . .

And tonight, the United States of America makes the following demands on the Taliban: Deliver to United States authorities all the leaders of al Qaeda who hide in your land. Release all foreign nationals, including American citizens, you have unjustly imprisoned. Protect foreign journalists, diplomats and aid workers in your country. Close immediately and permanently every terrorist training camp in Afghanistan, and hand over every terrorist, and every person in their support structure, to appropriate authorities. Give the United States full access to terrorist training camps, so we can make sure they are no longer operating.

These demands are not open to negotiation or discussion. The Taliban must act, and act immediately. They will hand over the terrorists, or they will share in their fate.

I also want to speak tonight directly to Muslims throughout the world. We respect your faith. It's practiced freely by many millions of Americans, and by millions more in countries that America counts as friends. Its teachings are good and peaceful, and those who commit evil in the name of Allah blaspheme the name of Allah. The terrorists are traitors to their own faith, trying, in effect, to hijack Islam itself. The enemy of America is not our many Muslim friends; it is not our many Arab friends. Our enemy is a radical network of terrorists, and every government that supports them.

Our war on terror begins with al Qaeda, but it does not end there. It will not end until every terrorist group of global reach has been found, stopped and defeated.

Americans are asking, why do they hate us? They hate what we see right here in this chamber—a democratically elected government. Their leaders are self-appointed. They hate our freedoms—our freedom of religion, our freedom of speech, our freedom to vote and assemble and disagree with each other.

They want to overthrow existing governments in many Muslim countries, such as Egypt, Saudi Arabia, and Jordan. They want to drive Israel out of the Middle East. They want to drive Christians and Jews out of vast regions of Asia and Africa.

These terrorists kill not merely to end lives, but to disrupt and end a way of life. With every atrocity, they hope that America grows fearful, retreating from the world and forsaking our friends. They stand against us, because we stand in their way.

We are not deceived by their pretenses to piety. We have seen their kind before. They are the heirs of all the murderous ideologies of the 20th century. By sacrificing human life to serve their radical visions—by abandoning every value except the will to power—they follow in the path of fascism, and Nazism, and totalitarianism. And they will follow that path all the way, to where it ends: in history's unmarked grave of discarded lies.

Americans are asking: How will we fight and win this war? We will direct every resource at our command—every means of diplomacy, every tool of intelligence, every instrument of law enforcement, every financial influence, and every necessary weapon of war—to the disruption and to the defeat of the global terror network.

This war will not be like the war against Iraq a decade ago, with a decisive liberation of territory and a swift conclusion. It will not look like the air war above Kosovo two years ago, where no ground troops were used and not a single American was lost in combat.

Our response involves far more than instant retaliation and isolated strikes. Americans should not expect one battle, but a lengthy campaign, unlike any other we have ever seen. It may include dramatic strikes, visible on TV, and covert operations, secret even in success. We will starve terrorists of funding, turn them one against another, drive them from place to place, until there is no refuge or no rest. And we will pursue nations that provide aid or safe haven to terrorism. Every nation, in every region, now has a decision to make. Either you are with us, or you are with the terrorists. From this day forward, any nation that continues to harbor or support terrorism will be regarded by the United States as a hostile regime.

Our nation has been put on notice: We are not immune from attack. We will take defensive measures against terrorism to protect Americans. Today, dozens of federal departments and agencies, as well as state and local governments, have responsibilities affecting homeland security. These efforts must be coordinated at the highest level. So tonight I announce the creation of a Cabinet-level position reporting directly to me—the Office of Homeland Security. . . .

This is not, however, just America's fight. And what is at stake is not just America's freedom. This is the world's fight. This is civilization's fight. This is the fight of all who believe in progress and pluralism, tolerance and freedom. . . .

Great harm has been done to us. We have suffered great loss. And in our grief and anger we have found our mission and our moment. Freedom and fear are at war. The advance of human freedom—the great achievement of our time, and the great hope of every time—now depends on us. Our nation—this generation—will lift a dark threat of violence from our people and our future. We will rally the world to this cause by our efforts, by our courage. We will not tire, we will not falter, and we will not fail. . . .

Joint Congressional Resolution on War with Iraq (October 2002)

Whereas in 1990 in response to Iraq's war of aggression against and illegal occupation of Kuwait, the United States forged a coalition of nations to liberate Kuwait and its people in order to defend the national security of the United States and enforce United Nations Security Council resolutions relating to Iraq;

Whereas after the liberation of Kuwait in 1991, Iraq entered into a United Nations sponsored cease-fire agreement pursuant to which Iraq unequivocally agreed, among other things, to eliminate its nuclear, biological, and chemical weapons programs and the means to deliver and develop them, and to end its support for international terrorism;

Whereas the efforts of international weapons inspectors, United States intelligence agencies, and Iraqi defectors led to the discovery that Iraq had large stockpiles of chemical weapons and a large scale biological weapons program, and that Iraq had an advanced nuclear weapons development program that was much closer to producing a nuclear weapon than intelligence reporting had previously indicated;

Whereas Iraq, in direct and flagrant violation of the cease-fire, attempted to thwart the efforts of weapons inspectors to identify and destroy Iraq's weapons of mass destruction stockpiles and development capabilities, which finally resulted in the withdrawal of inspectors from Iraq on October 31, 1998;

Whereas in 1998 Congress concluded that Iraq's continuing weapons of mass destruction programs threatened vital United States interests and international peace and security, declared Iraq to be in "material and unacceptable breach of its international obligations" and urged the President "to take appropriate action, in accordance with the Constitution and relevant laws of the United States, to bring Iraq into compliance with its international obligations"; . . .

Whereas Iraq both poses a continuing threat to the national security of the United States and international peace and security in the Persian Gulf region and remains in material and unacceptable breach of its international obligations by, among other things, continuing to possess and develop a significant chemical and biological weapons capability, actively seeking a nuclear weapons capability, and supporting and harboring terrorist organizations;

Whereas Iraq persists in violating resolutions of the United Nations Security Council by continuing to engage in brutal repression of its civilian population, thereby threatening international peace and security in the region, by refusing to release, repatriate, or account for non-Iraqi citizens wrongfully detained by Iraq, including an American serviceman, and by failing to return property wrongfully seized by Iraq from Kuwait;

Whereas the current Iraqi regime has demonstrated its capability and willingness to use weapons of mass destruction against other nations and its own people;

Whereas the current Iraqi regime has demonstrated its continuing hostility toward, and willingness to attack, the United States, including by attempting in 1993 to assassinate former President Bush and by firing on many thousands of occasions on United States and Coalition Armed Forces engaged in enforcing the resolutions of the United Nations Security Council;

Whereas members of al-Qaeda, an organization bearing responsibility for attacks on the United States, its citizens, and interests, including the attacks that occurred on September 11, 2001, are known to be in Iraq;

Whereas Iraq continues to aid and harbor other international terrorist organizations, including organizations that threaten the lives and safety of American citizens;

Whereas the attacks on the United States of September 11, 2001, underscored the gravity of the threat posed by the acquisition of weapons of mass destruction by international terrorist organizations;

Whereas Iraq's demonstrated capability and willingness to use weapons of mass destruction, the risk that the current Iraqi regime will either employ those weapons to launch a surprise attack against the United States or its Armed Forces or provide them to international terrorists who would do so, and the extreme magnitude of harm that would result to the United States and its citizens from such an attack, combine to justify action by the United States to defend itself;

Whereas United Nations Security Council Resolution 678 (1990) authorizes the use of all necessary means to enforce United Nations Security Council Resolution 660 (1991) and subsequent relevant resolutions and to compel Iraq to cease certain activities that threaten international peace and security, including the development of weapons of mass destruction and refusal or obstruction of United Nations weapons inspections in violation of United Nations Security Council Resolution 687 (1991), repression of its civilian population in violation of United Nations Security Council Resolution 688 (1991), and threatening its neighbors or United Nations operations in Iraq in violation of United Nations Security Council Resolution 949 (1994);

Whereas Congress in the Authorization for Use of Military Force Against Iraq Resolution (Public Law 102-1) has authorized the President "to use United States Armed Forces pursuant to United Nations Security Council Resolution 678 (1990) in order to achieve implementation of Security Council Resolutions 660, 661, 662, 664, 665, 666, 667, 669, 670, 674, and 677";

Whereas in December 1991, Congress expressed its sense that it "supports the use of all necessary means to achieve the goals of United Nations Security Council Resolution 687 as being consistent with the Authorization of Use of Military Force Against Iraq Resolution (Public Law 102-1)," that Iraq's repression of its civilian population violates United Nations Security Council Resolution 688 and "constitutes a continuing threat to the peace, security, and stability of the Persian Gulf region," and that Congress "supports the use of all necessary means to achieve the goals of United Nations Security Council Resolution 688";

Whereas the Iraq Liberation Act (Public Law 105-338) expressed the sense of Congress that it should be the policy of the United States to support efforts to remove from power the current Iraqi regime and promote the emergence of a democratic government to replace that regime;

Whereas on September 12, 2002, President Bush committed the United States to "work with the United Nations Security Council to meet our common challenge" posed by Iraq and to "work for the necessary resolutions," while also making clear that "the Security Council resolutions will be enforced, and the just demands of peace and security will be met, or action will be unavoidable";

Whereas the United States is determined to prosecute the war on terrorism and Iraq's ongoing support for international terrorist groups combined with its development of weapons of mass destruction in direct violation of its obligations under the 1991 cease-fire and other United Nations Security Council resolutions make clear that it is in the national security interests of the United States and in furtherance of the war on terrorism that all relevant United Nations Security Council resolutions be enforced, including through the use of force if necessary;

Whereas Congress has taken steps to pursue vigorously the war on terrorism through the provision of authorities and funding requested by the President to take the necessary actions against international terrorists and terrorist organizations, including those nations, organizations or persons who planned, authorized, committed or aided the terrorist attacks that occurred on September 11, 2001, or harbored such persons or organizations;

Whereas the President and Congress are determined to continue to take all appropriate actions against international terrorists and terrorist organizations, including those nations, organizations or persons who planned, authorized, committed or aided the terrorist attacks that occurred on September 11, 2001, or harbored such persons or organizations;

Whereas the President has authority under the Constitution to take action in order to deter and prevent acts of international terrorism against the United States, as Congress recognized in the joint resolution on Authorization for Use of Military Force (Public Law 107-40); and

Whereas it is in the national security of the United States to restore international peace and security to the Persian Gulf region: Now, therefore, be it

Resolved by the Senate and House of Representatives of the United States of America in Congress assembled,
SECTION 1. SHORT TITLE.

This joint resolution may be cited as the "Authorization for the Use of Military Force Against Iraq."

SEC. 2. SUPPORT FOR UNITED STATES DIPLOMATIC EFFORTS.

The Congress of the United States supports the efforts by the President to—

(1) strictly enforce through the United Nations Security Council all relevant Security Council resolutions applicable to Iraq and encourages him in those efforts; and

(2) obtain prompt and decisive action by the Security Council to ensure that Iraq abandons its strategy of delay, evasion and noncompliance and promptly and strictly complies with all relevant Security Council resolutions.

SEC. 3. AUTHORIZATION FOR USE OF UNITED STATES ARMED FORCES.

(a) AUTHORIZATION—The President is authorized to use the Armed Forces of the United States as he determines to be necessary and appropriate in order to—

(1) defend the national security of the United States against the continuing threat posed by Iraq; and

(2) enforce all relevant United Nations Security Council resolutions regarding Iraq.

(b) PRESIDENTIAL DETERMINATION—In connection with the exercise of the authority granted in subsection (a) to use force the President shall, prior to such exercise or as soon thereafter as may be feasible, but no later than 48 hours after exercising such authority, make available to the Speaker of the House of Representatives and the President pro tempore of the Senate his determination that—

(1) reliance by the United States on further diplomatic or other peaceful means alone either (A) will not adequately protect the national security of the United States against the continuing threat posed by Iraq or (B) is not likely to lead to enforcement of all relevant United Nations Security Council resolutions regarding Iraq; and

(2) acting pursuant to this resolution is consistent with the United States and other countries continuing to take the necessary actions against international terrorists and terrorist organizations, including those nations, organizations or persons who planned, authorized, committed or aided the terrorist attacks that occurred on September 11, 2001.

Key People, Laws, and Concepts

Abrams v. United States

Supreme Court case involving government suppression of antidraft language. The Court majority upheld the government's right to restrict such activities as a matter of national security, but in a dissenting opinion Justice Oliver Wendell Holmes Jr. pulled back from his own earlier opinion in *Schenck v. United States,* arguing that the nation's best interests, even in wartime, would best be protected by fostering an open marketplace of ideas.

Article I, Sections 8 and 9

Sections of the Constitution that outline most of Congress's military powers. Section 8 confers on Congress the power to declare war, to raise, fund, and make rules for an army and navy, and to call out and organize the state militias. Section 9 allows Congress to regulate suspension of the writ of habeas corpus in times of war or national emergency.

Articles of War

Rules for governing the conduct of U.S. military forces. The first Articles, adopted at the beginning of the American Revolution in 1775, were modeled on the rules used by the British to govern their land and naval forces.

Bas v. Tingy

An 1800 Supreme Court case addressing the disposition of cargo taken during the quasi war the United States had with France. The case established that a state of war can exist without a formal congressional declaration, although the justices disagreed on what that sort of war might look like in a legal sense.

Brandenburg v. Ohio

A 1969 Supreme Court case in which the conviction of a Klansman for inflammatory remarks made at a Klan rally was struck down. Although the case had little to do with wartime civil liberties, the justices explicitly rejected Holmes's "clear and present danger" doctrine as a test of free speech rights and laid the foundation for the modern court's libertarian reading of the First Amendment.

Clear and Present Danger Doctrine

First articulated by Justice Oliver Wendell Holmes Jr. in the 1919 Supreme Court case *Schenck v. United States,* this doctrine held that the government was justified in suppressing free speech when the words offered a clear and present danger of inciting illegal action. Often mistaken as an affirmation of free speech rights, the clear and present danger doctrine actually gave the government wide latitude—particularly during a war—to curb speech it considers to be inimical to national security.

CO Status

Conscientious objector status. A classification given to pacifists during World War II. Soldiers with CO status served as medics or in some nonviolent supporting role for the armed forces.

Cohen v. California

A 1971 Supreme Court case in which the justices struck down the conviction of a California man who displayed the words "Fuck the

Draft" on his jacket near a courthouse. The decision was an endorsement of free expression rights during wartime.

Committee on Military Affairs

Created by Congress during World War I to investigate various aspects of the national war effort. Also known as the Graham Committee, after its chairman, William J. Graham. Like its predecessor, the Civil War's Joint Committee on the Conduct of the War, the Committee on Military Affairs was seen by many as a source of partisan bickering against the Wilson administration.

Congressional Pearl Harbor Joint Committee

House and Senate joint committee formed to investigate the circumstances surrounding the Japanese attack on Pearl Harbor. After a lengthy investigation, the committee accused the two principal American military commanders on the scene, Admiral Husband Kimmel and General Walter Short, of committing "errors of judgment" in failing to adequately protect the Pearl Harbor base from attack.

Cramer v. United States

A 1945 case in which the Supreme Court struck down the conviction of a man accused of committing treason by plotting with German agents to commit acts of sabotage. Reinforced the Court's traditionally narrow interpretation of the Constitution's treason provisions.

Dynes v. Hoover

An 1858 Supreme Court case in which the justices upheld the power of the military justice system to discipline soldiers and sailors with relatively little civilian interference.

Enrollment Act of 1863

Primary legislation related to conscription in the North during the Civil War. The act authorized Union authorities to draft men between the ages of twenty and forty-five but provided for numerous loopholes, including the hiring of substitutes.

Ex parte Endo

A 1944 Supreme Court decision that struck down imprisonment of demonstrably loyal Americans of Japanese descent. The Court drew back somewhat from its generally supportive attitude toward the wartime treatment of Japanese-Americans.

Ex parte Merryman

An 1861 opinion issued by Supreme Court Chief Justice Roger B. Taney in his capacity as a U.S. circuit court judge for Maryland. In this opinion, Taney severely criticized President Abraham Lincoln's policy of martial law and suspension of the writ of habeas corpus in Maryland as an unconstitutional usurpation of congressional authority.

Ex parte Milligan

An 1866 Supreme Court decision declaring that civilians could not be tried by a military tribunal in areas where the civilian courts were still operating. In essence a reversal of *ex parte Vallandigham,* the *Milligan* decision could be seen as a vindication of wartime civil liberties, but it was also a serious legal setback for those Americans who wanted to use military courts to suppress the Ku Klux Klan and protect the rights of African-Americans.

Ex parte Vallandigham

Civil War Supreme Court decision (1864) upholding the banishment of Clement Vallandigham, a notorious Confederate sympathizer, to the South. Vallandigham's arrest and banishment were effected by the military justice system, and the Court held that during a time of war this was an acceptable practice.

Executive Order 9066

Signed by President Franklin Roosevelt in 1942, this order authorized the removal of thousands of Japanese-Americans from areas considered sensitive to national security, primarily along the West Coast.

Filipino Insurrection

Uprising of Filipino nationalists against American rule following the U.S. takeover of the Philippine Islands after the Spanish-American War. The uprising was a protracted guerrilla conflict, lasting from 1899 to 1901, and eventually involving thousands of American troops. Rumors of misconduct by U.S. soldiers sparked a congressional investigation in 1902.

Gulf of Tonkin Resolution

Passed by Congress in 1964 after an attack on a U.S. destroyer by North Vietnamese gunboats, this resolution gave President Johnson nearly unlimited authority to commit American troops, money, and resources to victory in the Vietnam conflict.

Habeas Corpus Act of 1863

First major piece of legislation related to the suspension of the writ of habeas corpus. Passed by Congress during the Civil War to authorize President Lincoln's suspension of the writ as well as to place legal boundaries on such suspensions.

Hirabayashi v. United States

A 1943 Supreme Court case in which the justices upheld the government's right to impose restrictions on a specific ethnic group—in this case, a curfew on Americans of Japanese descent—as a wartime security measure. The decision reinforced the government's discriminatory policies against Japanese-Americans during World War II.

Joint Committee on the Conduct of the War

Committee formed by congressional Republicans in late 1861 to oversee the North's war effort. It was the first prominent effort by Congress to involve itself directly in the day-to-day operations of a major American war. The brainchild of "Radical Republicans" who wanted a vigorous prosecution of the war and supported measures such as emancipation and confiscation of rebel property, the committee was viewed with ambivalence by President Lincoln and widely criticized in Democratic and conservative circles for being partisan and heavy-handed in its deliberations.

Korean War (1950–1953)

Begun by President Harry Truman, who committed American troops to the defense of South Korea when that nation was invaded by communist North Korea in 1950. Truman did not seek a formal declaration of war from Congress, arguing that a United Nations resolution mandated U.S. participation in South Korea's defense. This was the first time a U.S. president argued that he could commit American soldiers to a major war effort without a congressional declaration of war.

Lever Act of 1917

Gave the Woodrow Wilson administration broad regulatory powers over the wartime economy, including the ability to set market prices and regulate mechanisms of supply and demand.

Martial Law

The act of suspending the civilian justice system's operation in a given area, during a war or other serious emergency, and using the military justice system instead to preserve law and order. The Constitution defines martial law or specifies who may declare it and under what circumstances it may begin and end. Traditionally, it has been seen as a prerogative of the president, exercising his powers as commander in chief.

Martin v. Mott

An 1827 Supreme Court decision allowing the president to take command of state militias during war. Established presidential and federal supremacy over state military organizations.

Mexican War (1846–1848)

Begun with the declaration of war from Congress after President James Polk requested it. The war added the western third of the continent to the nation, but with significant political and moral controversy. Serious questions were raised, by Congressman Abraham Lincoln and others, concerning whether Polk misled Congress about a supposed Mexican invasion of the United States in order to get the declaration of war he needed.

Military Justice Act

A 1968 act by Congress that extended basic constitutional protections to defendants in the military justice system.

My Lai Massacre

A 1968 assault on Vietnamese civilians living in the small village of My Lai, in which U.S. soldiers killed more than 400 men, women, and children. Created a national uproar and resulted in the court-martial and conviction of one of the participants, Lieutenant William Calley.

New York Times Co. v. United States

A 1971 Supreme Court decision that rejected the Nixon administration's attempt to block publication of politically sensitive Pentagon documents in the name of national security. Generally seen as the foundation of the modern Court's expansive reading of freedom of the press and its generally restrictive reading of national security provisions when placed against First Amendment concerns.

Overman Act of 1918

A World War I act, named after its author, Senator Lee Overman, giving President Wilson nearly unlimited discretion in organizing the executive branch so that it might prosecute the war more efficiently.

Parker v. Levy

A 1974 case in which the Supreme Court upheld the court-martial of an army doctor who disobeyed orders and expressed antiwar sentiments. Although the trend during the 1960s and 1970s was generally toward expanding soldiers' rights under civilian rules of justice, this decision reaffirmed the Court's traditional disposition to leave military justice largely in the hands of soldiers themselves.

Persian Gulf War (1991)

A war fought by the United States in 1991 to defeat the forces of Iraqi dictator Saddam Hussein. Hussein invaded Kuwait in August 1990 and threatened to invade neighboring Saudi Arabia. After a massive military buildup and air bombing campaign, American forces retook Kuwait in a brief land campaign in February 1991, resulting in a lopsided victory against Hussein's clearly outmatched soldiers. Afterward, the United States and its allies imposed "no-fly zones" over large portions of northern and southern Iraq, and the United Nations imposed harsh economic sanctions on Hussein's regime that were aimed at either toppling the Iraqi leader or compelling his complete disarmament. The war reinforced the conviction among many Americans that it was both necessary and legal for a president to conduct a major military operation without a congressional declaration of war.

Prize Cases

The most important decisions by the Supreme Court during the Civil War, allowing the Lincoln administration to define Southerners as both treasonous Americans and alien enemies, as circumstances required. The case gave the federal government the legal flexibility necessary to win a war against enemies who both were and were not part of the American community.

Revolutionary War (1776–1781)

The war for America's independence gave the founding fathers the experiences that would govern the actions of those who drafted the nation's primary legal provisions for war making in the Constitutional Convention of 1787. For men like George Washington and Alexander Hamilton, the conduct of the Revolutionary War illustrated how desperately the United States would need a professional national military establishment and the legal capability to act with vigor and decisiveness during a war. For others, however, the war demonstrated the dangers of maintaining a professional military class and the need to retain civilian control over the military.

Schenck v. United States

A landmark World War I civil liberties case in which the Supreme Court upheld the conviction of a man accused of trying to subvert the draft system. In the court opinion, Justice Oliver Wendell Holmes Jr. articulated the doctrine whereby if words are held by government authorities to constitute a "clear and present danger" of inciting a dangerous act, then those words can be suppressed by the government.

Selective Draft Law Cases

Supreme Court rulings in 1918 that unanimously upheld the right of the federal government to conscript Americans into the armed forces during wartime.

Spanish-American War (1898)

Begun by a formal declaration of war by Congress after a series of events that heightened tensions between the United States and Spain. Created no significant litigation or constitutional issues, but did usher America's entry onto the world stage as an imperial power.

Standing Army

Eighteenth-century term for an army of professional soldiers. Many Americans feared standing armies, believing they were readily available tools of tyranny and oppression for an ambitious king, and preferred to rely on militias made up of citizen-soldiers.

Suspension of the Writ of Habeas Corpus

An extraordinary wartime measure, suspension of habeas corpus allows government officials to arrest and imprison individuals without being compelled to show that sufficient evidence exists. Article 2, Section 8 of the Constitution suggests that congressional authorization is needed before the president can suspend the writ.

Toth v. Quarles

A 1955 case in which the Supreme Court held that the military justice system could not try defendants for their actions once they had left the armed forces. The decision can be seen as an affirmation of soldiers' trial rights, but it also made more difficult the prosecution of soldiers who committed war crimes and then left military service.

Treason

Defined by Article III, Section 3 as consisting "only in levying war against [the United States], or in adhering to their enemies, giving them aid and comfort." It requires at least two witnesses to an overt act of treason. The Supreme Court has traditionally defined these provisions very narrowly, making treason convictions difficult to obtain.

United States v. Seeger

A 1965 Supreme Court decision that greatly expanded the legal definition of conscientious objector status for those who wished to avoid military service on moral or religious grounds.

Vietnam War (1945–1975)

U.S. involvement in Vietnam began during World War II, but the nation's involvement in a full-scale war began in the 1960s, when President Johnson committed significant numbers of American troops to the defense of South Vietnam against communist North Vietnam. The war raised a variety of legal issues, including the ongoing war powers debate between president and Congress, civil liberties issues, and questions related to the operation of the nation's draft system.

War of 1812 (1812–1814)

Begun by a formal congressional declaration of war after deterioration of relations between the United States and Great Britain. This nearly disastrous war (Washington, D.C., was burned by the British) generated little in the way of legal controversy, but the fact that President James Madison, widely known as the "father of the Constitution," felt compelled to request from Congress a declaration of war before initiating military action seemed to indicate that the framers intended Congress to be the nation's primary war-making authority.

War Powers Acts of 1941 and 1942

Broad grants of authority to President Franklin Roosevelt by Congress during World War II. These acts provided the legal basis by which the Roosevelt administration exercised broad discretionary authority over the nation's economic, political, and social life in the name of securing victory.

War Powers Act of 1973

Attempt by Congress to hold presidents accountable for military actions initiated without Congress's prior approval. Created in the shadow of the Vietnam War and the Gulf of Tonkin Resolution of 1964, which many felt had given President Lyndon Johnson too much latitude in expanding U.S. commitments in Vietnam. Required presidents to report to Congress their reasons for military actions within sixty days of initiating such actions or risk losing congressional funding. No president except Jimmy Carter has ever recognized the validity of the War Powers Act, and the Supreme Court has never ruled on its overall constitutionality.

West Virginia State Board of Education v. Barnette

A 1943 Supreme Court case in which the justices struck down a West Virginia law requiring schoolchildren to recite the pledge of allegiance. Reinforced rights of religious minorities to dissent from such obligations during wartime and affirmed free speech rights during time of war.

World War I (1914–1918)

U.S. involvement in the conflict began in 1917, after President Woodrow Wilson's request for a congressional declaration of war. During the war, Congress authorized significant grants of authority to the president, particularly regarding control over the wartime economy and suppression of dissent. The Espionage Act of 1917 authorized government suppression of words and actions that could be construed as obstruction of the national war effort, particularly the draft. Various Supreme Court decisions upheld these powers.

World War II (1941–1945)

U.S. involvement after Congress declared war at President Roosevelt's request in the wake of the Japanese assault on Pearl Harbor. The war fostered an unprecedented mobilization of the nation's economic resources and further enhanced the president's authority in many areas of American life. The war also witnessed the relocation of thousands of Japanese-Americans and their incarceration in camps, now widely considered to be the most egregious violation of wartime civil liberties in American history.

Youngstown Sheet and Tube Co. v. Sawyer

Rare instance in which the Supreme Court limited the president's war-making powers. In 1952, President Harry Truman, citing national security concerns, began a federal takeover of the nation's steel industry in an attempt to avert a possibly calamitous nationwide steel strike. The Supreme Court argued that such a measure was an unconstitutional assertion of presidential war-making authority.

Chronology

1782   Former Continental army officers form the Society of Cincinnatus, unintentionally stirring fears among the populace that the organization might become the nucleus of an aristocratic officer class.

1787   War-making provisions of the Constitution are drafted during the Philadelphia Constitutional Convention; federalists and antifederalists debate the wisdom of these measures.

1794   President George Washington considers taking the field as commander of the U.S. Army to suppress the Whiskey Rebellion; in the end he chooses not to do so, and no other American president has since thought seriously of taking direct command of soldiers in the field.

1800   The Supreme Court rules in *Bas v. Tingy* that the nation can be in a legally recognized state of war without a formal congressional declaration.

1801   President Thomas Jefferson authorizes a series of naval operations against the Barbary pirates without seeking prior congressional approval.

1812   President James Madison asks Congress to make a declaration of war against Great Britain. Congress does so, initiating the War of 1812.

1818   A special congressional committee investigates Andrew Jackson's treatment of Native Americans during recent military campaigns.

1827   The Supreme Court affirms in *Martin v. Mott* that the president can assume control of state militia organizations in his capacity as commander in chief.

1846   Congress declares war on Mexico.

1858   In *Dynes v. Hoover,* the Supreme Court allows the military justice system wide latitude in its control over military personnel.

1861   Supreme Court Chief Justice Roger B. Taney issues an opinion in *ex parte Merryman* that is severely critical of President Lincoln's record on civil liberties. Congress creates the Joint Committee on the Conduct of the War after a series of Union military disasters; the committee begins a general oversight role of the Union war effort.

1862   Both the Union and the Confederacy create the first military draft systems in American history.

1863   The Supreme Court in the *Prize Cases* gives the Lincoln administration much-needed legal flexibility to deal with the Confederates as rebels or as alien enemies, according to circumstances; draft riots in New York City leave 120 Americans dead.

1864   Colonel John M. Chivington leads a force of Colorado militiamen to a peaceful Cheyenne camp along the banks of Sand Creek; 133 Cheyenne lose their lives in the resulting massacre; the Supreme Court in *ex parte Vallandigham* upholds the conviction by a military court of a prominent Confederate sympathizer.

1866   The Supreme Court in *ex parte Milligan* rules that American civilians cannot be tried by a military court in areas where civilian courts are operating.

1898   Congress declares war on Spain, initiating the Spanish-American War.

1899   The U.S. Army begins operations in the Philippines that are designed to suppress rebels intent on resisting American rule over the islands.

1902   Congress's Committee on the Philippines holds hearings on the army's conduct in the Philippines.

1917   The United States enters World War I; Congress passes the Espionage Act, giving the federal government extraordinary power to suppress dissent; the Senate creates the Committee on Military Affairs, which holds hearings on the war effort.

1918   Congress passes the Overman Act, giving President Woodrow Wilson broad discretionary power to prosecute the national war effort; the Supreme Court in the *Selective Draft Law Cases* upholds the right of the government to conscript citizens; Robert Prager is murdered by a lynch mob in Collinsville, Illinois, for his alleged antiwar sympathies.

1919   Justice Oliver Wendell Holmes Jr. articulates the "clear and present danger" doctrine for addressing wartime civil liberties in *Schenck v. United States;* Holmes then pulls back from the more harsh implications of his *Schenck* opinion in *Abrams v. United States*

1940   President Franklin D. Roosevelt sells old destroyers to Great Britain under the Destroyer-Lease Deal.

1941   Congress declares war on Japan after a Japanese surprise attack on U.S. naval forces at Pearl Harbor, Hawaii; Germany declares war on the United States, thus drawing the nation into the European war; Congress passes the War Powers Act of 1941, giving the president authority over vast areas of America's economy and natural resources; Roosevelt authorizes the FBI to arrest anyone it deems a danger to the public safety.

1942   President Roosevelt signs Executive Order 9066, allowing the relocation of thousands of Japanese-Americans to internment camps.

1943   The Supreme Court in *Hirabayashi v. United States* allows the military to single out members of a given ethnic group in formulating wartime security measures; the Supreme Court in *West Virginia State Board of Education v. Barnette* upholds wartime free speech rights.

1944   In *ex parte Endo,* the Supreme Court restricts the power of the military to imprison American citizens under the pretext of national security with no clear reason for doing so.

1945   The Supreme Court narrowly construes wartime enforcement of the Constitution's treason language in *Cramer v. United States.*

1946   Congress's special committee investigating the Pearl Harbor attack releases its findings, which claim that the principal military commanders on the scene had been guilty of poor judgment; the Supreme Court in *in re Yamashita* allows the military to try accused war criminals, and in *Duncan v. Kahanamoku* allows the military wide latitude in using its justice system to try civilians.

1950   North Korean troops invade South Korea, sparking a war and a massive U.S. military buildup to protect South Korea and the nation's Cold War interests in the region; in the process, President Harry Truman is the first president to argue that an American president can initiate the nation's participation in a major war without congressional approval.

1952   President Truman fires popular General Douglas MacArthur, commander of U.S. forces in Korea, thus affirming civilian control over the military establishment but creating a political firestorm; the Supreme Court restricts the president's use of war powers during peacetime in *Youngstown Sheet and Tube Co. v. Sawyer.*

1955   In *Toth v. Quarles,* the Supreme Court rules that the military cannot try soldiers for military crimes after they leave the service.

1964   After the Gulf of Tonkin incident, during which North Vietnamese patrol boats fire on a U.S. destroyer, President Lyndon Johnson asks Congress for authorization for a major commitment of American troops and supplies for the defense of South Vietnam; with the Gulf of Tonkin Resolution, Congress gives the president a blanket authorization to use force.

1965   The United States begins a major buildup of its military forces in Vietnam to aid that nation's government in its struggle with Ho Chi Minh's communist North Vietnam; American air cavalry forces fight the first major engagement between U.S. and North Vietnamese troops in the Ia Drang valley; the Supreme Court expands the rights of conscientious objectors in *United States v. Seeger.*

1967   The Supreme Court refuses to hear a lawsuit *(Mara v. McNamara)* challenging the constitutionality of the Vietnam War.

1968   The Tet Offensive mounted by North Vietnam, although a military defeat for that country, proves to be a political victory, and marks the turning point for U.S. fortunes in Vietnam; Lieutenant William Calley and other American soldiers massacre hundreds of Vietnamese civilians in the village of My Lai.

1969   The Supreme Court in *Brandenburg v. Ohio* rejects the "clear and present danger" doctrine as a means for interpreting the First Amendment; in *O'Callahan v. Parker,* the Court restricts the power of the military justice system to try servicemen engaged in nonmilitary activities.

1970   William Calley is court-martialed and convicted of murder for his role in the My Lai massacre.

1971   The Supreme Court enlarges the grounds on which Americans can avoid military service by citing moral objections to war in *Gillette v. United States;* the Supreme Court overturns the conviction of a Vietnam War protester on First Amendment grounds in *Cohen v. California;* in *New York Times Co. v. United States,* the Court rejects the Nixon administration's attempt to block publication of the "Pentagon Papers" as a national security violation.

1973   In the wake of the Vietnam disaster, Congress tries to reassert its voice in war-making affairs by passing the War Powers Act of 1973, which requires the president to seek authorization from Congress for prolonged military operations.

1974   The Supreme Court in *Parker v. Levy* affirms the military's power to discipline its own soldiers in matters related to military behavior with relatively little civilian interference.

1975   The last American soldiers and personnel evacuate Vietnam as victorious North Vietnamese forces overrun South Vietnam.

1991   The United States embarks on its first large-scale military campaign since Vietnam when it initiates Operations Desert Shield and Desert Storm, designed to repel the forces of Iraq after that nation invades neighboring Kuwait; President George H. W. Bush authorizes this military buildup without a formal congressional declaration of war, but after a heated debate Congress passes a resolution supporting the president.

2001   On September 11, Islamic fundamentalist terrorists hijack passenger airliners to attack the World Trade Center in New York City, the Pentagon building in Washington, D.C., and another, unknown target (the latter airliner crashed into the Pennsylvania countryside); President George W. Bush declares that the United States is now involved in a war on terrorism.

2002   The nation debates a military assault against Iraq in order to oust Saddam Hussein and to disable Iraq's production of biological and chemical weapons and its efforts to develop nuclear weapons.

2003   Following lengthy and controversial debate at home and abroad, the United States leads a coalition of over thirty nations in an assault on Iraq to remove Saddam Hussein. After a brief decisive war, the Iraqi dictator is defeated and his regime is removed from power.

Table of Cases

Annotated Bibliography

Baker, Liva. 1991. *The Justice from Beacon Hill: The Life and Times of Oliver Wendell Holmes.* New York: HarperCollins.

    Lively general biography of Justice Holmes. Probably more accessible to students than most other studies of the subject. Good information on Holmes's thinking as he ruled on various civil liberties cases related to World War I.

Belknap, Michael. 2002. *The Vietnam War on Trial: The My Lai Massacre and the Court-Martial of Lieutenant Calley.* Lawrence: University Press of Kansas.

    Outstanding study of the My Lai massacre. Particularly strong on the legal issues and the various twists and turns of the court-martial process. Thorough, readable, and balanced, this is the best study of the subject available to students interested in the legal and political aspects of the massacre.

Bernath, Stuart L. 1970. *Squall across the Atlantic: American Civil War Prize Cases and Diplomacy.* Berkeley: University of California Press.

    Fairly useful study of the *Prize Cases.* Very good on diplomatic and legal contexts of the cases, but might be a bit dense for the average student. Still, this is the only book-length study of the subject.

Bishop, Joseph W., Jr. 1979. *Justice under Fire: A Study of Military Law.* New York: Charterhouse.

    Very useful overview of the military justice system, its history and development, and the ways in which court-martial procedures have developed over time.

Boot, Max. 2002. *The Savage Wars of Peace: Small Wars and the Rise of American Power.* New York: Basic.

    Very good study of America's "small wars," from the days of the early republic through the Persian Gulf War. Not much here on the legal issues of warfare, but an invaluable guide to the lesser-known military actions in American history.

Chafee, Zachariah, Jr. 1941. *Free Speech in the United States.* Cambridge, MA: Harvard University Press.

Classic study of free speech rights in America. A bit dated by now, but still quite useful for pre–World War II events and issues. Particularly good chapters on World War I–era cases.

Clausen, Henry C., and Bruce Lee. 1992. *Pearl Harbor: Final Judgement.* New York: Crown.

Exhaustive study of the investigations on the Pearl Harbor attack conducted by Congress. Perhaps a bit too detailed for those who want a succinct account, but nevertheless quite useful.

Detter, Ingrid. 2000. *The Law of War.* Cambridge, MA: Harvard University Press.

General theoretical overview of law and war in an international context. Useful for setting America in context of global developments.

Ely, John Hart. 1993. *War and Responsibility: Constitutional Lessons of Vietnam and Its Aftermath.* Princeton: Princeton University Press.

Very good study of modern war powers issues. Ely is highly critical of both the presidency and Congress in these matters, seeing the usurpation of war-making authority by modern presidents as dangerous, but also faulting Congress for abdicating its responsibilities. An excellent discussion of the Persian Gulf War, covert operations and their constitutional implications, and the strengths and weaknesses of the 1973 War Powers Act. A seminal book.

Freedman, Lawrence, and Efraim Karsh. 1995. *The Gulf Conflict, 1990–1991: Diplomacy and War in the New World Order.* Princeton: Princeton University Press.

A solid basic study of the Persian Gulf War. Outstanding on diplomatic and military issues, but surprisingly thin on debates between Congress and the Bush administration.

Generous, William T., Jr. 1973. *Swords and Scales: The Development of the Uniform Code of Military Justice.* Port Washington, NY: Kennikat.

Good general overview of the growth and development of the rules and procedures governing the operations of the military justice system. Some good history, but emphasizing twentieth-century issues.

Hall, Kermit. 1992. *The Oxford Companion to the Supreme Court.* New York: Oxford University Press.

An indispensable research guide to just about every possible topic related to the Supreme Court. Where law and war are concerned, it has particularly useful entries on the Civil War, World War II, and the War Powers Act of 1973.

Hyman, Harold M. 1975. *A More Perfect Union: The Impact of the Civil War and Reconstruction.* Boston: Houghton Mifflin.

Classic study of the legal and constitutional issues created by the Civil War. Offers a compelling case for expansion of federal authority during the war, and is particularly sympathetic to the Radical Republicans and the Lincoln administration.

Irons, Peter. 1983. *Justice at War.* New York: Oxford University Press.

Overview of cases involving civil liberties and warfare, weighted toward twentieth-century cases.

Kelly, Alfred H., Winfred A. Harbison, and Herman Belz. 1991. *The American Constitution: Its Origins and Development.* Vol. 1. New York: W. W. Norton.

Perhaps the best general constitutional history of the United States currently available. The chapters on Civil War constitutional issues and the jurisprudence of the Reconstruction era are particularly valuable, reflecting the interests of its authors.

Kennedy, David M. 1980. *Over Here: The First World War and American Society.* New York: Oxford University Press.

Best single-volume history of U.S. involvement in World War I. In the absence of a good, accessible study of the war's civil liberties cases, a valuable source of information on wartime legal developments. Particularly useful for its searching critique of relations between President Wilson and Congress.

Linfield, Michael. 1990. *Freedom under Fire: U.S. Civil Liberties in Times of War.* Boston: South End.

Study of civil liberties during war—broadly conceived—with a polemic bent, reflecting the author's belief that in times of war Americans routinely violate their most cherished safeguards for individual rights. This can be useful or tedious, depending on one's point of view, and the author's highly critical perspective slants his take on the evidence. Still, a generally useful book.

Livermore, Seward W. 1966. *Politics Is Adjourned: Woodrow Wilson and the War Congress, 1916–1918.* Middletown, CT: Wesleyan.

Good study of relations between Wilson and the wartime Congress. Particularly strong on matters related to regulation of the wartime economy and the operations of the Espionage Act of 1917.

Lurie, Jonathan. 1992. *Arming Military Justice: The Origins of the United States Military Court of Appeals, 1775–1950.* Vol. 1. Princeton: Princeton University Press.

By far the best available study of the early history and development of the nation's military justice system. The starting point for any serious study of the subject.

Maguire, Peter H. 2001. *Law and War: An American Story.* New York: Columbia University Press.

Very good discussion of legal issues related to World War II, with shorter sections on World War I and the nineteenth century. Generally a balanced account.

Neely, Mark E., Jr. 1992. *The Fate of Liberty: Abraham Lincoln and Civil Liberties.* New York: Oxford University Press.

Superior study of Lincoln's record on civil liberties. Offers both a useful general discussion of the broad legal issues involved in these matters and a grassroots view of individual arrests. Decisively refutes the old myth that Lincoln was a quasi dictator and offers instead a careful, balanced assessment of his actions.

Nufer, Harold E. 1981. *American Servicemembers' Supreme Court.* Washington, DC: University Press of America.

Reasonably useful study of the Court of Military Appeals, although a bit on the technical side and heavily weighted toward present-day issues.

Rehnquist, William H. 2000. *All the Laws but One: Civil Liberties in War.* New York: Vintage.

Our current chief justice has a scholarly, historical bent and has produced several works on constitutional history, including this study of American civil liberties during wartime. On the plus side, it is a fairminded, balanced assessment of the subject and is readable and quite accessible to the nonlawyer. On the downside, it focuses almost exclusively on the Civil War and World War II, particularly the former.

Robinson, Greg. 2001. *By Order of the President: FDR and the Internment of Japanese Americans.* Cambridge, MA: Harvard University Press.

Good recent study of the Japanese internment issue. Offers a thorough, fair assessment of these policies, including the political and legal rationales for Japanese-American internment as well as the human costs of those policies. Likely to become standard study.

Tap, Bruce. 1998. *Over Lincoln's Shoulder: The Committee on the Conduct of the War.* Lawrence: University Press of Kansas.

The only modern, book-length study of the subject, this is a mustread for anyone trying to understand congressional attempts to monitor the operations of war. Tap is generally quite critical of the committee and its members, but he marshals good evidence. A solid work.

White, G. Edward. 1993. *Justice Oliver Wendell Holmes: Law and the Inner Self.* New York: Oxford University Press.

A more scholarly, sophisticated study than Liva Baker's biography. A bit less useful on general details of Holmes's life, but an excellent chapter on his Civil War experiences and good discussion of the World War I civil liberties cases.

Wormuth, Francis D., and Edwin B. Firmage. 1989. *To Chain the Dog of War: The War Power of Congress in History and War.* Urbana: University of Illinois Press.

The starting point for any investigation of the war powers debate. This book is thorough, investigating the subject from the framers' intent in 1787 through the Reagan administration. Students new to the subject may find the book tough going at first, because it is so very exhaustive in its examination of all relevant court cases, statutes, and so on, but the patient reader will be rewarded with a complete knowledge of war powers issues. The authors make a strong case for a Congress-centered approach to war making.

Index

About the Author

Brian Dirck is assistant professor of American history at Anderson University in Anderson, Indiana. He specializes in the political, military, and legal history of the Civil War era. His first book was *Lincoln and Davis: Imagining America, 1809–1865* (University Press of Kansas, 2001), and he is currently working on a new study of Abraham Lincoln's law practice, which will be published by the University of Illinois Press.